TACITUS

IV

LCL 312

TACITUS

THE ANNALS

BOOKS IV–VI, XI–XII

WITH AN ENGLISH TRANSLATION BY

JOHN JACKSON

HARVARD UNIVERSITY PRESS

CAMBRIDGE, MASSACHUSETTS

LONDON, ENGLAND

First published 1937
Reprinted 1951, 1956, 1963, 1970, 1986, 1998

LOEB CLASSICAL LIBRARY® is a registered trademark
of the President and Fellows of Harvard College

ISBN 0-674-99345-4

Printed in Great Britain by St Edmundsbury Press Ltd,
Bury St Edmunds, Suffolk, on acid-free paper.
Bound by Hunter & Foulis Ltd, Edinburgh, Scotland.

CONTENTS

PREFACE

THESE volumes might no doubt have dispensed with a preface, but it seems to me a sad duty to acknowledge—though he would probably have forbidden me to do so—the great debt that it owes to the untiring kindness of the late Dr. Page ; who, almost to the end, helped me in the disheartening task of revising a translation made at an age which has begun to look like boyhood and only touched again after years of estrangement from the author and from the period.

A word, also, should perhaps be said about the few critical notes accompanying the text. As space hardly permitted, and the objects of the edition hardly required, the mention of every divergence from the written tradition, it was decided to omit the long list of those admirable corrections which, in the course of the sixteenth, seventeenth, and eighteenth centuries, converted the *Annals* into a legible book and have ever afterwards remained part and parcel of the text. On the other hand, later corrections, even in *minutiae*, have almost always been noticed ; and if the slightest doubt seemed to me to be attached to any emendation of any date, its author and the manuscript reading have been appended. Here and there, though seldom, a suggestion appears under my own name. If the ascription is ever erroneous—

PREFACE

and to one situated more or less ἔξω τῆς ἄρκτου καὶ τῆς οἰκουμένης ἁπάσης certainty on such points is a sheer impossibility—I can only express my regret.

J. JACKSON.

Caldbeck,
Cumberland.
December, 1936.

THE ANNALS OF TACITUS

BOOK IV

AB EXCESSU DIVI AUGUSTI

P. CORNELII TACITI

LIBER IV

I. C. Asinio C. Antistio consulibus nonus Tiberio
annus erat compositae rei publicae, florentis domus
(nam Germanici mortem inter prospera ducebat),
cum repente turbare fortuna coepit, saevire ipse aut
saevientibus viris praebere. Initium et causa penes
Aelium Seianum cohortibus praetoriis praefectum,
cuius de potentia supra memoravi: nunc originem,
mores, et quo facinore dominationem raptum ierit,
expediam.

Genitus Vulsiniis patre Seio Strabone equite Romano, et prima iuventa Gaium Caesarem divi
Augusti nepotem sectatus, non sine rumore Apicio
diviti et prodigo stuprum veno dedisse, mox Tiberium

---

[1] Gibbon's adaptation of the sentence to Constantine may
be quoted :— " If he reckoned, among the favours of fortune,
the death of his eldest son, of his nephew, and perhaps of his
wife, he enjoyed an uninterrupted flow of private as well as
public felicity, till the thirtieth year of his reign " (t. ii. 220
Bury).

[2] I. 24; III. 72.

[3] One of the Twelve Towns of Etruria, on the *via Cassia* :
now Bolsena.

[4] See I. 7; 24. He had since been raised to the prefecture
of Egypt (D. Cass. LVII. 19), and the sole praetorian commandant was now his son, adopted, as his name shows, by
an Aelius.

[5] M. Gavius—' Apicius ' being a sobriquet derived from a

2

THE ANNALS OF

TACITUS

BOOK IV

I. THE consulate of Gaius Asinius and Gaius A.V.C. 776=
Antistius was to Tiberius the ninth year of public A.D. 23
order and of domestic felicity (for he counted the
death of Germanicus among his blessings),[1] when
suddenly fortune disturbed the peace and he became
either a tyrant himself or the source of power to
the tyrannous. The starting-point and the cause
were to be found in Aelius Sejanus, prefect of the
praetorian cohorts. Of his influence I spoke above:[2]
now I shall unfold his origin, his character, and the
crime by which he strove to seize on empire.

Born at Vulsinii[3] to the Roman knight Seius
Strabo,[4] he became in early youth a follower of Gaius
Caesar, grandson of the deified Augustus; not without
a rumour that he had disposed of his virtue at a price
to Apicius,[5] a rich man and a prodigal. Before long,
by his multifarious arts, he bound Tiberius fast:

kindred spirit of the preceding century (Ath. 168 DE)—the
most famous gourmet of antiquity and the patron saint of
Roman cooks (Tert. *Apol.* 3). The well-known story of his
suicide on reaching the starvation limit of £100,000 (*velut
in ultima fame victurus, si in sestertio centiens vixisset*) is neatly
told by Seneca (*Ad Helv.* 10). He is credited by a scholium
on Juvenal with a monograph on gravies, but the plain cookery
book styled *Coelii Apicii de re coquinaria* is later than Com-
modus.

variis artibus devinxit, adeo ut obscurum adversum
alios sibi uni incautum intectumque efficeret, non
tam sollertia (quippe isdem artibus victus est) quam
deum ira in rem Romanam, cuius pari exitio viguit
ceciditque. Corpus illi laborum tolerans, animus
audax; sui obtegens, in alios criminator; iuxta
adulatio et superbia; palam compositus pudor, intus
summa apiscendi libido, eiusque causa modo largitio
et luxus, saepius industria ac vigilantia, haud minus
noxiae, quotiens parando regno finguntur.

II. Vim praefecturae modicam antea intendit,
dispersas per urbem cohortis una in castra condu-
cendo, ut simul imperia acciperent, numeroque et
robore et visu inter se fiducia ipsis, in ceteros metus
oreretur.[1] Praetendebat lascivire militem diductum;
si quid subitum ingruat, maiore auxilio pariter sub-
veniri; et severius acturos, si vallum statuatur
procul urbis inlecebris. Ut perfecta sunt castra,
inrepere paulatim militaris animos adeundo, appel-
lando; simul centuriones ac tribunos ipse deligere.
Neque senatorio ambitu abstinebat clientis suos
honoribus aut provinciis ornandi, facili Tiberio atque

---

[1] oreretur *Faërnus*: credetur *M*.

---

[1] Nine at this period, each under a tribune and comprising
1000 men with a complement of cavalry (*cohortes miliariae
equitatae*). The long tale of their feats in the making and
unmaking of Caesars begins with the elevation of Claudius
(41 A.D.), and ends with their declaration for Maxentius
(306 A.D.). Six years later, the corps, almost annihilated
by Constantine on the Mulvian Bridge, was disbanded and
its camp—close to the city on the east—destroyed.

[2] Three—*sine castris*—in Rome, the rest in neighbouring
towns (Suet. *Aug.* 49).

so much so that a man inscrutable to others became
to Sejanus alone unguarded and unreserved; and
this less by subtlety (in fact, he was beaten in the end
by the selfsame arts) than by the anger of Heaven
against that Roman realm for whose equal damnation
he flourished and fell. He was a man hardy by
constitution, fearless by temperament; skilled to
conceal himself and to incriminate his neighbour;
cringing at once and insolent; orderly and modest
to outward view, at heart possessed by a towering
ambition, which impelled him at whiles to lavishness
and luxury, but oftener to industry and vigilance—
qualities not less noxious when assumed for the winning of a throne.

II. The power of the prefectship, which had
hitherto been moderate, he increased by massing
the cohorts,[1] dispersed through the capital,[2] in one
camp; in order that commands should reach them
simultaneously, and that their numbers, their
strength, and the sight of one another, might in
themselves breed confidence and in others awe.
His pretext was that scattered troops became
unruly; that, when a sudden emergency called, help
was more effective if the helpers were compact;
and that there would be less laxity of conduct,
if an encampment was created at a distance from the
attractions of the city. Their quarters finished,
he began little by little to insinuate himself into the
affections of the private soldiers, approaching them
and addressing them by name, while at the same time
he selected personally their centurions and tribunes.
Nor did he fail to hold before the senate the tempta-
tion of those offices and governorships with which
he invested his satellites: for Tiberius, far from

5

ita prono, ut socium laborum non modo in sermonibus, sed apud patres et populum celebraret colique per theatra et fora effigies eius interque principia legionum sineret.

III. Ceterum plena Caesarum domus, iuvenis filius, nepotes adulti moram cupitis adferebant, quia[1] vi tot simul corripere intutum, dolus intervalla scelerum poscebat. Placuit tamen occultior via et a Druso incipere, in quem recenti ira ferebatur. Nam Drusus inpatiens aemuli et animo commotior orto forte iurgio intenderat Seiano manus et contra tendentis os verberaverat. Igitur cuncta temptanti promptissimum visum ad uxorem eius Liviam convertere, quae soror Germanici, formae initio aetatis indecorae, mox pulchritudine praecellebat. Hanc ut amore incensus adulterio pellexit, et postquam primi flagitii potitus est (neque femina amissa pudicitia alia abnuerit), ad coniugii spem, consortium regni et necem mariti impulit. Atque illa, cui avunculus Augustus, socer Tiberius, ex Druso liberi, seque ac maiores et posteros municipali adultero foedabat, ut pro honestis et praesentibus flagitiosa et incerta exspectaret. Sumitur in conscientiam Eudemus, amicus ac medicus Liviae, specie artis frequens

---

[1] quia *Nipperdey* : et quia.

---

[1] In the *principia*, the quasi-sacrosanct headquarters of a legionary camp: compare, for instance, I. 39; *Hist.* III. 13, 31.

[2] The male members, apart from Tiberius himself, consisted of (*a*) Drusus (*iuvenis filius*); (*b*) the sons of Germanicus (Nero, Drusus,—*nepotes adulti*,—with the young Caligula, aged eleven); (*c*) the twin sons of Drusus (Tiberius Gemellus and Germanicus, some four years old).

[3] Otherwise known as Livilla; grand-daughter of Augustus' sister Octavia and first cousin as well as wife to Drusus (see the stemmata, preceding Book I).

demurring, was complaisant enough to celebrate
" the partner of his toils " not only in conversation
but before the Fathers and the people, and to allow
his effigies to be honoured, in theatre, in forum,
and amid the eagles and altars of the legions.[1]

III. Still, the imperial house with its plentitude
of Caesars[2]—a son arrived at manhood, grandchildren
at the years of discretion—gave his ambition pause :
for to attack all at once by violence was hazardous,
while treachery demanded an interval between
crime and crime. He resolved, however, to take
the more secret way, and to begin with Drusus,
against whom he felt the stimulus of a recent anger ;
for Drusus, impatient of a rival, and quick-tempered
to a fault, had in a casual altercation raised his
hand against the favourite, and, upon a counter-
demonstration, had struck him in the face. On
exploring the possibilities, then, it appeared simplest
to turn to the prince's wife Livia,[3] sister of Germanicus, in her early days a harsh-favoured girl,
later a sovereign beauty. In the part of a fiery
lover, he seduced her to adultery : then, when the
first infamy had been achieved—and a woman,
who has parted with her virtue, will not refuse other
demands—he moved her to dream of marriage, a
partnership in the empire, and the murder of her
husband. And she, the grand-niece of Augustus,
the daughter-in-law of Tiberius, the mother of
Drusus' children, defiled herself, her ancestry,
and her posterity, with a market-town adulterer,
in order to change an honoured estate in the present
for the expectation of a criminal and doubtful
future. Eudemus, doctor and friend of Livia, was
made privy to the design, his profession supplying

7

secretis. Pellit domo Seianus uxorem Apicatam, ex qua tres liberos genuerat, ne paelici suspectaretur. Sed magnitudo facinoris metum, prolationes, diversa interdum consilia adferebat.

IV. Interim anni principio Drusus ex Germanici liberis togam virilem sumpsit, quaeque fratri eius Neroni decreverat senatus repetita. Addidit orationem Caesar, multa cum laude filii sui, quod patria benevolentia in fratris liberos foret. Nam Drusus, quamquam arduum sit eodem loci potentiam et concordiam esse, aequus adulescentibus aut certe non adversus habebatur. Exim vetus et saepe simulatum proficiscendi in provincias consilium refertur. Multitudinem veteranorum praetexebat imperator et dilectibus supplendos exercitus: nam voluntarium militem deesse, ac si suppeditet, non eadem virtute ac modestia agere, quia plerumque inopes ac vagi sponte militiam sumant. Percensuitque cursim numerum legionum et quas provincias tutarentur. Quod mihi quoque exsequendum reor, quae tunc Romana copia in armis, qui socii reges, quanto sit angustius imperitatum.

V. Italiam utroque mari duae classes, Misenum

---

[1] See I. 47; III. 47; Suet. *Tib.* 38. The motives assigned are reasonable enough, as there might be trouble with the veterans over the discharges and gratuities, while conscription was only in the sharpest emergencies applied in Italy and was unpopular in the provinces.

[2] Written, like II. 61 fin., between the extension of the Empire to the Persian Gulf under Trajan (115 A.D.) and the retrocession under Hadrian two years later. The principal annexations since Augustus were :—Mauretania (40 A.D.),

a pretext for repeated interviews. Sejanus, to forestall the suspicions of his mistress, closed his doors
on Apicata, the wife who had borne him three
children. Still the dimensions of the crime brought
tremors, adjournments, and occasionally a division
of counsels.

IV. Meanwhile, in the beginning of the year,
Drusus, one of Germanicus' children, assumed the
garb of manhood; and the senate repeated the compliments which it had decreed to his brother Nero.
The Caesar followed with a speech, comprising
a large encomium on his own son, " who showed a
fatherly benevolence towards the family of his
brother." For Drusus, difficult as it is for power and
concord to dwell together, had the reputation of
being well-disposed, or at least not inimical, to the
youths. Next, the old, oft-simulated project of an
excursion to the provinces[1] came up for discussion.
The Emperor alleged the multitude of time-expired
troops and the need of fresh conscriptions to maintain
the armies at strength. For there was a dearth, he
said, of volunteers; and, even when forthcoming,
they failed to show the old courage and discipline,
since it was too often the destitute and the vagrant
who enlisted of their own accord. He ran rapidly over
the number of the legions and the provinces beneath
their guardianship: a theme which I hold it my own
duty to pursue, in order that it may appear what
were the Roman forces then under arms, who the
kings in federation with the empire, and how narrow,
comparatively, the limits of our dominion.[2]

V. Italy, on either seaboard, was protected by

Britain (43 A.D.), Dacia (101–106 A.D.), Arabia Petraea (105
A.D.), Armenia and Mesopotamia (114 A.D.)

9

apud et Ravennam, proximumque Galliae litus
rostratae [1] naves praesidebant, quas Actiaca victoria
captas Augustus in oppidum Foroiuliense miserat
valido cum remige. Sed praecipuum robur Rhenum
iuxta, commune in Germanos Gallosque subsidium,
octo legiones erant. Hispaniae recens perdomitae
tribus habebantur. Mauros Iuba rex acceperat
donum populi Romani. Cetera Africae per duas
legiones parique numero Aegyptus, dehinc initio ab
Suriae [2] usque ad flumen Euphraten, quantum
ingenti terrarum sinu ambitur, quattuor legionibus
coercita, accolis Hibero Albanoque et aliis regibus,
qui magnitudine nostra proteguntur adversum
externa imperia. Et Thraeciam Rhoemetalces ac
liberi Cotyis, ripamque Danuvii legionum duae in
Pannonia, duae in Moesia attinebant, totidem apud
Delmatiam locatis, quae positu regionis a tergo illis,
ac si repentinum auxilium Italia posceret, haud
procul accirentur, quamquam insideret urbem pro-
prius miles, tres urbanae, novem praetoriae cohortes,
Etruria ferme Umbriaque delectae aut vetere Latio

---

[1] rostratae] constratae *Nipperdey.*
[2] Suriae *Muretus* : suria.

---

[1] Fréjus, a *chef-lieu de canton* in the département of Var;
now, owing to the silting of the Argens, a mile from the coast.
[2] By Agrippa in 19 B.C.
[3] Son of Juba I of Numidia; taken to Rome after Thapsus
and there educated; married to a daughter of Antony and
Cleopatra; famous as a polymath, and repeatedly cited as
such by writers like Pliny and Athenaeus.

fleets at Misenum and Ravenna; the adjacent coast of Gaul by a squadron of fighting ships, captured by Augustus at the victory of Actium and sent with strong crews to the town of Forum Julium.[1] Our main strength, however, lay on the Rhine—eight legions ready to cope indifferently with the German or the Gaul. The Spains, finally subdued not long before,[2] were kept by three. Mauretania, by the national gift, had been transferred to King Juba.[3] Two legions[4] held down the remainder of Africa; a similar number, Egypt: then, from the Syrian marches right up to the Euphrates, four sufficed for the territories enclosed in that enormous reach of ground; while, on the borders, the Iberian, the Albanian,[5] and other monarchs, were secured against alien power by the might of Rome. Thrace was held by Rhoemetalces and the sons of Cotys;[6] the Danube bank by two legions in Pannonia and two in Moesia; two more being posted in Dalmatia, geographically to the rear of the other four, and within easy call, should Italy claim sudden assistance—though, in any case, the capital possessed a standing army of its own: three urban[7] and nine praetorian cohorts, recruited in the main from Etruria and Umbria or

[4] One was usual, but owing to the war with Tacfarinas the *nona Hispana* had been brought over from Pannonia (III. 9).

[5] Small kingdoms between the Caucasus and Armenia, Albania touching the Caspian, Iberia separated from the Black Sea by Colchis.

[6] II. 64–67; III. 38 *sq.*

[7] Less distinguished than the praetorian cohorts, but numbered consecutively with them (*X, XI, XII*): a fourth served at Lyons (see III. 41 and *Hist.* I. 64, where Mommsen restored *cohortem XIII* for *c. XVIII*), and others were added later.

et coloniis antiquitus Romanis. At apud idonea provinciarum sociae triremes alaeque et auxilia cohortium, neque multo secus in iis virium: sed persequi incertum fuit,[1] cum ex usu temporis huc illuc mearent, gliscerent numero et aliquando minuerentur.

VI. Congruens crediderim recensere ceteras quoque rei publicae partis, quibus modis ad eam diem habitae sint, quoniam Tiberio mutati in deterius principatus initium ille annus attulit. Iam primum publica negotia et privatorum maxima apud patres tractabantur, dabaturque primoribus disserere, et in adulationem lapsos cohibebat ipse; mandabatque honores, nobilitatem maiorum, claritudinem militiae, inlustris domi artis spectando, ut satis constaret non alios potiores fuisse. Sua consulibus, sua praetoribus species; minorum quoque magistratuum exercita potestas; legesque, si maiestatis quaestio eximeretur, bono in usu. At frumenta et pecuniae vectigales, cetera publicorum fructuum societatibus equitum Romanorum agitabantur. Res suas Caesar spectatissimo cuique, quibusdam ignotis ex fama mandabat, semelque adsumpti tenebantur prorsus

---

[1] fuit] fuerit *Lipsius.*

[1] Towns possessed of 'Latin rights' before the extensions of the franchise at the close of the Social War (90–89 B.C.).

[2] Those in Italy proper—whence Otho's description of the guards as *Italiae alumni et Romana vere inventus* (*Hist.* I. 84). The limits mentioned were, however, soon overstepped, and ultimately, under Septimius Severus, recruiting for the cohorts was superseded by a system of promotion from the legions.

[3] The emperor, that is to say, abstained from trying *in camera* the cases—usually political and affecting culprits of rank—which would normally come before the senate in its capacity of a high court of criminal judicature.

Old Latium[1] and the earlier Roman colonies.[2] Again, at suitable points of the provinces, there were the federate warships, cavalry divisions and auxiliary cohorts in not much inferior strength : but to trace them was dubious, as they shifted from station to station, and, according to the exigency of the moment, increased in number or were occasionally diminished.

VI. It will be opportune, I take it, as this year brought the opening stages of deterioration in the principate of Tiberius, to review in addition the other departments of state and the methods by which they were administered up to that period. First, then, public affairs—together with private affairs of exceptional moment—were treated in the senate,[3] and discussion was free to the leading members, their lapses into subserviency being checked by the sovereign himself. In conferring offices, he took into view the nobility of a candidate's ancestry, the distinction of his military service, or the brilliance of his civil attainments, and left it sufficiently clear that no better choice had been available. The consulate had its old prestige ; so had the praetorship : the powers even of the minor magistracies were exercised ; and the laws, apart from the process in cases of treason, were in proper force. On the other hand, the corn-tribute, the monies from indirect taxation, and other public revenues, were handled by companies of Roman knights. The imperial property[4] was entrusted by the Caesar to men of tested merit, at times to a personal stranger on the strength of his reputation ; and his agents,

---

[4] The reference of the sentence is to the *fiscus*—a term which in its familiar sense appears not to be older than Claudius—and the procurators.

sine modo, cum plerique isdem negotiis insenescerent.
Plebes acri quidem annona fatigabatur, sed nulla
in eo culpa ex principe : quin infecunditati terrarum
aut asperis maris obviam iit, quantum impendio di-
ligentiaque poterat.   Et ne provinciae novis oneribus
turbarentur utque vetera sine avaritia aut crudelitate
magistratuum   tolerarent,   providebat: corporum
verbera, ademptiones bonorum aberant.   Rari per
Italiam Caesaris agri, modesta servitia, intra paucos
libertos domus ; ac si quando cum privatis disceptaret,
forum et ius.

VII. Quae cuncta non quidem comi via, sed
horridus ac plerumque formidatus, retinebat tamen,
donec morte Drusi verterentur: nam dum superfuit,
mansere, quia Seianus incipiente adhuc potentia
bonis consiliis notescere volebat, et ultor metuebatur
non occultus odii, set[1] crebro querens incolumi filio
adiutorem imperii alium vocari.   Et quantum superesse, ut collega dicatur ?   Primas dominandi spes
in arduo : ubi sis ingressus, adesse studia et ministros.
Exstructa iam sponte praefecti castra, datos in
manum milites ; cerni effigiem eius in monimentis
Cn. Pompei ; communis illi cum familia Drusorum

---

[1] odii set *Doederlein* : odii et.

---

[1] The *theatrum Magni* in the Campus Martius, the first
stone theatre in Rome, completed in 52 B.C., though opened
three years earlier. For the statue, see III. 72.

once installed, were retained quite indefinitely,
many growing grey in the service originally entered.
The populace, it is true, was harassed by exorbitant
food-prices, but in that point no blame attached
to the emperor: he spared, indeed, neither expense
nor pains in order to neutralize the effects of unfruitful soils or boisterous seas. He saw to it that
the provinces were not disturbed by fresh impositions
and that the incidence of the old was not aggravated
by magisterial avarice or cruelty: corporal punishment and the forfeiture of estates were not in vogue.
His demesnes in Italy were few, his establishment of
slaves unassuming, his household limited to a small
number of freedmen; and, in the event of a dispute
between himself and a private citizen, the decision
rested with a court of justice.

VII. All this, not gracefully indeed, but in his
grim and often dreaded fashion, he nevertheless
observed, until by the death of Drusus the whole
was overthrown. For, while the prince survived,
the old order remained; because Sejanus, yet in
the infancy of his power, desired to win a name
by good advice, and had still an avenger to dread—
an avenger careless to conceal his hatred, and complaining perpetually that, " in the lifetime of the
son, a stranger was styled coadjutor in the empire.
And how short a step till the coadjutor was termed
a colleague! The first designs upon a throne were
beset with difficulty; but, the first step made, a
faction and helpers were not far to seek. Already
an encampment had risen at the fiat of the prefect,
and the guards were delivered into his hand; his
effigy was visible in the monuments of Gnaeus
Pompeius;[1] his grandsons would mingle the blood

fore nepotes: precandam post haec modestiam, ut contentus esset. Neque raro neque apud paucos talia iaciebat, et secreta quoque eius corrupta uxore prodebantur.

VIII. Igitur Seianus maturandum ratus deligit venenum, quo paulatim inrepente fortuitus morbus adsimularetur. Id Druso datum per Lygdum spadonem, ut octo post annos cognitum est. Ceterum Tiberius per omnis valetudinis eius dies, nullo metu an ut firmitudinem animi ostentaret, etiam defuncto necdum sepulto, curiam ingressus est. Consulesque sede vulgari per speciem maestitiae sedentis honoris locique admonuit, et effusum in lacrimas senatum victo gemitu simul oratione continua erexit:—Non quidem sibi ignarum posse argui, quod tam recenti dolore subierit oculos senatus: vix propinquorum adloquia tolerari, vix diem aspici a plerisque lugentium. Neque illos inbecillitatis damnandos: se tamen fortiora solacia e complexu rei publicae petivisse. Miseratusque Augustae extremam senectam, rudem adhuc nepotum et vergentem aetatem suam, ut Germanici liberi, unica praesentium malorum levamenta, inducerentur petivit. Egressi consules firmatos adloquio adulescentulos deductosque ante Caesarem statuunt. Quibus adprensis

---

[1] By the projected marriage of Sejanus' daughter to the son of Claudius (iii. 29 n.).

[2] He was sixty-five; his mother eighty, if Dio's statement of her age at death is correct.

[3] Only the two elder, Caligula being excluded as too young.

of the Drusi with his own.[1] Henceforward they could only pray that he might be endowed with moderation, and rest content."—Views such as these he proclaimed neither on rare occasions nor to a few auditors; and, since the seduction of his wife, his very confidences were betrayed.

VIII. Sejanus, therefore, decided to lose no time, and chose a poison so gradual in its inroads as to counterfeit the progress of a natural ailment. It was adminstered to Drusus by help of the eunuch Lygdus, a fact brought to light eight years later. Tiberius, however, through all the days of his son's illness, either unalarmed or to advertise his firmness of mind, continued to visit the senate, doing so even after his death, while he was still unburied. The consuls were seated on the ordinary benches as a sign of mourning: he reminded them of their dignity and their place. The members broke into tears: he repressed their lamentation, and at the same time revived their spirits in a formal speech:— " He was not, indeed, unaware that he might be criticized for appearing before the eyes of the senate while his grief was still fresh. Mourners in general could hardly support the condolences of their own kindred—hardly tolerate the light of day. Nor were they to be condemned as weaklings; but personally he had sought a manlier consolation by taking the commonwealth to his heart." After deploring the extreme old age of his august mother, the still tender years of his grandsons, and his own declining days,[2] he asked for Germanicus' sons,[3] their sole comfort in the present affliction, to be introduced. The consuls went out, and, after reassuring the boys, brought them in and set them before the emperor.

"Patres conscripti, hos" inquit "orbatos parente
tradidi patruo ipsorum precatusque sum, quamquam
esset illi propria suboles, ne secus quam suum
sanguinem foveret, attolleret, sibique et posteris
conformaret. Erepto Druso preces ad vos converto
disque et patria coram obtestor: Augusti pronepotes,
clarissimis maioribus genitos, suscipite, regite,
vestram meamque vicem explete. Hi vobis, Nero et
Druse, parentum loco. Ita nati estis, ut bona
malaque vestra ad rem publicam pertineant."

IX. Magno ea fletu et mox precationibus faustis
audita; ac si modum orationi posuisset, misericordia
sui gloriaque animos audientium impleverat: ad
vana et totiens inrisa revolutus, de reddenda re
publica utque consules seu quis alius regimen
susciperent, vero quoque et honesto fidem dempsit.
Memoriae Drusi eadem quae in Germanicum
decernuntur, plerisque additis, ut ferme amat
posterior adulatio. Funus imaginum pompa maxime
inlustre fuit, cum origo Iuliae gentis Aeneas omnes-
que Albanorum reges et conditor urbis Romulus,
post Sabina nobilitas, Attus Clausus ceteraeque
Claudiorum effigies longo ordine spectarentur.

X. In tradenda morte Drusi quae plurimis maxi-

---

[1] The Sabine name of Appius Claudius Sabinus Regillensis,
consul, by the conventional chronology, in 495 B.C. and founder
of the patrician *gens Claudia*: cf. XI. 24; XII. 25. His traditional history may be found in Livy (II. 16; 21; 23, etc.).

" Conscript Fathers," he said, " when these children lost their parent, I gave them to their uncle, and begged him, though he had issue of his own, to use them as if they were blood of his blood—to cherish them, build up their fortunes, form them after his own image and for the welfare of posterity. With Drusus gone, I turn my prayers to you; I conjure you in the sight of Heaven and of your country:— These are the great-grandchildren of Augustus, scions of a glorious ancestry; adopt them, train them, do your part—and do mine! Nero and Drusus, these shall be your father and your mother: it is the penalty of your birth that your good and your evil are the good and the evil of the commonwealth."

IX. All this was listened to amid general tears, then with prayers for a happy issue; and, had he only set a limit to his speech, he must have left the minds of his hearers full of compassion for himself, and of pride: instead, by reverting to those vain and oft-derided themes, the restoration of the republic and his wish that the consuls or others would take the reins of government, he destroyed the credibility even of the true and honourable part of his statement.—The memorials decreed to Germanicus were repeated for Drusus, with large additions, such as sycophancy commonly favours at a second essay. The most arresting feature of the funeral was the parade of ancestral images, while Aeneas, author of the Julian line, with the whole dynasty of Alban kings, and Romulus, the founder of the city, followed by the Sabine nobles, by Attus Clausus,[1] and by the rest of the Claudian effigies, filed in long procession past the spectator.

X. In recording the death of Drusus, I have given

maeque fidei[1] auctoribus memorata sunt rettuli:
set non omiserim eorundem temporum rumorem,
validum adeo, ut nondum exolescat. Corrupta ad
scelus Livia Seianum Lygdi quoque spadonis animum
stupro vinxisse, quod is[2] aetate atque forma carus
domino interque primores ministros erat; deinde
inter conscios ubi locus veneficii tempusque conposita
sint, eo audaciae provectum, ut verteret et occulto
indicio Drusum veneni in patrem arguens moneret
Tiberium, vitandam potionem, quae prima ei apud
filium epulanti offerretur. Ea fraude *captum*[3]
senem, postquam convivium inierat, exceptum
poculum Druso tradidisse; atque illo ignaro et
iuveniliter hauriente auctam suspicionem, tamquam
metu et pudore sibimet inrogaret mortem, quam
patri struxerat.

XI. Haec vulgo iactata super id, quod nullo auctore
certo firmantur, prompte refutaveris. Quis enim
mediocri prudentia, nedum Tiberius tantis rebus
exercitus, inaudito filio exitium offerret, idque sua
manu et nullo ad paenitendum regressu? Quin
potius ministrum veneni excruciaret, auctorem
exquireret, insita denique etiam in extraneos
cunctatione et mora adversum unicum et nullius
ante flagitii conpertum uteretur? Sed quia Seianus

---

[1] maximaeque fidei *Ritter* : maximaeque fideis *Med.*.
maximeque fidis *Beroaldus*.   [2] is *Ernesti* : is *Lygdus*.
[3] captum *Muretus* : cum *Med.*, illectum *Nipperdey–Andresen*
(as at *Hist.* IV. 57 in.)

the version of the most numerous and trustworthy authorities; but I am reluctant to omit a contemporary rumour, so strong that it persists to-day. It asserts that, after seducing Livia to crime, Sejanus, by an indecent connection, also attached to himself the eunuch Lygdus, whose years and looks had won him the affection of his master and a prominent place among his attendants; that later, when the conspirators had agreed upon a place and time for the mortal dose, he carried audacity to the point of altering the arrangements, and, giving private warning to Tiberius that Drusus meditated the poisoning of his father, counselled him to avoid the first draught offered to him when he dined with his son; that, falling into the trap, the old emperor, on taking his place at the banquet, accepted the cup and passed it to Drusus; and that when Drusus, in complete ignorance, drained it as a young man would, suspicion only grew the darker—the assumption being that, out of fear and shame, he was inflicting upon himself the doom invented for his father.

XI. This commonly repeated account, apart from the fact that it is supported by no definite authority, may be summarily refuted. For what man of ordinary prudence, to say nothing of Tiberius with his training in great affairs, would force death upon a son whose defence was unheard—and force it by his own hand, with the door closed against any change of purpose? Why not, rather, torture the giver of the poison, search out the prompter behind him, proceed in short against an only son, never as yet found guilty of a crime, with that inveterate and scrupulous deliberation which he manifested even to strangers? But Sejanus was held the inventor

facinorum omnium repertor habebatur, ex nimia
caritate in eum Caesaris et ceterorum in utrumque
odio quamvis fabulosa et immania credebantur,
atrociore semper fama erga dominantium exitus.
Ordo alioqui sceleris per Apicatam Seiani proditus,
tormentis Eudemi ac Lygdi patefactus est. Neque
quisquam scriptor tam infensus extitit, ut Tiberio
obiectaret, cum omnia alia conquirerent intenderent-
que. Mihi tradendi arguendique rumoris causa fuit,
ut claro sub exemplo falsas auditiones depellerem
peteremque ab iis, quorum in manus cura nostra
venerit, *ne* divulgata atque incredibilia avide accepta
veris neque in miraculum corruptis antehabeant.

XII. Ceterum laudante filium pro rostris Tiberio
senatus populusque habitum ac voces dolentum
simulatione magis quam libens induebat, domumque
Germanici revirescere occulti laetabantur. Quod
principium favoris et mater Agrippina spem male
tegens perniciem adceleravere. Nam Seianus ubi
videt mortem Drusi inultam interfectoribus, sine
maerore publico esse, ferox scelerum, et quia prima
provenerant, volutare secum, quonam modo Germanici liberos perverteret, quorum non dubia suc-
cessio. Neque spargi venenum in tres poterat,
egregia custodum fide et pudicitia Agrippinae
inpenetrabili. Igitur contumaciam eius insectari,

---

[1] In a written statement to Tiberius, drawn up after the
fall of her husband and the execution of her children, and
immediately before her own suicide (D. Cass. LVIII. 11).
As she had been divorced, ὥστε μηκέτι συνοικεῖν (D. Cass.
l.l.), in the opening stages of Sejanus' intrigue with Livia,
her disclosures must have been at second hand, and the direct
evidence against the pair shrinks to the admissions extracted
by torture from their slaves eight years after the event.

of all villainies: therefore, as the Caesar loved him
over-well and the rest of the world hated both, the
most fabulous horrors found credence, rumour
being never so lurid as when princes quit the scene.
Moreover, the sequence of the crime was betrayed
by Sejanus' wife Apicata,[1] and disclosed in detail by
Eudemus and Lygdus under torture; nor was there
found one historian malevolent enough to lay it to
the charge of Tiberius at a time when historians
were collecting and aggravating all other circumstances. My own motive in chronicling and refuting
the scandal has been to discredit by one striking
instance the falsities of oral tradition, and to request
those into whose hands my work may have fallen
not too eagerly to accept a widely circulated and
incredible tale in place of truth not corrupted into
romance.

XII. However, while Tiberius on the Rostra was
pronouncing the panegyric upon his son, the senate
and people, from hypocrisy more than impulse,
assumed the attitude and accents of mourning,
and exulted in secret that the house of Germanicus
was beginning again to flourish. This incipient
popularity, together with Agrippina's failure to hide
her maternal hopes, hastened its destruction. For
Sejanus, when he saw the death of Drusus passing
unrevenged upon the murderers, unlamented by
the nation, grew bolder in crime, and, since his
first venture had prospered, began to revolve ways
and means of eliminating the children of Germanicus,
whose succession was a thing undoubted. To dis-
tribute poison among the three was impossible; for
their custodians were patterns of fidelity, Agrippina's
chastity impenetrable. He proceded, therefore, to

vetus Augustae odium, recentem Liviae conscientiam exagitare, ut superbam fecunditate, subnixam popularibus studiis inhiare dominationi apud Caesarem arguerent. Atque haec callidis criminatoribus, inter quos delegerat Iulium Postumum, per adulterium Mutiliae Priscae inter intimos aviae et consiliis suis peridoneum, quia Prisca in animo Augustae valida anum suapte natura potentiae anxiam insociabilem nurui efficiebat. Agrippinae quoque proximi inliciebantur pravis sermonibus tumidos spiritus perstimulare.

XIII. At Tiberius nihil intermissa rerum cura, negotia pro solaciis accipiens, ius civium, preces sociorum tractabat; factaque auctore eo senatus consulta, ut civitati Cibyraticae apud Asiam, Aegiensi apud Achaiam, motu terrae labefactis, subveniretur remissione tributi in triennium. Et Vibius Serenus pro consule ulterioris Hispaniae, de vi publica damnatus, ob atrocitatem morum in insulam Amorgum deportatur. Carsidius Sacerdos, reus tamquam fru-

---

[1] Livia Drusilla, wife first of Ti. Claudius Nero, then of Augustus; mother by the former of Tiberius and the elder Drusus. For her relationship to the younger Livia and Agrippina, see the genealogical table (vol. ii. p. 241); for her feud with the latter, I. 33 and II. 43.

[2] If *haec* is feminine, as assumed here after Ryck and others, then *aviae* is Augusta as grandmother in the strict sense of the term to Livia : if it is neuter (sc. *efficiebat Seianus*), then *aviae* is loosely used of Augusta's relationship to Agrippina, her husband's grandchild and grandson's wife.

[3] Cibyra Magna, at the southern extremity of Phrygia Magna, a centre of the iron trade (Hor. *Ep.* I. 6, 32; Strab. 651).

[4] Now Vostizza, on the Corinthian Gulf.

[5] II. 30; IV. 28-30.

[6] Subdivided since 25 B.C. into Baetica and Lusitania. The former—a senatorial province—is here meant.

declaim against her contumacity, and, by playing upon Augusta's[1] old animosity and Livia's recent sense of guilt, induced them to carry information to the Caesar that, proud of her fruitfulness and confident in the favour of the populace, she was turning a covetous eye to the throne. In addition, Livia,[2] with the help of skilled calumniators—one of the chosen being Julius Postumus, intimate with her grandmother owing to his adulterous connection with Mutilia Prisca, and admirably suited to her own designs through Prisca's influence over Augusta—kept working for the total estrangement from her grandson's wife of an old woman, by nature anxious to maintain her power. Even Agrippina's nearest friends were suborned to infuriate her haughty temper by their pernicious gossip.

XIII. Meanwhile Tiberius had in no way relaxed his attention to public business, but, accepting work as a consolation, was dealing with judicial cases at Rome and petitions from the provinces. On his proposal, senatorial resolutions were passed to relieve the towns of Cibyra[3] in Asia and Aegium[4] in Achaia, both damaged by earthquake, by remitting their tribute for three years. Vibius Serenus,[5] too, the proconsul of Further Spain,[6] was condemned on a charge of public violence, and deported, as the result of his savage character, to the island of Amorgus.[7] Carsidius Sacerdos, accused of supplying grain

---

[7] The *lex Iulia de vi publica* (8 B.C.) prohibited the scourging, torture, imprisonment or execution of a Roman citizen appealing to the Caesar, under pain of interdiction from fire and water (exile at choice in any island—with four exceptions —lying 50 miles from the mainland). Deportation to a specified place was, therefore, at this period an aggravation of the penalty : later it became normal.

mento hostem Tacfarinatem iuvisset, absolvitur, eiusdemque criminis C. Gracchus. Hunc comitem exilii admodum infantem pater Sempronius in insulam Cercinam tulerat. Illic adultus inter extorris et liberalium artium nescios, mox per Africam ac Siciliam mutando sordidas merces sustentabatur; neque tamen effugit magnae fortunae pericula. Ac ni Aelius Lamia et L. Apronius, qui Africam obtinuerant, insontem protexissent, claritudine infausti generis et paternis adversis foret abstractus.

XIV. Is quoque annus legationes Graecarum civitatium habuit, Samiis Iunonis, Cois Aesculapii delubro vetustum asyli ius ut firmaretur petentibus. Samii decreto Amphictyonum nitebantur, quis praecipuum fuit rerum omnium iudicium, qua tempestate Graeci conditis per Asiam urbibus ora maris potiebantur. Neque dispar apud Coos antiquitas, et accedebat meritum ex loco: nam civis Romanos templo Aesculapii induxerant, cum iussu regis Mithridatis apud cunctas Asiae insulas et urbes trucidarentur. Variis dehinc et saepius inritis praetorum questibus, postremo Caesar de inmodestia histrionum rettulit: multa ab iis in publicum seditiose, foeda per domos temptari; Oscum quondam

---

[1] I. 53.

[2] VI. 27; Hor. *Carm.* I. 26; III. 17; *Ep.* I. 14, 6.

[3] In 88 B.C. Sanctuaries, including at least one other of Aesculapius, were violated wholesale during the massacre (App. *Mithr.* 22 *sq.*).

to a public enemy in the person of Tacfarinas, was acquitted; and the same charge failed against Gaius Gracchus. Gracchus had been taken in earliest infancy by his father Sempronius [1] to share his banishment in the island of Cercina. There he grew to manhood in the company of landless men, destitute of all liberal accomplishments; later, he eked out a livelihood by mean trading transactions in Africa and Sicily: yet even so he failed to escape the hazards reserved for rank and fortune. Indeed, had not Aelius Lamia [2] and Lucius Apronius, former governors of Africa, come to the rescue of his innocence, he would have been swept to ruin by the fame of his calamitous house and the disasters of his father.

XIV. This year also brought delegations from two Greek communities, the Samians and Coans desiring the confirmation of an old right of asylum to the temples of Juno and Aesculapius respectively. The Samians appealed to a decree of the Amphictyonic Council, the principal tribunal for all questions in the period when the Greeks had already founded their city-states in Asia and were dominant upon the sea-coast. The Coans had equal antiquity on their side, and, in addition, a claim associated with the place itself: for they had sheltered Roman citizens in the temple of Aesculapius at a time when, by order of King Mithridates, they were being butchered in every island and town of Asia. [3] Next, after various and generally ineffective complaints from the praetors, the Caesar at last brought up the question of the effrontery of the players:—"They were frequently the fomenters of sedition against the state and of debauchery in private houses; the

ludicrum, levissimae apud vulgum oblectationis, eo
flagitiorum et virium venisse, *ut* auctoritate patrum
coercendum sit.   Pulsi tum histriones Italia.

XV. Idem annus alio quoque luctu Caesarem
adfecit,[1] alterum ex geminis Drusi liberis extingu-
endo, neque minus morte amici.   Is fuit Lucilius
Longus, omnium illi tristium laetorumque socius
unusque e senatoribus Rhodii secessus comes.   Ita
quamquam novo homini censorium funus, effigiem
apud forum Augusti publica pecunia patres decrevere,
apud quos etiam tum cuncta tractabantur, adeo ut
procurator Asiae Lucilius Capito accusante provincia
causam dixerit, magna cum adseveratione principis,
non se ius nisi in servitia et pecunias familiaris
dedisse : quod si vim praetoris usurpasset mani-
busque militum usus foret, spreta in eo mandata sua :
audirent socios.   Ita reus cognito negotio damnatur.
Ob quam ultionem, et quia priore anno in C. Silanum
vindicatum erat, decrevere Asiae urbes templum
Tiberio matrique eius ac senatui.   Et permissum
statuere ; egitque Nero gratis ea causa patribus
atque avo, laetas inter audientium adfectiones, qui
recenti memoria Germanici illum aspici, illum audiri

<hr/>

¹ adfecit *Ritter* : adficit.

<hr/>

¹ Campanian amateur farces (*fabulae Atellanae*), with stock
characters and a country-town setting ; transplanted to Rome
after the Hannibalian War, given a literary treatment later, and
represented by professional actors.   In vogue under the early
empire as after-pieces (*exodia*), they were apt to be seasoned
with very thinly disguised references to the foibles of the reign-
ing emperor : e.g., the excesses of Tiberius at Capreae, Nero's
matricide, Galba's avarice, Domitian's divorce (Suet. *Tib.* 45 ;
Ner. 39 ; *Galb.* 13 ; *Dom.* 10).

² From 6. B.C. to the death of Lucius Caesar in 2 A.D.

³ A state funeral (*publicum funus*), though the exact force
of the adjective is in doubt.

old Oscan farce,[1] the trivial delight of the crowd, had come to such a pitch of indecency and power that it needed the authority of the senate to check it." The players were then expelled from Italy.

XV. The same year brought still another bereavement to the emperor, by removing one of the twin children of Drusus, and an equal affliction in the death of a friend. This was Lucilius Longus, his comrade in evil days and good, and the one member of the senate to share his isolation at Rhodes.[2] Hence, in spite of his modest antecedents, a censorian funeral[3] and a statue erected in the Forum of Augustus at the public expense were decreed to him by the Fathers, before whom, at that time, all questions were still dealt with; so much so, that Lucilius Capito, the procurator[4] of Asia, was obliged, at the indictment of the province, to plead his cause before them, the emperor asserting forcibly that " any powers he had given to him extended merely to the slaves and revenues of the imperial domains; if he had usurped the governor's authority and used military force, it was a flouting of his orders: the provincials must be heard." The case was accordingly tried and the defendant condemned. In return for this act of retribution, as well as for the punishment meted out to Gaius Silanus[5] the year before, the Asiatic cities decreed a temple to Tiberius, his mother, and the senate. Leave to build was granted, and Nero returned thanks on that score to the senate and his grandfather—a pleasing sensation to his listeners, whose memory of Germanicus was fresh enough to permit the fancy that his were the features they saw and the accents to which they listened.

[4] Of the *res privata* of the emperor.   [5] III. 66 *sqq.*

rebantur. Aderantque iuveni modestia ac forma principe viro digna, notis in eum Seiani odiis ob periculum gratiora.

XVI. Sub idem tempus de flamine Diali in locum Servi Maluginensis defuncti legendo, simul roganda nova lege disseruit Caesar. Nam patricios confarreatis parentibus genitos tres simul nominari, ex quis unus legeretur, vetusto more; neque adesse, ut olim, eam copiam, omissa confarreandi adsuetudine aut inter paucos retenta: (plurisque eius rei causas adferebat, potissimam penes incuriam virorum feminarumque; accedere ipsius caerimoniae difficultates, quae consulto vitarentur) . . . [1] et quod exiret e iure patrio, qui id flamonium apisceretur quaeque in manum flaminis conveniret. Ita medendum senatus decreto aut lege, sicut Augustus quaedam ex horrida illa antiquitate ad praesentem usum flexisset. Igitur tractatis religionibus placitum instituto flaminum nihil demutari: sed lata lex, qua flaminica Dialis sacrorum causa in potestate viri, cetera promisco feminarum iure ageret. Et filius Maluginensis patri suffectus. Utque glisceret dig-

[1] . . . *Lipsius.*

---

[1] III. 58 n.

[2] The chief of the three modes of marriage *cum conventione in manum* (the bride passing entirely from the jurisdiction of her father into that of her husband, to whom she stood henceforward in the legal position of daughter). The name comes from the cake of spelt (*panis farreus*) consumed or offered at the ceremony in presence of the pontifex maximus, the flamen Dialis, and at least ten witnesses.

[3] A feature naturally regarded with disfavour by the parents.

The youth had, in fact, a modesty and beauty worthy of a prince: endowments the more attractive from the peril of their owner, since the hatred of Sejanus for him was notorious.

XVI. Nearly at the same date, the Caesar spoke on the need of choosing a flamen of Jupiter,[1] to replace the late Servius Maluginensis, and of also passing new legislation. "Three patricians," he pointed out, "children of parents wedded ' by cake of spelt,'[2] were nominated simultaneously; and on one of them the selection fell. The system was old-fashioned, nor was there now as formerly the requisite supply of candidates, since the habit of marrying by the ancient ritual had been dropped, or was retained in few families."—Here he offered several explanations of the fact, the principal one being the indifference of both sexes, though there was also a deliberate avoidance of the difficulties of the ceremony itself.—". . . and since both the man obtaining this priesthood and the woman passing into the marital control of a flamen were automatically withdrawn from paternal jurisdiction.[3] Consequently, a remedy must be applied either by a senatorial resolution or by special law, precisely as Augustus had modified several relics of the rough old world to suit the needs of the present." It was decided, then, after a discussion of the religious points, that no change should be made in the constitution of the flamenship; but a law was carried, that the flamen's wife, though under her husband's tutelage in respect of her sacred duties, should otherwise stand upon the same legal footing as any ordinary woman. Maluginensis' son was elected in the room of his father; and to enhance the dignity of

natio sacerdotum atque ipsis promptior animus foret ad capessendas caerimonias, decretum Corneliae virgini, quae in locum Scantiae capiebatur, sestertium viciens, et quotiens Augusta theatrum introisset, ut sedes inter Vestalium consideret.

XVII. Cornelio Cethego Visellio Varrone consulibus pontifices eorumque exemplo ceteri sacerdotes, cum pro incolumitate principis vota susciperent, Neronem quoque et Drusum isdem dis commendavere non tam caritate iuvenum quam adulatione, quae moribus corruptis perinde anceps, si nulla et ubi nimia est. Nam Tiberius haud umquam domui Germanici mitis, tum vero aequari adulescentes senectae suae inpatienter indoluit; accitosque pontifices percontatus est, num id precibus Agrippinae aut minis tribuissent. Et illi quidem, quamquam abnuerent, modice perstricti; etenim pars magna e propinquis ipsius aut primores civitatis erant: ceterum in senatu oratione monuit in posterum, ne quis mobiles adulescentium animos praematuris honoribus ad superbiam extolleret. Instabat quippe Seianus incusabatque diductam civitatem ut civili bello: esse qui se partium Agrippinae vocent, ac ni resistatur, fore pluris; neque aliud gliscentis discordiae remedium, quam si unus alterve maxime prompti subverterentur.

XVIII. Qua causa C. Silium et Titium Sabinum

---

[1] On the third of January, the *vota pro incolumitate rei publicae* being on the first.

the priests and increase their readiness to perform
the ritual of the various cults, two million sesterces
were voted to the Virgin Cornelia, who was being
appointed to succeed Scantia; while Augusta, whenever she entered the theatre, was to take her place
among the seats reserved for the Vestals.

XVII. In the consulate of Cornelius Cethegus and
Visellius Varro, the pontiffs and—after their example
—the other priests, while offering the vows for the life
of the emperor,[1] went further and commended Nero
and Drusus to the same divinities, not so much from
affection for the princes as in that spirit of sycophancy,
of which the absence or the excess is, in a corrupt
society, equally hazardous. For Tiberius, never
indulgent to the family of Germanicus, was now
stung beyond endurance to find a pair of striplings
placed on a level with his own declining years. He
summoned the pontiffs, and asked if they had made
this concession to the entreaties—or should he say
the threats?—of Agrippina. The pontiffs, in spite
of their denial, received only a slight reprimand
(for a large number were either relatives of his own
or prominent figures in the state); but in the senate,
he gave warning that for the future no one was to
excite to arrogance the impressionable minds of the
youths by such precocious distinctions. The truth
was that Sejanus was pressing him hard:—"The
state," so ran his indictment, "was split into two
halves, as if by civil war. There were men who
proclaimed themselves of Agrippina's party: unless
a stand was taken, there would be more; and the
only cure for the growing disunion was to strike
down one or two of the most active malcontents."

XVIII. On this pretext he attacked Gaius Silius

A.V.C. 777 =
A.D. 24

33

adgreditur. Amicitia Germanici perniciosa utrique, Silio et quod ingentis exercitus septem per annos moderator partisque apud Germaniam triumphalibus Sacroviriani belli victor, quanto maiore mole procideret, plus formidinis in alios dispergebatur. Credebant plerique auctam offensionem ipsius intemperantia, immodice iactantis suum militem in obsequio duravisse, cum alii ad seditiones prolaberentur; neque mansurum Tiberio imperium, si iis quoque legionibus cupido novandi fuisset. Destrui per haec fortunam suam Caesar inparemque tanto merito rebatur. Nam beneficia eo usque laeta sunt, dum videntur exsolvi posse: ubi multum antevenere, pro gratia odium redditur.

XIX. Erat uxor Silio Sosia Galla, caritate Agrippinae invisa principi. Hos corripi dilato ad tempus Sabino placitum, inmissusque Varro consul, qui paternas inimicitias obtendens odiis Seiani per dedecus suum gratificabatur. Precante reo brevem moram, dum accusator consulatu abiret, adversatus est Caesar: solitum quippe magistratibus diem privatis dicere: nec infringendum consulis ius, cuius vigiliis niteretur, ne quod res publica detrimentum caperet. Proprium id Tiberio fuit scelera nuper

---

[1] He appears as *legatus pro praetore* in Upper Germany in 14 A.D. (I. 31), and his defeat of Sacrovir was in 21 A.D. (III. 42 *sqq.*). For his triumphal insignia (15 A.D.) and the nature of that distinction, see I. 72 n.

[2] III. 43 fin.

[3] Tiberius employs the phrasing (*viderent consules ne quid detrimenti res publica caperet*) of the old *senatus consultum ultimum*—first used against C. Gracchus and later, for instance, against Catiline—investing the consuls with quasi-dictatorial powers for the duration of a crisis, and tantamount more or less to a proclamation of martial law.

and Titius Sabinus. The friendship of Germanicus was fatal to both; but in the case of Silius there was the further point that, as he had commanded a great army for seven years,[1] had earned the emblems of triumph in Germany, and was the victor of the war with Sacrovir, the greater ruin of his fall must spread a wider alarm among others. Many considered his offence to have been aggravated by his own indiscretion: he boasted too loudly that " his troops had stood loyal while others were rushing into mutiny; nor could Tiberius have retained the throne, if those legions too had caught the passion for revolution." Such claims, the Caesar thought, were destructive of his position, and left it inadequate to cope with such high deserts. For services are welcome exactly so long as it seems possible to requite them: when that stage is left far behind, the return is hatred instead of gratitude.

XIX. Silius had a wife, Sosia Galla, who by her affection for Agrippina had incurred the detestation of the emperor. On these two, it was decided, the blow should fall: Sabinus could be postponed awhile. Varro, the consul, was unleashed, and, under the pretext of continuing his father's feud,[2] gratified the animosities of Sejanus at the price of his own degradation. The defendant asked a short adjournment till the prosecutor could lay down his consulate, but the Caesar opposed:—" It was quite usual for magistrates to take legal action against private citizens, nor must there be any infraction of the prerogatives of the consul, on whose vigilance it depended 'that the commonwealth should take no harm.' "[3] It was a characteristic of Tiberius to shroud his latest discoveries in crime under the

reperta priscis verbis obtegere. Igitur multa adseveratione, quasi aut legibus cum Silio ageretur aut
Varro consul aut illud res publica esset, coguntur
patres. Silente reo, vel si defensionem coeptaret,
non occultante cuius ira premeretur, conscientia belli
Sacrovir diu dissimulatus, victoria per avaritiam
foedata et uxor socia arguebantur. Nec dubie
repetundarum criminibus haerebant, sed cuncta
quaestione maiestatis exercita, et Silius imminentem
damnationem voluntario fine praevertit.

XX. Saevitum tamen in bona, non ut stipendiariis
pecuniae redderentur, quorum nemo repetebat, sed
liberalitas Augusti avulsa, conputatis singillatim
quae fisco petebantur. Ea prima Tiberio erga
pecuniam alienam diligentia fuit. Sosia in exilium
pellitur Asinii Galli sententia, qui partem bonorum
publicandam, pars ut liberis relinqueretur censuerat.
Contra M'. Lepidus quartam accusatoribus secundum
necessitudinem legis, cetera liberis concessit.

Hunc ego Lepidum temporibus[1] illis gravem et
sapientem virum fuisse comperior: nam pleraque ab
saevis adulationibus aliorum in melius flexit. Neque

---

[1] ⟨ut⟩ temporibus *C. F. W. Mueller.*

---

[1] As a rule—though one with exceptions—suicide before
condemnation saved the estate (*pretium festinandi,* VI. 29).
[2] VI. 4. n.

phrases of an older world. With scrupulous gravity, therefore, as though Silius were on his trial before the law, as though Varro were a consul or that state of things a commonwealth, the Fathers were convened. With the defendant either holding his peace, or, if he essayed a defence, making no secret of the person under whose resentment he was sinking, the indictment was presented: Sacrovir long screened through complicity in his revolt, a victory besmirched by rapine, a wife the partner of his sins. Nor was there any doubt that, on the charges of extortion, the pair were inextricably involved; but the entire case was handled as an impeachment for treason, and Silius anticipated the impending condemnation by a voluntary end.

XX. Nevertheless, no mercy was shown to his estate:[1] not that any sums were to be refunded to the provincial tribute-payers, none of whom lodged a claim; but the bounty of Augustus was summarily deducted and the claims of the imperial exchequer calculated item by item: the first instance in which Tiberius had given so sharp an eye to property other than his own. Sosia was driven into exile on the motion of Asinius Gallus, who had proposed to confiscate one half of her estate, while leaving the other to her children. A countermotion by Manius Lepidus[2] assigned a quarter, which was legally necessary, to the accusers, and the residue to the family.

This Lepidus, I gather, was, for his period, a man of principle and intelligence: for the number of motions to which he gave a more equitable turn, in opposition to the cringing brutality of others, is very considerable. Nor yet did he lack discretion,

37

tamen temperamenti egebat, cum aequabili auctoritate et gratia apud Tiberium viguerit. Unde dubitare cogor, fato et sorte nascendi, ut cetera, ita principum inclinatio in hos, offensio in illos, an sit aliquid in nostris consiliis liceatque inter abruptam contumaciam et deforme obsequium pergere iter ambitione ac periculis vacuum. At Messalinus Cotta haud minus claris maioribus, sed animo diversus, censuit cavendum senatus consulto, ut quamquam insontes magistratus et culpae alienae nescii provincialibus uxorum criminibus perinde quam suis plecterentur.

XXI. Actum dehinc de Calpurnio Pisone, nobili ac feroci viro. Is namque, ut rettuli, cessurum se urbe ob factiones accusatorum in senatu clamitaverat et spreta potentia Augustae trahere in ius Urgulaniam domoque principis excire ausus erat. Quae in praesens Tiberius civiliter habuit: sed in animo revolvente iras, etiam si impetus offensionis languerat, memoria valebat. Pisonem Q. Granius secreti sermonis incusavit adversum maiestatem habiti, adiecitque in domo eius venenum esse eumque gladio accinctum introire curiam. Quod ut atrocius vero tramissum; ceterorum, quae multa cumulabantur, receptus est reus, neque peractus ob mortem

---

[1] Son of the famous M. Valerius Messala Corvinus—*magni Messalae lippa propago* Pers. ii. 72. A patron of Ovid, and almost proverbial for his wealth and liberality (Juv. v. 109; vii. 95), he bears none the less a dubious character in the *Annals* (cf. II. 32, and especially V. 3 and VI. 5).

[2] II. 34.

since with Tiberius he stood uniformly high in influence and in favour : a circumstance which compels me to doubt whether, like all things else, the sympathies and antipathies of princes are governed in their incidence by fate and the star of our nativity, or whether our purposes count and we are free, between the extremes of bluff contumacy and repellent servility, to walk a straight road, clear of intrigues and of perils.   On the other side, Messalinus Cotta,[1] with an equally distinguished lineage but a contrasted character, pressed for a senatorial decree ruling that magistrates, even if personally innocent and not aware of guilt in others, should be penalized for the misdeeds of their wives in the provinces precisely as for their own.

XXI. Next there was treated the case of Calpurnius Piso, a man of birth and courage : it was he who, as I have stated already,[2] had exclaimed to the senate that he would retire from the capital as a protest against the cabals of the informers, and, contemptuous of the influence of Augusta, had dared to bring Urgulania before a court and to summon her from under the imperial roof. For the moment, Tiberius took the incidents in good part ; but in his heart, brooding over its grounds for wrath, though the first transport of resentment might have died down, memory lived. It was Quintus Granius, who charged Piso with holding private conversations derogatory to majesty ; and added that he kept poison at his house and wore a sword when entering the curia. The last count was allowed to drop as too atrocious to be true ; on the others, which were freely accumulated, he was entered for trial, and was only saved from undergoing it by a well-timed death.

opportunam. Relatum et de Cassio Severo exule,
qui sordidae originis, maleficae vitae, sed orandi
validus, per immodicas inimicitias ut iudicio iurati
senatus Cretam amoveretur effecerat; atque illic
eadem actitando recentia veteraque odia advertit,
bonisque exutus, interdicto igni atque aqua, saxo
Seripho consenuit.

XXII. Per idem tempus Plautius Silvanus praetor
incertis causis Aproniam coniugem in praeceps iecit,
tractusque ad Caesarem ab L. Apronio socero
turbata mente respondit, tamquam ipse somno
gravis atque eo ignarus, et uxor sponte mortem
sumpsisset. Non cunctanter Tiberius pergit in domum, visit cubiculum, in quo reluctantis et impulsae
vestigia cernebantur. Refert ad senatum, datisque
iudicibus Urgulania Silvani avia pugionem nepoti
misit. Quod perinde creditum, quasi principis
monitu, ob amicitiam Augustae cum Urgulania.
Reus frustra temptato ferro venas praebuit exsol-
vendas. Mox Numantina, prior uxor eius, accusata
iniecisse carminibus et veneficiis vaecordiam marito,
insons iudicatur.

XXIII. Is demum annus populum Romanum
longo adversum Numidam Tacfarinatem bello absolvit.
Nam priores duces, ubi impetrando triumphalium

---

[1] l. 72 n.

The case, also, of the exiled Cassius Severus [1] was brought up in the senate. Of sordid origin and mischievous life, but a powerful orator, he had made enemies on such a scale that by a verdict of the senate under oath he was relegated to Crete. There, by continuing his methods, he drew upon himself so many animosities, new or old, that he was now stripped of his estate, interdicted from fire and water, and sent to linger out his days on the rock of Seriphos.

XXII. About this time, the praetor Plautius Silvanus, for reasons not ascertained, flung his wife Apronia out of the window, and, when brought before the emperor by his father-in-law, Lucius Apronius, gave an incoherent reply to the effect that he had himself been fast asleep and was therefore ignorant of the facts; his wife, he thought, must have committed suicide. Without any hesitation, Tiberius went straight to the house and examined the bedroom, in which traces were visible of resistance offered and force employed. He referred the case to the senate, and a judicial committee had been formed, when Silvanus' grandmother Urgulania sent her descendant a dagger. In view of Augusta's friendship with Urgulania, the action was considered as equivalent to a hint from the emperor: the accused, after a fruitless attempt with the weapon, arranged for his arteries to be opened. Shortly afterwards, his first wife Numantina, charged with procuring the insanity of her husband by spells and philtres, was adjudged innocent.

XXIII. This year at last freed the Roman nation from the long-drawn war with the Numidian Tacfarinas. For earlier commanders, once they con-

insigni sufficere res suas crediderant, hostem omitte-
bant; iamque tres laureatae in urbe statuae,[1] et
adhuc raptabat Africam Tacfarinas, auctus Maurorum auxiliis, qui, Ptolemaeo Iubae filio[2] iuventa
incurioso, libertos regios et servilia imperia bello
mutaverant. Erat illi praedarum receptor ac socius
populandi rex Garamantum,[3] non ut cum exercitu
incederet, sed missis levibus copiis, quae ex longinquo
in maius audiebantur; ipsaque e provincia, ut quis
fortuna inops, moribus turbidus, promptius ruebant,
quia Caesar post res a Blaeso gestas, quasi nullis iam
in Africa hostibus, reportari nonam legionem iusserat,[4]
nec pro consule eius anni P. Dolabella retinere ausus
erat, iussa principis magis quam incerta belli metuens.

XXIV. Igitur Tacfarinas disperso rumore rem
Romanam aliis quoque ab nationibus lacerari eoque
paulatim Africa decedere, ac posse reliquos circum-
veniri, si cuncti, quibus libertas servitio potior,
incubuissent, auget viris positisque castris Thubuscum oppidum[5] circumsidet. At Dolabella contracto
quod erat militum, terrore nominis Romani et quia
Numidae peditum aciem ferre nequeunt, primo sui
incessu solvit obsidium locorumque opportuna permu-

---

[1] Those of Furius Camillus (II. 52), Lucius Apronius (III.
21), and Junius Blaesus (III. 72).

[2] He appears to have succeeded his father a year previously,
and reigned till 40 A.D., when he was summoned to Rome and
executed by his cousin Caligula (Suet. *Cal.* 26).

[3] In Fezzan (III. 74).

[4] To Pannonia (III. 9; IV. 5 n.).

[5] Identified with Thubusuctu (*Tiklat*) near Saldae (*Bougie*)
on the Mauretanian frontier.

sidered their exploits sufficient for a grant of triumphal decorations, usually left the enemy in peace; and already three laurelled statues[1] adorned the capital, while Tacfarinas was still harrying Africa, reinforced by contingents of Moors, who, during the heedless youth of Juba's son Ptolemy,[2] had sought in war a change from royal freedmen and servile despotism. The Garamantian king[3] acted as the receiver of his booty and the partner of his forays, not to the extent of taking the field with an army, but by despatching light-armed troops, whose numbers report magnified in proportion to the distance; and from the province itself every man of broken fortunes or turbulent character rushed to his standard with an alacrity all the greater because, after the successes of Blaesus, the Caesar, as though no enemies were left in Africa, had ordered the ninth legion back,[4] nor had Publius Dolabella, proconsul for the year and more apprehensive of the emperor's orders than of the chances of war, ventured to detain it.

XXIV. Accordingly, after launching a report that other nations as well were engaged on the dismemberment of the Roman empire, which on that account was step by step evacuating Africa, while the garrison remaining might be cut off by the combined onslaught of all who preferred liberty to bondage, Tacfarinas increased his strength, established a camp, and invested the town of Thubuscum.[5] Dolabella, on the other hand, mustered every available man, and, through the terrors of the Roman name and the inability of the Numidians to face embattled infantry, raised the siege at his first advance and fortified the various strategic points:

43

nivit; simul principes Musulamiorum defectionem coeptantes securi percutit. Dein, quia pluribus adversum Tacfarinatem expeditionibus cognitum, non gravi nec uno incursu consectandum hostem vagum, excito cum popularibus rege Ptolemaeo quattuor agmina parat, quae legatis aut tribunis data; et praedatorias manus delecti Maurorum duxere: ipse consultor aderat omnibus.

XXV. Nec multo post adfertur Numidas apud castellum semirutum, ab ipsis quondam incensum, cui nomen Auzea, positis mapalibus consedisse, fisos loco, quia vastis circum saltibus claudebatur. Tum expeditae cohortes alaeque, quam in partem ducerentur ignarae, cito agmine rapiuntur. Simulque coeptus dies et concentu tubarum ac truci clamore aderant semisomnos in barbaros, praepeditis Numidarum equis aut diversos pastus pererrantibus. Ab Romanis confertus pedes, dispositae turmae, cuncta proelio provisa: hostibus contra omnium nesciis non arma, non ordo, non consilium, sed pecorum modo trahi, occidi, capi. Infensus miles memoria laborum et adversum eludentis optatae totiens pugnae se quisque ultione et sanguine explebant. Differtur per manipulos, Tacfarinatem omnes, notum tot proeliis, consectentur: non nisi

---

[1] II. 52 n.   [2] Aumale.

at the same time he brought to the block the
Musulamian[1] chieftains who were contemplating
rebellion. Then, as several expeditions against
Tacfarinas had shown that a nomadic enemy was not
to be brought to bay by a single incursion carried
out by heavy-armed troops, he summoned King
Ptolemy with his countrymen, and arranged four
columns under the command of legates or tribunes;
companies of raiders were led by picked Moors;
he himself was present as adviser to all the divisions.

XXV. Before long, word came in that the
Numidians had pitched their tents and were lying
close by a half-ruined fort called Auzea,[2] to which
they had themselves set fire some time ago: they
felt confident of their ground, as it was encircled by
enormous woods. On this, the light cohorts and
mounted squadrons, without being informed of
their destination, were hurried off at full speed.
Day was just breaking when with a fierce yell and
a blast of trumpets they came on the half-awakened
barbarians, while the Numidian horses were still
shackled or straying through distant pasture-grounds.
On the Roman side, the infantry were in massed
formation, the cavalry disposed in troops, every
provision made for battle: the enemy, in contrast,
were aware of nothing, without weapons, without
order, without a plan, dragged to slaughter or to
captivity like cattle. The soldiers, embittered by
the memory of hardships undergone and of battle
so often hoped for against this elusive foe, took every
man his fill of revenge and blood. Word was passed
round the maniples that all were to make for
Tacfarinas, a familiar figure after so many engagements: there would be no rest from war till the arch-

duce interfecto requiem belli fore. At ille deiectis circum stipatoribus vinctoque iam filio et effusis undique Romanis, ruendo in tela captivitatem haud inulta morte effugit isque finis armis impositus.

XXVI. Dolabellae petenti abnuit triumphalia Tiberius, Seiano tribuens, ne Blaesi avunculi eius laus obsolesceret. Sed neque Blaesus ideo inlustrior, et huic negatus honor gloriam intendit: quippe minore exercitu insignis captivos, caedem ducis bellique confecti famam deportarat. Sequebantur et Garamantum legati, raro in urbe visi, quos Tacfarinate caeso perculsa gens, et [1] culpae conscia [2] ad satis faciendum populo Romano miserat. Cognitis dehinc Ptolemaei per id bellum studiis repetitus ex vetusto more honos missusque [3] e senatoribus, qui scipionem eburnum, togam pictam, antiqua patrum munera, daret regemque et socium atque amicum appellaret.

XXVII. Eadem aestate mota [4] per Italiam servilis belli semina fors oppressit. Auctor tumultus T. Curtisius,[5] quondam praetoriae cohortis miles, primo coetibus clandestinis apud Brundisium et circumiecta oppida, mox positis propalam libellis ad libertatem

---

[1] et] set *Halm* (*with* nescia).
[2] conscia *Lipsius* (socia *Nipperdey*): nescia.
[3] honos missusque *Doederlein*: omissusque.
mota] moti *Pluygers*.   [5] Curtisius] Curtilius *Reinesius*.

---

[1] The triumphal toga with golden stars on a purple ground. The ivory sceptre figures on the reverse of a coin of Ptolemy's,

rebel was slain. He, with his guards cut down around him, his son already in chains, and Romans streaming up on all hands, rushed on the spears and escaped captivity by a death which was not unavenged. This marked the close of hostilities.

XXVI. The request of Dolabella for triumphal distinctions was rejected by Tiberius: a tribute to Sejanus, whose uncle Blaesus might otherwise have found his glories growing dim. But the step brought no added fame to Blaesus, and the denial of the honour heightened the reputation of Dolabella, who, with a weaker army, had credited himself with prisoners of note, a general slain, and a war concluded. He was attended also—a rare spectacle in the capital— by a number of Garamantian deputies, whom the tribesmen, awed by the fate of Tacfarinas and conscious of their delinquencies, had sent to offer satisfaction to the Roman people. Then, as the campaign had demonstrated Ptolemy's good-will, an old-fashioned distinction was revived, and a member of the senate was despatched to present him with the traditional bounty of the Fathers, an ivory sceptre with the embroidered robe,[1] and to greet him by the style of king, ally, and friend.

XXVII. During the same summer, the seeds of a slave war, which had begun to stir in Italy, were rendered harmless by an accident. The instigator of revolt was Titus Curtisius, a former private in a praetorian cohort. First at clandestine meetings in the neighbourhood of Brundisium and the adjacent towns, then by openly posted manifestoes, he kept

together with a curule chair, which must also have been part of the gift (cf. *e.g.* Liv. XXX. 15; XLII. 14).

vocabat agrestia per longinquos saltus et ferocia
servitia, cum velut munere deum tres biremes ad-
pulere ad usus commeantium illo mari. Et erat
isdem regionibus Cutius Lupus quaestor, cui provincia
vetere ex more calles [1] evenerant [2]: is disposita
classiariorum copia coeptantem cum maxime coniura-
tionem disiecit. Missusque a Caesare propere
Staius tribunus cum valida manu ducem ipsum et
proximos audacia in urbem traxit, iam trepidam ob
multitudinem familiarum, quae gliscebat inmensum,
minore in dies plebe ingenua.

XXVIII. Isdem consulibus miseriarum ac saevitiae
exemplum atrox, reus pater, accusator filius (nomen
utrique Vibius Serenus) in senatum inducti sunt.
Ab exilio retractus inluvieque ac squalore obsitus et
tum catena vinctus peroranti filio pater comparatur.[3]
Adulescens multis munditiis, alacri vultu, structas
principi insidias, missos in Galliam concitores belli
index idem et testis dicebat, adnectebatque Cae-
cilium Cornutum praetorium ministravisse pecuniam;

[1] calles] Cales *Lipsius* (*supported by Mommsen*).

[2] evenerant *Haase* : evenerat.

[3] pater comparatur *Madvig* : praeparatur *Med.* (pater
oranti f. comparatur *Halm*).

---

[1] " The reference is to the troops of armed and mounted
herdsmen (*pastores*) maintained by the great proprietors on
their extensive ranches (*saltus*) in Apulia and Calabria. These
pastores had been notorious as early as the days of Catiline
(63 B.C., Sall. *Cat.* 46). Under Tiberius a quaestor was
stationed in S. Italy to check their excesses, especially when
moving along the tracks (*calles*) leading from the lowland to
the highland grazing-grounds " (Pelham, on XII. 65).

[2] For the obscure quaestorian ' provinces ' in Italy, the
reader may be referred to Nipperdey or Furneaux. With
Lipsius' emendation, the sense of the passage is unchanged,
but it is assumed that Cales (*Calvi*), the first Latin colony in

summoning the fierce country slaves[1] of the outlying ranches to strike for freedom, when almost providentially three biremes for the protection of sea-borne traffic put in to port. As in addition the quaestor Cutius Lupus, who in accordance with an old custom had been assigned the " grazing-tracks " for his province,[2] happened to be in the district, he drew up a force of marines and shattered the conspiracy at the very outset. The tribune Staius, hurriedly sent by the Caesar with a strong force, dragged the leader and the bolder of his subordinates to Rome, where tremors were already felt at the size of the slave-establishments, which were assuming huge dimensions while the free-born populace dwindled day by day.

XXVIII. In the same consulate, as an appalling example of the miseries and heartlessness of the age, there appeared before the senate as defendant a father and a son as prosecutor, each bearing the name of Vibius Serenus.[3] The father, haled back from exile, a mass of filth and rags, and now in irons, stood pitted against the invective of his son: the youth, a highly elegant figure with a cheerful countenance, informer at once and witness, told his tale of treason plotted against the sovereign and missionaries of rebellion sent over to Gaul;[4] adding that the funds had been supplied by the ex-praetor, Caecilius

Campania, had originally been important enough to be taken as the headquarters of a quaestorian district running from coast to coast of the peninsula and so including the Calabrian town of Brundisium.

[3] For the father, see chap. 13 above; for the son, chap. 36 below.

[4] From Baetica—his father's province—at the time of the rising of Sacrovir.

qui taedio curarum, et quia periculum pro exitio
habebatur, mortem in se festinavit. At contra reus
nihil infracto animo obversus in filium quatere vincla,
vocare ultores deos, ut sibi quidem redderent exilium,
ubi procul tali more ageret, filium autem quandoque
supplicia sequerentur. Adseverabatque innocentem
Cornutum et falso exterritum; idque facile intellectu,
si proderentur alii: non enim se caedem principis et
res novas uno socio cogitasse.

XXIX. Tum accusator Cn. Lentulum et Seium
Tuberonem nominat, magno pudore Caesaris, cum
primores civitatis, intimi ipsius amici, Lentulus
senectutis extremae, Tubero defecto corpore,
tumultus hostilis et turbandae rei publicae accerse-
rentur. Sed hi quidem statim exempti: in patrem
ex servis quaesitum, et quaestio adversa accusatori
fuit. Qui scelere vaecors, simul vulgi rumore territus,
robur et saxum aut parricidarum poenas minitantium,
cessit urbe. Ac retractus Ravenna exsequi accusationem adigitur, non occultante Tiberio vetus odium
adversum exulem Serenum. Nam post damnatum
Libonem missis ad Caesarem litteris exprobraverat
suum tantum studium sine fructu fuisse, addideratque
quaedam contumacius quam tutum apud aures

---

[1] I. 27 n. [2] The legate of Germanicus (II. 20).
[3] The *Tullianum*, described by Sallust (*Cat.* 55), and still in
existence.
[4] The Tarpeian Rock: cf. II. 32; VI. 19.
[5] The so-called *poena cullei*—the parricide being sewn into a
sack in company with a dog, a cock, a viper, and an ape, then
flung into the sea: see, for instance, Juv. viii. 214 (Mayor)
and Cic. *Rosc. Am.* § 70 (Landgraf).

Cornutus. Cornutus, as he was weary of his anxieties and risk was considered tantamount to ruin, lost no time in making away with himself. The prisoner on the other hand, with a spirit totally unbroken, faced his son, clanked his chains, and called upon the avenging gods :—" For himself, let them give him back his exile, where he could live remote from these fashions ; as for his son, let retribution attend him in its own time ! " He insisted that Cornutus was guiltless, the victim of an unfounded panic, and that the fact would be patent if other names were divulged : for certainly he himself had not contemplated murder of the emperor and revolution with a solitary ally !

XXIX. The accuser then named Gnaeus Lentulus[1] and Seius Tubero,[2] greatly to the discomfiture of the Caesar, who found two most prominent nobles, close friends of his own, the former far advanced in years, the latter in failing health, charged with armed rebellion and conspiracy against the peace of the realm. These, however, were at once exempted : against the father resort was had to examination of his slaves under torture—an examination which proved adverse to the prosecutor ; who, maddened by his crime and terrified also by the comments of the multitude, threatening him with the dungeon[3] and the rock[4] or the penalties of parricide,[5] left Rome. He was dragged back from Ravenna and forced to proceed with his accusation, Tiberius making no effort to disguise his old rancour against the exile. For, after the condemnation of Libo, Serenus had written to the emperor, complaining that his zeal alone had gone without reward, and concluding with certain expressions too defiant to be safely addressed

superbas et offensioni proniores. Ea Caesar octo post annos rettulit, medium tempus varie arguens, etiam si tormenta pervicacia servorum contra evenissent.

XXX. Dictis dein sententiis ut Serenus more maiorum puniretur, quo molliret invidiam, intercessit. Gallus Asinius *cum*[1] Gyaro aut Donusa claudendum censeret, id quoque aspernatus est, egenam aquae utramque insulam referens dandosque vitae usus, cui vita concederetur. Ita Serenus Amorgum reportatur. Et quia Cornutus sua manu ceciderat, actum de praemiis accusatorum abolendis, si quis maiestatis postulatus ante perfectum iudicium se ipse vita privavisset. Ibaturque in eam sententiam, ni durius contraque morem suum palam pro accusatoribus Caesar inritas leges, rem publicam in praecipiti conquestus esset: subverterent potius iura quam custodes eorum amoverent. Sic delatores, genus hominum publico exitio repertum et *ne*[2] poenis quidem umquam satis coercitum, per praemia eliciebantur.

XXXI. His tam adsiduis tamque maestis modica laetitia intericitur, quod C. Cominium equitem Romanum, probrosi in se carminis convictum, Caesar precibus fratris, qui senator erat, concessit. Quo magis mirum habebatur gnarum meliorum, et quae

---

[1] ⟨cum⟩ *Muretus.*   [2] ⟨ne⟩ *Bekker.*

---

[1] By decapitation after flogging—the penalties symbolized by the *fasces* and *secures*.
[2] III. 68 n.—Donusa, if rightly identified with *Stenosa*, lay E. of Naxos.

to that proud and lightly offended ear. To this grievance the Caesar harked back after eight years; finding in the interval materials for a variety of charges, even though, through the obduracy of the slaves, the torture had disappointed expectations.

XXX. When members then expressed the view that Serenus should be punished according to ancestral custom,[1] he sought to mitigate the odium by interposing his veto. A motion of Asinius Gallus, that the prisoner should be confined in Gyarus[2] or Donusa, he also negatived: both islands, he reminded him, were waterless, and, if you granted a man his life, you must also allow him the means of living. Serenus was, therefore, shipped back to Amorgus. And since Cornutus had fallen by his own hand, a proposal was discussed that the accuser's reward should be forfeited whenever the defendant in a charge of treason had resorted to suicide before the completion of the trial. The resolution was on the point of being adopted, when the Caesar, with considerable asperity and unusual frankness, took the side of the accusers, complaining that the laws would be inoperative, the country on the edge of an abyss: they had better demolish the constitution than remove its custodians. Thus the informers, a breed invented for the national ruin and never adequately curbed even by penalties, were now lured into the field with rewards.

XXXI. The round of tragedies was broken by a relatively cheerful interlude when the emperor spared Gaius Cominius, a Roman knight convicted of a poetical lampoon upon himself, as a concession to the prayers of his brother, a member of the senate. The fact heightened the general wonder that,

fama clementiam sequeretur, tristiora malle. Neque
enim socordia peccabat; nec occultum est, quando
ex veritate, quando adumbrata laetitia facta imperatorum celebrentur. Quin ipse, conpositus alias et
velut eluctantium verborum, solutius promptiusque
eloquebatur, quotiens subveniret. At P. Suillium,
quaestorem quondam Germanici, cum Italia arcere-
tur convictus pecuniam ob rem iudicandam cepisse,
amovendum in insulam censuit, tanta contentione
animi, ut iure iurando obstringeret e re publica id
esse. Quod aspere acceptum ad praesens mox in
laudem vertit regresso Suillio; quem vidit sequens
aetas praepotentem, venalem et Claudii principis
amicitia diu prospere, numquam bene usum. Eadem
poena in Catum Firmium senatorem statuitur,
tamquam falsis maiestatis criminibus sororem petivisset. Catus, ut rettuli, Libonem inlexerat insidiis,
deinde indicio perculerat. Eius operae memor
Tiberius, sed alia praetendens, exilium deprecatus
est: quo minus senatu pelleretur non obstitit.

XXXII. Pleraque eorum, quae rettuli quaeque
referam, parva forsitan et levia memoratu videri non
nescius sum: sed nemo annales nostros cum scriptura
eorum contenderit, qui veteres[1] populi Romani res

---

[1] veteres] veteris *Freinsheim (cf.* I. 1).

---

[1] Publius Suillius Rufus, half-brother of Corbulo; married
to a daughter of Ovid's third wife (*nam tibi quae coniunx,
eadem mihi filia paene est: Et quae te generum, me vocat illa
virum,* ex P. iv. 8); a conspicuous accuser—*continuus ac saevus
accusandis reis*—under Claudius (XI. 5); banished by the
agency of Seneca to the Balearic Isles in 58 A.D. (XIII.
42 *sq.*).
[2] ii. 27.

cognizant as he was of better things and of the fame that attended mercy, he should still prefer the darker road. For neither did he err by thoughtlessness; nor, indeed, is it difficult to divine when the acts of emperors are applauded with sincerity and when with feigned enthusiam. Moreover, he himself, otherwise an artificial speaker whose every word had apparently to struggle for utterance, spoke out with more fluency and promptness whenever he spoke in charity. On the other hand, when Publius Suillius,[1] an old quaestor of Germanicus, was about to escape with banishment from Italy after being convicted of judicial corruption, he moved for his deportation to an island, with so much earnestness as to make a declaration on oath that the change was demanded by national interests. His intervention, severely criticized at the time, redounded before long to his credit: for Suillius returned, and the succeeding generation viewed him in the plenitude of power, the venal favourite of Claudius, exploiting the imperial friendship long profitably, never well. The same penalty was invoked upon Firmius Catus, a member of the senate, for laying a false charge of treason against his sister. Catus, as I have said,[2] had laid the trap for Libo and afterwards destroyed him by his evidence. In the recollection of that service, Tiberius, though producing other reasons, now procured a remission of his banishment: to his ejection from the senate he raised no hindrance.

XXXII. I am not unaware that very many of the events I have described, and shall describe, may perhaps seem little things, trifles too slight for record; but no parallel can be drawn between these chronicles of mine and the work of the men who composed the

conposuere. Ingentia illi bella, expugnationes urbium, fusos captosque reges, aut si quando ad interna praeverterent, discordias consulum adversum tribunos, agrarias frumentariasque leges, plebis et optimatium certamina libero egressu memorabant: nobis in arto et inglorius labor; immota quippe aut modice lacessita pax, maestae urbis res et princeps proferendi imperi incuriosus erat. Non tamen sine usu fuerit introspicere illa primo aspectu levia, ex quis magnarum saepe rerum motus oriuntur.

XXXIII. Nam cunctas nationes et urbes populus aut primores aut singuli regunt: delecta ex iis et consociata rei publicae forma laudari facilius quam evenire, vel si evenit, haud diuturna esse potest. Igitur ut olim plebe valida, vel cum patres pollerent, noscenda vulgi natura et quibus modis temperanter haberetur, senatusque et optimatium ingenia qui maxime perdidicerant, callidi temporum et sapientes credebantur, sic converso statu neque alia re Romana, quam si unus imperitet, haec conquiri tradique in rem fuerit, quia pauci prudentia honesta ab deterioribus, utilia ab noxiis discernunt, plures aliorum eventis docentur. Ceterum ut profutura, ita minimum oblectationis adferunt. Nam situs gentium,

ancient history of the Roman people. Gigantic wars, cities stormed, routed and captive kings, or, when they turned by choice to domestic affairs, the feuds of consul and tribune, land-laws and corn-laws, the duel of nobles and commons—such were the themes on which *they* dwelt, or digressed, at will. Mine is an inglorious labour in a narrow field: for this was an age of peace unbroken or half-heartedly challenged, of tragedy in the capital, of a prince careless to extend the empire. Yet it may be not unprofitable to look beneath the surface of those incidents, trivial at the first inspection, which so often set in motion the great events of history.

XXXIII. For every nation or city is governed by the people, or by the nobility, or by individuals: a constitution selected and blended from these types is easier to commend than to create; or, if created, its tenure of life is brief. Accordingly, as in the period of alternate plebeian dominance and patrician ascendancy it was imperative, in one case, to study the character of the masses and the methods of controlling them; while, in the other, those who had acquired the most exact knowledge of the temper of the senate and the aristocracy were accounted shrewd in their generation and wise; so to-day, when the situation has been transformed and the Roman world is little else than a monarchy, the collection and the chronicling of these details may yet serve an end: for few men distinguish right and wrong, the expedient and the disastrous, by native intelligence; the majority are schooled by the experience of others. But while my themes have their utility, they offer the minimum of pleasure. Descriptions of countries, the vicissitudes of battles, com-

THE ANNALS OF TACITUS

varietates proeliorum, clari ducum exitus retinent ac
redintegrant legentium animum: nos saeva iussa,
continuas accusationes, fallaces amicitias, perniciem
innocentium et easdem exitu [1] causas coniungimus,
obvia rerum similitudine et satietate. Tum quod
antiquis scriptoribus rarus obtrectator, neque refert
cuiusquam Punicas Romanasne [2] acies laetius extu-
leris: at multorum, qui Tiberio regente poenam vel
infamias [3] subiere, posteri manent. Utque familiae
ipsae iam extinctae sint, reperies qui ob similitudinem
morum aliena malefacta sibi obiectari putent. Etiam
gloria ac virtus infensos habet, ut nimis ex propinquo diversa arguens. Sed ad inceptum [4] redeo.

XXXIV. Cornelio Cosso Asinio Agrippa consulibus
Cremutius Cordus postulatur, novo ac tunc primum
audito crimine, quod editis annalibus laudatoque
M. Bruto C. Cassium Romanorum ultimum dixisset.
Accusabant Satrius Secundus et Pinarius Natta,
Seiani clientes. Id perniciabile reo, et Caesar truci
vultu defensionem accipiens, quam Cremutius,
relinquendae vitae certus, in hunc modum exorsus
est:—"Verba mea, patres conscripti, arguuntur:
adeo factorum innocens sum. Sed neque haec in

[1] exitu] exitii *Pichena.*
[2] Romanasne *Nipperdey* : Romanasve.
[3] poenam vel infamias] poenas vel infamiam *Heraeus.*
[4] ad inceptum *Halm* : ancepto *Med.*, ad incepta *Beroaldus.*

---

[1] Author of a history of Augustus, ἥν αὐτὸς ἐκεῖνος ἀνεγνώκει
(D. Cass. LVII. 24). Seneca's *Consolatio ad Marciam* (on the
death of a son) is addressed to his daughter.
[2] There were to be parallels later under Domitian : cf. *e.g.
Agr.* 2, Suet. *Dom.* 10 *Iunium Rusticum* (sc. interemit),
*quod Paeti Thraseae et Helvidii Prisci laudes edidisset appellas-
setque eos sanctissimos viros.*

manders dying on the field of honour, such are the
episodes that arrest and renew the interest of the
reader: for myself, I present a series of savage
mandates, of perpetual accusations, of traitorous
friendships, of ruined innocents, of various causes and
identical results—everywhere monotony of subject,
and satiety. Again, the ancient author has few
detractors, and it matters to none whether you
praise the Carthaginian or the Roman arms with the
livelier enthusiasm. But of many, who underwent
either the legal penalty or a form of degradation
in the principate of Tiberius, the descendants remain;
and, assuming the actual families to be now extinct,
you will still find those who, from a likeness of
character, read the ill deeds of others as an innuendo
against themselves. Even glory and virtue create
their enemies—they arraign their opposites by too
close a contrast. But I return to my subject.

XXXIV. The consulate of Cornelius Cossus and
Asinius Agrippa opened with the prosecution of
Cremutius Cordus [1] upon the novel and till then [2]
unheard-of charge of publishing a history, eulogizing
Brutus, and styling Cassius the last of the Romans. [3]
The accusers were Satrius Secundus and Pinarius
Natta, clients of Sejanus. That circumstance sealed
the defendant's fate—that and the lowering brows
of the Caesar, [4] as he bent his attention to the defence;
which Cremutius, resolved to take his leave of life,
began as follows :—" Conscript Fathers, my words
are brought to judgement—so guiltless am I of deeds !
Nor are they even words against the sole persons

A.V.C. 778 =
A.D. 25

---

[3] In Plutarch it is Brutus himself who calls the dead Cassius
ἔσχατον ἄνδρα Ῥωμαίων (*Brut.* 44 *init.*).

[4] The trial takes place before the senate, with the emperor
presiding.

principem aut principis parentem, quos lex maiestatis
amplectitur: Brutum et Cassium laudavisse dicor,
quorum res gestas cum plurimi composuerint, nemo
sine honore memoravit. Titus Livius, eloquentiae ac
fidei praeclarus in primis, Cn. Pompeium tantis
laudibus tulit, ut Pompeianum eum Augustus
appellaret; neque id amicitiae eorum offecit.
Scipionem, Afranium, hunc ipsum Cassium, hunc
Brutum nusquam latrones et parricidas, quae nunc
vocabula inponuntur, saepe ut insignis viros nominat.
Asinii Pollionis scripta egregiam eorundem memoriam
tradunt; Messalla Corvinus imperatorem suum
Cassium praedicabat: et uterque opibus atque honoribus perviguere. Marci Ciceronis libro, quo Catonem
caelo aequavit, quid aliud dictator Caesar quam
rescripta oratione, velut apud iudices, respondit?
Antonii epistulae, Bruti contiones falsa quidem in
Augustum probra, set multa cum acerbitate habent;
carmina Bibaculi et Catulli referta contumeliis
Caesarum leguntur: sed ipse divus Iulius, ipse divus
Augustus et tulere ista et reliquere, haud facile

---

[1] Scipio and Afranius—Pompey's father-in-law and lieutenant respectively. Both perished, the former by suicide, the
latter after pursuit and capture, after the disaster of Thapsus
in 46 B.C.

[2] The famous man of letters and affairs of the Augustan
period (70 B.C.–4 A.D.). His history—the *periculosae plenum
opus aleae* of Hor. *Carm.* II. 1—opened with the first triumvirate (60 B.C.).

[3] See III. 34 n. He had followed successively Cassius,
Antony, and Augustus.

embraced by the law of treason, the sovereign or the
parent of the sovereign: I am said to have praised
Brutus and Cassius, whose acts so many pens have
recorded, whom not one has mentioned save with
honour. Livy, with a fame for eloquence and
candour second to none, lavished such eulogies on
Pompey that Augustus styled him ' the Pompeian ':
yet it was without prejudice to their friendship.
Scipio, Afranius,[1] this very Cassius, this Brutus—
not once does he describe them by the now fashionable
titles of brigand and parricide, but time and again
in such terms as he might apply to any distinguished
patriots. The works of Asinius Pollio[2] transmit
their character in noble colours; Messalla Corvinus[3]
gloried to have served under Cassius: and Pollio
and Corvinus lived and died in the fulness of wealth
and honour! When Cicero's book[4] praised Cato to
the skies, what did it elicit from the dictator Caesar
but a written oration as though at the bar of public
opinion? The letters of Antony, the speeches of
Brutus, contain invectives against Augustus, false
undoubtedly yet bitter in the extreme; the poems—
still read—of Bibaculus[5] and Catullus[6] are packed
with scurrilities upon the Caesars: yet even the
deified Julius, the divine Augustus himself, tolerated
them and left them in peace; and I hesitate whether

[4] A lost panegyric of Cato Uticensis (*Laus Catonis*, A. Gell.
XIII. 19), answered by Caesar in two books of *Anticatones*
(Suet. *Caes.* 56).

[5] M. Furius (' *Bibaculus* erat et vocabatur,' Plin. *H.N.*,
praef. 24). The scanty fragments, chiefly from Suetonius,
may be found in Baehrens *F.P.R.* 317 *sq.*; the references of
Horace, at *Sat.* II. 5, 41 and I. 10, 36.

[6] *Valerium Catullum, a quo sibi versiculis de Mamurra*
(Cat. 57) *perpetua stigmata imposita non dissimulaverat, eodem
die adhibuit cenae* (Suet. *Caes.* 73).

dixerim, moderatione magis an sapientia. Namque
spreta exolescunt: si irascare, adgnita videntur."

XXXV. " Non attingo Graecos, quorum non modo
libertas, etiam libido impunita; aut si quis advertit,
dictis dicta ultus est. Sed maxime solutum et sine
obtrectatore fuit prodere de iis, quos mors odio aut
gratiae exemisset. Num enim[1] armatis Cassio et
Bruto ac Philippenses campos optinentibus belli
civilis causa populum per contiones incendo? An
illi quidem septuagensimum ante annum peremti,
quo modo imaginibus suis noscuntur, quas ne victor
quidem abolevit, sic partem memoriae apud scriptores
retinent? Suum cuique decus posteritas rependit;
nec deerunt, si damnatio ingruit, qui non modo
Cassii et Bruti, set etiam mei meminerint." Egressus
dein senatu vitam abstinentia finivit. Libros per
aediles cremandos censuere patres: set manserunt,
occultati et editi. Quo magis socordiam eorum
inridere libet, qui praesenti potentia credunt extingui
posse etiam sequentis aevi memoriam. Nam contra
punitis ingeniis gliscit auctoritas, neque aliud externi
reges aut qui eadem saevitia usi sunt, nisi dedecus
sibi atque illis gloriam peperere.

XXXVI. Ceterum postulandis reis tam continuus
annus fuit, ut feriarum Latinarum diebus praefectum

---

[1] enim *Halm*: eum.

---

[1] But in an expurgated edition—*circumcisis quae dixisse
ei nocuerat* (Quint. X. 1, 104). A fragment survives in the
elder Seneca (*Suas.* 6, 19), to confute the prophecy of his
son that the work would be unforgotten *quamdiu fuerit in
pretio Romana cognosci* (Cons. ad Marc. 1).
[2] The son of Germanicus. For the urban prefectship see
VI. 11, with the note.

to ascribe their action to forbearance or to wisdom. For things contemned are soon things forgotten: anger is read as a recognition.

XXXV. " I leave untouched the Greeks; with them not liberty only but licence itself went unchastised, or, if a man retaliated, he avenged words by words. But what above all else was absolutely free and immune from censure was the expression of an opinion on those whom death had removed beyond the range of rancour or of partiality. Are Brutus and Cassius under arms on the plains of Philippi, and I upon the platform, firing the nation to civil war? Or is it the case that, seventy years since their taking-off, as they are known by their effigies which the conqueror himself did not abolish, so a portion of their memory is enshrined likewise in history?—To every man posterity renders his wage of honour; nor will there lack, if my condemnation is at hand, those who shall remember, not Brutus and Cassius alone, but me also! " He then left the senate, and closed his life by self-starvation. The Fathers ordered his books to be burned by the aediles; but copies remained, hidden and afterwards published:[1] a fact which moves us the more to deride the folly of those who believe that by an act of despotism in the present there can be extinguished also the memory of a succeeding age. On the contrary, genius chastised grows in authority; nor have alien kings or the imitators of their cruelty effected more than to crown themselves with ignominy and their victims with renown.

XXXVI. For the rest, the year was so continuous a chain of impeachments that in the days of the Latin Festival, when Drusus,[3] as urban prefect,

urbis Drusum, auspicandi gratia tribunal ingressum, adierit Calpurnius Salvianus in Sextum Marium: quod a Caesare palam increpitum causa exilii Salviano fuit. Obiecta publice Cyzicenis incuria caerimoniarum divi Augusti, additis violentiae criminibus adversum civis Romanos. Et amisere libertatem, quam bello Mithridatis meruerant, circumsessi nec minus sua constantia quam praesidio Luculli pulso rege. At Fonteius Capito, qui pro consule Asiam curaverat, absolvitur, conperto ficta in eum crimina per Vibium Serenum. Neque tamen id Sereno noxae fuit, quem odium publicum tutiorem faciebat. Nam ut quid destrictior accusator, velut sacrosanctus erat: leves, ignobiles poenis adficiebantur.

XXXVII. Per idem tempus Hispania ulterior missis ad senatum legatis oravit, ut exemplo Asiae delubrum Tiberio matrique eius exstrueret. Qua occasione Caesar, validus alioqui spernendis honoribus et respondendum ratus iis, quorum rumore arguebatur in ambitionem flexisse, huiusce modi orationem coepit:—" Scio, patres conscripti, constantiam meam a plerisque desideratam, quod Asiae civitatibus nuper idem istud petentibus non sim adversatus. Ergo et prioris silentii defensionem, et quid in futurum statuerim, simul aperiam. Cum divus Augustus sibi

---

[1] See VI. 19. One or two shreds of evidence indicate that Salvianus was also of Spanish extraction.

[2] In Lesser Phrygia. The siege, ended by a crushing defeat of Mithridates, was in 74–73 B.C. (Plut. *Lucull.*, 9–11).

[3] See above, chap. 28 *sq.*

[4] See chap. 15.

mounted the tribunal to inaugurate his office, he was approached by Calpurnius Salvianus with a suit against Sextus Marius:[1] an action which drew a public reprimand from the Caesar and occasioned the banishment of Salvianus. The community of Cyzicus[2] were charged with neglecting the cult of the deified Augustus; allegations were added of violence to Roman citizens; and they forfeited the freedom earned during the Mithridatic War, when the town was invested and they beat off the king as much by their own firmness as by the protection of Lucullus. On the other hand, Fonteius Capito, who had administered Asia as proconsul, was acquitted upon proof that the accusations against him were the invention of Vibius Serenus. The reverse, however, did no harm to Serenus, who was rendered doubly secure by the public hatred.[3] For the informer whose weapon never rested became quasi-sacrosanct: it was on the insignificant and unknown that punishments descended.

XXXVII. About the same time, Further Spain sent a deputation to the senate, asking leave to follow the example of Asia[4] by erecting a shrine to Tiberius and his mother. On this occasion, the Caesar, sturdily disdainful of compliments at any time, and now convinced that an answer was due to the gossip charging him with a declension into vanity, began his speech in the following vein:—" I know, Conscript Fathers, that many deplored my want of consistency because, when a little while ago the cities of Asia made this identical request, I offered no opposition. I shall therefore state both the case for my previous silence and the rule I have settled upon for the future. Since the deified Augustus had not forbidden

atque urbi Romae templum apud Pergamum sisti
non prohibuisset, qui omnia facta dictaque eius vice
legis observem, placitum iam exemplum promptius
secutus sum, quia cultui meo veneratio senatus
adiungebatur. Ceterum ut semel recepisse veniam
habuerit, ita omnes per [1] provincias effigie numinum
sacrari ambitiosum, superbum; et vanescet Augusti
honor, si promiscis adulationibus vulgatur."

XXXVIII. "Ego me, patres conscripti, mortalem
esse et hominum officia fungi satisque habere, si
locum principem impleam, et vos testor et meminisse
posteros volo; qui satis superque memoriae meae
tribuent, ut maioribus meis dignum, rerum vestrarum
providum, constantem in periculis, offensionum pro
utilitate publica non pavidum credant. Haec mihi
in animis vestris templa, hae pulcherrimae effigies et
mansurae. Nam quae saxo struuntur, si iudicium
posterorum in odium vertit, pro sepulchris spernuntur.
Proinde socios civis et deos ipsos precor, hos ut mihi
ad finem usque vitae quietam et intellegentem
humani divinique iuris mentem duint, illos ut,
quandoque concessero, cum laude et bonis recorda-
tionibus facta atque famam nominis mei prose-
quantur." Perstititque posthac secretis etiam ser-

---

[1] omnes per *Nipperdey* : per oms per.

---

[1] III. 63 n. The temple dates from 29 B.C., and is instanced
by Tiberius as marking the definite inauguration of emperor
worship in the provinces : see Suet. *Aug.* 52; D. Cass. LI. 20;
Boissier, *Religion romaine*[8] i. 129 *sqq.*
[2] Since the only immortality, according to Tiberius, is the
kindly memory of mankind, a temple to a hated prince is not
the shrine of a living god, but the tomb of a dead man. Compare Amm. Marc. XXII. 11, 7 *flexis ad aedem ipsam* (a Christian

the construction of a temple at Pergamum[1] to himself and the City of Rome, observing as I do his every action and word as law, I followed the precedent already sealed by his approval, with all the more readiness that with worship of myself was associated veneration of the senate. But, though once to have accepted may be pardonable, yet to be consecrated in the image of deity through all the provinces would be vanity and arrogance, and the honour paid to Augustus will soon be a mockery, if it is vulgarized by promiscuous experiments in flattery.

XXXVIII. " As for myself, Conscript Fathers, that I am mortal, that my functions are the functions of men, and that I hold it enough if I fill the foremost place among them—this I call upon you to witness, and I desire those who shall follow us to bear it in mind. For they will do justice, and more, to my memory, if they pronounce me worthy of my ancestry, provident of your interests, firm in dangers, not fearful of offences in the cause of the national welfare. These are my temples in your breasts, these my fairest and abiding effigies : for those that are reared of stone, should the judgement of the future turn to hatred, are scorned as sepulchres![2] And so my prayer to allies and citizens and to Heaven itself is this : to Heaven, that to the end of my life it may endow me with a quiet mind, gifted with understanding of law human and divine ; and to my fellow-men, that, whenever I shall depart, their praise and kindly thoughts may still attend my deeds and the memories attached to my name." And, in fact, from now onward, even in his private conversations,

church) *luminibus, ' Quam diu,' inçuit, ' sepulchrum hoc stabit ? '*

monibus aspernari talem sui cultum. Quod alii modestiam, multi, quia diffideret, quidam ut degeneris animi interpretabantur. Optumos quippe mortalium altissima cupere: sic Herculem et Liberum apud Graecos, Quirinum apud nos deum numero additos: melius Augustum, qui speraverit. Cetera principibus statim adesse: unum insatiabiliter parandum, prosperam sui memoriam; nam contemptu famae contemni virtutes.

XXXIX. At Seianus nimia fortuna socors et muliebri insuper cupidine incensus, promissum matrimonium flagitante Livia, componit ad Caesarem codicillos: moris quippe tum erat quamquam praesentem scripto adire. Eius talis forma fuit:—Benevolentia patris Augusti et mox plurimis Tiberii iudiciis ita insuevisse, ut spes votaque sua non prius ad deos quam ad principum auris conferret. Neque fulgorem honorum umquam precatum: excubias ac labores, ut unum e militibus, pro incolumitate imperatoris malle. Ac tamen quod pulcherrimum adeptum, ut coniunctione Caesaris dignus crederetur: hinc initium spei. Et quoniam audiverit Augustum in conlocanda filia non nihil etiam de equitibus Romanis consultavisse, ita, si maritus Liviae quaereretur,

---

[1] But not quite inflexibly, as one or two inscriptions show.
[2] III. 29 n.   [3] Julia (I. 53 n.).

he persisted [1] in a contemptuous rejection of these divine honours to himself: an attitude by some interpreted as modesty, by many as self-distrust, by a few as degeneracy of soul :—" The best of men," they argued, " desired the greatest heights : so Hercules and Liber among the Greeks, and among ourselves Quirinus, had been added to the number of the gods. The better way had been that of Augustus—who hoped! To princes all other gratifications came instantly : for one they must toil and never know satiety—the favourable opinion of the future. For in the scorn of fame was implied the scorn of virtue ! "

XXXIX. Meanwhile Sejanus, blinded by overgreat good fortune and fired to action by feminine passion as well—Livia was demanding the promised marriage—drafted a memorial to the Caesar : it was a convention of the period to address him in writing even when he was in the capital. The gist of the document was that " owing to the benevolence of the prince's father Augustus, followed by so many expressions of approval from Tiberius, he had formed the habit of carrying his hopes and his vows to the imperial ears as readily as to the gods. He had never asked for the baubles of office : he would rather stand sentry and work like the humblest soldier for the security of the emperor. And yet he had reached the supreme goal—he had been counted worthy of an alliance with the Caesar.[2] This had taught him to hope; and since he had heard that Augustus, when settling his daughter,[3] had to some extent considered the claims even of Roman knights, so, if a husband should be required for Livia, he begged that Tiberius would bear in mind a friend

haberet in animo amicum sola necessitudinis gloria usurum. Non enim exuere inposita munia: satis aestimare firmari domum adversum iniquas Agrippinae offensiones, idque liberorum causa; nam sibi multum superque vitae fore, quod tali cum principe explevisset.

XL. Ad ea Tiberius laudata pietate Seiani suisque in eum beneficiis modice percursis, cum tempus tamquam ad integram consultationem petivisset, adiunxit:—Ceteris mortalibus in eo stare consilia, quid sibi conducere putent; principum diversam esse sortem, quibus praecipua rerum ad famam derigenda. Ideo se non illuc decurrere, quod promptum rescriptu, posse ipsam Liviam statuere, nubendum post Drusum an in penatibus isdem tolerandum haberet; esse illi matrem et aviam, propiora consilia. Simplicius acturum, de inimicitiis primum Agrippinae, quas longe acrius arsuras, si matrimonium Liviae velut in partis domum Caesarum distraxisset. Sic quoque erumpere aemulationem feminarum, eaque discordia nepotes suos convelli: quid si intendatur certamen tali coniugio? "Falleris enim, Seiane, si te mansurum in eodem ordine putas, et Liviam, quae Gaio Caesari, mox Druso nupta fuerit, ea mente acturam, ut cum equite Romano senescat. Ego ut

who would derive nothing from the connection but
its glory. For he did not seek to divest himself of
the duties laid on him: it was enough, in his estima-
tion, if his family was strengthened against the unfounded animosities of Agrippina; and that simply
for the sake of his children. As to himself, whatever
the term of years he might complete under such
a sovereign, it would be life enough and to spare!"

XL. In reply, Tiberius praised Sejanus' devotion,
touched not too heavily on his own services to him,
and asked for time, in order, he said, to consider
the matter fully and freely. Then he wrote again:—
"With other men, the standpoint for their decisions
was what was in their own interests: the lot of
princes was very different, as their weightiest affairs
had to be regulated with an eye upon public opinion.
Therefore he did not take refuge in the answer
which came most readily to the pen—that Livia could
determine for herself whether she ought to marry
after Drusus or rest content with her old home, and
that she had a mother and grandmother who were
more natural advisers. He would deal more openly:
and first with regard to Agrippina's enmity, which
would blaze out far more fiercely if Livia's marriage
divided, as it were, the Caesarian house into two
camps. Even as matters stood, there were outbreaks
of feminine jealousy, and the feud was unsettling
his grandchildren. What then if the strife was
accentuated by the proposed union?"—"For,
Sejanus," he continued, "you delude yourself,
if you imagine that you can keep your present rank,
or that the Livia who has been wedded successively
to Gaius Caesar and to Drusus will be complaisant
enough to grow old at the side of a Roman knight.

71

sinam, credisne passuros qui fratrem eius, qui patrem
maioresque nostros in summis imperiis videre?
Vis tu quidem istum intra locum sistere: sed illi
magistratus et primores, qui te invitum perrumpunt
omnibusque de rebus consulunt, excessisse iam
pridem equestre fastigium longeque antisse patris
mei amicitias non occulti ferunt perque invidiam tui
me quoque incusant. At enim Augustus filiam
suam equiti Romano tradere meditatus est. Mirum
hercule, si cum in omnis curas distraheretur immen-
sumque attolli provideret quem coniunctione tali
super alios extulisset, C. Proculeium et quosdam in
sermonibus habuit insigni tranquillitate vitae, nullis
rei publicae negotiis permixtos. Sed si dubitatione
Augusti movemur, quanto validius est quod Marco
Agrippae, mox mihi conlocavit? Atque ego haec
pro amicitia non occultavi: ceterum neque tuis
neque Liviae destinatis adversabor. Ipse quid intra
animum volutaverim, quibus adhuc necessitudinibus
inmiscere te mihi parem, omittam ad praesens
referre: id tantum aperiam, nihil esse tam excelsum,
quod non virtutes istae tuusque in me animus mere-
antur, datoque tempore vel in senatu vel in contione
non reticebo."

XLI. Rursum Seianus, non iam de matrimonio, sed

---

[1] With members of the equestrian order—Maecenas,
Sallustius Crispus (III. 30), and their like.

[2] An intimate friend of Augustus, and his emissary to
Antony and Cleopatra after Actium (Plut. *Ant.* 77–79);
coupled with Maecenas by Juvenal (vii. 94), and with Sallustius Crispus by Horace (*Carm.* II. 2).

Assuming that I myself consent, do you suppose the position will be tolerated by those who have seen her brother, her father, and our ancestors, in the supreme offices of state? You wish, for your own part, to stop short at the station you hold: but those magistrates and men of distinction who take you by storm and consult you on any and every subject make no secret of their opinion that you have long since transcended the heights of the equestrian order and left the friendships[1] of my father far behind; and in their envy of you they censure myself as well. —You make the point that Augustus considered the possibility of bestowing his daughter on a Roman knight. Astonishing, certainly, that, tugged at by every sort of anxiety, and foreseeing an immense accession of dignity to the man whom he should have raised above his peers by such an alliance, his conversation ran on Gaius Proculeius[2] and a few others, remarkable for their quietude of life and implicated in none of the business of the state! But, if we are to be moved by the hesitancy of Augustus, how much more cogent the fact that he affianced her to Marcus Agrippa and later to myself!—I have spoken openly, as was due to our friendship; but I shall oppose neither your decisions nor those of Livia. Of the result of my own reflections, and the further ties by which I propose to cement our union, I shall at present forbear to speak. One point only I shall make clear: no station, however exalted, would be unearned by your qualities and your devotion to myself; and when the occasion comes, either in the senate or before the public, I shall not be silent."

XLI. In rejoinder, Sejanus—now alarmed not for his marriage but on deeper grounds—urged him to

altius metuens, tacita suspicionum, vulgi rumorem, ingruentem invidiam deprecatur. Ac ne adsiduos in domum coetus arcendo infringeret potentiam aut receptando facultatem criminantibus praeberet, huc flexit, ut Tiberium ad vitam procul Roma amoenis locis degendam impelleret. Multa quippe providebat: sua in manu aditus litterarumque magna ex parte se arbitrum fore, cum per milites commearent; mox Caesarem vergente iam senecta secretoque loci mollitum munia imperii facilius tramissurum: et minui sibi invidiam adempta salutantum turba, sublatisque inanibus veram potentiam augeri.[1] Igitur paulatim negotia urbis, populi adcursus, multitudinem adfluentium increpat, extollens laudibus quietem et solitudinem, quis abesse taedia et offensiones ac praecipua rerum maxime agitari.

XLII. Ac forte habita per illos dies de Votieno Montano, celebris ingenii viro, cognitio cunctantem iam Tiberium perpulit, ut vitandos crederet patrum coetus vocesque, quae plerumque verae et graves coram ingerebantur. Nam postulato Votieno ob contumelias in Caesarem dictas, testis Aemilius e militaribus viris dum studio probandi cuncta refert et quamquam inter obstrepentis magna adsevera-

---

[1] veram potentiam augeri *Marcilius*: vera potentia augere *Med.*

---

[1] Despatches would be carried from Rome by the *speculatores*, a special mounted corps of the praetorian guard, and, as such, directly under the influence of Sejanus.

[2] A Narbonese orator and declaimer; described by the elder Seneca as *homo rarissimi, etiamsi non emendatissimi ingenii* (*Contr.* 28, 15), and by Mamercus Scaurus as *inter oratores Ovidius* (*ib.* 17).

disregard the still voice of suspicion, the babble of
the multitude, the attacks of his maligners. At
the same time, unwilling either to enfeeble his influence by prohibiting the throngs which besieged his
doors or to give a handle to his detractors by receiving them, he turned to the idea of inducing
Tiberius to spend his days in some pleasant retreat
at a distance from Rome. The advantages, he foresaw, were numerous. Interviews would lie in his
own bestowal; letters he could largely supervise, as
they were transmitted by soldiers:[1] before long, the
Caesar, who was already in the decline of life and
would be rendered laxer by seclusion, would be
readier to transfer the functions of sovereignty;
while his own unpopularity would diminish with the
abolition of his great levées, and the realities of his
power be increased by the removal of its vanities.
Little by little, therefore, he began to denounce the
drudgeries of the capital, its jostling crowds, the end-
less stream of suitors, and to give his eulogies to
quiet and solitude, where tedium and bickering were
unknown and a man's chief attention could be centred
on affairs of first importance.

XLII. As chance would have it, the trial at this
juncture of the popular and talented Votienus Montanus [2] forced Tiberius (who was already wavering)
to the conviction that he must avoid the meetings
of the senate and the remarks, often equally true and
mordant, which were there repeated to his face.
For, during the indictment of Votienus for the use
of language offensive to the emperor, the witness
Aemilius, a military man, in his anxiety to prove the
case, reported the expressions in full, and, disregard-
ing the cries of protest, struggled on with his tale

tione nititur, audivit Tiberius probra, quis per
occultum lacerabatur, adeoque perculsus est, ut se
vel statim vel in cognitione purgaturum clamitaret
precibusque proximorum, adulatione omnium aegre
componeret animum. Et Votienus quidem maiestatis poenis adfectus est: Caesar obiectam sibi
adversus reos inclementiam eo pervicacius amplexus,
Aquiliam adulterii delatam cum Vario Ligure, quamquam Lentulus Gaetulicus¹ consul designatus lege
Iulia damnasset, exilio² punivit Apidiumque Me-
rulam, quod in acta divi Augusti non iuraverat, albo³
senatorio erasit.

XLIII. Auditae dehinc Lacedaemoniorum et Mes-
seniorum legationes de iure templi Dianae Limna-
tidis, quod suis a maioribus suaque in terra dicatum
Lacedaemonii firmabant annalium memoria vatum-
que carminibus, sed Macedonis Philippi, cum quo
bellassent, armis ademptum ac post C. Caesaris
et M. Antonii sententia redditum. Contra Messenii
veterem inter Herculis posteros divisionem Pelo-
ponnesi protulere, suoque regi Denthaliatem⁴ agrum
in quo id delubrum, cessisse; monimentaque eius rei
sculpta saxis et aere prisco manere. Quod si vatum,

---

¹ Younger brother of Cornelius Cossus, consul in this year;
epigrammatist (*sic scribit Catullus, sic Marsus, sic Pedo, sic
Gaetulicus, sic quicumque perlegitur*, Mart. I. *praef.*), and probably historian (Suet. *Cal.* 8); in command later of the legions
of Upper Germany (VI. 30); executed for conspiracy under
Caligula (D. Cass. LIX. 22; Suet. *Claud.* 9).
² For the penalties under this law, see II. 50 with the notes.
' Exile ' involved the confiscation of the delinquent's estate
and the forfeiture of his civic rights.
³ I. 72 n.
⁴ A border shrine on the upper course of the Nedon; according to tradition, the scene of the affray which led to the first
Messenian War.

with great earnestness. Tiberius thus heard the
scurrilities with which he was attacked in private; and
such was the shock that he kept crying out he would
refute them, either on the spot or in the course of the
trial; his equanimity being restored with difficulty
by the entreaties of his friends and the adulation of
all. Votienus himself suffered the penalties of
treason. The Caesar, as he had been reproached
with ruthlessness to defendants, adhered to his
methods with all the more tenacity; punishing
Aquilia by exile on the charge of adultery with
Varius Ligus, though Lentulus Gaetulicus,[1] the
consul designate, had pressed only for conviction
under the Julian Law;[2] and expunging Apidius
Merula from the senatorial register because he had
not sworn allegiance to the acts of the deified
Augustus.[3]

XLIII. A hearing was now given to embassies from
Lacedaemon and Messene upon the legal ownership
of the temple of Diana Limnatis.[4] That it had been
consecrated by their own ancestors, and on their
own ground, the Lacedaemonians sought to establish
by the records of history and the hymns of the poets:
it had been wrested from them, however, by the
Macedonian arms during their war with Philip,[5]
and had been returned later by the decision of
Julius Caesar and Mark Antony. In reply, the
Messenians brought forward the old partition of the
Peloponnese between the descendants of Hercules:—
" The Denthaliate district, in which the shrine stood,
had been assigned to their king, and memorials
of the fact, engraved on rock and ancient bronze,
were still extant. But if they were challenged to

[5] In the invasion of Laconia after Chaeronea (337 B.C.).

annalium ad testimonia vocentur, pluris sibi ac
locupletiores esse; neque Philippum potentia, sed
ex vero statuisse: idem regis Antigoni, idem imperatoris Mummii iudicium; sic Milesios permisso
publice arbitrio, postremo Atidium Geminum praetorem Achaiae decrevisse. Ita secundum Messenios
datum.

Et Segestani aedem Veneris montem apud Erycum,
vetustate dilapsam, restaurari postulavere, nota
memorantes de origine eius et laeta Tiberio. Susce-
pit curam libens ut consanguineus.

Tunc tractatae Massiliensium preces probatumque
P. Rutilii exemplum; namque eum legibus pulsum
civem sibi Zmyrnaei addiderant. Quo iure Vulcacius
Moschus exul in Massilienses receptus bona sua rei
publicae eorum ut patriae reliquerat.

XLIV. Obiere eo anno viri nobiles Cn. Lentulus
et L. Domitius. Lentulo super consulatum et
triumphalia de Getis gloriae fuerat bene tolerata
paupertas, dein magnae opes innocenter partae [1]
et modeste habitae. Domitium decoravit pater

---

[1] partae *Lipsius*: paratae.

---

[1] Antigonus Doson of Macedonia (229–220 B.C.). The decision would be posterior to his defeat of Cleomenes III of
Sparta at Sellasia (222 B.C.).

[2] By a majority of 584 to 16: The terms of the award
(135 B.C.) survive.

[3] For the connection of Segesta and Eryx, in N.W. Sicily,
with Troy, Aeneas, and the Julii, see, for instance, Thuc. VI.
2, 3; Virg. *Aen.* V. 718, 759. The actual restoration seems to
have been carried out by Claudius *ex aerario populi Romani*
(Suet. *Claud.* 25).

[4] *P. Rutilius, vir summae innocentiae, quoniam legatus Q.
Mucii proconsulis a publicanorum iniuriis Asiam defenderat,
invisus equestri ordini, penes quem iudicia erant, repetundarum*

adduce the evidences of poetry and history, the more numerous and competent witnesses were on their side, nor had Philip decided by arbitrary power, but on the merits of the case: the same had been the judgement of King Antigonus[1] and the Roman commander Mummius; and a similar verdict was pronounced both by Miletus,[2] when that state was commissioned to arbitrate, and, last of all, by Atidius Geminus, the governor of Achaia." The point was accordingly decided in favour of Messene.

The Segestans also demanded the restoration of the age-worn temple of Venus on Mount Eryx, and told the familiar tale of its foundation: much to the pleasure of Tiberius, who as a relative willingly undertook the task.[3]

At this time, a petition from Massilia was considered, and sanction was given to the precedent set by Publius Rutilius.[4] For, after his banishment by form of law, Rutilius had been presented with the citizenship of Smyrna; on the strength of which, the exile Vulcacius Moschus had naturalized himself at Massilia and bequeathed his estate to the community, as his fatherland.

XLIV. This year saw the end of the great nobles, Gnaeus Lentulus[5] and Lucius Domitius.[6] Lentulus, over and above his consulate and the triumphal distinctions he had won against the Getae, could claim the glories, first of honest poverty gallantly carried, then of a great fortune innocently acquired and temperately employed. Domitius derived distinction

---

damnatus in exilium missus est (93 or 92 B.C., Liv. *Epit.* 70). The case is mentioned also at III. 66.

[5] See I. 27 n. and chap. 29 above.

[6] L. Domitius Ahenobarbus, grandfather of the emperor Nero.

civili bello maris potens, donec Antonii partibus,
mox Caesaris misceretur. Avus Pharsalica acie pro
optumatibus ceciderat. Ipse delectus, cui minor
Antonia, Octavia genita, in matrimonium daretur,
post exercitu flumen Albim transcendit, longius
penetrata Germania, quam quisquam priorum,
easque ob res insignia triumphi adeptus est. Obiit
et L. Antonius, multa claritudine generis, sed
inprospera. Nam patre eius Iullo[1] Antonio ob
adulterium Iuliae morte punito hunc admodum
adulescentulum, sororis nepotem, seposuit Augustus
in civitatem Massiliensem, ubi specie studiorum
nomen exilii tegeretur. Habitus tamen supremis
honor, ossaque tumulo Octaviorum inlata per
decretum senatus.

XLV. Isdem consulibus facinus atrox in citeriore
Hispania admissum a quodam agresti nationis
Termestinae. Is praetorem provinciae L. Pisonem,
pace incuriosum, ex inproviso in itinere adortus uno
vulnere in mortem adfecit; ac pernicitate equi
profugus, postquam saltuosos locos attigerat, dimisso
equo per derupta et avia sequentis frustratus est.

---

[1] Iullo *Andresen* (Iulo *Lipsius*) : iulio.

---

[1] Octavian.

[2] The two sisters Antonia were daughters of the triumvir
Antony and Augustus' sister Octavia : it is practically certain,
however, that, both here and at XII. 64, Tacitus' statement is
erroneous, and that the elder married L. Domitius; the younger,
Tiberius' brother Drusus.

[3] Son of Antony and Fulvia; brought up at Rome by his
stepmother Octavia; condemned to death in 2 B.C.

[4] I. 53 n.

[5] As Autun (III. 43 n.) was a Latin university for the north,
so Marseilles was a Greek university for the south, with a

from a father who had held the command of the
sea during the Civil War, until he attached himself
to the cause of Antony, and, later, to that of the
Caesar:[1] his grandfather had fallen on the aristo-
cratic side upon the field of Pharsalia. Himself
chosen to receive the hand of Octavia's daughter,
the younger Antonia,[2] he crossed the Elbe with an
army, penetrating deeper into Germany than any
of his predecessors, and was rewarded for his exploit
by the emblems of triumph. Lucius Antonius also
passed away, the bearer of a great but luckless
name: for, little more than a boy when his father
Iullus[3] paid the extreme penalty for his adultery with
Julia,[4] he had been relegated by Augustus to the city
of Massilia, where the name of exile could be veiled
under the pretext of study.[5] His funeral, however,
was celebrated with honour, and by a senatorial
decree his bones were laid in the family tomb of the
Octavii.

XLV. Under the same consuls, an audacious crime
was committed in Hither Spain[6] by a rustic of the
Termestine tribe. Making a surprise attack on the
governor of the province, Lucius Piso, who was
travelling with a carelessness due to the peaceful
conditions, he struck him dead with one blow.
Carried clear by the speed of his horse, he turned it
loose on reaching wooded country, and eluded the
hue and cry in the rugged and trackless wilds. But

fame rivalling that of Athens (Strab. IV. 1, 4; Cic. *Flacc.*
26 etc.). It was the *sedes ac magistra studiorum* of Agricola
(*Agr.* 4).
  [6] The east and north of the peninsula (*Hispania Tarraconensis*).—The Termestine capital, Termes, is identified with
Tiermes, near the sources of the Duero in the Sierra de Urbión.

Neque diu fefellit: nam prenso ductoque per proximos pagos equo, cuius foret cognitum. Et repertus cum tormentis edere conscios adigeretur, voce magna sermone patrio frustra se interrogari clamitavit: adsisterent socii ac spectarent; nullam vim tantam doloris fore, ut veritatem eliceret. Idemque cum postero ad quaestionem retraheretur, eo nisu proripuit se custodibus saxoque caput adflixit, ut statim exanimaretur. Sed Piso Termestinorum dolo caesus habetur; qui*ppe*[1] pecunias e publico interceptas acrius quam ut tolerarent barbari cogebat.

XLVI. Lentulo Gaetulico C. Calvisio consulibus decreta triumphi insignia Poppaeo Sabino contusis Thraecum gentibus, qui montium editis sine cultu[2] atque eo ferocius agitabant. Causa motus super hominum ingenium, quod pati dilectus et validissimum quemque militiae nostrae dare aspernabantur, ne regibus quidem parere nisi ex libidine soliti, aut si mitterent auxilia, suos ductores praeficere nec nisi adversum accolas belligerare. Ac tum rumor incesserat fore ut disiecti aliisque nationibus permixti diversas in terras traherentur. Sed antequam arma inciperent, misere legatos amicitiam obsequiumque

---

[1] quippe *Bezzenberger*: qui.
[2] sine cultu *Bezzenberger*: incultu *Med.*, *Nipperdey, Fisher,* incultius *Georges* (*from* Sall. *Iug.*, 19, 6; 89, 7).

---

[1] Maternal grandfather of Nero's mistress and wife, Poppaea: see I. 80, V. 10, and the obituary notice in VI. 39.

detection was not long deferred: the horse was caught and led round the villages in the neighbourhood till the ownership was ascertained. After discovery, when the torture was applied in order to force him to disclose his confederates, he cried aloud in his native tongue that " questions were useless: his partners might stand by and watch—for pain would have no terrors capable of extracting the truth." Next day, as he was being dragged again to the torture, he threw himself clear of the warders and dashed his head against a rock, with such an exertion of strength that he expired on the spot. It is believed nevertheless, that Piso fell a victim to a Termestine conspiracy: for public monies had gone astray, and he was exacting restitution with a vigour too much for barbarian patience.

XLVI. In the consulate of Lentulus Gaetulicus and Gaius Calvisius, triumphal decorations were voted to Poppaeus Sabinus,[1] for crushing the Thracian tribesmen, who, on their mountain peaks, lived uncivilized, and proportionately bold. The cause of the insurrection, apart from the temper of the insurgents, was that they refused to tolerate the military levies and to devote the whole of their able-bodied manhood to the Roman service. Their obedience, indeed, even to their kings was usually a matter of caprice, and the occasional contingents they sent were led by their own chiefs and acted only against neighbouring clans. In this case, too, a rumour was current that the clans were to be broken up and incorporated with other stocks, then dragged into distant countries. Still, before appealing to arms they sent a deputation to insist on their former friendship and loyalty. "Both," they said, "would be

A.V.C. 779 = A.D. 26

memoraturos, et mansura haec, si nullo novo onere
temptarentur: sin ut victis servitium indiceretur,
esse sibi ferrum et iuventutem et promptum libertati
aut ad mortem animum. Simul castella rupibus
indita conlatosque illuc parentes et coniuges ostenta-
bant bellumque impeditum arduum cruentum
minitabantur.

XLVII. At Sabinus, donec exercitus in unum
conduceret, datis mitibus responsis, *post*quam Pomponius Labeo e Moesia cum legione, rex Rhoemetalces
cum auxiliis popularium, qui fidem non mutaverant,
venere, addita praesenti copia ad hostem pergit,
compositum iam per angustias saltuum. Quidam
audentius apertis in collibus visebantur, quos dux
Romanus acie suggressus haud aegre pepulit, sanguine
barbarorum modico ob propinqua suffugia. Mox
castris in loco communitis valida manu montem
occupat, angustum et aequali dorso continuum usque
ad proximum castellum, quod magna vis armata aut
incondita tuebatur. Simul in ferocissimos, qui ante
vallum more gentis cum carminibus et tripudiis
persultabant, mittit delectos sagittariorum. Ii dum
eminus grassabantur, crebra et inulta vulnera fecere:
propius incedentes eruptione subita turbati sunt
receptique subsidio Sugambrae cohortis, quam

---

[1] An imperial province, corresponding more or less to the
old Servia and Bulgaria.
[2] II. 67 n.

continued if they were not tried by fresh impositions. But if they were sentenced to slavery as a vanquished race, they had steel and young men, and souls resolute for freedom or for death." At the same time, they pointed to their strongholds perched upon the crags, and to the parents and wives placed in them for refuge, and threatened a war intricate, arduous, and bloody.

XLVII. Sabinus, till he could muster his forces, returned soft answers; but when Pomponius Labeo arrived from Moesia[1] with a legion, and King Rhoemetalces[2] with a body of native auxiliaries who had not renounced their allegiance, he added his own available troops and moved against the enemy, by now concentrated in the wooded gorges. A few, more daring, showed themselves on the open hills, but were driven from them without difficulty, when the Roman commander advanced in battle-order, though cover was so near that little barbarian blood was spilt. Then, after fortifying a camp on the spot, Sabinus with a strong detachment made himself master of a narrow mountain-ridge running without a break to the nearest tribal fortress, which was held by a considerable force of armed men and irregulars. Simultaneously, he sent a picked body of archers to deal with the bolder spirits who, true to the national custom, were gambolling with songs and war-dances in front of the rampart. The bowmen, so long as they operated at long range, inflicted many wounds with impunity; on advancing closer, they were thrown into disorder by an unlooked-for sally, and fell back on the support of a Sugambrian cohort,[3]

[3] One of four or five auxiliary cohorts of the name, recruited on the Rhine bank.

Romanus promptam ad pericula nec minus cantuum et armorum tumultu trucem haud procul instruxerat.

XLVIII. Translata dehinc castra hostem propter, relictis apud priora munimenta Thraecibus, quos nobis adfuisse memoravi. Iisque permissum vastare, urere, trahere praedas, dum populatio lucem intra sisteretur noctemque in castris tutam et vigilem capesserent. Id primo servatum: mox versi in luxum et raptis opulenti omittere stationes lascivia epularum aut somno et vino procumbere. Igitur hostes incuria eorum conperta duo agmina parant, quorum altero populatores invaderentur, alii castra Romana adpugnarent, non spe capiendi, sed ut clamore, telis suo quisque periculo intentus sonorem alterius proelii non acciperet. Tenebrae insuper delectae augendam ad formidinem. Sed qui vallum legionum temptabant, facile pelluntur; Thraecum auxilia repentino incursu territa, cum pars munitionibus adiacerent, plures extra palarentur, tanto infensius caesi, quanto perfugae et proditores ferre arma ad suum patriaeque servitium incusabantur.

XLIX. Postera die Sabinus exercitum aequo loco ostendit, si barbari successu noctis alacres proelium

drawn up a short distance away by the Roman general, since the men were prompt in danger, and, as regards the din produced by their songs and weapons, not less awe-inspiring than the enemy.

XLVIII. The camp was then moved a stage nearer the adversary; and the Thracians, whom I mentioned as having joined us, were left in charge of the earlier lines. They had licence to ravage, burn, and plunder, so long as their depredations were limited to the daylight, and the night spent safely and wakefully behind entrenchments. At first, the rule was kept: then, turning to luxury and enriched by their booty, they began to leave their posts for some wild orgy, or lay tumbled in drunken slumber. The enemy, therefore, who had information of their laxity, arranged two columns, by one of which the raiders were to be attacked, while another band demonstrated against the Roman encampment; not with any hope of capture, but in order that, amid the shouting and the missiles, every man engrossed by his own danger might be deaf to echoes of the other conflict. Darkness, moreover, was chosen for the blow, so as to intensify the panic. The attempt on the earthworks of the legions was, however, easily repelled: the Thracian auxiliaries, a few of whom were lying along their lines, while the majority were straggling outside, lost their nerve at the sudden onset, and were cut down all the more ruthlessly because they were branded as renegades and traitors carrying arms for the enslavement of themselves and their fatherland.

XLIX. On the following day, Sabinus paraded his army in the plain, in the hope that the barbarians, elated by the night's success might venture battle.

auderent. Et postquam castello aut coniunctis tumulis non degrediebantur, obsidium coepit per praesidia, quae opportune iam muniebat;[1] dein fossam loricamque contexens quattuor milia passuum ambitu amplexus est; tum paulatim, ut aquam pabulumque eriperet, contrahere claustra artaque circumdare; et struebatur agger, unde saxa hastae ignes propinquum iam in hostem iacerentur. Sed nihil aeque quam sitis fatigabat, cum ingens multitudo bellatorum inbellium uno reliquo fonte uterentur; simul equi[2] armenta, ut mos barbaris, iuxta clausa, egestate pabuli exanimari; adiacere corpora hominum, quos vulnera, quos sitis peremerat; pollui cuncta sanie, odore, contactu.

L. Rebusque turbatis malum extremum discordia accessit, his deditionem, aliis mortem et mutuos inter se ictus parantibus; et erant qui non inultum exitium, sed eruptionem suaderent. Neque ignobiles tantum his[3] diversi sententiis, verum e ducibus Dinis, provectus senecta et longo usu vim atque clementiam Romanam edoctus, ponenda arma, unum adflictis id remedium disserebat, primusque se cum coniuge et liberis victori permisit: secuti aetate aut sexu inbecilli et quibus maior vitae quam gloriae

---

[1] muniebat] immuniebat *Freinsheim* (*from* XI. 19).
[2] simul equi *Lipsius*: simuleque *Med.*, simulque *Med*[1].
[3] tantum his *Madvig*: quamvis.

As they showed no signs of descending from their
stronghold or from the adjacent hills, he began
their investment, with the help of the fortified
posts which, opportunely enough, he was already
constructing; then drew a continuous fosse and
breastwork, with a circumference of four miles;
and lastly, step by step, contracted and tightened
his lines of circumvallation, so as to cut off the supplies
of water and forage; while an embankment began
to rise, from which stones, spears, and fire-brands
could be showered on the no longer distant enemy.
But nothing told on the defence so much as thirst,
since the one spring remaining had to serve the whole
great multitude of combatants and non-combatants.
At the same time, horses and cattle—penned up
with their owners in the barbarian style—were
dying for lack of fodder; side by side with them lay
the bodies of men, victims of wounds or thirst, and
the whole place was an abomination of rotting blood,
stench, and infection.

L. To the confusion was added the last calamity,
discord; some proposing surrender, some to fall
on each other and die; while there were those, again,
who commended, not unavenged destruction, but
a last sortie. Others, and not the multitude only,
dissented from each of these views: one of the
leaders, Dinis, now advanced in years, and familiar
through long experience with the power and the
clemency of Rome, urged them to lay down their
arms—it was the one resource in their extremity—
and took the initiative by placing himself, his wife,
and his children, at the disposal of the victor. He was
followed by those who laboured under the disabilities
of age or sex, or who were more passionately attached

cupido. At iuventus Tarsam inter et Turesim distrahebatur. Utrique destinatum cum libertate occidere, sed Tarsa properum finem, abrumpendas pariter spes ac metus clamitans, dedit exemplum demisso in pectus ferro; nec defuere qui eodem modo oppeterent. Turesis sua cum manu noctem opperitur, haud nescio duce nostro; igitur firmatae stationes densioribus globis. Et ingruebat nox nimbo atrox, hostisque clamore turbido, modo per vastum silentium, incertos obsessores effecerat, cum Sabinus circumire, hortari, ne ad ambigua sonitus aut simulationem quietis casum insidiantibus aperirent, sed sua quisque munia servarent immoti telisque non in falsum iactis.

LI. Interea barbari catervis decurrentes nunc in vallum manualia saxa, praeustas sudes, decisa robora iacere, nunc virgultis et cratibus et corporibus exanimis complere fossas, quidam pontis et scalas ante fabricati inferre propugnaculis eaque prensare, detrahere et adversum resistentis comminus niti. Miles contra deturbare telis, pellere umbonibus, muralia pila, congestas lapidum moles provolvere. His partae victoriae spes et, si cedant, insignitius

to life than to glory. On the other hand, the younger fighting men were divided between Tarsa and Turesis. Both were resolute not to outlive their freedom; but Tarsa, crying out for a quick despatch, a quietus to hope and fear alike, gave the example by plunging his weapon into his breast: nor were others lacking to choose the same mode of death. Turesis and his followers waited for the night: a fact of which the Roman commander was not ignorant. The outposts, accordingly, were secured by denser masses of men.—Night was falling, with a storm of rain; and the wild shouting on the enemy's side, alternating as it did with deathly stillnesses, had begun to perplex the besiegers, when Sabinus made a tour of his lines and urged the men to be misled neither by ambiguous sound nor by simulated quiet into giving the ambuscaded foe his opening: every man should attend to his duties without budging from his post or expending javelins on an illusory mark.

LI. Meanwhile, the barbarians, speeding down in their bands, now battered the palisade with hand-flung stones, stakes pointed in the fire, and oak-boughs hewn from the tree; now filled the moats with brushwood, hurdles, and lifeless bodies; while a few with bridges and ladders, fabricated before-hand, advanced against the turrets, clutching them, tearing them down, and struggling hand to hand with the defenders. The troops, in return, struck them down with spears, dashed them back with their shield-bosses, hurled on them siege-javelins and piles of massive stone. On each side were incentives enough to courage: on ours, the hope that victory was won, and the more flagrant ignominy which

flagitium, illis extrema iam salus et adsistentes
plerisque matres et coniuges earumque lamenta
addunt animos. Nox aliis in audaciam, aliis ad
formidinem opportuna; incerti ictus, vulnera inpro-
visa; suorum atque hostium ignoratio et montis
anfractu repercussae velut a tergo voces adeo cuncta
miscuerant, ut quaedam munimenta Romani quasi
perrupta omiserint. Neque tamen pervasere hostes
nisi admodum pauci: ceteros, deiecto [1] promptissimo
quoque aut saucio, adpetente iam luce trusere in
summa castelli, ubi tandem coacta deditio. Et
proxima sponte incolarum recepta: reliquis, quo
minus vi aut obsidio subigerentur, praematura
montis Haemi et saeva hiems subvenit.

LII. At Romae commota principis domo, ut series
futuri in Agrippinam exitii inciperet, Claudia Pulchra
sobrina eius postulatur accusante Domitio Afro. Is
recens praetura, modicus dignationis et quoquo
facinore properus clarescere, crimen inpudicitiae,
adulterum Furnium, veneficia in principem et
devotiones obiectabat. Agrippina semper atrox,
tum et periculo propinquae accensa, pergit ad
Tiberium ac forte sacrificantem patri repperit.[2] Quo

---

[1] deiecto *Orelli* : delecto.
[2] repperit] reperit *Ernesti*.

---

[1] Great niece of Agrippina's grandfather, Augustus;
formerly wife of Quintilius Varus (I. 3 n.).
[2] As a member of the college *sodalium Augustalium* (I. 54).

would attend a defeat; on theirs, the fact that
they were striking the last blow for deliverance
—many with their wives and mothers close at hand
and their lamentations sounding in their ears.
Night, screening the audacity of some, the panic of
others; blows dealt at random, wounds unforeseen;
the impossibility of distinguishing friend from foe;
cries echoed back from the mountain ravines, and
so coming apparently from the rear—all this had
produced such general confusion that the Romans
abandoned some of their positions as forced. Yet
actually none but a handful of the enemy made their
way through; while the remainder, with their
bravest either dead or disabled, were at the approach
of daylight pushed back to their stronghold on the
height, where surrender at last became compulsory.
The districts adjoining were taken over with the
concurrence of the inhabitants: the rest were saved
from reduction, whether by assault or investment,
by the premature and stern winter of the Haemus
range.

LII. But in Rome, the imperial house was already
shaken; and now, to open the train of events leading
to the destruction of Agrippina, her second cousin,
Claudia Pulchra,[1] was put on trial, with Domitius
Afer as accuser. Fresh from a praetorship, with
but a modest standing in the world, and hurrying
towards a reputation by way of any crime, he indicted her for unchastity, for adultery with Furnius,
for practices by poison and spell against the life of
the sovereign. Agrippina, fierce-tempered always
and now inflamed by the danger of her kinswoman,
flew to Tiberius, and, as chance would have it, found
him sacrificing to his father.[2] This gave the occasion

initio invidiae non eiusdem ait mactare divo Augusto victimas et posteros eius insectari. Non in effigies mutas divinum spiritum transfusum: se imaginem veram, caelesti sanguine ortam, intellegere discrimen, suscipere sordes. Frustra Pulchram praescribi, cui sola exitii causa sit, quod Agrippinam stulte prorsus ad cultum delegerit, oblita Sosiae ob eadem adflictae. Audita haec raram occulti pectoris vocem elicuere, correptamque Graeco versu admonuit non ideo laedi, quia non regnaret. Pulchra et Furnius damnantur. Afer primoribus oratorum additus, divulgato ingenio et secuta adseveratione Caesaris, qua suo iure disertum eum appellavit. Mox capessendis accusationibus aut reos tutando prosperiore eloquentiae quam morum fama fuit, nisi quod aetas extrema multum etiam eloquentiae dempsit, dum fessa mente retinet silentii inpatientiam.

LIII. At Agrippina pervicax irae et morbo corporis inplicata, cum viseret eam Caesar, profusis diu ac per silentium lacrimis, mox invidiam et preces orditur: subveniret solitudini, daret maritum; habilem adhuc iuventam sibi, neque aliud probis quam ex matrimonio solacium; esse in civitate,

---

[1] See chap. 19.

[2] Suetonius translates :—*Si non dominaris, inquit, filiola, iniuriam te accipere existimas?* (*Tib.* 53). The obvious retranslation:—Εἰ μὴ τυραννεῖς, τέκνον, ἀδικεῖσθαι δοκεῖς; dates from the sixteenth century.

[3] *Vidi ego longe omnium, quos mihi cognoscere contigit, summum oratorem, Domitium Afrum, valde senem, quotidie aliquid ex ea quam meruerat fama perdentem . . . quae occasio fuit dicendi malle eum deficere quam desinere* (Quint. XII. 11, 3).

for a reproachful outburst:—" It was not," she said,
" for the same man to offer victims to the deified
Augustus and to persecute his posterity. Not into
speechless stone had that divine spirit been trans-
fused: *she*, his authentic effigy, the issue of his
celestial blood, was aware of her peril and assumed
the garb of mourning. It was idle to make a pretext
of Pulchra, the only cause of whose destruction
was that in utter folly she had chosen Agrippina
as the object of her affection, forgetful of Sosia,[1]
who was struck down for the same offence." Her
words elicited one of the rare deliverances of that
impenetrable breast. He seized her, and admonished
her in a line of Greek [2] that she was not necessarily
" A woman injured, if she lacked a throne." Pulchra
and Furnius were condemned. Afer took rank with
the great advocates: his genius had found publicity,
and there had followed a pronouncement from the
Caesar, styling him " an orator by natural right."
Later, whether as conductor of the prosecution or
as mainstay of the defence, he enjoyed a fame which
stood higher for eloquence than for virtue. Yet
even of that eloquence age took heavy toll, sapping
as it did his mental power and leaving his incapacity
for silence.[3]

LIII. Meanwhile Agrippina, obstinately nursing
her anger, and attacked by physical illness, was
visited by the emperor. For long her tears fell in
silence; then she began with reproaches and entreaties:—" He must aid her loneliness and give
her a husband; she had still the requisite youth,[4] and
the virtuous had no consolation but in marriage—
the state had citizens who would stoop to receive the

[4] By Mommsen's reckoning, her age would be about forty.

qui . . .[1] Germanici coniugem ac liberos eius recipere dignarentur. Sed Caesar non ignarus, quantum ea re[2] peteretur, ne tamen offensionis aut metus manifestus foret, sine responso quamquam instantem reliquit. Id ego, a scriptoribus annalium non traditum, repperi in commentariis Agrippinae filiae, quae Neronis principis mater vitam suam et casus suorum posteris memoravit.

LIV. Ceterum Seianus maerentem et inprovidam altius perculit, immissis qui per speciem amicitiae monerent paratum ei venenum, vitandas soceri epulas. Atque illa simulationum nescia, cum propter discumberet, non vultu aut sermone flecti, nullos attingere cibos, donec advertit Tiberius, forte an quia audiverat; idque quo acrius experiretur, poma, ut erant adposita, laudans nurui sua manu tradidit. Aucta ex eo suspicio Agrippinae, et intacta ore servis tramisit. Nec tamen Tiberii vox coram secuta, sed obversus ad matrem non mirum ait, si quid severius in eam statuisset, a qua veneficii insimularetur. Inde rumor parari exitium, neque id imperatorem palam audere, secretum ad perpetrandum quaeri.

LV. Sed Caesar quo famam averteret, adesse frequens senatui legatosque Asiae, ambigentis

---

[1] *About fourteen letters are omitted in Med. at the end of a line   Haase supplied :*—'⟨qui divo Augusto ortam⟩.'

[2] ea re *Madvig*: ex re publica *Med.* (*by dittography of the* p *in* peteretur).

---

[1] They are mentioned only once elsewhere—by Pliny (*H.N.* VII. 8, 46), as authority for a statement with regard to the birth of Nero.

wife of Germanicus and his children." The Caesar,
however, though he saw all that was implied in the
request, was reluctant to betray either fear or resentment, and therefore, in spite of her insistence,
left her without an answer.—This incident, not
noticed by the professed historians, I found in the
memoirs of her daughter Agrippina [1] (mother of the
emperor Nero), who recorded for the after-world
her life and the vicissitudes of her house.

LIV. Sejanus, however, struck a deeper dismay
into her harassed and improvident breast by sending
agents to warn her, under the colour of friendship,
that poison was ready for her: she would do well to
avoid the dinners of her father-in-law. And she,
a stranger to all pretence, as she reclined next to
him at table, relaxed neither her features nor her
silence, and refused to touch her food; until at last,
either by accident or from information received,
Tiberius' attention was arrested, and, to apply a
more searching test, he took some fruit as it had
been set before him and with his own hand passed
it to his daughter-in-law, with a word of praise. The
act increased Agrippina's suspicions, and without
tasting the dish she passed it over to the slaves.
Even so, no overt remark followed from Tiberius:
he turned, however, to his mother, and observed
that it was not strange if he had resolved on
slightly rigorous measures against a lady who accused
him of murder by poison. Hence a rumour that her
destruction was in preparation, and that the emperor
lacked courage to do the deed openly: a quiet
setting for the crime was being considered.

LV. To divert criticism, the Caesar attended the
senate with frequency, and for several days listened

quanam in civitate templum statueretur pluris per
dies audivit. Undecim urbes certabant, pari ambitione, viribus diversae. Neque multum distantia
inter se memorabant de vetustate generis, studio
in populum Romanum per bella Persi et Aristonici
aliorumque regum. Verum Hypaepeni Trallianique
Laodicenis ac Magnetibus simul tramissi ut parum
validi; ne Ilienses quidem, cum parentem urbis
Romae Troiam referrent, nisi antiquitatis gloria
pollebant. Paulum addubitatum, quod Halicarnasii
mille et ducentos per annos nullo motu terrae
nutavisse sedes suas vivoque in saxo fundamenta
templi adseveraverant. Pergamenos (eo ipso nitebantur) aede Augusto ibi sita satis adeptos creditum.
Ephesii Milesiique, hi Apollinis, illi Dianae caeri-
monia occupavisse civitates visi. Ita Sardianos inter
Zmyrnaeosque deliberatum. Sardiani decretum
Etruriae recitavere ut consanguinei : nam Tyrrhenum
Lydumque Atye rege genitos ob multitudinem
divisisse gentem; Lydum patriis in terris resedisse,
Tyrrheno datum novas ut conderet sedes; et ducum
e nominibus indita vocabula illis per Asiam, his in
Italia; auctamque adhuc Lydorum opulentiam

---

[1] See chap. 15.

[2] The Macedonian war with Perseus was closed by the battle
of Pydna (168 B.C.); the rising of Aristonicus, a natural son
of Eumenes II of Pergamum, was suppressed by M. Perpenna
and M'. Aquilius (130–129 B.C.). The " other kings " are presumably Mithridates and Pharnaces of Pontus and various
Arsacidae of Parthia.

[3] Hypaepa—a plural form—was in Lydia; Tralles, in Caria;
Laodicea " ad Lycum," in Phrygia; Magnesia, not " a Sipylo "

to the deputies from Asia debating which of their communities was to erect his temple.[1] Eleven cities competed, with equal ambition but disparate resources. With no great variety each pleaded national antiquity, and zeal for the Roman cause in the wars with Perseus, Aristonicus, and other kings.[2] But Hypaepa and Tralles,[3] together with Laodicea and Magnesia, were passed over as inadequate to the task: even Ilium, though it appealed to Troy as the parent of Rome, had no significance apart from the glory of its past. Some little hesitation was caused by the statement of the Halicarnassians that for twelve hundred years no tremors of earthquake had disturbed their town, and the temple foundations would rest on the living rock. The Pergamenes were refuted by their main argument: they had already a sanctuary of Augustus, and the distinction was thought ample. The state-worship in Ephesus and Miletus was considered to be already centred on the cults of Diana and Apollo respectively: the deliberations turned, therefore, on Sardis and Smyrna. The Sardians read a decree of their " kindred country " of Etruria. " Owing to its numbers," they explained, " Tyrrhenus and Lydus, sons of King Atys, had divided the nation. Lydus had remained in the territory of his fathers, Tyrrhenus had been allotted the task of creating a new settlement; and the Asiatic and Italian branches of the people had received distinctive titles from the names of the two leaders; while a further advance in the Lydian power had come with the despatch

(II. 47) but " ad Maeandrum " (III. 62), in Lydia.—Tralles, at all events, might have alleged a Caesarian miracle in support of its claim (Caes. *B. C.* III. 105).

missis in insulam [1] populis, cui mox a Pelope nomen. Simul litteras imperatorum et icta nobiscum foedera bello Macedonum ubertatemque fluminum suorum, temperiem caeli ac ditis circum terras memorabant.

LVI. At Zmyrnaei repetita vetustate, seu Tantalus Iove ortus illos, sive Theseus divina et ipse stirpe, sive una Amazonum condidisset, transcendere ad ea, quis maxime fidebant, in populum Romanum officiis, missa navali copia non modo externa ad bella, sed quae in Italia tolerabantur; seque primos templum urbis Romae statuisse, M. Porcio consule, magnis quidem iam populi Romani rebus, nondum tamen ad summum elatis, stante adhuc Punica urbe et validis per Asiam regibus. Simul L. Sullam testem adferebant, gravissimo in discrimine exercitus ob asperitatem hiemis et penuriam vestis, cum id Zmyrnam in contionem nuntiatum foret, omnis qui adstabant detraxisse corpori tegmina nostrisque legionibus misisse. Ita rogati sententiam patres Zymrnaeos praetulere. Censuitque Vibius Marsus, ut M'.[2] Lepido, cui ea provincia obvenerat, super numerum legaretur, qui templi curam susciperet. Et quia Lepidus ipse deligere per modestiam abnuebat, Valerius Naso e praetoriis sorte missus est.

----

[1] insulam *Urlichs* : Graeciam.
[2] M'. *Borghesi* : M.

----

[1] Against Antiochus III of Syria (191–188 B.C.).
[2] In the Social War (90–87 B.C.).
[3] The elder Cato—M. Porcius Cato Censorius; consul with L. Valerius Flaccus in 195 B.C.

of colonists to the peninsula which afterwards took its name from Pelops." At the same time, they recalled the letters from Roman commanders, the treaties concluded with us in the Macedonian war, their ample rivers, tempered climate, and the richness of the surrounding country.

LVI. The deputies from Smyrna, on the other hand, after retracing the antiquity of their town— whether founded by Tantalus, the seed of Jove; by Theseus, also of celestial stock; or by one of the Amazons—passed on to the arguments in which they rested most confidence: their good offices towards the Roman people, to whom they had sent their naval force to aid not merely in foreign wars [1] but in those with which we had to cope in Italy,[2] while they had also been the first to erect a temple to the City of Rome, at a period (the consulate of Marcus Porcius) [3] when the Roman fortunes stood high indeed, but had not yet mounted to their zenith, as the Punic capital was yet standing and the kings were still powerful in Asia. At the same time, Sulla was called to witness that " with his army in a most critical position through the inclement winter and scarcity of clothing, the news had only to be announced at a public meeting in Smyrna, and the whole of the bystanders stripped the garments from their bodies and sent them to our legions." The Fathers accordingly, when their opinion was taken, gave Smyrna the preference. Vibius Marsus proposed that a supernumerary legate, to take responsibility for the temple, should be assigned to Manius Lepidus, to whom the province of Asia had fallen; and since Lepidus modestly declined to make the selection himself, Valerius Naso was chosen by lot among the ex-praetors and sent out.

LVII. Inter quae diu meditato prolatoque saepius consilio tandem Caesar in Campaniam [1] specie dedicandi templa apud Capuam Iovi, apud Nolam Augusto, sed certus procul urbe degere. Causam abscessus quamquam secutus plurimos auctorum ad Seiani artes rettuli, quia tamen caede eius patrata sex postea annos pari secreto coniunxit, plerumque permoveor, num ad ipsum referri verius sit, saevitiam ac libidinem cum factis promeret, locis occultantem. Erant qui crederent in senectute corporis quoque habitum pudori fuisse: quippe illi praegracilis et incurva proceritas, nudus capillo vertex, ulcerosa facies ac plerumque medicaminibus interstincta; et Rhodi secreto vitare coetus, recondere voluptates insuerat. Traditur etiam matris inpotentia extrusum, quam dominationis sociam aspernabatur neque depellere poterat, cum dominationem ipsam donum eius accepisset. Nam dubitaverat Augustus Germanicum, sororis nepotem et cunctis laudatum, rei Romanae inponere, sed precibus uxoris evictus Tiberio Germanicum, sibi Tiberium adscivit. Idque Augusta exprobrabat, reposcebat.

LVIII. Profectio arto comitatu fuit: unus senator

[1] Campaniam] Campaniam ⟨concessit⟩ *Otto.*

---

[1] The house in which he had died was consecrated (D. Cass. LVI. 46).

LVII. Meanwhile, after long meditating and often deferring his plan, the Caesar at length departed for Campania, ostensibly to consecrate one temple to Jupiter at Capua and one to Augustus at Nola,[1] but in the settled resolve to fix his abode far from Rome. As to the motive for his withdrawal, though I have followed the majority of historians in referring it to the intrigues of Sejanus, yet in view of the fact that his isolation remained equally complete for six consecutive years after Sejanus' execution, I am often tempted to doubt whether it could not with greater truth be ascribed to an impulse of his own, to find an inconspicuous home for the cruelty and lust which his acts proclaimed to the world. There were those who believed that in his old age he had become sensitive also to his outward appearances. For he possessed a tall, round-shouldered, and abnormally slender figure, a head without a trace of hair, and an ulcerous face generally variegated with plasters; while, in the seclusion of Rhodes, he had acquired the habit of avoiding company and taking his pleasures by stealth. The statement is also made that he was driven into exile by the imperious temper of his mother, whose partnership in his power he could not tolerate, while it was impossible to cut adrift one from whom he held that power in fee. For Augustus had hesitated whether to place Germanicus, his sister's grandson and the theme of all men's praise, at the head of the Roman realm, but, overborne by the entreaties of his wife, had introduced Germanicus into the family of Tiberius, and Tiberius into his own: a benefit which the old empress kept recalling and reclaiming.

LVIII. His exit was made with a slender retinue:

consulatu functus, Cocceius Nerva, cui legum peritia, eques Romanus praeter Seianum ex inlustribus Curtius Atticus, ceteri liberalibus studiis praediti, ferme Graeci, quorum sermonibus levaretur. Ferebant periti caelestium iis motibus siderum excessisse Roma Tiberium, ut reditus illi negaretur. Unde exitii causa multis fuit properum finem vitae coniectantibus vulgantibusque; neque enim tam incredibilem casum providebant, ut undecim per annos libens patria careret. Mox patuit breve confinium artis et falsi, veraque quam obscuris tegerentur. Nam in urbem non regressurum haud forte dictum: ceterorum nescii egere, cum propinquo rure aut litore et saepe moenia urbis adsidens extremam senectam compleverit.

LIX. Ac forte illis diebus oblatum Caesari anceps periculum auxit vana rumoris praebuitque ipsi materiem, cur amicitiae constantiaeque Seiani magis fideret. Vescebantur in villa, cui vocabulum Speluncae, mare Amunclanum inter *et*[1] Fundanos montes, nativo in specu. Eius os lapsis repente saxis obruit quosdam ministros: hinc metus in omnis et fuga eorum, qui convivium celebrabant. Seianus genu vultuque et manibus super Caesarem suspensus

---

[1] ⟨et⟩ *Bezzenberger.*

---

[1] The grandfather of the future emperor : for his death, see VI. 26.

[2] II. 59 n.

[3] A friend of Ovid, who addresses a couple of letters to him (*ex P.* II. 4 and 7). He succumbed later to the enmity of Sejanus (VI. 10).

[4] For the half-belief of Tacitus in the profession, as distinct from its practitioners, the *locus classicus* is VI. 20–22.

[5] Golfo di Terracina.

one senator who had held a consulship (the jurist
Cocceius Nerva)[1] and—in addition to Sejanus—
one Roman knight of the higher rank,[2] Curtius
Atticus;[3] the rest being men of letters, principally
Greeks, in whose conversation he was to find amuse-
ment. The astrologers declared that he had left
Rome under a conjunction of planets excluding the
possibility of return: a fatal assertion to the many
who concluded that the end was at hand and gave
publicity to their views. For they failed to foresee
the incredible event, that through eleven years he
would persist self-exiled from his fatherland. It
was soon to be revealed how close are the confines
of science and imposture, how dark the veil that
covers truth.[4] That he would never return to Rome
was not said at venture: of all else, the seers were
ignorant; for in the adjacent country, on neighbouring beaches, often hard under the city-walls, he
reached the utmost limit of old age.

LIX. It chanced in those days that a serious
accident which occurred to the Caesar encouraged
these idle speculations and gave the prince himself
a reason for greater faith in the friendship and
firmness of Sejanus. They were at table in a villa
known as the Grotto, built in a natural cavern between the Gulf of Amyclae[5] and the mountains of
Fundi.[6] A sudden fall of rock at the mouth buried
a number of servants, the consequence being a
general panic and the flight of the guests present.
Sejanus alone hung over the Caesar with knee, face
and hands, and opposed himself to the falling stones—

[6] Fondi.—Strabo notices the great caves of the district,
accommodating κατοικίας μεγάλας καὶ πολυτελεῖς (V. 3, 6).
The name of the villa survives in the modern Sperlonga.

opposuit sese incidentibus, atque habitu tali repertus
est a militibus, qui subsidio venerant. Maior ex
eo, et quamquam exitiosa suaderet, ut non sui
anxius, cum fide audiebatur. Adsimulabatque iudi-
cis partis adversum Germanici stirpem, subditis qui
accusatorum nomina sustinerent maximeque in-
sectarentur Neronem proximum successioni et,
quamquam modesta iuventa, plerumque tamen quid
in praesentiarum conduceret oblitum, dum a libertis
et clientibus, apiscendae potentiae properis, exstimu-
latur ut erectum et fidentem animi [1] ostenderet:
velle id populum Romanum, cupere exercitus, neque
ausurum contra Seianum, qui nunc patientiam senis
et segnitiam iuvenis iuxta insultet.

LX. Haec atque talia audienti nihil quidem
pravae cogitationis, sed interdum voces procedebant
contumaces et inconsultae, quas adpositi custodes
exceptas auctasque cum deferrent neque Neroni
defendere daretur, diversae insuper sollicitudinum
formae oriebantur. Nam alius occursum eius vitare,
quidam salutatione reddita statim averti, plerique inceptum sermonem abrumpere, insistentibus contra
inridentibusque qui Seiano fautores aderant.
Enimvero Tiberius torvus aut falsum renidens vultu:
seu loqueretur seu taceret iuvenis, crimen ex silentio,
ex voce. Ne nox quidem secura, cum uxor vigilias

---

[1] animi] animi se *Ritter,* animum *Pichena.*

an attitude in which he was found by the soldiers who had come to their assistance. This brought an accession of greatness, and, fatal though his advice might be, yet, as a man whose thoughts were not for himself, he found a confiding listener. Towards the family of Germanicus he began to assume the pose of judge, suborning agents to support the character of accusers, their main attack to be delivered on Nero, who stood next in the line of succession, and, in spite of the modesty of his youth, too often forgot what the times demanded, while his freedmen and clients, bent on the rapid acquisition of power, urged him to a display of spirit and confidence:—" It was this the nation desired and the armies yearned for, and Sejanus, who now trampled alike on the patience of an old man and the tameness of a young one, would not risk a counter-stroke! "

LX. To all this and the like he listened with no malice in his mind; but at intervals there fell from him defiant and unconsidered phrases; and as these were seized upon and reported with enlargements by the watchers posted round his person, no chance of refutation being allowed him, other forms of anxiety began in addition to make their appearance. One man would avoid meeting him; some went through the formality of salutation, then promptly turned away; many broke off any attempt at conversation; while, in contrast, any adherents of Sejanus who happened to be present stood their ground and jeered. As to Tiberius, he met him either with gloomy brows or with a hypocritical smile on his countenance; whether the boy spoke or held his peace, there was guilt in silence, guilt in speech. Even night itself was not secure, since his

somnos suspiria matri Liviae atque illa Seiano pate-
faceret; qui fratrem quoque Neronis Drusum traxit
in partes, spe obiecta principis loci, si priorem aetate
et iam labefactum demovisset. Atrox Drusi ingenium super cupidinem potentiae et solita fratribus
odia accendebatur invidia, quod mater Agrippina
promptior Neroni erat. Neque tamen Seianus ita
Drusum fovebat, ut non in eum quoque semina
futuri exitii meditaretur, gnarus praeferocem et
insidiis magis opportunum.

LXI. Fine anni excessere insignes viri Asinius
Agrippa, claris maioribus quam vetustis vitaque non
degener, et Q. Haterius, familia senatoria, eloquentiae, quoad vixit, celebratae: monimenta
ingeni eius haud perinde retinentur. Scilicet impetu
magis quam cura vigebat; utque aliorum meditatio
et labor in posterum valescit, sic Haterii canorum
illud et profluens cum ipso simul extinctum est.

LXII. M. Licinio L. Calpurnio consulibus ingentium bellorum cladem aequavit malum inprovisum:

---

[1] Drusus' daughter, Julia (III. 29). As there is no hint of
reprobation in the mention of her at VI. 27, Nipperdey charit-
ably inferred that her disclosures were made with the best of
motives.

[2] Consul two years previously (chap. 34). The reference
to his ancestry bears upon his two famous grandfathers, M.
Agrippa and Asinius Pollio, the former of obscure, the latter
of undistinguished origins.

[3] *Q. Haterii cursum, suis temporibus oratoris celeberrimi,
longe abesse ab homine sano volo. Nunquam dubitavit, nunquam
intermisit: semel incipiebat, semel desinebat* (Sen. *Ep.* 40).
Similar verdicts are passed by the elder Seneca and Jerome.

wakeful hours, his slumbers, his sighs, were communicated by his wife[1] to her mother Livia, and by Livia to Sejanus; who had actually made a convert of his brother Drusus by holding before his eyes the prospect of supremacy, once he should have ousted his senior from his already precarious position. Over and above the lust of power and the hatred habitual to brothers, the savage temper of Drusus was inflamed by envy, as the preferences of his mother Agrippina were for Nero. None the less, Sejanus' solicitude for Drusus was not so great but that, even against him, he was pondering the measures which should ripen to his destruction: for he knew the rash hardihood which laid him peculiarly open to treachery.

LXI. At the close of the year, two distinguished men passed away: Asinius Agrippa,[2] of an ancestry more honourable than old, from which his life had not degenerated; and Quintus Haterius, a member of a senatorial family, and master of an eloquence famous in his lifetime, though the extant memorials of his talent are not retained in equal esteem. The truth is that his strength lay more in vigour than in care;[3] and, as the study and labour of others take an added value with time, so the melody and fluency of Haterius were extinguished with himself.

LXII. In the consulate of Marcus Licinius[4] and Lucius Calpurnius,[5] the casualties of some great wars were equalled by an unexpected disaster. It began

A.V.C. 780 = A.D. 27

[4] M. Licinius Crassus Frugi; conjectured to be the adoptive name (with his old cognomen) of the younger of the Pisos, to whom Horace addressed the *Ars Poetica*.

[5] L. (originally, Cn.) Calpurnius Piso (III. 17 n.).

eius initium simul et finis exstitit. Nam coepto apud
Fidenam amphitheatro Atilius quidam libertini
generis, quo spectaculum gladiatorum celebraret,
neque fundamenta per solidum subdidit, neque
firmis nexibus ligneam compagem superstruxit, ut
qui non abundantia pecuniae nec municipali ambitione, sed in sordidam mercedem id negotium
quaesivisset. Adfluxere avidi talium, imperitante
Tiberio procul voluptatibus habiti, virile ac muliebre
secus, omnis aetas, ob propinquitatem loci effusius;
unde gravior pestis fuit, conferta mole, dein convulsa, dum ruit intus aut in exteriora effunditur
inmensamque vim mortalium, spectaculo intentos aut
qui circum adstabant, praeceps trahit atque operit.
Et illi quidem, quos principium stragis in mortem
adflixerat, ut tali sorte, cruciatum effugere: miserandi
magis quos abrupta parte corporis nondum vita
deseruerat; qui per diem visu, per noctem ululatibus
et gemitu coniuges aut liberos noscebant. Iam
ceteri fama exciti, hic fratrem, propinquum ille,
alius, parentes lamentari. Etiam quorum diversa
de causa amici aut necessarii aberant, pavere tamen;
nequedum comperto, quos illa vis perculisset, latior
ex incerto metus.

LXIII. Ut coepere dimoveri obruta, concursus ad
exanimos complectentium, osculantium; et saepe
certamen, si confusior facies, sed par forma aut aetas

---

[1] A Sabine town some five miles from Rome, but sunk to
little more than a hamlet (*Gabiis desertior atque/Fidenis vicus*,
Hor. *Ep.* I. 11, 7).

and ended in a moment. A certain Atilius, of the freedman class, who had begun an amphitheatre at Fidena,[1] in order to give a gladiatorial show, failed both to lay the foundation in solid ground and to secure the fastenings of the wooden structure above; the reason being that he had embarked on the enterprise, not from a superabundance of wealth nor to court the favours of his townsmen, but with an eye to sordid gain. The amateurs of such amusements, debarred from their pleasures under the reign of Tiberius, poured to the place, men and women, old and young, the stream swollen because the town lay near. This increased the gravity of the catastrophe, as the unwieldy fabric was packed when it collapsed, breaking inward or sagging outward, and precipitating and burying a vast crowd of human beings, intent on the spectacle or standing around. Those, indeed, whom the first moment of havoc had dashed to death, escaped torture, so far as was possible in such a fate: more to be pitied were those whose mutilated bodies life had not yet abandoned, who by day recognized their wives or their children by sight, and at night by their shrieks and moans. The news brought the absent to the scene—one lamenting a brother, one a kinsman, another his parents. Even those whose friends or relatives had left home for a different reason still felt the alarm, and, as it was not yet known whom the catastrophe had destroyed, the uncertainty gave wider range for fear.

LXIII. When the fallen materials came to be removed, the watchers rushed to their dead, embracing them, kissing them, not rarely quarrelling over them, in cases where the features had been obliterated but a parity of form or age had led to

errorem adgnoscentibus fecerat. Quinquaginta hominum milia eo casu debilitata vel obtrita sunt;
cautumque in posterum senatus consulto, ne quis
gladiatorium munus ederet, cui minor quadringentorum milium res, neve amphitheatrum inpone-
retur nisi solo firmitatis spectatae. Atilius in exilium
actus est. Ceterum sub recentem cladem patuere
procerum domus, fomenta et medici passim praebiti,
fuitque urbs per illos dies quamquam maesta facie
veterum institutis similis, qui magna post proelia
saucios largitione et cura sustentabant.

LXIV. Nondum ea clades exoleverat, cum ignis
violentia urbem ultra solitum adfecit, deusto monte
Caelio; feralemque annum ferebant et ominibus
adversis susceptum principi consilium absentiae, qui
mos vulgo, fortuita ad culpam trahentes, ni Caesar
obviam isset tribuendo pecunias ex modo detrimenti.
Actaeque ei grates apud senatum ab inlustribus
famaque apud populum, quia sine ambitione aut
proximorum precibus ignotos etiam et ultro accitos
munificentia iuverat. Adduntur sententiae, ut mons
Caelius in posterum Augustus appellaretur, quando
cunctis circum flagrantibus sola Tiberii effigies, sita
in domo Iunii senatoris, inviolata mansisset. Evenisse

---

[1] The killed, according to Suetonius (*Tib.* 40), exceeded
20,000; but the figures will not bear a moment's examination.
[2] The second ward (*Caelimontium*) of the fourteen into which
the capital was divided by Augustus (10 B.C.).

mistaken identification. Fifty thousand persons[1] were maimed or crushed to death in the disaster; and for the future it was provided by a decree of the senate that no one with a fortune less than four hundred thousand sesterces should present a gladiatorial display, and that no amphitheatre was to be built except on ground of·tried solidity. Atilius was driven into banishment. It remains to be said that, on the morrow of the accident, the great houses were thrown open; dressings and doctors were supplied to all comers; and Rome throughout those days, however tragic her aspect, yet offered a parallel to the practice of the ancients, who were accustomed, after a stricken field, to relieve the wounded by their liberality and their care.

LXIV. The disaster had not yet faded from memory, when a fierce outbreak of fire affected the city to an unusual degree by burning down the Caelian Hill.[2] "It was a fatal year, and the sovereign's decision to absent himself had been adopted under an evil star"—so men began to remark, converting, as is the habit of the crowd, the fortuitous into the culpable, when the Caesar checked the critics by a distribution of money in proportion to loss sustained. Thanks were returned to him; in the senate, by the noble; in the streets, by the voice of the people: for without respect of persons, and without the intercession of relatives, he had aided with his liberality even unknown sufferers whom he had himself encouraged to apply. Proposals were added that the Caelian Hill should for the future be known as the Augustan, since, with all around on fire, the one thing to remain unscathed had been a bust of Tiberius in the house of the senator Junius. "The same,"

id olim Claudiae Quintae, eiusque statuam vim ignium
bis elapsam maiores apud aedem matris deum
consecravisse. Sanctos acceptosque numinibus Claudios et augendam caerimoniam loco, in quo tantum in
principem honorem di ostenderint.

LXV. Haud fuerit absurdum tradere montem eum
antiquitus Querquetulanum cognomento fuisse, quod
talis silvae frequens fecundusque erat, mox Caelium
appellitatum a Caele Vibenna, qui dux gentis
Etruscae cum auxilium tulisset,[1] sedem eam acceperat a Tarquinio Prisco, seu quis alius regum dedit:
nam scriptores in eo dissentiunt. Cetera non
ambigua sunt, magnas eas copias per plana etiam ac
foro propinqua habitavisse, unde Tuscum vicum e
vocabulo advenarum dictum.

LXVI. Sed ut studia procerum et largitio
principis adversum casus [2] solacium tulerant, ita
accusatorum maior in dies et infestior vis sine leva-
mento grassabatur; corripueratque Varum Quinti-
lium, divitem et Caesari propinquum, Domitius Afer,
Claudiae Pulchrae matris eius condemnator, nullo

---

[1] tulisset *Lipsius*: appellatum tavisset *Med.*, portavisset
Doederlein, adportavisset *Croll*.
[2] casus *Heinsius*: casum.

---

[1] Probably a grand-daughter of Appius Claudius Caecus,
and possibly a Vestal. The miracle, which vindicated her
chastity on the arrival of the Mother of the Gods from Pessinus
in 204 B.C., is accorded a hundred lines by Ovid (*Fast.* IV. 247
sqq.).
[2] This passage is the sole authority for the name. The con-
flicting legends as to the hill and the *vicus Tuscus* (between the
Capitoline and the Palatine) may be seen in Nipperdey: the
only version with some slight accidental interest is that of
Claudius in the Lyons fragment of his speech on the *ius
honorum* of the Gauls.

it was said, " had happened formerly to Claudia Quinta;[1] whose statue, twice escaped from the fury of the flames, our ancestors had dedicated in the temple of the Mother of the Gods. The Claudian race was sacrosanct and acceptable to Heaven, and additional solemnity should be given to the ground on which the gods had shown so notable an honour to the sovereign."

LXV. It may not be out of place to state that the hill was originally named the " Querquetulanus,"[2] from the abundance of oak produced on it, and only later took the title of " Caelius " from Caeles Vibenna, an Etruscan chief; who, for marching to the aid of Rome, had received the district as a settlement, either from Tarquinius Priscus or by the gift of another of our kings. On that point the authors disagree: the rest is not in doubt—that Vibenna's numerous forces established themselves on the level also, and in the neighbourhood of the forum, with the result that the Tuscan Street has taken its name from the immigrants.

LXVI. But while the good-will of the nobles and the liberality of the emperor had been able to mitigate accidents, the violence of the informers, more pronounced and more venomous every day, ran riot without a palliative. Quintilius Varus,[3] a rich man and a relation of the Caesar, had been attacked by the same Domitius Afer who procured the condemnation of his mother Claudia Pulchra. No surprise was felt that Afer, who after years of indigence had now

---

[3] Son of Augustus' ill-starred general, and once affianced to a daughter of Germanicus (M. Sen. *Contr.* 3, 10). For his mother's connection with the imperial family, see chap. 52.

mirante quod diu egens et parto nuper praemio
male usus plura ad flagitia accingeretur. P. Dola-
bellam socium delationis extitisse miraculo erat,
quia claris maioribus et Varo conexus suam ipse
nobilitatem, suum sanguinem perditum ibat. Restitit
tamen senatus et opperiendum imperatorem censuit,
quod unum urguentium malorum suffugium in
tempus erat.

LXVII. At Caesar dedicatis per Campaniam
templis, quamquam edicto monuisset, ne quis
quietem eius inrumperet, concursusque oppidanorum
disposito milite prohiberentur, perosus tamen muni-
cipia et colonias omniaque in continenti sita, Capreas
se in insulam abdidit, trium milium freto ab extremis
Surrentini promunturii diiunctam. Solitudinem eius
placuisse maxime crediderim, quoniam inportuosum
circa mare et vix modicis navigiis pauca subsidia;
neque adpulerit quisquam nisi gnaro custode. Caeli
temperies hieme mitis obiectu montis, quo saeva
ventorum arcentur; aestas in favonium obversa et
aperto circum pelago peramoena; prospectabatque
pulcherrimum sinum, antequam Vesuvius mons
ardescens faciem loci verteret. Graecos ea tenuisse

---

[1] The accuser's legal bounty (chap. 20). The archaeologists
have discovered a more reputable source of income in the
shape of his extensive brickyards—the industry ranked as
agricultural, and was therefore open to a senator—which
ultimately became the property of the mother of Marcus
Aurelius.

[2] Capri.—The island had been imperial property since 29
B.C., when Augustus acquired it from Naples in exchange
for Ischia (Suet. *Aug.* 92; D. Cass. LII. 43).

[3] Sorrento.

made a scandalous use of his recently earned reward,[1] should be girding himself to fresh enormities : the astonishing point was that Publius Dolabella should have come forward as his partner in the accusation : for, with his high descent and his family connection with Varus, he was now setting out to destroy his own nobility and his own blood. The senate, however, stood its ground, and decided to await the emperor, the only course offering a momentary respite from the imminent horrors.

LXVII. Meanwhile, the Caesar, after dedicating the temples in Campania ; though he had warned the public by edict not to invade his privacy, and the crowds from the country-towns were being kept at distance by troops appropriately disposed ; yet conceived so intense a loathing for the municipalities, the colonies, and all things situated on the mainland, that he vanished into the Isle of Capreae,[2] which three miles of strait divide from the extreme point of the Surrentine promontory.[3] The solitude of the place I should suppose to have been its principal commendation, as it is surrounded by a harbourless sea, with a few makeshift roadsteads hardly adequate for small-sized vessels, while it is impossible to land unobserved by a sentry. In winter, the climate is gentle, owing to the mountain barrier which intercepts the cold sweep of the winds ; its summers catch the western breeze and are made a delight by the circling expanse of open sea ; while it overlooked the most beautiful of bays, until the activity of Vesuvius [4] began to change the face of the landscape. The tradition goes that Campania was held by Greek

[4] In the great eruption of 79 A.D., which destroyed Pompeii and Herculaneum.

Capreasque Telebois habitatas fama tradit. Sed
tum Tiberius duodecim villarum nominibus et molibus
insederat, quanto intentus olim publicas ad curas,
tanto occultiores [1] in luxus et malum otium resolutus.
Manebat quippe suspicionum et credendi temeritas,
quam Seianus augere etiam in urbe suetus acrius
turbabat, non iam occultis adversum Agrippinam et
Neronem insidiis. Quis additus miles nuntios,
introitus, aperta secreta velut in annalis referebat,
ultroque struebantur, qui monerent perfugere ad
Germaniae exercitus vel celeberrimo fori effigiem divi
Augusti amplecti populumque ac senatum auxilio
vocare. Eaque spreta ab illis, velut pararent,
obiciebantur.

LXVIII. Iunio Silano et Silio Nerva consulibus
foedum anni principium incessit tracto in carcerem
inlustri equite Romano, Titio Sabino, ob amicitiam
Germanici: neque enim omiserat coniugem liberos-
que eius percolere, sector domi, comes in publico,
post tot clientes unus eoque apud bonos laudatus et
gravis iniquis. Hunc Latinius Latiaris, Porcius Cato,

---

[1] occultiores *Weissenborn*: occultior *Med.*, occultos *J. F.
Gronovius.*

---

[1] From the Echinades off Acarnania: the legend is casually
mentioned by Virgil (*Aen.* VII. 735).

[2] They were probably named, as Lipsius saw, after the
Twelve Gods: one, at all events, was the *villa Iovis* (Suet.
Tib. 65).

[3] Ap. Junius Silanus, son presumably of C. Silanus (III.
66, 69), and later the stepfather of Messalina (D. Cass. LX. 14).
His death (*Appiana caedes* XI. 29), in 42 A.D., was one of the
earliest scandals of Claudius' principate (Suet. *Claud.* 37, D.
Cass. *l.l.*).

settlers, Capreae being inhabited by Teleboans.[1]
At this time, however, the islet was occupied by the
imposing fabric of the twelve villas—with their
twelve names[2]—of Tiberius; who, once absorbed in
the cares of state, was now unbending with equal
zest in hidden vice and flagitious leisure. For his
rashness of suspicion and belief remained, and
Sejanus, who even in the capital had habitually
encouraged it, was now more actively unsettling his
mind; for there was no longer any concealment of his
plots against Agrippina and Nero. Soldiers dogged
their steps, and recorded their messages, their
interviews, their doings open and secret, with the
exactitude of annalists; while agents were even set
at work to advise the pair to take refuge with the
armies of Germany, or, at the most crowded hour of
the forum, to clasp the effigy of the deified Augustus
and call the senate and people to aid. And, since
they rejected any such action, it was imputed to
them as in contemplation.

LXVIII. With the consulate of Junius Silanus[3] and
Silius Nerva, the opening year came charged with
disgrace; and the great Roman knight, Titius
Sabinus,[4] was dragged to the dungeon to expiate
his friendship with Germanicus. For he had abated
nothing of his scrupulous attentions to the widow and
children of the dead, but remained their visitor at
home, their companion in public—the one survivor
of that multitude of clients, and rewarded, as such,
by the admiration of the good and the hatred of the
malevolent. He was singled out for attack by
Latinius Latiaris, Porcius Cato, Petilius Rufus, and

A.V.C. 781 =
A.D. 28

---

[4] Marked down for destruction four years earlier, then
respited (chap. 18 *sq.*).

Petilius Rufus, M. Opsius praetura functi adgrediuntur, cupidine consulatus, ad quem non nisi per Seianum aditus; neque Seiani voluntas nisi scelere quaerebatur. Compositum inter ipsos, ut Latiaris, qui modico usu Sabinum contingebat, strueret dolum, ceteri testes adessent, deinde accusationem inciperent. Igitur Latiaris iacere fortuitos primum sermones, mox laudare constantiam, quod non, ut ceteri, florentis domus amicus adflictam deseruisset; simul honora de Germanico, Agrippinam miserans, disserebat. Et postquam Sabinus, ut sunt molles in calamitate mortalium animi, effudit lacrimas, iunxit questus, audentius iam onerat Seianum, saevitiam, superbiam, spes eius. Ne in Tiberium quidem convicio abstinet; iique sermones, tamquam vetita miscuissent, speciem artae amicitiae fecere. Ac iam ultro Sabinus quaerere Latiarem, ventitare domum, dolores suos quasi ad fidissimum deferre.

LXIX. Consultant quos memoravi, quonam modo ea plurium auditu acciperentur. Nam loco, in quem coibatur, servanda solitudinis facies; et si pone fores adsisterent, metus visus, sonitus aut forte ortae suspicionis erat. Tectum inter et laquearia tres senatores, haud minus turpi latebra quam detestanda fraude, sese abstrudunt, foraminibus et rimis aurem

Marcus Opsius, ex-praetors enamoured of the consulate: an office to which there was no avenue but through Sejanus, while the complaisance of Sejanus was only to be purchased by crime. The arrangement among the four was that Latiaris, who was connected with Sabinus by some little intimacy, should lay the trap; that the rest should be present as witnesses; and that only then should the accusation be set on foot. Latiaris, therefore, began with casual remarks in conversation, then passed to eulogies on the constancy of Sabinus, who, unlike the rest, had not abandoned in its affliction the house to which he had been attached in its prosperity: at the same time, he referred to Germanicus in terms of honour, and to Agrippina in a strain of pity. Then, as Sabinus, with the usual weakness of the human heart in sorrow, broke into tears coupled with complaints, he grew bolder and showered reproaches on Sejanus, his cruelty, his arrogance, his ambition. Even Tiberius was not spared, and these conversations, regarded as an exchange of forbidden sentiments, gave the appearance of intimate friendship.—And now Sabinus began himself to seek the company of Latiaris, to frequent his house, and to convey his griefs to that seemingly faithful breast.

LXIX. The partners, whom I have mentioned, now discussed the means of ensuring that these conversations should have a wider audience. For the trysting-place had necessarily to retain an air of solitude; and, if they stood behind the doors, there was a risk of detection by sight, by sound, or by a casually roused suspicion. Between roof and ceiling —an ambuscade as humiliating as the ruse was detestable—three senators inserted themselves, and

admovent. Interea Latiaris repertum in publico
Sabinum, velut recens cognita narraturus, domum et
in cubiculum trahit; praeteritaque et instantia,
quorum adfatim copia, ac novos terrores cumulat.
Eadem ille et diutius, quanto maesta, ubi semel
prorupere, difficilius reticentur. Properata inde
accusatio, missisque ad Caesarem litteris ordinem
fraudis suumque ipsi dedecus narravere. Non alias
magis anxia et pavens civitas, *sui t*egens [1] adversum
proximos; congressus, conloquia, notae ignotaeque
aures vitari; etiam muta atque inanima, tectum et
parietes circumspectabantur.

LXX. Sed Caesar sollemnia incipientis anni ka-
lendis Ianuariis epistula precatus, vertit in Sabinum,
corruptos quosdam libertorum et petitum se arguens,
ultionemque haud obscure poscebat. Nec mora
quin decerneretur; et trahebatur damnatus, quantum
obducta veste adstrictis faucibus niti poterat, clamitans sic inchoari annum, has Seiano victimas cadere.
Quo intendisset oculos, quo verba acciderent, fuga
vastitas, deseri itinera fora. Et quidam regredie-

---

[1] ⟨sui t⟩egens *Mueller*: egens *Med.*, tegens *Lipsius*,
reticens *Weissenborn*.

---

[1] Chap. 17 n.

applied their ears to chinks and openings. Meanwhile, Latiaris had discovered Sabinus in the streets, and, on the pretext of communicating news just received, dragged him home and into the bedroom, where he rehearsed a list of troubles past and present —there was no paucity of material!—accompanied by newly-arisen motives of terror. Sabinus replied in the same vein, but at greater length: for grief, when once it has overflowed, becomes more difficult to repress. The accusation was now hurried forward; and in a letter to the Caesar the associates exposed the sequence of the plot together with their own degradation. In Rome, the anxiety and panic, the reticences of men towards their nearest and dearest, had never been greater: meetings and conversations, the ears of friend and stranger were alike avoided; even things mute and inanimate— the very walls and roofs—were eyed with circumspection.

LXX. However, in a letter read on the first of January,[1] the Caesar, after the orthodox prayers for the new year, turned to Sabinus, charging him with the corruption of several of his freedmen, and with designs against himself; and demanded vengeance in terms impossible to misread. Vengeance was decreed without loss of time; and the doomed man was dragged to his death, crying with all the vigour allowed by the cloak muffling his head and the noose around his neck, that " these were the ceremonies that inaugurated the year, these the victims that bled to propitiate Sejanus ! " In whatever direction he turned his eyes, wherever his words reached an ear, the result was flight and desolation, an exodus from street and forum. Here and there a man re-

bantur ostentabantque se rursum, id ipsum paventes,
quod timuissent. Quem enim diem vacuum poena,
ubi inter sacra et vota, quo tempore verbis etiam
profanis abstineri mos esset, vincla et laqueus
inducantur? Non inprudentem Tiberium tantam
invidiam adisse, set[1] quaesitum meditatumque, ne
quid impedire credatur, quo minus novi magistratus,
quo modo delubra et altaria, sic carcerem recludant.
Secutae insuper litterae grates agentis, quod homi-
nem infensum rei publicae punivissent, adiecto
trepidam sibi vitam, suspectas inimicorum insidias,
nullo nominatim conpellato; neque tamen dubitabatur in Neronem et Agrippinam intendi.

LXXI. Ni mihi destinatum foret suum quaeque
in annum referre, avebat animus antire statimque
memorare exitus, quos Latinius atque Opsius ceteri-
que flagitii eius repertores habuere, non modo
postquam Gaius Caesar rerum potitus est, sed
incolumi Tiberio, qui scelerum ministros ut perverti
ab aliis nolebat, ita plerumque satiatus et oblatis in
eandem operam recentibus veteres et praegravis
adflixit: verum has atque alias sontium poenas in
tempore trademus. Tum censuit Asinius Gallus,
cuius liberorum Agrippina matertera erat, petendum
a principe, ut metus suos senatui fateretur amoveri-
que sineret. Nullam aeque Tiberius, ut rebatur, ex

---

[1] adisse, set *Wurm* : adisset.

---

[1] On Robespierre's principle :—' Quiconque tremble est
coupable ' (*Discours à la Convention du* 31 *mars* 1794).

[2] By the first execution.

[3] For Latiaris, see VI. 4. Of Cato, it is known from Fron-
tinus (*Aq.* 102) that he was *curator aquarum* for one month in
38 A.D., and the brevity of his term of office may obviously
have a sinister explantion.

[4] She was the half-sister of Tiberius' first wife Vipsania,
who, after her divorce, had married Gallus (I. 12 fin.).

traced his steps and showed himself again, pale at
the very thought that he had manifested alarm.[1]
" For what day would find the killers idle, when amid
sacrifices and prayers, at a season when custom
prohibited so much as an ominous word, chains and
the halter came upon the scene? Not from want of
thought had odium such as this been incurred by
Tiberius: it was a premeditated and deliberate act,
that none might think that the new magistrates were
precluded from inaugurating the dungeon[2] as they
did the temples and the altars."—A supplementary
letter followed: the sovereign was grateful that they
had punished a man who was a danger to his country.
He added that his own life was full of alarms, and
that he suspected treachery from his enemies. He
mentioned none by name; but no doubt was felt
that the words were levelled at Agrippina and
Nero.

LXXI. If it were not my purpose to enter each
event under its year, I should be tempted to anticipate, and to record at once the endings made by
Latinius and Opsius and the remaining inventors of
this atrocity, not only after the accession of Gaius
Caesar, but in the lifetime of Tiberius;[3] who, disinclined though he was to see the ministers of his
villainy destroyed by others, yet often wearied of
their ministrations, and, when fresh workers in the
same field presented themselves, struck down the
old and burdensome. However, these and other
punishments of the guilty I shall chronicle at their
proper time. Now, Asinius Gallus, of whose children
Agrippina was the aunt,[4] proposed that the emperor
should be requested to disclose his fears to the senate
and permit their removal. Of all his virtues, as he
regarded them, there was none which Tiberius held

virtutibus suis quam dissimulationem diligebat: eo aegrius accepit recludi quae premeret. Sed mitigavit Seianus, non Galli amore, verum ut cunctationes principis opperiretur,[1] gnarus lentum in meditando, ubi prorupisset, tristibus dictis atrocia facta coniungere.

Per idem tempus Iulia mortem obiit, quam neptem Augustus convictam, adulterii damnaverat, proieceratque in insulam Trimerum,[2] haud procul Apulis litoribus. Illic viginti annis exilium toleravit Augustae ope sustentata, quae florentes privignos cum per occultum subvertisset, misericordiam erga adflictos palam ostentabat.

LXXII. Eodem anno Frisii, transrhenanus populus, pacem exuere, nostra magis avaritia quam obsequii inpatientes. Tributum iis Drusus iusserat modicum pro angustia rerum, ut in usus militares coria boum penderent, non intenta cuiusquam cura, quae firmitudo, quae mensura, donec Olennius e primipilaribus regendis Frisiis inpositus terga urorum delegit, quorum ad formam acciperentur. Id aliis quoque nationibus arduum apud Germanos difficilius tolerabatur, quis ingentium beluarum feraces saltus,

---

[1] opperiretur *J. F. Gronovius* (opperirentur *Muretus*): aperirentur *Med., Kiessling, Halm.*

[2] Tremetum *Freinsheim.—The present name of the group is Isole di Tremiti.*

---

[1] Daughter of M. Vipsanius Agrippa and the elder Julia, therefore sister to Agrippina. Her banishment for the intrigue with D. Silanus (III. 24) synchronized with that of Ovid, but the theories spun from the coincidence are highly doubtful.

[2] On the North Sea coast, west of the Chauci, between the Zuydersee and the Ems (*Friesland*). They had remained

in such esteem as his power of dissimulation; whence the chagrin with which he received this attempt to reveal what he chose to suppress. Sejanus, however, mollified him; not from love of Gallus, but in order to await the issue of the emperor's hesitations: for he knew that, leisurely as he was in deliberation, once he had broken out, he left little interval between ominous words and ruthless deeds.

About this time, Julia[1] breathed her last. Convicted of adultery, she had been sentenced by her grandfather Augustus, and summarily deported to the island of Trimerus, a little way from the Apulian coast. There she supported her exile for twenty years, sustained by the charity of Augusta; who had laboured in the dark to destroy her step-children while they flourished, and advertised to the world her compassion when they fell.

LXXII. In the same year, the Frisians,[2] a tribe on the further bank of the Rhine, violated the peace, more from our cupidity than from their own impatience of subjection. In view of their narrow resources, Drusus had imposed on them a moderate tribute, consisting in a payment of ox-hides for military purposes. No one had given particular attention to their firmness or size, until Olennius, a leading centurion appointed to the Frisian governorship selected the hide of the aurochs[3] as the standard for the contributions. The demand, onerous enough to any people, was the less endurable in Germany; where the forests teem with huge animals, but the

consistently loyal to Rome since their submission to Tiberius' brother Drusus (12 B.C.).

[3] The extinct European wild ox, which survived in Lithuania up to the sixteenth century.

modica domi armenta sunt. Ac primo boves ipsos,
mox agros, postremo corpora coniugum aut liberorum
servitio tradebant. Hinc ira et questus, et postquam
non subveniebatur, remedium ex bello. Rapti qui
tributo aderant milites et patibulo adfixi: Olennius
infensos fuga praevenit, receptus castello, cui nomen
Flevum; et haud spernenda illic civium sociorumque
manus litora Oceani praesidebat.

LXXIII. Quod ubi L. Apronio inferioris Germaniae
pro praetore cognitum, vexilla legionum e superiore
provincia peditumque et equitum auxiliarium delectos accivit ac simul utrumque exercitum Rheno
devectum Frisiis intulit, soluto iam castelli obsidio et
ad sua tutanda degressis rebellibus. Igitur proxima
aestuaria aggeribus et pontibus traducendo graviori
agmini firmat. Atque interim repertis vadis alam
Canninefatem et quod peditum Germanorum inter
nostros merebat circumgredi terga hostium iubet,
qui iam acie compositi pellunt turmas socialis
equitesque legionum subsidio missos. Tum tres
leves cohortes ac rursum duae, dein tempore interiecto alarius eques inmissus: satis validi, si simul

---

[1] I. 56; III. 21.

[2] Recruited from the Canninefates (the orthography is
variable) in the Kennemar district of North Holland (*Hist.* IV.
15 etc.).

[3] The *ala C.*

[4] The regular legionary cavalry—four *turmae* of thirty men
apiece to each of the four legions (the army of Lower Germany)
at the disposal of Apronius.

[5] The whole body, of which the Canninefates formed part.

domesticated herds are of moderate size. First their cattle only, next their lands, finally the persons of their wives or children, were handed over to servitude. Hence, indignation and complaints; then, as relief was not accorded, an appeal to arms. The soldiers stationed to supervise the tribute were seized and nailed to the gibbet. Olennius forestalled the rage of his victims by flight, finding shelter in a fort by the name of Flevum, where a respectable force of Romans and provincials was mounting guard on the coast of the North Sea.

LXXIII. As soon as the intelligence reached Lucius Apronius,[1] the governor of Lower Germany, he summoned detachments of legionaries from the Upper Province, with picked bodies of auxiliary foot and horse, and conveyed both armies simultaneously down the Rhine into Frisian territory; where the siege of the fortress had already been raised, and the insurgents had left for the defence of their own possessions. He therefore provided a solid road of causeways and bridges through the neighbouring estuaries, to facilitate the transit of his heavy columns: in the meantime, as a ford had been discovered, he gave orders for the Canninefate cavalry,[2] with the whole of the German foot serving in our ranks, to work round the rear of the enemy; who, now drawn up in order of battle, forced back the auxiliary squadrons[3] and the legionary horse[4] despatched to their help. Next, three light-armed cohorts, then two more, and finally, after some time had intervened, the whole of the mounted auxiliaries[5] were thrown into the struggle. The forces were powerful enough, if they had been launched on the enemy simultaneously; but, arriving as they did at

incubuissent, per intervallum adventantes neque constantiam addiderant turbatis et pavore fugientium auferebantur. Cethego Labeoni legato quintae legionis quod reliquum auxiliorum tradit. Atque ille dubia suorum re in anceps tractus missis nuntiis vim legionum inplorabat. Prorumpunt quintani ante alios et acri pugna hoste pulso recipiunt cohortis alasque fessas vulneribus. Neque dux Romanus ultum iit aut corpora humavit, quamquam multi tribunorum praefectorumque et insignes centuriones cecidissent. Mox compertum a transfugis nongentos Romanorum apud lucum, quem Baduhennae vocant, pugna in posterum extracta confectos, et aliam quadringentorum manum occupata Cruptorigis [1] quondam stipendiarii villa, postquam proditio metuebatur, mutuis ictibus procubuisse.

LXXIV. Clarum inde inter Germanos Frisium nomen, dissimulante Tiberio damna, ne cui bellum permitteret. Neque senatus in eo cura, an imperii extrema dehonestarentur: pavor internus occupaverat animos, cui remedium adulatione quaerebatur. Ita quamquam diversis super rebus consulerentur, aram clementiae, aram amicitiae effigiesque circum Caesaris ac Seiani censuere, crebrisque

---

[1] Cruptorigis *Otto* : cruptoricis.

---

[1] Presumably a goddess—of war, according to Grimm.

intervals, so far from communicating steadiness to the broken troops, they were on the point of being carried away by the panic of the fugitives, when Apronius put the last of the auxiliaries under the command of Cethegus Labeo, the legate of the fifth legion. Labeo, whom the critical position of his side involved in serious danger, sent off messengers with an urgent request for the full strength of the legions. The men of the fifth dashed forward in advance of the others, drove back the enemy in a sharp engagement, and brought off the cohorts and cavalry squadrons in a state of exhaustion from their wounds. The Roman general made no attempt at revenge; nor did he bury his dead, though a considerable number of tribunes, prefects, and centurions of mark had fallen. Shortly afterwards, it was ascertained from deserters that nine hundred Romans, who had prolonged the struggle till next day, had been despatched in the so-called Grove of Baduhenna; [1] while another detachment of four hundred, after occupying the villa of Cruptorix, formerly a soldier in our pay, had been driven by fears of treachery to die on each other's swords.

LXXIV. Thus the Frisian name won celebrity in Germany; while Tiberius, rather than entrust anyone with the conduct of the war, suppressed our losses. The senate, too, had other anxieties than a question of national dishonour on the confines of the empire: an internal panic had preoccupied all minds, and the antidote was being sought in sycophancy. Thus, although their opinion was being taken on totally unrelated subjects, they voted an altar of Mercy and an altar of Friendship with statues of the Caesar and Sejanus on either hand, and with reiterated

precibus efflagitabant visendi sui copiam facerent.
Non illi tamen in urbem aut propinqua urbi degressi
sunt: satis visum omittere insulam et in proximo
Campaniae aspici. Eo venire patres, eques, magna
pars plebis, anxii erga Seianum, cuius durior congressus, atque eo per ambitum et societate con-
siliorum parabatur. Satis constabat auctam ei
adrogantiam foedum illud in propatulo servitium
spectanti; quippe Romae sueti discursus, et magnitudine urbis incertum, quod quisque ad negotium
pergat: ibi campo aut litore iacentes nullo discrimine noctem ac diem iuxta gratiam aut fastus
ianitorum perpetiebantur, donec id *quo*que vetitum:
et revenere in urbem trepidi, quos non sermone, non
visu dignatus erat, quidam male alacres, quibus
infaustae amicitiae gravis exitus inminebat.

LXXV. Ceterum Tiberius neptem Agrippinam
Germanico ortam cum coram Cn. Domitio tradidisset,
in urbe celebrari nuptias iussit. In Domitio super
vetustatem generis propinquum Caesaribus sanguinem delegerat; nam is aviam Octaviam et per eam
Augustum avunculum praeferebat.

---

[1] Father, by the younger Agrippina, of the emperor Nero,
and "detestable in every point of his life," according to
Suetonius, who produces satisfactory evidence (*Ner.* 5).—For
his connection with the imperial family, see chap. 44.

petitions conjured the pair to vouchsafe themselves
to sight. Neither of them, however, came down so far
as Rome or the neighbourhood of Rome: it was
deemed enough to emerge from their isle and present
themselves to view on the nearest shore of Campania.
To Campania went senators and knights, with a
large part of the populace, their anxieties centred
round Sejanus; access to whom had grown harder,
and had therefore to be procured by interest and
by a partnership in his designs. It was evident
enough that his arrogance was increased by the sight
of this repulsive servility so openly exhibited. At
Rome, movement is the rule, and the extent of the
city leaves it uncertain upon what errand the passer-
by is bent: there, littering without distinction the
plain or the beach, they suffered day and night
alike the patronage or the insolence of his janitors,
until that privilege, too, was vetoed, and they
retraced their steps to the capital—those whom he
had honoured neither by word nor by look, in fear
and trembling; a few, over whom hung the fatal
issue of that infelicitous friendship, with misplaced
cheerfulness of heart.

LXXV. For the rest, Tiberius, after personally
conferring on Gnaeus Domitius[1] the hand of his
grandchild Agrippina, ordered the marriage to be
celebrated in Rome. In Domitius, to say nothing of
the antiquity of his family, he had chosen a blood-
connection of the Caesars: for he could boast
Octavia as his grandmother, and, through Octavia,
Augustus as his great-uncle.

BOOK V
FRAGMENT

LIBRI V. FRAGMENTUM

I. RUBELLIO et Fufio consulibus, quorum utrique Geminus cognomentum erat, Iulia Augusta mortem obiit, aetate extrema, nobilitatis per Claudiam familiam et adoptione Liviorum Iuliorumque clarissimae. Primum ei matrimonium et liberi fuere cum Tiberio Nerone, qui bello Perusino profugus, pace inter Sex. Pompeium ac triumviros pacta in urbem rediit. Exim Caesar cupidine formae aufert marito, incertum an invitam, adeo properus, ut ne spatio quidem ad enitendum dato penatibus suis gravidam induxerit. Nullam posthac subolem edidit, sed sanguini Augusti per coniunctionem Agrippinae et Germanici adnexa communis pronepotes habuit. Sanctitate domus priscum ad morem, comis ultra quam antiquis feminis probatum, mater inpotens, uxor facilis et cum artibus mariti, simulatione filii bene composita. Funus eius modicum, testamentum diu inritum

---

[1] She was eighty-six (D. Cass. LVIII. 1).

[2] Her father was a Claudius, adopted by M. Livius Drusus, the reforming tribune of 91 B.C., and therefore bore the name M. Livius Drusus Claudianus, she herself being Livia Drusilla, until by the will of Augustus she was adopted *in familiam Iuliam nomenque Augustum* (I. 8).

[3] Father of the emperor. Suetonius devotes a chapter to his career (*Tib.* 4).

[4] Between Octavian and L. Antonius, brother of the triumvir; terminated by the starving of Perusia (*Perugia*) into surrender (40 B.C.).

BOOK V.   1–5

I. In the consulate of Rubellius and Fufius, both
surnamed Geminus, Julia Augusta departed this life
in extreme old age;[1] by membership of the Claudian
family and by adoption into the Livian and Julian
houses,[2] associated with the proudest nobility of
Rome. Her first marriage and only children were
to Tiberius Nero;[3] who, exiled in the Perusian War,[4]
returned to the capital on the conclusion of peace[5]
between Sextus Pompeius and the triumvirate. In
the sequel, Augustus, smitten by her beauty, took her
from her husband. Her regrets are doubtful, and his
haste was such that, without even allowing an interval
for her confinement, he introduced her to his hearth
while pregnant. After this, she had no issue; but
the union of Agrippina and Germanicus created a
blood connection between herself and Augustus, so
that her great-grandchildren were shared with the
prince.[6] In domestic virtue she was of the old school,
though her affability went further than was approved
by women of the elder world. An imperious mother,
she was an accommodating wife, and an excellent
match for the subtleties of her husband and the
insincerity of her son. Her funeral was plain, her

---

[5] In 39 B.C.
[6] Germanicus was her own grandson, Agrippina the grand-
daughter of Augustus.

fuit. Laudata est pro rostris a Gaio Caesare
pronepote, qui mox rerum potitus est.

II. At Tiberius, quod supremis in matrem officiis
defuisset, nihil mutata amoenitate vitae, magni
tudinem negotiorum per litteras excusavit, honores-
que memoriae eius ab senatu large decretos quasi
per modestiam imminuit, paucis admodum receptis
et addito, ne caelestis religio decerneretur: sic
ipsam maluisse. Quin et parte eiusdem epistulae
increpuit amicitias muliebris, Fufium consulem
oblique perstringens. Is gratia Augustae floruerat,
aptus adliciendis feminarum animis, dicax idem et
Tiberium acerbis facetiis inridere solitus, quarum
apud praepotentis in longum memoria est.

III. Ceterum ex eo praerupta iam et urguens
dominatio: nam incolumi Augusta erat adhuc
perfugium, quia Tiberio inveteratum erga matrem
obsequium, neque Seianus audebat auctoritati
parentis antire: tunc velut frenis exsoluti pro-
ruperunt, missaeque in Agrippinam ac Neronem
litterae, quas pridem adlatas et cohibitas ab Augusta
credidit vulgus: haud enim multum [1] post mortem
eius recitatae sunt. Verba inerant quaesita asperi-
tate: sed non arma, non rerum novarum studium,
amores iuvenum et inpudicitiam nepoti obiectabat.

---

[1] multum] multo *Heinsius, Halm.*

---

[1] Her legacies were paid in full by Caligula (Suet. *Cal.* 16).
[2] She was deified, however, by Claudius.

will long unexecuted: her eulogy was delivered at
the rostra by her great-grandson Gaius Caesar, soon
to occupy the throne.

II. Tiberius, however, without altering the amenities
of his life, excused himself by letter, on the score of
important affairs, for neglecting to pay the last
respects to his mother, and, with a semblance
of modesty, curtailed the lavish tributes decreed to
her memory by the senate. Extremely few passed
muster, and he added a stipulation that divine
honours were not to be voted:[2] such, he observed,
had been her own wish. More than this, in a part
of the same missive he attacked " feminine friendships ": an indirect stricture upon the consul
Fufius, who had risen by the favour of Augusta, and,
besides his aptitude for attracting the fancy of the
sex, had a turn for wit and a habit of ridiculing
Tiberius with those bitter pleasantries which linger
long in the memory of potentates.

III. In any case, there followed from now onward
a sheer and grinding despotism: for, with Augusta
still alive, there had remained a refuge; since
deference to his mother was ingrained in Tiberius,
nor did Sejanus venture to claim precedence over
the authority of a parent. But now, as though freed
from the curb, they broke out unrestrained, and a
letter denouncing Agrippina and Nero was forwarded
to Rome; the popular impression being that it was
delivered much earlier and suppressed by the old
empress, since it was publicly read not long after
her death. Its wording was of studied asperity,
but the offences imputed by the sovereign to his
grandson were not rebellion under arms, not meditated
revolution, but unnatural love and moral depravity.

THE ANNALS OF TACITUS

In nurum ne id quidem confingere ausus, adrogantiam
oris et contumacem animum incusavit, magno
senatus pavore ac silentio, donec pauci, quis nulla
ex honesto spes (et publica mala singulis in occa-
sionem gratiae trahuntur), ut referretur postulavere,
promptissimo Cotta Messalino cum atroci sententia.
Sed aliis a primoribus maximeque a magistratibus
trepidabatur: quippe Tiberius etsi infense invectus
cetera ambigua reliquerat.

IV. Fuit in senatu Iunius Rusticus, conponendis
patrum actis delectus a Caesare, eoque meditationes
eius introspicere creditus. Is fatali quodam motu
(neque enim ante specimen constantiae dederat) seu
prava sollertia, dum imminentium oblitus incerta
pavet, inserere se dubitantibus ac monere consules,
ne relationem inciperent; disserebatque brevibus
momentis summa verti: posse quandoque *domus* [1]
Germanici exitium [2] paenitentiae *esse* seni.[3] Simul
populus effigies Agrippinae ac Neronis gerens
circumsistit curiam faustisque [4] in Caesarem ominibus
falsas litteras et principe invito exitium domui eius
intendi clamitat. Ita nihil triste illo die patratum.
Ferebantur etiam sub nominibus consularium fictae
in Seianum sententiae, exercentibus plerisque per

[1] ⟨domus⟩ *Halm (after Orelli)* : om.
[2] Germanici exitium *Ruperti* : Germanicis titium.
[3] ⟨esse⟩ seni *Walther* : senis.
[4] faustisque *Muretus* : festisque.

---

[1] *Inito honore* (Caesar's first consulate, 59 B.C.) *primus
omnium instituit ut tam senatus quam populi diurna acta
confierent et publicarentur* (Suet. *Jul.* 20 init.).
[2] Purporting to have been delivered in the senate.

Against his daughter-in-law he dared not fabricate even such a charge, but arraigned her haughty language and refractory spirit; the senate listening in profound alarm and silence, until a few who had nothing to hope from honesty (and public misfortunes are always turned by individuals into stepping-stones to favour) demanded that a motion be put—Cotta Messalinus being foremost with a drastic resolution. But among other leading members, and especially the magistrates, alarm prevailed: for Tiberius, bitter though his invective had been, had left all else in doubt.

IV. There was in the senate a certain Junius Rusticus, chosen by the Caesar to compile the official journal of its proceedings,[1] and therefore credited with some insight into his thoughts. Under some fatal impulse—for he had never before given an indication of courage—or possibly through a mis-applied acuteness which made him blind to dangers imminent and terrified of dangers uncertain, Rusticus insinuated himself among the doubters and warned the consuls not to introduce the question—" A touch," he insisted, " could turn the scale in the gravest of matters: it was possible that some day the extinction of the house of Germanicus might move the old man's penitence." At the same time, the people, carrying effigies of Agrippina and Nero, surrounded the curia, and, cheering for the Caesar, clamoured that the letter was spurious and that it was contrary to the Emperor's wish that destruction was plotted against his house. On that day, therefore, no tragedy was perpetrated. There were circulated, also, under consular names, fictitious attacks upon Sejanus:[2] for authors in plenty exercised

occultum atque eo procacius libidinem ingeniorum. Unde illi ira violentior et materies criminandi: spretum dolorem principis ab senatu, descivisse populum; audiri iam et legi novas contiones, nova patrum consulta: quid reliquum nisi ut caperent ferrum et, quorum imagines pro vexillis secuti forent, duces imperatoresque deligerent?

V. Igitur Caesar repetitis adversum nepotem et nurum probris increpitaque per edictum plebe, questus apud patres quod fraude unius senatoris imperatoria maiestas elusa publice foret, integra tamen sibi cuncta postulavit. Nec ultra deliberatum, quo minus non quidem extrema decernerent (id enim vetitum), sed paratos ad ultionem vi principis impediri testarentur. . . .

---

[1] A summary of the events related in the lost portions of this and the following books will be found in the chronological table (pp. 419–22).

their capricious imagination with all the petulance of anonymity. The result was to fan his anger and to supply him with the material for fresh charges :—
" The senate had spurned the sorrow of its emperor, the people had forsworn its allegiance. Already disloyal harangues, disloyal decrees of the Fathers, were listened to and perused: what remained but to take the sword and in the persons whose effigies they had followed as their ensigns to choose their generals and their princes ? "

V. The Caesar, therefore, after repeating the scandalous allegations against his grandson and daughter-in-law and rebuking the populace by edict, expressed his regret to the senate " that by the dishonesty of a single member the imperial majesty should have been publicly turned to scorn," but demanded that the entire affair should be left in his own hands. Further deliberation was needless, and they proceeded, not indeed to decree the last penalties (that course was forbidden) but to assert their readiness for vengeance, from which they were debarred by compulsion of the sovereign. . . .[1]

BOOK VI

LIBER VI

V. 6. . . . Quattuor et quadraginta orationes
super ea re habitae, ex quis ob metum paucae, plures
adsuetudine . . .

" . . . Mihi pudorem aut Seiano invidiam adlaturum censui.   Versa est fortuna, et ille quidem, qui
collegam et generum adsciverat, sibi ignoscit :
ceteri, quem per dedecora fovere, cum scelere
insectantur.   Miserius sit ob amicitiam accusari
an amicum accusare, haud discreverim.   Non crude-
litatem, non clementiam cuiusquam experiar, sed
liber et mihi ipsi probatus antibo periculum.   Vos
obtestor, ne memoriam nostri per maerorem quam

---

¹ After *testarentur* (V. 5 fin.), the Mediceus leaves vacant a
space sufficient for three or four letters, then proceeds with
quattuor et quadraginta (V. 6 init.), no indication being given
of the commencement of a fresh book.   Hence, all from
V. 1 to VI. 51 was printed as Book V until the edition of Justus
Lipsius; who saw that two books were necessary, and began
the sixth with the consulate of Domitius and Scribonianus
(VI. 1).   Haase's view, that the fifth closed with the fall of
Sejanus and that the opening of the sixth is lost, is now
universally accepted, though Lipsius' numeration is generally
retained.

² The occasion of the forty-four speeches is unknown, but
is conjectured to have been the punishment of Livia for her
part in the death of Drusus (IV. 3 sqq.)—After the next lacuna,
the narrative has passed to an unnamed friend of Sejanus,
addressing the company at a last social gathering before

BOOK VI[1]

V. 6 . . . Forty-four speeches were delivered on A.V.C. 784 = the subject, a few dictated by alarm, the majority A.D. 31 by the habit of adulation. . . .[2]

". . . I considered likely to result in my own disgrace or the odium of Sejanus. The tide has turned, and while he who designated the fallen as colleague[3] and son-in-law[4] pronounces his own exculpation, the rest, who fawned upon him in their degradation, now persecute him in their villainy. Which is the more pitiful thing—to be arraigned for a friendship or to arraign the friend—I do not seek to determine. I shall experiment with the cruelty of none, the mercy of none: a free man, approved by my own conscience, I shall anticipate my danger. I conjure you to preserve my memory not more with sorrow than in joy, and to add me,

suicide. Compare, among others, the cases of Libo (II. 31), Petronius (XVI. 19), and Thrasea XVI. 34).

[3] Actually, in the consulate; prospectively, as was generally believed in the empire.

[4] So, at VI. 8, Terentius calls him *tuum, Caesar, generum.* The passages were first explained by Reimar (on D. Cass. LVIII. 11) from a statement in Zonaras, drawn from Dio :— τὸν δὲ Σηϊανὸν . . . κηδεστὴν ἐπὶ Ἰουλίᾳ τῇ τοῦ Δρούσου θυγατρὶ ποιησάμενος ὕστερον ἔκτεινεν (XI. 2). In that case, the marriage projected for the favourite was with a grand-daughter of Tiberius, and *generum adsciverat* should, in accuracy, have been *progenerum destinaverat.*

laeti retineatis, adiciendo me quoque iis, qui fine egregio publica mala effugerunt."

V. 7. Tunc singulos, ut cuique absistere,[1] adloqui animus erat, retinens aut dimittens partem diei absumpsit, multoque adhuc coetu et cunctis intrepidum vultum eius spectantibus, cum superesse tempus novissimis crederent, gladio, quem sinu abdiderat, incubuit. Neque Caesar ullis criminibus aut probris defunctum insectatus est, cum in Blaesum multa foedaque incusavisset.

V. 8. Relatum inde de P. Vitellio et Pomponio Secundo. Illum indices arguebant claustra aerarii, cui praefectus erat, et militarem pecuniam rebus novis obtulisse; huic a Considio[2] praetura functo obiectabatur Aelii Galli amicitia, qui punito Seiano in hortos Pomponii quasi fidissimum ad subsidium perfugisset. Neque aliud periclitantibus auxilii quam in fratrum constantia fuit, qui vades exstitere. Mox crebris prolationibus spem ac metum iuxta gravatus Vitellius petito per speciem studiorum scalpro levem ictum venis intulit vitamque aegritudine animi finivit. At Pomponius multa morum elegantia et ingenio inlustri, dum adversam fortunam aequus tolerat, Tiberio superstes fuit.

---

[1] absistere *Pfitzner, Draeger* : adsistere.
[2] ⟨C.⟩ Considio *Wurm*.

---

[1] Uncle of Sejanus (I. 16 sqq.; III. 35; 73–75).
[2] I. 70 n.
[3] P. Pomponius Secundus—*vatis civisque clarissimus*, according to his friend Pliny, who wrote his biography (Plin. min. *Ep.* III. 5). Most of the known facts of his life are gleaned from the Annals (cf. XI. 13; XII. 27 sq.; *Dial.* 13).
[4] The *aerarium militare* : see I. 78 n.

one name more, to the roll of those who by a notable ending found an escape from public calamity."

V. 7. He now spent part of the day in detaining or dismissing his visitors, as each was inclined to take his leave or to speak with him; and while the gathering was still thronged, while all eyes were fixed on his intrepid countenance, and the belief prevailed that some time remained before the last act, he fell on a sword which he had concealed in the fold of his dress. No accusation or calumny from the Caesar, who had laid many revolting charges against Blaesus,[1] followed him to the grave.

V. 8. Next, Publius Vitellius[2] and Pomponius Secundus[3] came under discussion. The first-named was accused by the informers of offering the keys of the treasury,[4] of which he was prefect, together with the army fund, to the cause of revolution: against the latter the offence alleged by the ex-praetor Considius was his friendship with Aelius Gallus,[5] who after the execution of Sejanus had taken shelter in Pomponius' garden as his surest resource. Their only help in the hour of danger was in the firmness of their brothers, who came forward as securities. Later, as adjournment followed adjournment, Vitellius, anxious to be rid alike of hope and fear, asked for a pen-knife on the ground that he wished to write, slightly incised an artery, and in the sickness of his heart made an end of life. On the other hand, Pomponius, a man of great refinement of character and shining talents,[6] bore the reverses of fortune with equanimity and outlived Tiberius.

[5] Almost certainly the eldest son of Sejanus.
[6] Chiefly as a tragic poet: cf. Quint. XI. 98. He was kept in confinement for seven years, then released by Caligula.

V. 9. Placitum posthac, ut in reliquos Seiani liberos adverteretur, vanescente quamquam plebis ira ac plerisque per priora supplicia lenitis. Igitur portantur in carcerem, filius imminentium intellegens, puella adeo nescia, ut crebro interrogaret, quod ob delictum et quo traheretur; neque facturam ultra, et posse se puerili verbere moneri. Tradunt temporis eius auctores, quia triumvirali supplicio adfici virginem inauditum habebatur, a carnifice laqueum iuxta conpressam; exim oblisis faucibus id aetatis corpora in Gemonias abiecta.

V. 10. Per idem tempus Asia atque Achaia exterritae sunt acri magis quam diuturno rumore, Drusum Germanici filium apud Cycladas insulas, mox in continenti visum. Et erat iuvenis haud dispari aetate, quibusdam Caesaris libertis velut adgnitus; per dolumque comitantibus adliciebantur ignari fama nominis et promptis Graecorum animis ad nova et mira. Quippe elapsum custodiae pergere ad paternos exercitus, Aegyptum aut Suriam invasurum, fingebant simul credebantque. Iam iuventutis concursu, iam publicis studiis frequentabatur, laetus praesentibus et inanium spe, cum auditum id Poppaeo Sabino: is Macedoniae tum intentus

---

[1] Between the Capitol and Forum Romanum (cf.III. 14 n.).
[2] Now a prisoner *in ima parte Palatii* (Suet. *Tib.* 54). See VI. 23.
[3] IV. 46 n.

V. 9. It was then determined that the surviving children of Sejanus should pay the penalty, though the anger of the populace was nearly spent and the majority of men had been placated by the earlier executions. They were therefore carried to the dungeon, the boy conscious of the fate in store for him, the girl so completely ignorant that she asked repeatedly what her offence had been and to what place they were dragging her: she would do wrong no more, and she could be cautioned with the usual childish beating. It is recorded by authors of the period that, as it was considered an unheard-of thing for capital punishment to be inflicted on a virgin, she was violated by the executioner with the halter beside her: they were then strangled, and their young bodies thrown on to the Gemonian Stairs.[1]

V. 10. Towards the same time, Asia and Achaia were thrown into panic by a rumour, more vigorous than durable, that Drusus,[2] the son of Germanicus, had been seen in the Cyclades and, not long afterwards, on the continent. There was, in fact, a youth of not dissimilar age, whom a few of the emperor's freedmen had pretended to recognize. In pursuance of the plot, they acted as his escort, and ignorant recruits began to be drawn in, allured by the prestige of his name, aided by Greek avidity for the new and strange; for the tale they no sooner coined than credited was that he had escaped from watch and ward and was making for his father's armies with the intention of invading Egypt or Syria. Already a rallying-point for youthful volunteers and popular enthusiasm, he was flushed with actual success and groundless hope, when the affair came to the ear of Poppaeus Sabinus.[3] He was now

THE ANNALS OF TACITUS

Achaiam quoque curabat. Igitur quo vera seu
falsa antiret, Toronaeum Thermaeumque sinum
praefestinans, mox Euboeam Aegaei maris insulam et
Piraeum Atticae orae, dein Corinthiense litus
angustiasque Isthmi evadit; marique Ionio [1] Nico-
polim Romanam coloniam ingressus, ibi demum
cognoscit sollertius interrogatum, quisnam foret,
dixisse M. Silano genitum, et multis sectatorum
dilapsis ascendisse navem tamquam Italiam peteret.
Scripsitque haec Tiberio, neque nos originem finemve
eius rei ultra comperimus.

V. 11. Exitu anni diu aucta discordia consulum
erupit. Nam Trio, facilis capessendis inimicitiis et
foro exercitus, ut segnem Regulum ad opprimendos
Seiani ministros oblique perstrinxerat: ille, nisi
lacesseretur, modestiae retinens, non modo rettu-
dit collegam, sed ut noxium coniurationis ad disquisi-
tionem traheret. Multisque patrum orantibus
ponerent odia in perniciem itura, mansere infensi ac
minitantes, donec magistratu abirent.

VI.—I. Cn. Domitius et Camillus Scribonianus
consulatum inierant, cum Caesar tramisso quod

---

[1] Ionio *Barthold* (*cf.* II. 53) : alio.

---

[1] The gulfs of Kassandra and Saloniki.
[2] II. 53 n.
[3] Probably the future father-in-law of Caligula (III. 24;
VI. 20).
[4] Dio, whatever his authority, states that he was sent to
Tiberius, and dates the incident three years later.
[5] Both *suffecti*. For Trio, see II. 28 n.; for Regulus, VI. 4;
XII. 22; XIV. 47.
[6] IV. 75 n.

occupied in Macedonia, but responsible also for Achaia. Determined, therefore, to take the story— true or false—in time, he hastened past the bays of Torone and Thermae,[1] left behind him the Aegean island of Euboea, Piraeus on the Attic sea-board, then the Corinthian coast and the narrow neck of the Isthmus, and made his way by the Ionian Sea into the Roman colony of Nicopolis.[2] There at last he discovered that the adventurer, when questioned more skilfully as to his identity, had declared himself the son of Marcus Silanus;[3] and that, as many of his adherents had slipped away, he had boarded a ship, bound ostensibly for Italy. Sabinus sent a written report to Tiberius, nor have I further information as to the origin or end of the incident.[4]

V. 11. At the close of the year, the chronic disagreement between the consuls[5] came to a head. For Trio, always ready to enter upon a quarrel, and versed in the methods of the courts, had indirectly censured Regulus for slowness in crushing the creatures of Sejanus: Regulus, tenacious of his self-control except under deliberate provocation, not merely parried his colleague's attack but proposed to call him to account for criminal complicity in the plot; and, in spite of entreaties from many members of the senate that they would lay aside an enmity bound to have a fatal issue, they maintained their hostile and threatening attitude till they went out of office.

VI.—I. Gnaeus Domitius[6] and Camillus Scribonianus[7] had entered on their consulate, when the A.V.C. 785 = A.D. 32

---

[7] M. Furius Camillus Scribonianus, *legatus pro praetore* of Illyricum in 42 A.D.; committed suicide on the collapse of a four days' rising against Claudius (Suet. *Claud.* 13).

Capreas et Surrentum interluit freto Campaniam
praelegebat, ambiguus an urbem intraret, seu, quia
contra destinaverat, speciem venturi simulans. Et
saepe in propinqua degressus, aditis iuxta Tiberim
hortis, saxa rursum et solitudinem maris repetiit,
pudore scelerum et libidinum, quibus adeo indomitis
exarserat, ut more regio pubem ingenuam stupris
pollueret. Nec formam tantum et decora corpora,
set in his modestam pueritiam, in aliis imagines
maiorum incitamentum cupidinis habebat. Tuncque
primum ignota antea vocabula reperta sunt sellari-
orum et spintriarum ex foeditate loci ac multiplici
patientia ; praepositique servi, *qui con*quirerent[1]
pertraherent, dona in promptos, minas adversum
abnuentis, et si retinerent propinquus aut parens,
vim raptus suaque ipsi libitia velut in captos exerce-
bant.

II. At Romae principio anni, quasi recens cognitis
Liviae flagitiis ac non pridem etiam punitis, atroces
sententiae dicebantur, in effigies quoque ac memoriam
eius, et bona Seiani ablata aerario ut in fiscum co-
gerentur, tam*quam* referret. Scipiones haec et
Silani et Cassii isdem ferme aut paulum inmutatis
verbis adseveratione multa censebant, cum repente

---

[1] ⟨qui con⟩quirerent *Doederlein* : quirerent.

---

[1] " Strange and new-commented lusts For which wise Nature
hath not left a name " (Ben Jonson, *Sejanus* IV. 5). Details
might be expected, and will be found, in Suetonius (*Tib.*
43–45).—The commonsense objections to the traditional
account of these debaucheries are stated forcibly enough—
though perhaps rather less so than might have been anticipated
—by Voltaire (*Oeuvres*, xxiii. p. 455, Geneva, 1772). They
were ably developed by the French advocate Linguet, and
little has been, or can be, added either to his presentment of
the case or to Boissier's attempted answer (*Tacite*[6], pp. 108

Caesar crossed the channel that flows between Capreae and Surrentum, and skirted the shores of Campania, in doubt whether to enter the capital or no,—or, possibly, affecting the intention of arrival because he had decided not to arrive. After landing frequently at neighbouring points and visiting the Gardens by the Tiber, he resorted once more to his rocks and the solitude of the sea, in shame at the sins and lusts whose uncontrollable fires had so inflamed him that, in the kingly style, he polluted with his lecheries the children of free-born parents. Nor were beauty and physical charm his only incitements to lasciviousness, but sometimes a boyish modesty and sometimes a noble lineage. And now were coined the names, hitherto unknown, of *sellarii* and *spintriae*,[1] one drawn from the obscenity of a place, one from the versatility of the pathic; while slaves, commissioned to seek and fetch, plied the willing with gratuities, the reluctant with threats, and, if a kinsman or parent refused compliance, resorted to force, abduction, and the slaking of their own desires as if in a captured city.

II. But in Rome, at the opening of the year, as though the offences of Livia were crimes but recently detected, not crimes actually punished long before, stern measures were advocated even against her statues and her memory; while the estate of Sejanus was to be withdrawn from the treasury and confiscated to the imperial exchequer, as though a difference existed. The proposals were being supported with great earnestness, in identical or slightly varied terms, by men of the rank of Scipio, Cassius, and

sqq.). It remains impossible that all can be true and incredible that all can be false.

Togonius Gallus, dum ignobilitatem suam magnis nominibus inserit, per deridiculum auditur. Nam principem orabat deligere senatores, ex quis viginti sorte ducti et ferro accincti, quotiens curiam inisset, salutem eius defenderent. Crediderat nimirum epistulae subsidio sibi alterum ex consulibus poscentis, ut tutus a Capreis urbem peteret. Tiberius tamen, ludibria seriis permiscere solitus, egit gratis benevolentiae patrum: sed quos omitti posse, quos deligi? Semperne eosdem an subinde alios? Et honoribus perfunctos an iuvenes, privatos an e magistratibus? Quam deinde speciem fore sumentium in limine curiae gladios? Neque sibi vitam tanti, si armis tegenda foret. Haec, adversus Togonium verbis moderans, neque ut [1] ultra abolitionem sententiae suaderet.

III. At Iunium Gallionem, qui censuerat, ut praetoriani actis stipendiis ius apiscerentur in quattuordecim ordinibus sedendi, violenter increpuit, velut coram rogitans, quid illi cum militibus, quos neque dicta nisi imperatoris [2] neque praemia nisi ab imperatore accipere par esset. Repperisse prorsus quod divus Augustus non providerit: an potius discordiam et seditionem a satellite Seiani quaesitam, qua rudis

---

[1] ⟨ut⟩ Doederlein.
[2] ⟨nisi⟩ Rhenanus.—[imperatoris] Lipsius, vulg.

---

[1] A prominent declaimer of the period (Dial. 26; M. Sen. Contr. X. pr. 13); a friend of Ovid (ex P. IV. 11), and adoptive father of the Gallio of Acts xviii. 12–17.

[2] In the theatre, the fourteen lowest rows of the cavea, appropriated to the knights by the lex Roscia of 67 B.C., the orchestra being reserved for the senate.

Silanus, when suddenly Togonius Gallus thrust his insignificance into the series of great names and was heard with derision. For he begged the emperor to choose a number of senators, twenty of whom, drawn by lot and carrying weapons, were to protect his safety whenever he had entered the curia. He had believed, forsooth, the Caesar's letter, when he demanded the support of one of the consuls, in order that he might make the journey from Capreae to Rome in safety. None the less, Tiberius, with his habit of blending jest and earnest, expressed his thanks for the good-will of the Fathers:—" But who could be passed over—who chosen? Were the chosen to be always the same, or with now and then a change? Men with their career behind them, or youths? Private individuals or officials? Finally, what sort of figure would his protectors make when assuming their swords on the threshold of the curia? Nor, indeed, did he hold his life to be worth the price, if it had to be shielded by arms."—This answer was studiously moderate in its references to Togonius, and avoided any suggestion beyond the deletion of the proposal.

III. On the other hand, Junius Gallio,[1] who had moved that the Praetorians, on finishing their service, should acquire the right to a seat in the Fourteen Rows,[2] drew down a fierce rebuke:— " What," demanded Tiberius, as if addressing him to his face, " had *he* to do with the soldiers, who had no right to take any but their master's orders or any but their master's rewards? He had certainly hit upon something not taken into consideration by the deified Augustus! Or was it a minion of Sejanus, fostering disaffection and sedition, in order by a

animos nomine honoris ad corrumpendum militiae
morem propelleret? Hoc pretium Gallio meditatae
adulationis tulit, statim curia, deinde Italia exactus;
et quia incusabatur facile toleraturus exilium delecta
Lesbo, insula nobili et amoena, retrahitur in urbem
custoditurque domibus magistratuum. Isdem litteris
Caesar Sextium Paconianum praetorium perculit
magno patrum gaudio, audacem, maleficum, omnium
secreta rimantem delectumque ab Seiano, cuius ope
dolus Gaio Caesari pararetur. Quod postquam
patefactum, prorupere concepta pridem odia, et
summum supplicium decernebatur, ni professus
indicium foret.

IV. Ut vero Latinium Latiarem ingressus est,
accusator ac reus iuxta invisi gratissimum spectaculum praebebant. Latiaris, ut rettuli, praecipuus
olim circumveniendi Titii Sabini et tunc luendae
poenae primus fuit. Inter quae Haterius Agrippa
consules anni prioris invasit, cur mutua accusatione
intenta nunc silerent: metum prorsus et noxae
conscientiam [1] pro foedere haberi; at non patribus
reticenda quae audivissent. Regulus manere tempus
ultionis, seque coram principe exsecuturum; Trio
aemulationem inter collegas et si qua discordes

---

[1] noxae conscientiam *Groslot*: noxam conscientiae.

nominal compliment to drive simple souls into a
breach of discipline?" Such was the reward of
Gallio's studied adulation: he was ejected at once
from the senate; later from Italy; and, as the charge
was made that he would carry his exile lightly, since
he had chosen the famous and pleasant island of
Lesbos, he was dragged back to the capital and
detained under the roof of various magistrates.
In the same letter, the Caesar, to the intense pleasure
of the senate, struck at the former praetor Sextius
Paconianus—fearless, mischievous, a searcher into
all men's secrets, and the chosen helper of Sejanus
in the laying of his plot against Gaius Caesar. On
the announcement followed an explosion of long-
cherished hatreds, and the last penalty was all but
decreed, when he offered to turn informer.

IV. However, when he began upon Latinius
Latiaris, accuser and accused—impartially detested
as they were—furnished the most grateful of spec-
tacles.—Latiaris, as I have recorded,[1] had formerly
been the chief agent in entrapping Titius Sabinus;
and he was now the first to make atonement.

In the midst of all this, Haterius Agrippa attacked
the consuls of the year before:—"Why," he demanded, " after preferring their charges and counter-
charges,[2] were they silent now? The truth was that
they were treating their fears and their conscious-
ness of guilt as a bond of alliance; but the senate
could not keep silence upon the statements to which
it had listened." Regulus answered that he was
awaiting the proper time for his vengeance, and would
pursue his case in the presence of the emperor;
Trio, that this rivalry between colleagues, together
with any words they might have let fall during the

iecissent melius oblitterari respondit. Urguente
Agrippa Sanquinius Maximus e consularibus oravit
senatum, ne curas imperatoris conquisitis insuper
acerbitatibus augerent: sufficere ipsum statuendis
remediis. Sic Regulo salus et Trioni dilatio exitii
quaesita. Haterius invisior fuit, quia somno aut
libidinosis vigiliis marcidus et ob segnitiam quamvis
crudelem principem non metuens inlustribus viris
perniciem inter ganeam ac stupra meditabatur.

V. Exim Cotta Messalinus, saevissimae cuiusque
sententiae auctor eoque inveterata invidia, ubi
primum facultas data, arguitur pleraque *in* C. Caesarem quasi incertae[1] virilitatis, et cum die natali
Augustae inter sacerdotes epularetur, novendialem
eam cenam dixisse; querensque de potentia M'.
Lepidi ac L. Arruntii, cum quibus ob rem pecunia-
riam disceptabat, addidisse: "Illos quidem senatus,
me autem tuebitur Tiberiolus meus." Quae[2] cuncta
a primoribus civitatis revincebatur, iisque instantibus
ad imperatorem provocavit. Nec multo post litterae
adferuntur, quibus in modum defensionis, repetito
inter se atque Cottam amicitiae principio crebrisque

---

[1] incertae *Lipsius*: incerta *Med.*, inchstae *Rhenanus*,
Nipperdey.
[2] quae *Nipperdey*: neque.

---

[1] Till 35 A.D. : see chap. 38.
[2] For *pudicitiae neque suae neque alienae pepercit* (Suet. *Cal.*
36).
[3] The *cena novendialis* was a meal of *puls*, bread, and wine,
laid on the tomb nine days after the interment. Cotta's
remark has lost clarity with the years, but would appear to
combine a hint that he found his sacerdotal banquet both
funereal and frugal with a sneer at the emperor, who had left
his mother a dead woman, when he might have converted her
into a goddess (V. 2).

feud, would be better blotted from memory. As
Agrippa urged the point, the consular Sanquinius
Maximus begged the members not to augment the
cares of the emperor by raking up fresh vexations:
he was competent to prescribe a remedy by himself.
To Regulus this brought salvation; to Trio, a respite
from doom:[1] Haterius was detested all the more,
because, enervated by sleep or the wakeful hours
of lust, and so lethargic as to have no fear of the
emperor however great his cruelty, he yet amid his
gluttony and lecheries could plot the ruin of the
famous.

V. Next Cotta Messalinus, father of every bar-
barous proposal and therefore the object of inveterate dislike, found himself, on the first available
occasion, indicted for hinting repeatedly that the
sex of Gaius Caesar was an open question;[2] for dining
with the priests on Augusta's birthday and describing
the function as a wake;[3] for adding, when he was
complaining of the influence of Manius Lepidus and
Lucius Arruntius,[4] his opponents in a money dispute:
—" The senate will side with them, but my pretty
little Tiberius with me." The whole of the charges
were proved against him by men of the highest
position; and, as they pressed their case, he appealed
to the emperor. Before long came a letter; in
which Tiberius, by way of defence, harked back to
the origin of the friendship between himself and
Cotta, commemorated his many services, and desired

[4] Both Lepidus (for the praenomen see Nipperdey on III.
22) and Arruntius figure prominently and creditably in the
first half of the Annals. For the former compare, for instance,
I. 13; III. 11, 22, 50; IV. 20, 56; VI. 27: for the latter, I. 13,
76; VI. 27, 47 sq.

eius officiis commemoratis, ne verba prave detorta neu convivalium fabularum simplicitas in crimen duceretur postulavit.

VI. Insigne visum est earum Caesaris litterarum initium ; nam his verbis exorsus est : " Quid scribam vobis, patres conscripti, aut quo modo [1] scribam aut quid omnino non scribam hoc tempore, di me deaeque peius perdant, quam perire me cotidie sentio, si scio." Adeo facinora atque flagitia sua ipsi quoque in supplicium verterant. Neque frustra praestantissimus sapientiae firmare solitus est, si recludantur tyrannorum mentes, posse aspici laniatus et ictus, quando ut corpora verberibus, ita saevitia, libidine, malis consultis animus dilaceretur. Quippe Tiberium non fortuna, non solitudines protegebant, quin tormenta pectoris suasque ipse poenas fateretur.

VII. Tum facta patribus potestate statuendi de *C.*[2] Caeciliano senatore, qui plurima adversum Cottam prompserat, placitum eandem poenam inrogari quam in Aruseium et Sanquinium, accusatores L. Arruntii : quo non aliud honorificentius Cottae evenit, qui nobilis quidem, set egens ob luxum, per flagitia infamis, sanctissimis Arruntii artibus dignitate ultionis aequabatur.

Q. Servaeus posthac et Minucius Thermus inducti, Servaeus praetura functus et quondam Germanici comes, Minucius equestri loco, modeste habita

---

[1] quo modo *Suetonius (Tib.* 67) : quando.   [2] ⟨C⟩ *Wurm.*

---

[1] Socrates.—Tacitus paraphrases a famous and much imitated passage of Plato (*Gorg.* 524 E). Julian, as it happens, turns it to the same account :—ἐπιστραφέντος δὲ (*sc.* Τιβερίου) . . . ὤφθησαν ὠτειλαὶ κατὰ τὸν νῶτον μυρίαι, καυτῆρές τινες καὶ ξέσματα καὶ πληγαὶ χαλεπαὶ καὶ μώλωπες ὑπό τε ἀκολασίας καὶ ὠμότητος ψῶραί τινες καὶ λειχῆνες οἷον ἐγκεκαυμέναι (*Caes.* 309 C).

[2] The account of this accusation is lost.

[3] II. 56 ; III. 13 and 19.

that mischievously perverted phrases and the frankness of table-talk should not be turned into evidence of guilt.

VI. The beginning of this letter from the Caesar was considered notable; for he opened with the following words:—*If I know what to write to you, Conscript Fathers, or how to write it, or what not to write at all at this time, may gods and goddesses destroy me more wretchedly than I feel myself to be perishing every day!* So surely had his crimes and his infamies turned to the torment even of himself; nor was it in vain that the first of sages [1] was accustomed to affirm that, could the souls of tyrants be laid open, lacerations and wounds would meet the view; since, as the body is torn by the lash, so is the spirit of man by cruelty and lust and evil purposes. For not his station nor his solitudes could save Tiberius from himself confessing the rack within his breast and his own punishments.

VII. The Fathers were then empowered to decide upon the case of Gaius Caecilianus, a senator who had produced most of the evidence against Cotta; and it was agreed that the same penalty should be inflicted as on Aruseius and Sanquinius, the accusers of Lucius Arruntius.[2] It was the most signal compliment that ever fell to the share of Cotta; who, noble undoubtedly, but beggared by his prodigality and degraded by his vices, was now honoured with a vengeance that placed him on a level with the spotless character of Arruntius.

Next, Quintus Servaeus and Minucius Thermus were brought to judgement—Servaeus, an ex-praetor formerly included in Germanicus' suite; [3] Minucius, of equestrian rank. Each had refrained

Seiani amicitia; unde illis maior miseratio. Contra Tiberius praecipuos ad scelera increpans admonuit C. Cestium patrem [1] dicere senatui quae sibi scripsisset, suscepitque Cestius accusationem. Quod maxime exitiabile tulere illa tempora, cum primores senatus infimas etiam delationes exercerent, alii propalam, multi per occultum; neque discerneres alienos a coniunctis, amicos ab ignotis, quid recens aut vetustate obscurum : perinde in foro, in convivio, quaque de re locuti incusabantur, ut quis praevenire et reum destinare properat, pars ad subsidium sui, plures infecti quasi valetudine et contactu. Sed Minucius et Servaeus damnati indicibus accessere. Tractique sunt in casum eundem Iulius Africanus e Santonis Gallica civitate, Seius Quadratus : originem non repperi. Neque sum ignarus a plerisque scriptoribus omissa multorum pericula et poenas, dum copia fatiscunt aut, quae ipsis nimia et maesta fuerant, ne pari taedio lecturos adficerent verentur : nobis pleraque digna cognitu obvenere, quamquam ab aliis incelebrata.

VIII. Nam ea tempestate, qua Seiani amicitiam ceteri falso exuerant, ausus est eques Romanus M. Terentius, ob id reus, amplecti, ad hunc modum apud

---

[1] patrem] praetorem *Lipsius.*

---

[1] The name survives in the former French province of Saintonge (part of Charente-Inférieure).
[2] Otherwise unknown.

from abusing his friendship with Sejanus: a fact which gained them peculiar sympathy. Tiberius, on the other hand, denouncing them as ringleaders in crime, instructed the elder Gaius Cestius to repeat to the senate what he had written to himself; and Cestius duly undertook the prosecution. It was, indeed, the most deadly blight of the age that prominent senators practised even the basest forms of delation, some with perfect openness, and many in private. Nor could any distinction be traced between alien and relative, between friend and stranger, between the events of to-day and those of the dim past. Alike in the Forum or at a dinnerparty, to speak of any subject was to be accused: for every man was hastening to be first in the field and to mark down his victim, occasionally in selfdefence, generally through infection with what seemed a contagious disease. However, Minucius and Servaeus, on being found guilty, joined the informers; and the same ruin involved Julius Africanus, from the Gallic community of the Santones,[1] and Seius Quadratus, whose antecedents I have not discovered.—Nor am I unaware that the perils and penalties of many are passed over by a number of historians; who either lose heart from the abundance of their materials or apprehend that a list which they themselves found long and depressing may produce equal disgust in their readers. For my own part, much has come my way that deserves a record, even though unchronicled by others.

VIII. For instance, at the very period when all others had falsely disclaimed the friendship of Sejanus, the Roman knight Marcus Terentius,[2] accused on that score, dared to embrace

senatum ordiendo :—" Fortunae quidem meae fortasse minus expediat adgnoscere crimen quam abnuere ; sed utcumque casura res est, fatebor et fuisse me Seiano amicum, et ut essem expetisse, et postquam adeptus eram laetatum.   Videram collegam patris regendis praetoriis cohortibus, mox urbis et militiae munia simul obeuntem.   Illius propinqui et adfines honoribus augebantur ; ut quisque Seiano intimus, ita ad Caesaris amicitiam validus : contra quibus infensus esset, metu ac sordibus conflictabantur. Nec quemquam exemplo adsumo : cunctos, qui novissimi consilii expertes fuimus, meo unius discrimine defendam.   Non enim Seianum Vulsiniensem set Claudiae et Iuliae domus partem, quas adfinitate occupaverat, tuum, Caesar, generum, tui consulatus socium, tua officia in re publica capessentem colebamus.   Non est nostrum aestimare, quem supra ceteros et quibus de causis extollas : tibi summum rerum iudicium di dedere, nobis obsequii gloria relicta est.   Spectamus porro quae coram habentur, cui ex te opes honores, quis plurima iuvandi nocendive potentia, quae Seiano fuisse nemo negaverit.   Abditos principis sensus, et si quid occultius parat, exquirere inlicitum, anceps : nec ideo adsequare. Ne, patres conscripti, ultimum Seiani diem, sed sedecim annos cogitaveritis.   Etiam Satrium atque

---

[1] See III. 29 and V. 6, with the notes.

the accusation:—" In my plight," so ran his
exordium in the senate, " it may perhaps be less
profitable to avow than to deny the charge; but, however the event is to fall, I shall confess that not only
was I the friend of Sejanus, but that I strove for
his friendship, and that, when I attained it, I rejoiced. I had seen him the colleague of his father
in command of the praetorian cohorts; and, later,
discharging civil duties as well as military. His
relatives by blood and marriage were honoured with
offices; the closer a man's intimacy with Sejanus,
the stronger his claim to the emperor's friendship;
while, in contrast, danger and the garb of supplica-
tion were the troubled lot of his enemies. I take no
man for my text: all who, like myself, were without
part in his ultimate design, I shall defend at my own
risk only. For we courted, not Sejanus of Vulsinii,
but the member of those Claudian and Julian
houses[1] into which his alliances had won him entry;
your son-in-law, Caesar; the partner of your consulate; the agent who discharged your functions
in the state. It is not ours to ask whom you exalt
above his fellows, or why: you the gods have made
the sovereign arbiter of things; to us has been left
the glory of obedience. Moreover, we see only
what is laid before our eyes,—the person who holds
wealth and dignities from you,—those who have the
greatest power to help or to injure,—and that Sejanus
had all, no man will deny! To search out the hidden
thoughts of the emperor and the designs he may
shape in secret, is unlawful and is dangerous: nor
would the searcher necessarily find. Conscript
Fathers, think not of the last day of Sejanus, but of
the sixteen years of Sejanus! We venerated even

Pomponium[1] venerabamur; libertis quoque ac
ianitoribus eius notescere pro magnifico accipiebatur.
Quid ergo? Indistincta haec defensio et promisca
dabitur? Immo iustis terminis dividatur. Insidiae
in rem publicam, consilia caedis adversum imperatorem puniantur: de amicitia et officiis idem finis
et te, Caesar, et nos absolverit."

IX. Constantia orationis, et quia repertus erat,
qui efferret quae omnes animo agitabant, eo usque
potuere, ut accusatores eius, additis quae ante
deliquerant, exilio aut morte multarentur.

Secutae dehinc Tiberii litterae in Sex. Vistilium[2]
praetorium, quem Druso fratri percarum in cohortem
suam transtulerat. Causa offensionis Vistilio fuit,
seu composuerat quaedam in Gaium Caesarem ut
impudicum, sive ficto habita fides. Atque ob id
convictu principis prohibitus cum senili manu ferrum
temptavisset, obligat[3] venas; precatusque per codicillos, immiti rescripto venas resolvit. Acervatim
ex eo Annius Pollio, Appius Silanus Scauro Mamerco
simul ac Sabino Calvisio maiestatis postulantur, et
Vinicianus Pollioni patri adiciebatur, clari genus et
quidam summis honoribus. Contremuerantque
patres (nam quotus quisque adfinitatis aut amicitiae

[1] Pomponium] Pinarium *Ritter* (*from* IV. 34).
[2] Vistilium *Nipperdey*: Vestilium.
[3] obligat *Baiter*: ob legatu.

---

[1] IV. 34; VI. 47.—Pomponius, if the name is rightly
transmitted, must have appeared in the lost part of Book V.

Satrius[1] and Pomponius; it was accounted nobly
done, if we grew known to his very freedmen and
his janitors! What then? Is this defence to be
allowed without discrimination to all and sundry?
Not so: let the dividing line be drawn true; let
treason against the realm, projected assassination
of the sovereign, meet their punishment; but,
when friendship and its duties are in question, if
we terminate them at the same moment as you, we
are vindicated, Caesar, along with yourself!"

IX. The firmness of his speech, and the fact
that a man had been discovered to utter what the
world was thinking, made so powerful an impression
that his accusers, whose former delinquencies were
added to the reckoning, were penalized by banishment
or death.

Now followed a letter from Tiberius directed
against the former praetor Sextus Vistilius, whom,
as the close friend of his brother Drusus, he had
transferred to his own retinue. The ground of
displeasure against Vistilius was either his author-
ship of certain attacks on the morals of Gaius Caesar
or a false statement credited by the emperor. Excluded on this score from the emperor's society, after
first making trial of the dagger with a senile hand,
he bound up his veins, then sent a written plea for
pardon, and, on receiving a pitiless reply, opened
them again. Next, in one group, Annius Pollio
and Appius Silanus were indicted for treason side
by side with Mamercus Scaurus and Calvisius Sabinus, while Vinicianus was coupled with his father
Pollio. All were of distinguished family, some of
the highest official standing; and the Fathers had
begun to tremble—for how few were clear of a

tot inlustrium virorum expers erat?), ni Celsus urbanae cohortis tribunus, tum inter indices, Appium et Calvisium discrimini exemisset. Caesar Pollionis ac Viniciani Scaurique causam, ut ipse cum senatu nosceret, distulit, datis quibusdam in Scaurum tristibus notis.

X. Ne feminae quidem exsortes periculi. Quia occupandae rei publicae argui non poterant, ob lacrimas incusabantur; necataque est anus Vitia,[1] Fufii Gemini mater, quod filii necem flevisset. Haec apud senatum: nec secus apud principem Vescularius Flaccus ac Iulius Marinus ad mortem aguntur, e vetustissimis familiarium, Rhodum secuti et apud Capreas individui, Vescularius insidiarum in Libonem internuntius; Marino participe Seianus Curtium Atticum oppresserat. Quo laetius acceptum sua exempla in consultores recidisse.

Per idem tempus L. Piso pontifex, rarum in tanta claritudine, fato obiit, nullius servilis sententiae sponte auctor, et quotiens necessitas ingrueret, sapienter moderans. Patrem ei censorium fuisse memoravi; aetas ad octogensimum annum processit; decus triumphale in Thraecia meruerat. Sed praecipua ex eo gloria, quod praefectus urbi recens

---

[1] Vitia] Vibia *Nipperdey,* Fufia *Ritter.*

---

[1] II. 28. [2] IV. 58.

[3] L. Calpurnius Piso Caesoninus, son of the Piso (Caesar's father-in-law) attacked by Cicero, and probably father of the youths addressed in the *Ars Poetica.*

[4] In a lost passage. The father's censorship was in 50 B.C.

connection by marriage or by friendship with so many famous men!—when Celsus, tribune of an urban cohort, and now among the prosecutors, freed Appius and Calvisius from danger. The cases of Pollio, Vinicianus, and Scaurus were adjourned by the emperor for his personal decision in company with the senate, though there were certain ominous indications attached to his mention of Scaurus.

X. Even women were not exempt from peril. As they could not be accused of grasping at sovereignty, they were indicted for their tears; and the aged Vitia, mother of Fufius Geminus, was put to death because she had wept at the killing of her son. This in the senate: similarly, at the emperor's tribunal, Vescularius Flaccus and Julius Marinus were hurried to their death—two of his ancient friends, who had followed him to Rhodes and at Capreae, were not divided from him: Vescularius, his intermediary in the plot against Libo;[1] Marinus, the partner of Sejanus in the destruction of Curtius Atticus;[2] whence the greater joy, when it was learned that the precedents had recoiled upon their contrivers.

About the same time, the pontiff Lucius Piso[3]— rare accident in one of his great fame—died in the course of nature. Never the willing author of any slavish proposal, if ever necessity pressed too hard, he was still a discreet and restraining influence. His father, as I have mentioned,[4] had held the censorship; his life was prolonged to the eightieth year; and he had earned in Thrace the honour of a triumph. But his main distinction was the remarkable judgement with which, as Urban Prefect, he exercised an authority, only of late continuous, and disliked

continuam potestatem et insolentia parendi gravi-
orem mire temperavit.

XI. Namque antea, profectis domo regibus ac
mox magistratibus, ne urbs sine imperio foret, in
tempus deligebatur, qui ius redderet ac subitis
mederetur; feruntque ab Romulo Dentrem Romu-
lium, post ab Tullo Hostilio NumamMarcium et ab
Tarquinio Superbo Spurium Lucretium inpositos.
Dein consules mandabant; duratque simulacrum,
quotiens ob ferias Latinas praeficitur qui consulare
munus usurpet. Ceterum Augustus bellis civilibus
Cilnium Maecenatem equestris ordinis cunctis apud
Romam atque Italiam praeposuit: mox rerum
potitus ob magnitudinem populi ac tarda legum
auxilia sumpsit e consularibus qui coerceret servitia
et quod civium audacia turbidum, nisi vim metuat.
Primusque Messala Corvinus eam potestatem et
paucos intra dies finem accepit, quasi nescius exer-
cendi; tum Taurus Statilius, quamquam provecta
aetate, egregie toleravit; dein Piso viginti [1] per

---

[1] XX] XV *Ernesti, Halm, Nipperdey* (*cf.* Suet. *Tib.* 42);
VI *Corsinus* (*cf.* Sen. *ep.* 83).

---

[1] Roughly speaking, the prefectship begins as an emergency
office, to provide for the contingency of the king, or later both
consuls, being absent from Rome. With the creation of the
urban praetorship (367 B.C.), it becomes unnecessary, but its
shadow remains, as a prefect is appointed annually during the
absence of the high magistrates and senate at the Latin Festival on the Alban Mount. Under Augustus, the office is revived as need arises; with the retirement of Tiberius to
Capreae, it becomes a standing office, reserved for consulars

the more because the habit of obedience was lacking.[1]

XI. For previously, to avoid leaving the capital without a competent authority, when the kings—or, later, the magistrates—had to absent themselves from home, it was usual to choose a temporary official to preside in the courts and deal with emergencies; and the tradition runs that Denter Romulius was appointed by Romulus, and, subsequently, Numa Marcius by Tullus Hostilius, and Spurius Lucretius by Tarquinius Superbus. Then the right of delegation passed to the consuls; and a shade of the old order lingers whenever, on account of the Latin Festival, a Prefect is commissioned to discharge the consular functions.[2] Again, in the civil wars, Augustus placed Cilnius Maecenas of the equestrian order at the head of all affairs in Rome and Italy.[3] Then, upon his advent to power, as the population was large and legal remedies dilatory, he took from the body of ex-consuls an official to coerce the slaves as well as that class of the free-born community whose boldness renders it turbulent, unless it is overawed by force. Messala Corvinus was the first to receive those powers, only to forfeit them within a few days on the ground of his incapacity to exercise them. Next, Statilius Taurus upheld the position admirably in spite of his advanced age; and finally Piso, after acquitting himself with equal credit for twenty

and tenable during the pleasure of the emperor making the appointment, but vacated necessarily at his death.

[2] The simulacrum coexisted with the substantial office, but chiefly as a means of complimenting distinguished young men under senatorial age, e.g. Drusus (IV. 36) or Nero (Suet. Ner. 7).

[3] But not under the specific title of praefectus urbi.

annos pariter probatus, publico funere ex decreto
senatus celebratus est.

XII. Relatum inde ad patres a Quintiliano tribuno
plebei de libro Sibullae, quem Caninius Gallus
quindecimvirum recipi inter ceteros eiusdem vatis
et ea de re senatus consultum postulaverat. Quo
per discessionem facto misit litteras Caesar, modice
tribunum increpans ignarum antiqui moris ob
iuventam. Gallo exprobrabat, quod scientiae caeri-
moniarumque vetus incerto auctore, ante sententiam
collegii, non, ut adsolet, lecto per magistros aesti-
matoque carmine, apud infrequentem senatum
egisset. Simul commonefecit, quia multa vana sub
nomine celebri vulgabantur, sanxisse Augustum,
quem intra diem ad praetorem urbanum deferrentur
neque habere privatim liceret. Quod a maioribus
quoque decretum erat post exustum sociali bello[1]
Capitolium, quaesitis Samo, Ilio, Erythris, per Africam
etiam ac Siciliam et Italicas colonias carminibus
Sibullae, una seu plures fuere, datoque sacerdotibus
negotio, quantum humana ope potuissent, vera

---

[1] [sociali bello] *Nipperdey*, civili b. *Lipsius*, Sullano b.
Heraeus.

---

[1] If the manuscript reading were genuine, his appointment
would fall in the reign of Augustus; which contradicts the
story given by Pliny (*H.N.* XIV. 22, 145) and Suetonius
(*Tib.* 42)—supported to some extent by Seneca's account
of his habits (*Ep.* 83)—that he received it after a drinking-
bout with Tiberius.

[2] III. 64 n.

years,[1] was honoured by decree of the senate with a public funeral.

XII. A proposal was now put to the Fathers by the plebeian tribune Quintilianus with regard to a Sibylline book; Caninius Gallus, of the Fifteen,[2] demanding its admission among the other verses of the same prophetess, and a senatorial decree on the point. This had been accorded without discussion,[3] when the emperor forwarded a letter, in which he passed a lenient criticism on the tribune "whose youth accounted for his ignorance of old custom": to Gallus he expressed his displeasure that he, "long familiar with religious theory and ritual, had on dubious authority forestalled the decision of his College, and, before the poem had, as usual, been read and considered by the Masters, had brought up the question in a thinly attended senate." He reminded him at the same time that, because of the many apocryphal works circulated under the famous name, Augustus had fixed a day within which they were to be delivered to the Urban Praetor, private ownership becoming illegal.—A similar decision had been taken even at an earlier period, after the burning of the Capitol during the Social War;[4] when the verses of the Sibyl, or Sibyls, as the case may be, were collected from Samos, Ilium, and Erythrae, and even in Africa, Sicily, and the Graeco-Italian colonies; the priests being entrusted with the task of sifting out the genuine specimens, so far as should have been possible by

[3] III. 69 n.
[4] A slip, probably due to a copyist, as the date is correctly given at *Hist.* III. 72 *arserat et ante Capitolium civili bello* (in the conflict between Sulla and the Marians, 83 B.C.).

discernere. Igitur tunc quoque notioni quindecimvirum is liber subicitur.

XIII. Isdem consulibus gravitate annonae iuxta
seditionem ventum, multaque et pluris per dies in
theatro licentius efflagitata, quam solitum adversum
imperatorem. Quis commotus incusavit magistratus
patresque, quod non publica auctoritate populum
coercuissent, addiditque quibus ex provinciis et
quanto maiorem quam Augustus rei frumentariae
copiam advectaret. Ita castigandae plebi compositum senatus consultum prisca severitate, neque
segnius consules edixere. Silentium ipsius non
civile, ut crediderat, sed in superbiam accipiebatur.

XIV. Fine anni Geminius, Celsus, Pompeius,
equites Romani, cecidere coniurationis crimine; ex
quis Geminius prodigentia opum ac mollitia vitae
amicus Seiano, nihil ad serium. Et Iulius Celsus
tribunus in vinclis laxatam catenam et circumdatam
in diversum tendens suam ipse cervicem perfregit.
At Rubrio Fabato, tamquam desperatis rebus
Romanis Parthorum ad misericordiam fugeret,
custodes additi. Sane is repertus apud fretum
Siciliae retractusque per centurionem nullas proba-
biles causas longinquae peregrinationis adferebat:

human means. Hence, in this case also, the book in question was submitted to the examination of the Quindecimvirate.

XIII. Under the same consuls, the excessive price of corn all but ended in rioting; and large demands were for several days made in the theatre with a freedom not usually employed towards the sovereign. Aroused by this, he upbraided the magistrates and the senate for having failed to restrain the populace by the authority of the state; and, in addition, pointed to the provinces from which he imported the corn-supply, and to the fact that he did so on a far greater scale than Augustus. In the hope, then, of reducing the commons to order, the senate framed a resolution of old-fashioned severity; while an edict not less drastic was issued by the consuls. The silence of Tiberius himself was not, as he had thought, taken for democratic forbearance but for pride.

XIV. At the end of the year, the Roman knights, Geminius, Celsus, and Pompeius, succumbed to the charge of conspiracy. One of them, Geminius, through his prodigal expenditure and effeminacy of life, was certainly a friend of Sejanus, but to no serious purpose. The tribune Julius Celsus, again, when imprisoned, slackened his chain, and by slipping it over his head and pulling at the two ends broke his neck. On the other hand, Rubrius Fabatus was placed under surveillance on the ground that, in despair at the state of Rome, he was contemplating flight to the mercy of the Parthians. Certainly he was discovered in the neighbourhood of the Sicilian Strait, and, when haled back by a centurion, could give no plausible reasons for his distant pilgrimage.

mansit tamen incolumis, oblivione magis quam
clementia.

XV. Ser. Galba L. Sulla consulibus diu quaesito,
quos neptibus suis maritos destinaret Caesar, postquam instabat virginum aetas, L. Cassium, M.
Vinicium legit. Vinicio oppidanum genus: Calibus
ortus, patre atque avo consularibus, cetera equestri
familia erat, mitis ingenio et comptae facundiae.
Cassius plebeii Romae generis, verum antiqui hono-
ratique, et severa patris disciplina eductus facilitate
saepius quam industria commendabatur. Huic Dru-
sillam, Vinicio Iuliam Germanico genitas coniungit
superque ea re senatui scribit, levi cum honore
iuvenum. Dein redditis absentiae causis admodum
vagis flexit ad graviora et offensiones ob rem publicam
coeptas, utque Macro praefectus tribunorumque et
centurionum pauci secum introirent, quotiens curiam
ingrederetur, petivit. Factoque large et sine prae-
scriptione generis aut numeri senatus consulto ne
tecta quidem urbis, adeo publicum consilium numquam adiit, deviis plerumque itineribus ambiens
patriam et declinans.

XVI. Interea magna vis accusatorum in eos inru-
pit, qui pecunias faenore auctitabant adversum legem

---

[1] The future emperor, though his praenomen was at this
time Lucius (Suet. *Galb.* 4).

[2] The third sister, Agrippina, had already married Cn.
Domitius (IV. fin.).—Of the two bridegrooms, Cassius—
brother of the celebrated jurist (XII. 12 n.)—was executed
eight years later by Caligula; Vinicius was poisoned in 46 A.D.
by Messalina (D. Cass. LIX. 29; LX. 27).

[3] Naevius Sertorius Macro, who carried through the arrest
of Sejanus, replaced him as praetorian prefect, and proved,
according to Lucius Arruntius, the worse villain of the pair
(chap. 48). For his courtship of Caligula, see below (chap.
45 sq.); for his suicide at his protégé's order, D. Cass. LIX. 10.

He kept his life, however, more through forgetfulness than through clemency.

XV. In the consulate of Servius Galba[1] and Lucius Sulla, the Caesar, after long debating whom to appoint as husbands for his grand-daughters, found the age of the girls advancing, and selected Lucius Cassius and Marcus Vinicius. Vinicius came of country stock: born at Cales, with a father and grandfather of consular rank, but of equestrian family otherwise, he was gentle in disposition and the master of a polished eloquence. Cassius, of a plebeian but old and honoured house at Rome, and trained under strict paternal discipline, recommended himself more often by an accommodating temper than by energy. To him and to Vinicius Tiberius plighted respectively Drusilla and Julia,[2] the daughters of Germanicus, and wrote to the senate on the subject with a perfunctory eulogy of the young men. Then, after giving a number of extremely indefinite reasons for his absence, he turned to the graver subject of " enmities incurred for his country's good," and asked that the prefect Macro[3] and a few tribunes and centurions should be admitted with himself as often as he entered the curia. Yet, notwithstanding that the senate passed a comprehensive decree without any proviso as to the composition or numbers of his escort, not once did he even approach the roofs of Rome, far less the deliberative assembly of the state, but time and again, by devious roads, encircled, and avoided, his native city

XVI. Meanwhile, an army of accusers broke loose on the persons who habitually increased their riches by usury, in contravention of a law of the dictator

dictatoris Caesaris, qua de modo credendi possidendique intra Italiam cavetur, omissam olim, quia privato usui bonum publicum postponitur. Sane vetus urbi faenebre malum et seditionum discordiarumque creberrima causa, eoque cohibebatur antiquis quoque et minus corruptis moribus. Nam primo duodecim tabulis sanctum, ne quis unciario faenore amplius exerceret, cum antea ex libidine locupletium agitaretur; dein rogatione tribunicia ad semuncias redactum,[1] postremo vetita versura. Multisque plebi scitis obviam itum fraudibus, quae totiens repressae miras per artis rursum oriebantur. Sed tum Gracchus praetor, cui ea quaestio evenerat, multitudine periclitantium subactus rettulit ad senatum, trepidique patres (neque enim quisquam tali culpa vacuus) veniam a principe petivere; et concedente annus in posterum sexque menses dati, quis secundum iussa legis rationes familiaris quisque componerent.

XVII. Hinc inopia rei nummariae, commoto simul omnium aere alieno, et quia tot damnatis bonisque

---

[1] redactum *Halm* : redactu.

---

[1] Nothing certain is known of this law, which must have been distinct from the emergency measures of 48 B.C. (Caes. *B.C.* III. 1).

[2] In 450 B.C. The statement rests on the authority of Tacitus : Livy's date is 357 B.C. (VII. 16).

[3] In 347 B.C. (Livy, VII. 27).

[4] *Invenio apud quosdam L. Genucium, tr-pl., tulisse ad populum ne faenerare liceret* (342 B.C., Livy, *ib.* 42).—By the Roman system of naming rates of interest, *unciarium faenus* must mean $\frac{1}{12}$ per cent. per month, or 1 per cent. per annum. Holding such a rate to be impossibly low, Niebuhr—forcibly controverted by Nipperdey, but followed by Mommsen—took

Caesar,[1] regulating the conditions of lending money and holding property within the boundaries of Italy: a measure dropped long ago, since the public good ranks second to private utility. The curse of usury, it must be owned, is inveterate in Rome, a constant source of sedition and discord; and attempts were accordingly made to repress it even in an older and less corrupt society. First came a provision of the Twelve Tables[2] that the rate of interest, previously governed by the fancy of the rich, should not exceed one-twelfth per cent. for the month; later[3] a tribunician rogation lowered it to one-half of that amount; and at length usufruct was unconditionally banned;[4] while a series of plebiscites strove to meet the frauds which were perpetually repressed, only, by extraordinary evasions, to make their appearance once more. In the present instance, however, the praetor Gracchus, to whose jurisdiction the case had fallen, was forced by the numbers implicated to refer it to the senate; and the Fathers in trepidation —for not one member was clear from such a charge— asked an indulgence from the prince. It was granted; and the next eighteen months were assigned as a term of grace within which all accounts were to be adjusted in accordance with the prescriptions of the law.

XVII. The result was a dearth of money: for not only were all debts called in simultaneously; but after so many convictions and sales of forfeited

the sense of the words to be $\frac{1}{12}$th of the capital, *i.e.* $8\frac{1}{3}$ per cent. per annum, which he ingeniously raised to 10 ($= 8\frac{1}{3} \times \frac{12}{10}$) per cent., by accepting the tradition of a primitive year of ten months.

eorum divenditis signatum argentum fisco vel aerario attinebatur. Ad hoc senatus praescripserat, duas quisque faenoris partis in agris per Italiam conlocaret, *debitores totidem aeris alieni statim solverent.*[1] Sed creditores in solidum appellabant, nec decorum appellatis minuere fidem. Ita primo concursatio et preces, dein strepere praetoris tribunal, eaque quae remedio quaesita, venditio et emptio, in contrarium mutari, quia faeneratores omnem pecuniam mercandis agris condiderant. Copiam vendendi secuta vilitate, quanto quis obaeratior, aegrius distrahebant, multique fortunis provolvebantur; eversio rei familiaris dignitatem ac famam praeceps dabat, donec tulit opem Caesar disposito per mensas miliens sestertio factaque mutuandi copia sine usuris per triennium, si debitor populo in duplum praediis cavisset. Sic refecta fides, et paulatim privati quoque creditores reperti. Neque emptio agrorum exercita ad formam senatus consulti, acribus, ut ferme talia, initiis, incurioso fine.

XVIII. Dein redeunt priores metus postulato maiestatis Considio Proculo, qui nullo pavore diem

---

[1] ⟨debitores . . . solverent⟩ *Nipperdey.* (*The words, necessary to the sense, are preserved in* Suet. *Tib.* 48).

---

[1] Strictly, the proceeds of the sale of confiscated properties went, like unclaimed legacies, to the senatorial treasury (*aerarium*), but frequently enough they were diverted to the *fiscus*: an instance follows shortly (chap. 19 init.).

[2] Special public banks under the charge of a senatorial commission (D. Cass. LVIII. 21).

estates, the cash which had been realized was locked in the treasury or the imperial exchequer.[1] To meet this difficulty, the senate had prescribed that every creditor was to invest two-thirds of his capital, now lying at interest, in landed property in Italy; ⟨the debtor to discharge immediately an equivalent proportion of his liability.⟩ The lenders, however, called in the full amounts, and the borrowers could not in honour refuse to answer the call. Thus, at first there were hurryings to and fro, and appeals for mercy; then a hum of activity in the praetor's court; and the very scheme which had been devised as a remedy—the sale and purchase of estates— began to operate with the contrary effect, since the usurers had withdrawn their capital from circulation in order to buy land. As the glutting of the market was followed by a fall in prices, the men with the heaviest debts experienced the greatest difficulty in selling, and numbers were ejected from their properties. Financial ruin brought down in its train both rank and reputation, till the Caesar came to the rescue by distributing a hundred million sesterces among various counting-houses,[2] and facilities were provided for borrowing free of interest for three years, if the borrower had given security to the state to double the value in landed property. Credit was thus revived, and by degrees private lenders also began to be found. Nor was the purchase of estates practised in accordance with the terms of the senatorial decree, a vigorous beginning lapsing as usual into a careless end.

XVIII. The old fears now returned with the indictment for treason of Considius Proculus; who, while celebrating his birthday without a qualm,

natalem celebrans raptus in curiam pariterque damnatus interfectusque est.[1] Sorori eius Sanciae aqua atque igni interdictum accusante Q. Pomponio. Is moribus inquies haec et huiusce modi a se factitari praetendebat, ut parta apud principem gratia periculis Pomponii Secundi fratris mederetur. Etiam in Pompeiam Macrinam exilium statuitur, cuius maritum Argolicum, socerum Laconem e primoribus Achaeorum Caesar adflixerat. Pater quoque inlustris eques Romanus ac frater praetorius, cum damnatio instaret, se ipsi interfecere. Datum erat crimini, quod Theophanen Mytilenaeum proavum eorum Cn. Magnus inter intimos habuisset, quodque defuncto Theophani caelestis honores Graeca adulatio tribuerat.

XIX. Post quos Sex. Marius Hispaniarum ditissimus defertur incestasse filiam et saxo Tarpeio deicitur. Ac ne dubium haberetur magnitudinem pecuniae malo vertisse, *aerarias*[2] aurariasque eius, quamquam publicarentur, sibimet Tiberius seposuit. Inritatusque suppliciis cunctos, qui carcere attinebantur accusati societatis cum Seiano, necari iubet. Iacuit inmensa strages, omnis sexus, omnis aetas, in-

---

[1] est *Bezzenberger* : et.
[2] ⟨aerarias⟩ *Ritter.—Compare* Plin. *H.N.* xxxiv 2, 4 aes Marianum quod et Cordubense dicitur.

---

[1] V. 8 n.
[2] References are frequent to his friendship and influence with Pompey, to whom he owed his Roman citizenship, and whose history he wrote : see, for instance, Cic. *pro Arch.* § 24; *ad Att.* V. 11; Caes. *B.C.* III. 18. Strabo, writing about 18 A.D., mentions the intimacy of his son with Tiberius (XIII. 2, 3).
[3] At Mytilene, for which he had secured from Pompey the privileges of a free town, in spite of the city's dubious record in the Mithridatic War (Plut. *Pomp.* 42).

was swept off to the senate-house and in the same
moment condemned and executed. His sister
Sancia was banned from fire and water, the accuser
being Quintus Pomponius: a restless character,
who pleaded that the object of his activity in this
and similar cases was, by acquiring favour with
the emperor, to palliate the dangers of his brother
Pomponius Secundus.[1] Exile was also the sentence
of Pompeia Macrina, whose husband Argolicus and
father-in-law Laco, two of the most prominent men
in Achaia had been struck down by the Caesar.
Her father, too, a Roman knight of the highest
rank, and her brother, a former praetor, finding their
condemnation at hand, committed suicide. The
crime laid to their account was that Theophanes
of Mytilene [2] (great-grandfather of Pompeia and her
brother) had been numbered with the intimates of
Pompey, and that, after his death, Greek sycophancy
had paid him the honour of deification.[3]

XIX. After these, Sextus Marius,[4] the richest
man of Spain, was arraigned for incest with his
daughter and flung from the Tarpeian Rock; while,
to leave no doubt that it was the greatness of his
wealth which had redounded to his ruin, his copper-
mines and gold-mines, though forfeit to the state,
were reserved by Tiberius for himself. And as
executions had whetted his appetite, he gave orders
for all persons in custody on the charge of complicity
with Sejanus to be killed. On the ground lay the
huge hecatomb of victims:[5] either sex, every age;

---

[4] IV. 36.
[5] Twenty in one day, according to the manuscripts of
Suetonius (*Tib.* 61).

lustres ignobiles, dispersi aut aggerati. Neque
propinquis aut amicis adsistere, inlacrimare, ne visere
quidem diutius dabatur, sed circumiecti custodes et
in maerorem cuiusque intenti corpora putrefacta
adsectabantur, dum in Tiberim traherentur, ubi
fluitantia aut ripis adpulsa non cremare quisquam,
non contingere. Interciderat sortis humanae com-
mercium vi metus, quantumque saevitia glisceret,
miseratio arcebatur.

XX. Sub idem tempus Gaius Caesar, discedenti
Capreas avo comes, Claudiam, M. Silani filiam,
coniugio accepit, immanem animum subdola modestia
tegens, non damnatione matris, non exitio [1] fratrum
rupta voce; qualem diem [2] Tiberius induisset, pari
habitu, haud multum distantibus verbis. Unde
mox scitum Passieni oratoris dictum percrebruit
neque meliorem umquam servum neque deteriorem
dominum fuisse.

Non omiserim praesagium Tiberii de Servio Galba
tum consule; quem accitum et diversis sermonibus
pertemptatum postremo Graecis verbis in hanc
sententiam adlocutus *est* " et tu, Galba, quandoque
degustabis imperium," seram ac brevem potentiam

---

[1] exitio *Nipperdey* : exilio.
[2] qualem [diem] *Acidalius. The metaphor is, in fact, more
than harsh, and dittography would be easy: cf. e.g.* alii = dii,
III. 38.

---

[1] V. 10 n. He stood high in the opinion of Tiberius (D.
Cass. LIX. 8), but was forced to suicide by his son-in-law
(Suet. *Cal.* 23).
[2] He is praised by Seneca (*N.Q.* IV. pr. 6), was consul twice,
and through his marriage later with Agrippina had the double
distinction of being brother-in-law to Caligula and stepfather
to Nero.

the famous, the obscure; scattered or piled in mounds. Nor was it permitted to relatives or friends to stand near, to weep over them, or even to view them too long; but a cordon of sentries, with eyes for each beholder's sorrow, escorted the rotting carcasses, as they were dragged to the Tiber, there to float with the current or drift to the bank, with none to commit them to the flames or touch them. The ties of our common humanity had been dissolved by the force of terror; and before each advance of cruelty compassion receded.

XX. About the same time, Gaius Caesar, who had accompanied his grandfather on the departure to Capreae, received in marriage Claudia, the daughter of Marcus Silanus.[1] His monstrous character was masked by a hypocritical modesty: not a word escaped him at the sentencing of his mother or the destruction of his brethren; whatever the mood assumed for the day by Tiberius, the attitude of his grandson was the same, and his words not greatly different. Hence, a little later, the epigram of the orator Passienus[2]—that the world never knew a better slave, nor a worse master.

I cannot omit the prophecy of Tiberius with regard to Servius Galba, then consul. He sent for him, sounded him in conversations on a variety of subjects, and finally addressed him in a Greek sentence, the purport of which was, " Thou, too, Galba, shalt one day have thy taste of empire ":[3] a hint of belated and short-lived power,[4] based on knowledge

[3] Suetonius, who mistakenly makes Augustus the prophet, gives the Greek as :—καὶ σύ, τέκνον, τῆς ἀρχῆς ἡμῶν παρατρώξῃ. Dio has: καὶ σύ ποτε τῆς ἡγεμονίας γεύσῃ (LVII. 19).

[4] Born in 3 B.C., he tasted empire from June, 68 A.D., to January, 69 A.D.

significans, scientia Chaldaeorum artis, cuius apiscendae otium apud Rhodum, magistrum Thrasullum
habuit, peritiam eius hoc modo expertus.

XXI. Quotiens super tali negotio consultaret,
edita domus parte ac liberti unius conscientia utebatur. Is litterarum ignarus, corpore valido, per
avia ac derupta (nam saxis domus imminet) praeibat
eum, cuius artem experiri Tiberius statuisset, et
regredientem, si vanitatis aut fraudum suspicio
incesserat, in subiectum mare praecipitabat, ne index
arcani exsisteret. Igitur Thrasullus isdem rupibus
inductus postquam percontantem commoverat, imperium ipsi et futura sollerter patefaciens, interro-
gatur an suam quoque genitalem horam comperisset,
quem tum annum, qualem diem haberet. Ille
positus siderum ac spatia dimensus haerere primo,
dein pavescere, et quantum introspiceret, magis ac
magis trepidus admirationis et metus, postremo
exclamat ambiguum sibi ac prope ultimum discrimen
instare. Tum complexus eum Tiberius praescium
periculorum et incolumem fore gratatur, quaeque
dixerat oracli vice accipiens inter intimos amicorum
tenet.

XXII. Sed mihi haec ac talia audienti in incerto
iudicium est, fatone res mortalium et necessitate
immutabili an forte volvantur. Quippe sapientissi-

---

[1] He retained that precarious position, received—as is
shown by his name, Ti. Claudius Thrasyllus—the citizenship
from his patron, and, after accompanying him to Rome, lived
with him till his death in 36 A.D., one year before that of the
emperor.

of the Chaldean art, the acquirement of which he owed to the leisure of Rhodes and the instructions of Thrasyllus. His tutor's capacity he had tested as follows.

XXI. For all consultations on such business he used the highest part of his villa and the confidential services of one freedman. Along the pathless and broken heights (for the house overlooks a cliff) this illiterate and robust guide led the way in front of the astrologer whose art Tiberius had resolved to investigate, and on his return, had any suspicion arisen of incompetence or of fraud, hurled him into the sea below, lest he should turn betrayer of the secret. Thrasyllus, then, introduced by the same rocky path, after he had impressed his questioner by adroit revelations of his empire to be and of the course of the future, was asked if he had ascertained his own horoscope—what was the character of that year—what the complexion of that day. A diagram which he drew up of the positions and distances of the stars at first gave him pause; then he showed signs of fear: the more careful his scrutiny, the greater his trepidation between surprise and alarm; and at last he exclaimed that a doubtful, almost a final, crisis was hard upon him. He was promptly embraced by Tiberius, who, congratulating him on the fact that he had divined, and was about to escape, his perils, accepted as oracular truth, the predictions he had made, and retained him among his closest friends.[1]

XXII. For myself, when I listen to this and similar narratives, my judgement wavers. Is the revolution of human things governed by fate and changeless necessity, or by accident? You will

mos veterum quique sectas[1] eorum aemulantur
diversos reperies, ac multis insitam opinionem non
initia nostri, non finem, non denique homines dis
curae; ideo creberrime tristia in bonos, laeta apud
deteriores esse. Contra alii fatum quidem congruere
rebus putant, sed non e vagis stellis, verum apud
principia et nexus naturalium causarum; ac tamen
electionem vitae nobis relinquunt, quam ubi elegeris,
certum imminentium ordinem. Neque mala vel
bona, quae vulgus putet: multos, qui conflictari
adversis videantur, beatos, at plerosque quamquam
magnas per opes miserrimos. si illi gravem fortunam
constanter tolerent, hi prospera inconsulte utantur.
Ceterum plurimis mortalium non eximitur, quin
primo cuiusque ortu ventura destinentur, sed quaedam secus quam dicta sint cadere, fallaciis ignara
dicentium: ita corrumpi fidem artis, cuius clara
documenta et antiqua aetas et nostra tulerit. Quippe
a filio eiusdem Thrasulli praedictum Neronis imperium in tempore memorabitur, ne nunc incepto
longius abierim.

XXIII. Isdem consulibus Asinii Galli mors vulgatur, quem egestate cibi peremptum haud dubium,

<hr>

[1] sectas *Wurm* : sectam.

<hr>

[1] The Epicureans.
[2] The Stoics.
[3] The best ancient presentation of the sceptical case is a
lecture of Favorinus, heard and recorded by Aulus Gellius
(*N.A.* XIV. 1).
[4] Possibly at XIV. 9.
[5] Eldest son of Asinius Pollio (IV. 34 n.). Three years earlier,
while visiting Tiberius in Capreae, he was condemned by the
senate in obedience to a letter of the emperor, and had since
then been held in *custodia libera* by the consuls ' to prevent
not his escape but his death ' (D. Cass. LVIII. 3).

find the wisest of the ancients, and the disciples
attached to their tenets, at complete variance; in
many of them[1] a fixed belief that Heaven concerns
itself neither with our origins, nor with our ending,
nor, in fine, with mankind, and that so adversity
continually assails the good, while prosperity dwells
among the evil. Others[2] hold, on the contrary, that,
though there is certainly a fate in harmony with
events, it does not emanate from wandering stars,
but must be sought in the principles and processes
of natural causation. Still, they leave us free to
choose our life: that choice made, however, the
order of the future is certain. Nor, they maintain,
are evil and good what the crowd imagines: many
who appear to be the sport of adverse circumstances
are happy; numbers are wholly wretched though in
the midst of great possessions—provided only that
the former endure the strokes of fortunes with firmness, while the latter employ her favours with
unwisdom. With most men, however, the faith is
ineradicable that the future of an individual is
ordained at the moment of his entry into life; but
at times a prophecy is falsified by the event, through
the dishonesty of the prophet who speaks he knows
not what; and thus is debased the credit of an art, of
which the most striking evidences have been furnished
both in the ancient world and in our own.[3] For the
forecast of Nero's reign, made by the son of this very
Thrasyllus, shall be related at its fitting place:[4]
at present I do not care to stray too far from my
theme.

XXIII. Under the same consulate, the death of
Asinius Gallus[5] became common knowledge. That
he died from starvation was not in doubt; but

sponte an[1] necessitate, incertum habebatur. Con-
sultusque Caesar an sepeliri sineret, non erubuit
permittere ultroque incusare casus, qui reum abstu-
lissent, antequam coram convinceretur: scilicet
medio triennio defuerat tempus subeundi iudicium
consulari seni, tot consularium parenti. Drusus
deinde exstinguitur, cum se miserandis alimentis,
mandendo e cubili tomento, nonum ad diem deti-
nuisset. Tradidere quidam praescriptum fuisse
Macroni, si arma ab Seiano temptarentur, extractum
custodiae iuvenem (nam in Palatio attinebatur)
ducem populo imponere. Mox, quia rumor incede-
bat fore ut nuru ac nepoti conciliaretur Caesar,
saevitiam quam paenitentiam maluit.

XXIV. Quin et invectus in defunctum probra
corporis, exitiabilem in suos, infensum rei publicae
animum obiecit recitarique factorum dictorumque
eius descripta per dies iussit, quo non aliud atrocius
visum: adstitisse tot per annos, qui vultum, gemitus,
occultum etiam murmur exciperent, et potuisse avum
audire, legere, in publicum promere vix fides, nisi
quod Attii centurionis et Didymi liberti epistulae servorum nomina praeferebant, ut quis egredientem
cubiculo Drusum pulsaverat, exterruerat. Etiam

---

[1] an *Orsini*: vel.

[1] Pronounced a public enemy by the senate, *criminante
Tiberio* (Suet. *Cal.* 7), and still imprisoned in an underground
chamber of the Palatium.

whether of free will or by compulsion was held uncertain. The Caesar, when asked if he allowed him burial, did not blush to accord permission and to go out of his way to deplore the accidents which had carried off the accused before he could be convicted in his own presence. In a three years' interval, that is to say, time had been lacking for this aged consular, father of so many consular sons, to be brought to judgement! Next, Drusus[1] passed away, after sustaining life through eight full days by the pitiable resource of chewing the stuffing of his mattress. The statement has been made that Macro's orders were, if Sejanus appealed to arms, to withdraw the youth from custody (he was confined in the Palace) and to place him at the head of the people. Then, as a rumour gained ground that the Caesar was about to be reconciled with his daughter-in-law and grandson, he preferred cruelty to repentance.

XXIV. More than this, he inveighed against the dead, reproaching him with unnatural vice and with sentiments pernicious to his family and dangerous to the state; and ordered the reading of the daily register of his doings and sayings. This was regarded as the crowning atrocity. That for so many years the watchers should have been at his side, to catch his looks, his sighs, even his half-articulated murmurs, and that his grandfather should have endured to hear all, read all, and divulge it to the public, might have passed belief but for the fact that the reports of the centurion Attius and the freedman Didymus paraded the names of this or the other slave who had struck or terrorized the prince whenever he attempted to leave his room.

sua verba centurio saevitiae plena, tamquam egregium, vocesque deficientis adiecerat, quis primo[1]
quasi per dementiam, funesta Tiberio, mox, ubi
exspes vitae fuit, meditatas compositasque diras
inprecabatur, ut, quem ad modum nurum filiumque
fratris et nepotes domumque omnem caedibus
complevisset, ita poenas nomini generique maiorum
et posteris exsolveret. Obturbabant quidem patres
specie detestandi : sed penetrabat pavor et admiratio,
callidum olim et tegendis sceleribus obscurum huc
confidentiae venisse, ut tamquam dimotis parietibus
ostenderet nepotem sub verbere centurionis, inter
servorum ictus extrema vitae alimenta frustra
orantem.

XXV. Nondum is dolor exoleverat, cum de
Agrippina auditum, quam interfecto Seiano spe
sustentatam provixisse reor, et postquam nihil de
saevitia remittebatur, voluntate exstinctam, nisi si
negatis alimentis adsimulatus est finis, qui videretur
sponte sumptus. Enimvero Tiberius foedissimis
criminationibus exarsit, impudicitiam arguens et
Asinium Gallum adulterum, eiusque morte ad taedium vitae conpulsam. Sed Agrippina aequi inpatiens,
dominandi avida, virilibus curis feminarum vitia

---

[1] primo *Bahrdt* : primo alienationem mentis simulans.

---

[1] The victims are Agrippina, her husband Germanicus
(at once the nephew and the adopted son of Tiberius), and their
children, Nero—banished in 29 A.D. to the island of Pontia
and there starved to death—and Drusus himself.

The centurion had even added his own brutal remarks, as a point to his credit; along with the
dying words of his prisoner, who had begun by cursing
Tiberius in apparent delirium, and then, when all
hope of life was gone, had denounced him with a
meditated and formal imprecation: that as he had
done to death his daughter-in-law, his brother's son,
his grandchildren,[1] and had filled his whole house
with blood, so he might pay the penalty due to the
name and line of his ancestors, and to his posterity.
The Fathers interrupted, indeed, with a pretence
of horror: in reality, they were penetrated with
terror and astonishment that, once so astute, so
impenetrable in the concealment of his crimes, he
had attained such a pitch of confidence that he
could, as it were, raze his palace-walls and exhibit
his grandson under the scourge of a centurion, among
the blows of slaves, imploring in vain the humblest
necessaries of life.

XXV. This tragedy had not yet faded from memory,
when news came of Agrippina;[2] who, after the death
of Sejanus, had continued, I take it, to live, because
sustained by hope, and then, as there was no abatement of cruelty, had perished by her own will; unless
food was withheld, so that her death should present
features which might be taken for those of suicide.
The point certain is that Tiberius broke out in
abominable calumnies, accusing her of unchastity
and adultery with Asinius Gallus, by whose death
she had been driven to tire of life. Yet Agrippina,
impatient of equality and athirst for power, had sunk
female frailty in masculine ambition. She had died,

[2] Banished simultaneously with Nero, but to the island of
Pandateria (I. 53 n.).

exuerat. Eodem die defunctam, quo biennio ante
Seianus poenas luisset, memoriaeque id prodendum
addidit Caesar iactavitque, quod non laqueo strangu-
lata neque in Gemonias proiecta foret. Actae ob id
grates decretumque, ut quintum decumum kal.
Novembris, utriusque necis die, per omnis annos
donum Iovi sacraretur.

XXVI. Haud multo post Cocceius Nerva, continuus
principi, omnis divini humanique iuris sciens, integro
statu, corpore inlaeso, moriendi consilium cepit.
Quod ut Tiberio cognitum, adsidere, causas requirere,
addere preces, fateri postremo grave conscientiae,
grave famae suae, si proximus amicorum nullis
moriendi rationibus vitam fugeret. Aversatus sermonem Nerva abstinentiam cibi coniunxit. Ferebant
gnari cogitationum eius, quanto propius mala rei
publicae viseret, ira et metu, dum integer, dum
intemptatus, honestum finem voluisse.

Ceterum Agrippinae pernicies, quod vix credibile,
Plancinam traxit. Nupta olim Cn. Pisoni et palam
laeta morte Germanici, cum Piso caderet, precibus
Augustae nec minus inimicitiis Agrippinae defensa
erat. Ut odium et gratia desiere, ius valuit; petita-
que criminibus haud ignotis sua manu sera magis
quam inmerita supplicia persolvit.

---

[1] IV. 58 n.
[2] II. 43 sqq.; 75 fin.; III. 15.

the Caesar pursued, on the very day on which, two years earlier, Sejanus had expiated his crimes, a fact which ought to be transmitted to memory; and he mentioned with pride that she had not been strangled or thrown on to the Gemonian Stairs. Thanks were returned for the mercy, and it was decreed that on the eighteenth of October, the day of both the killings, an offering should be consecrated to Jupiter for all years to come.

XXVI. A little later, Cocceius Nerva,[1] the inseparable friend of the emperor, versed in all law divine or secular, his position intact, his health unimpaired, adopted the resolution of dying. Tiberius, on discovering the fact, sat down by his side, inquired his reasons, proceeded to entreaties, and in the last resort confessed that it would be a serious matter for his conscience and a serious matter for his reputation, if the nearest of his friends were to flee from life with no motive for dying. Declining all conversation, Nerva continued his abstention from food till the end. It was stated by those acquainted with his thoughts that, moved by his closer view of the calamities of his country, he had, in indignation and fear, whilst yet unscathed, yet unassailed, decided for an honourable end.

To proceed, the destruction of Agrippina, scarcely credible though it seems, brought down Plancina.[2] Once wedded to Gnaeus Piso and openly exulting in the death of Germanicus, upon her husband's fall she had been saved by the intercessions of Augusta, and, not less so, by the enmity of Agrippina. When both hatred and favour ceased, justice prevailed: she was arraigned on charges notorious to the world, and paid by her own hand a penalty more overdue than undeserved.

XXVII. Tot luctibus funesta civitate pars maeroris fuit, quod Iulia Drusi filia, quondam Neronis uxor, denupsit in domum Rubellii Blandi, cuius avum Tiburtem equitem Romanum plerique meminerant.

Extremo anni mors Aelii Lamiae funere censorio celebrata, qui administrandae Suriae imagine tandem exsolutus urbi praefuerat. Genus illi decorum, vivida senectus; et non permissa provincia dignationem addiderat. Exim Flacco Pomponio Suriae pro praetore defuncto recitantur Caesaris litterae, quis incusabat egregium quemque et regendis exercitibus idoneum abnuere id munus, seque ea necessitudine ad preces cogi, per quas consularium aliqui capessere provincias adigerentur, oblitus Arruntium, ne in Hispaniam pergeret, decumum iam annum attineri. Obiit eodem anno et M'. Lepidus, de cuius moderatione atque sapientia in prioribus libris satis conlocavi. Neque nobilitas diutius demonstranda est: quippe Aemilium genus fecundum bonorum civium, et qui eadem familia corruptis moribus, inlustri tamen fortuna egere.

---

[1] This ' contributory regret ' seems something of an anticlimax; but even a knight of the respectability of Atticus was held *dedecere Claudiorum imagines* (II. 43). For the issue of the mésalliance, see XIII. 19 n.

[2] And as a teacher of rhetoric at Rome—the first knight, according to the elder Seneca, to embrace a profession till then reserved for freedmen (*turpe erat docere quod honestum erat discere*, Contr. II. pr. 5).

[3] IV. 13 n.—He would seem to have been appointed governor of Syria in 20 A.D., in succession to Cn. Sentius (II. 74), but to have been detained in Rome by Tiberius, while the province was administered by Sentius' legate Pacuvius (II. 79). In 32 A.D., he followed Piso as *praefectus urbi*, and Syria was entrusted to Pomponius Flaccus.

XXVII. Among all the griefs of a melancholy realm, it was a contributory regret[1] that Julia, daughter of Drusus and formerly wife of Nero, now married into the family of Rubellius Blandus, whose grandfather was remembered by many as a Roman knight from Tibur.[2]

At the very close of the year, the death of Aelius Lamia,[3] whose belated release from his phantom administration of Syria had been followed by the Urban Prefectship, was celebrated by a censorian funeral. His birth was noble, his age vigorous, and he had derived from the withholding of his province an added dignity. Then, on the decease of Pomponius Flaccus, propraetor of Syria, a letter was read from the emperor; who complained that every outstanding man, capable of commanding armies,[4] refused that duty; and such was his need that he was reduced to entreaties, in the hope that here and there a former consul might be driven to undertake a governorship; while he failed to recollect that for the tenth successive year Arruntius was being kept at home for fear that he should start for Spain.[5] Still in the same year died Manius Lepidus, to whose moderation and wisdom I have given space enough in the previous books. Nor does his nobility call for long demonstration: the Aemilian race has been prolific of patriots, and those of the family who have borne degenerate characters have yet played their part with the brilliance of their high fortunes.

---

[4] As the governor of a major imperial province.

[5] He must have been appointed to *Hispania Tarraconensis* after the murder of L. Piso in 25 A.D. (IV. 45): *decimum*, therefore, is only a round number.

THE ANNALS OF TACITUS

XXVIII. Paulo Fabio L. Vitellio consulibus post longum saeculorum ambitum avis phoenix in Aegyptum venit praebuitque materiem doctissimis indigenarum et Graecorum multa super eo miraculo disserendi. De quibus congruunt et plura ambigua, sed cognitu non absurda promere libet. Sacrum Soli id animal et ore ac distinctu pinnarum a ceteris avibus diversum consentiunt qui formam eius effinxere: de numero annorum varia traduntur. Maxime vulgatum quingentorum spatium: sunt qui adseverent mille quadringentos sexaginta unum interici, prioresque alios tres [1] Sesoside primum, post Amaside dominantibus, dein Ptolemaeo, qui ex Macedonibus tertius regnavit, in civitatem, cui Heliopolis nomen, advolavisse, multo ceterarum volucrum comitatu novam faciem mirantium. Sed antiquitas quidem obscura: inter Ptolemaeum ac Tiberium minus ducenti quinquaginta anni fuerunt. Unde nonnulli falsum hunc phoenicem neque Arabum e terris credidere, nihilque usurpavisse ex his,[2] quae vetus memoria firmavit. Confecto quippe annorum numero, ubi mors propinquet, suis in terris struere nidum eique vim genitalem

----

[1] alios tres *Halm* : aliter.   [2] his] iis Ritter.

----

[1] Both Pliny and Dio place the visit two years later.

[2] This is the length, not of one of the phoenix-cycles, but of the Sothic or Canicular, period ($\kappa \upsilon \nu \iota \kappa \grave{o} \varsigma \ \kappa \acute{\upsilon} \kappa \lambda o \varsigma$), at the end of which the error arising from the difference between a calendar year of 365 days and a solar year of 365¼ redresses itself without intercalation. The period owes its name to the fact that at the beginning of each cycle the heliacal rising of Sothis—the Dog Star—occurred on the first of Thoth, the opening day of the year. That one such cycle is known from Censorinus to have ended in 139 A.D. in a point of cardinal importance for Egyptian chronology.

XXVIII. In the consulate of Paulus Fabius and A.U.C. 787 =
Lucius Vitellius, after a long period of ages, the A.D. 34
bird known as the phoenix visited Egypt,[1] and
supplied the learned of that country and of Greece
with the material for long disquisitions on the
miracle. I propose to state the points on which they
coincide, together with the larger number that are
dubious, yet not too absurd for notice. That the
creature is sacred to the sun and distinguished from
other birds by its head and the variegation of its
plumage, is agreed by those who have depicted its
form: as to its term of years, the tradition varies.
The generally received number is five hundred;
but there are some who assert that its visits fall at
intervals of 1461 years,[2] and that it was in the reigns,
first of Sesosis,[3] then of Amasis,[4] and finally of Ptolemy[5]
(third of the Macedonian dynasty), that the three
earlier phoenixes flew to the city called Heliopolis[6]
with a great escort of common birds amazed at the
novelty of their appearance. But while antiquity is
obscure, between Ptolemy and Tiberius there were
less than two hundred and fifty years: whence the
belief has been held that this was a spurious phoenix,
not originating on the soil of Arabia, and following
none of the practices affirmed by ancient tradition.
For—so the tale is told—when its sum of years is
complete and death is drawing on, it builds a nest
in its own country and sheds on it a procreative in-

[3] II. 60 n.
[4] See Hdt. II. 172 sqq. The accepted date of his reign
is 569–526 B.C.
[5] 247–222 B.C.
[6] Egypt *Pe-ra* (*Anu*), Hebr. *On*. The ruins are near
Matarieh, six miles N.N.E. of Cairo.

adfundere, ex qua fetum oriri; et primam adulto
curam sepeliendi patris, neque id temere, sed sublato
murrae pondere temptatoque per longum iter, ubi
par oneri, par meatui sit, subire patrium corpus inque
Solis aram perferre atque adolere. Haec incerta et
fabulosis aucta: ceterum aspici aliquando in Aegypto
eam volucrem non ambigitur.

XXIX. At Romae caede continua Pomponius
Labeo, quem praefuisse Moesiae rettuli, per abruptas
venas sanguinem effudit; aemulataque est coniunx
Paxaea. Nam promptas eius modi mortes metus
carnificis faciebat, et quia damnati publicatis bonis
sepultura prohibebantur, eorum, qui de se statuebant,
humabantur corpora, manebant testamenta, pretium
festinandi. Sed Caesar missis ad senatum litteris
disseruit morem fuisse maioribus, quotiens diri-
merent amicitias, interdicere domo eumque finem
gratiae ponere: id se repetivisse in Labeone, atque
illum, quia male administratae provinciae aliorumque
criminum urgebatur,[1] culpam invidia velavisse,
frustra conterrita uxore, quam etsi nocentem periculi
tamen expertem fuisse. Mamercus dein Scaurus
rursum postulatur, insignis nobilitate et orandis

---

[1] urgebatur] arguebatur *Ernesti.*

[1] IV. 47 init.   [2] See chap. 9.

fluence, from which springs a young one, whose first care on reaching maturity is to bury his sire. Nor is that task performed at random, but, after raising a weight of myrrh and proving it by a far flight, so soon as he is a match for his burden and the course before him, he lifts up his father's corpse, conveys him to the Altar of the Sun, and consigns him to the flames.—The details are uncertain and heightened by fable; but that the bird occasionally appears in Egypt is unquestioned.

XXIX. But at Rome the carnage proceeded without a break; and Pomponius Labeo, whose governorship of Moesia I mentioned earlier,[1] opened his veins and bled to death, his example being emulated by his wife Paxaea. For these modes of dying were rendered popular by fear of the executioner and by the fact that a man legally condemned forfeited his estate and was debarred from burial; while he who passed sentence upon himself had his celerity so far rewarded that his body was interred and his will respected. The Caesar, however, in a letter addressed to the senate, explained that " it had been the custom of our ancestors, as often as they broke off a friendship, to interdict their house to the offender and to make this the close of amicable relations. To that method he had himself reverted in the case of Labeo: but Labeo, arraigned for maladministration of his province, as well as on other counts, had veiled his guilt by casting a slur upon his sovereign, while inspiring a baseless terror in his wife, who, though guilty had still stood in no danger." Then came the second impeachment[2] of Mamercus Scaurus, distinguished by birth and by his talent as an advocate, but in life a re-

causis, vita probrosus. Nihil hunc amicitia Seiani,
sed labefecit haud minus validum ad exitia Marconis
odium, qui easdem artis occultius exercebat;
detuleratque argumentum tragoediae a Scauro
scriptae, additis versibus, qui in Tiberium flecterentur:
verum ab Servilio et Cornelio accusatoribus adulterium Liviae, magorum sacra obiectabantur. Scaurus,
ut dignum veteribus Aemiliis, damnationem anteiit,[1]
hortante Sextia uxore, quae incitamentum mortis et
particeps fuit.

XXX. Ac tamen accusatores, si facultas incideret,
poenis adficiebantur, ut Servilius Corneliusque
perdito Scauro famosi, quia pecuniam a Vario Ligure
omittendae delationis ceperant, in insulas interdicto
igni atque aqua demoti sunt. Et Abudius Ruso
functus aedilitate, dum Lentulo Gaetulico, sub quo
legioni praefuerat, periculum facessit, quod is Seiani
filium generum destinasset, ultro damnatur atque
urbe exigitur. Gaetulicus ea tempestate superioris
Germaniae legiones curabat mirumque amorem
adsecutus erat, effusae clementiae, modicus severitate et proximo quoque exercitui per L. Apronium
socerum non ingratus. Unde fama constans ausum
mittere ad Caesarem litteras, adfinitatem sibi cum
Seiano haud sponte, sed consilio Tiberii coeptam;

---

[1] anteiit *Halm*: anteit.

---

[1] The subject, according to Dio (LVIII. 24), was Atreus
one of the objectionable lines a variant upon Eur. *Phoen.*
393 τὰς τῶν κρατούντων ἀμαθίας φέρειν χρεών, and the comment
of Tiberius :—Κἀγὼ οὖν αὐτὸν Αἴαντα ποιήσω.
[2] IV. 42 n.   [3] IV. 73.

probate. His fall was brought about, not by the friendship of Sejanus but by something equally potent for destruction, the hatred of Macro; who practised the same arts with superior secrecy, and had laid an information turning on the plot of a tragedy written by Scaurus; from which he appended a number of verses capable of being referred to Tiberius.[1] The charges, however, brought by the actual accusers, Servilius and Cornelius, were adultery with Livia and addiction to magic rites. Scaurus, adopting the course worthy of the old Aemilii, forestalled his condemnation, encouraged by his wife Sextia, who was the abettor and sharer of his death.

XXX. And yet the accusers, if opportunity arose, experienced the pains of the law. Thus Servilius and Cornelius, notorious for the ruin of Scaurus, were banned from fire and water and sequestrated in the islands for accepting the money of Varius Ligus as the price of dropping a delation. So, too, Abudius Ruso, a former aedile, while threatening a prosecution of Lentulus Gaetulicus,[2] under whom he had commanded a legion, on the ground that he had destined his daughter's hand for a son of Sejanus, was actually condemned himself and expelled from Rome. Gaetulicus at the time was in charge of the legions of Upper Germany, and had gained an extraordinary hold on their affections as an officer of large clemency, chary of severity, and, thanks to his father-in-law Lucius Apronius,[3] not unacceptable even to the next army. Hence the steady tradition that he ventured to send a letter to the Caesar, pointing out that " his connection with Sejanus was begun not by his own will but upon the advice of

perinde se quam Tiberium falli potuisse, neque
errorem eundem illi sine fraude, aliis exitio habendum. Sibi fidem integram et, si nullis insidiis
peteretur, mansuram; successorem non aliter quam
indicium mortis accepturum. Firmarent velut foedus, quo princeps ceterarum rerum poteretur, ipse
provinciam retineret. Haec, mira quamquam, fidem
ex eo trahebant, quod unus omnium Seiani adfinium
incolumis multaque gratia mansit, reputante Tiberio
publicum sibi odium, extremam aetatem magisque
fama quam vi stare res suas.

XXXI. C. Cestio M. Servilio consulibus nobiles
Parthi in urbem venere, ignaro rege Artabano. Is
metu Germanici fidus Romanis, aequabilis in suos,
mox superbiam in nos, saevitiam in populares sumpsit,
fretus bellis, quae secunda adversum circumiectas
nationes exercuerat, et senectutem Tiberii ut
inermem despiciens avidusque Armeniae, cui defuncto rege Artaxia Arsacen liberorum suorum
veterrimum inposuit, addita contumelia et missis,
qui gazam a Vonone relictam in Suria Ciliciaque
reposcerent; simul veteres Persarum ac Macedonum
terminos, seque invasurum possessa primum Cyro [1]

---

[1] primum Cyro *Baiter* : icyro.

---

[1] Partho-Armenian affairs were touched on in II. 1–4, 56,
58, 68, and doubtless in the lost part of Book V. The situation
is now roughly this :—In Rome are three members of the Parthian royal house—a son (Phraates) of Phraates IV, and two
grandsons (Tiridates and Meherdates). Of the other three sons
of Phraates IV, sent by their father as hostages, two have died
in Italy ; the eldest, Vonones, after a short tenure of the throne
first of Parthia, then of Armenia, has perished in an attempt
to escape from his detention in Cilicia.—In Parthia, the energetic half-Scythian king, Artabanus III, who ejected Vonones,
still reigns, but there is disaffection among the grandees.—In
Armenia, the Greek prince Zeno, raised to the throne by Ger-

Tiberius. It had been as easy for himself to be deceived as for Tiberius; and the same error should not be treated as harmless in one case and fatal in others. His loyalty was inviolate, and, if he was not treacherously attacked, would so remain: a successor he would not take otherwise than as indicative of his doom. Best would be to ratify a kind of treaty, by which the emperor would be supreme elsewhere, while he himself kept his province." The tale, though remarkable, drew credibility from the fact that, alone of all the family connections of Sejanus, Gaetulicus remained unscathed and high in favour; Tiberius reflecting that he was the object of public hatred, that his days were numbered, and that his fortunes stood more by prestige than by real strength.

XXXI. In the consulate of Gaius Cestius and A.V.C. 788 = A.D. 35 Marcus Servilius, a number of Parthian nobles made their way to the capital without the knowledge of King Artabanus.[1] That prince, loyal to Rome and temperate towards his subjects while he had Germanicus to fear, soon adopted an attitude of arrogance to ourselves and of cruelty to his countrymen. For he was emboldened by the campaigns he had successfully prosecuted against the surrounding nations; he disdained the old age of Tiberius as no longer fit for arms; and he coveted Armenia, on the throne of which (after the death of Artaxias) he installed his eldest son Arsaces, adding insult to injury by sending envoys to reclaim the treasure[2] left by Vonones in Syria and Cilicia. At the same time, he referred in boastful and menacing terms to the old boundaries of the Persian and Macedonian empires, and to his intention of seizing the territories held first by

manicus as Artaxias III, is dead, and has been replaced by the eldest son of Artabanus.   [2] Doubtless mentioned in Book V.

et post Alexandro per vaniloquentiam ac minas
iaciebat. Sed Parthis mittendi secretos nuntios
validissimus auctor fuit Sinnaces, insigni familia ac
perinde opibus, et proximus huic Abdus ademptae
virilitatis. Non despectum id apud barbaros ultroque
potentiam habet. Ii adscitis et aliis primoribus, quia
neminem gentis Arsacidarum summae rei inponere
poterant, interfectis ab Artabano plerisque aut
nondum adultis, Phraaten regis Phraatis filium Roma
poscebant: nomine tantum et auctore opus, [ut] [1]
sponte Caesaris ut genus Arsacis ripam apud
Euphratis cerneretur.

XXXII. Cupitum id Tiberio: ornat Phraaten
accingitque paternum ad fastigium, destinata retinens
consiliis et astu res externas moliri, arma procul
habere. Interea cognitis insidiis Artabanus tardari
metu, modo cupidine vindictae inardescere. Et
barbaris cunctatio servilis, statim exsequi regium
videtur: valuit tamen utilitas, ut Abdum specie
amicitiae vocatum ad epulas lento veneno inligaret,
Sinnacen dissimulatione ac donis, simul per negotia
moraretur. Et Phraates apud Suriam dum omisso
cultu Romano, cui per tot annos insueverat, instituta
Parthorum sumit, patriis moribus impar morbo

---

[1] [ut] *Joh. Mueller.*

Cyrus and afterwards by Alexander. The most influential advocate, however, for the despatch of the secret legation by the Parthians was Sinnaces, a man of noted family and corresponding wealth; and, next to him, the eunuch Abdus: for among barbarians that condition brings with it not contempt but actual power. Other magnates also were admitted into their counsels; then, as they were unable to bestow the crown on a scion of the Arsacidae, many of whom had been killed by Artabanus while others were under age, they demanded from Rome Phraates, the son of King Phraates:—" Only a name and a warrant were necessary—only that, with the Caesar's permission, a descendant of Arsaces should be seen upon the bank of Euphrates! "

XXXII. This was what Tiberius had desired; and, faithful to his rule of manipulating foreign affairs by policy and craft without a resort to arms, he gave Phraates the means and equipment for mounting his father's throne. Meanwhile, the conspiracy had come to the knowledge of Artabanus, who was alternately checked by his fears and inflamed by the lust of revenge. To barbarians hesitancy is the vice of a slave, immediate action the quality of a king: yet expediency so far prevailed that Abdus, under the cloak of friendship, was invited to a banquet and incapacitated by a slow poison, while Sinnaces was delayed by pretexts, by presents, and at the same time by continuous employment. In Syria, too, Phraates, who had discarded the Roman style of life, to which he had been habituated for years, in order to conform to Parthian usage, proved unequal to the customs of his fatherland, and was taken off by disease. Still,

absumptus est. Sed non Tiberius omisit incepta:
Tiridatem sanguinis eiusdem aemulum Artabano
reciperandaeque Armeniae Hiberum Mithridaten
deligit conciliatque fratri Pharasmani, qui gentile
imperium obtinebat; et cunctis, quae apud Orientem
parabantur, L. Vitellium praefecit. Eo de homine
haud sum ignarus sinistram in urbe famam, pleraque
foeda memorari, ceterum *in* regendis provinciis
prisca virtute egit. Unde regressus et formidine Gai
Caesaris, familiaritate Claudii turpe in servitium
mutatus exemplar apud posteros adulatorii dedecoris
habetur, cesseruntque prima postremis, et bona
iuventae senectus flagitiosa oblitteravit.

XXXIII. At ex regulis prior Mithridates Pharasmanem perpulit dolo et vi conatus suos iuvare,
repertisque corruptores ministros Arsacis multo auro
ad scelus cogunt; simul Hiberi magnis copiis Armeniam inrumpunt et urbe Artaxata potiuntur. Quae
postquam Artabano cognita. filium Oroden ultorem
parat; dat Parthorum[1] copias, mittit qui auxilia
mercede facerent: contra Pharasmanes adiungere
Albanos, accire Sarmatas, quorum sceptuchi utrimque
donis acceptis more gentico diversa induere. Sed

---

[1] Parthorum *Duebner*: Parthorumque *Med.—Probably a
genitive is lost, e.g.* Parth⟨orum Hyrcan⟩orumque. *Nipperdey
proposed :*—⟨Hyrcanorum⟩ Parthorumque.

---

[1] IV. 5 n.

[2] The notorious favourite of Claudius, consul in the previous
year, and father of the future emperor.

[3] Suetonius (*Vit.* 2) gives two or three instances. One was
deservedly famous :—*Huius et illa vox est,* ' *Saepe facias,*' *cum
saecularis ludos edenti Claudio gratularetur.*

[4] II. 56 n.

[5] IV. 5 n.

[6] A loose designation for various trans-Caucasian tribes.

Tiberius declined to renounce his plans. In Tiridates (a member of the same family) he found a competitor for Artabanus; as the recoverer of Armenia he selected the Iberian[1] Mithridates, and reconciled him to his brother Pharasmanes, who held the crown of their native country; and as director of the whole of his eastern projects he appointed Lucius Vitellius.[2] The man, I am aware, bore a sinister reputation at Rome, and is the subject of many a disgraceful tale; yet, as a governor of provinces, he acted with a primitive integrity. Then came his return; and through dread of Caligula and intimacy with Claudius he declined into repulsive servility, and is regarded to-day as a type of obsequious ignominy:[3] his beginnings have been forgotten in his end, the virtues of his youth have been obliterated by the scandals of his age.

XXXIII. Of the chieftains, Mithridates was the first to induce Pharasmanes to support his attempts by fraud and by force; and bribery agents were discovered, who at a heavy price in gold tempted the attendants of Arsaces to murder. Simultaneously the Iberians in great strength broke into Armenia and gained possession of the town of Artaxata.[4] As soon as the news reached Artabanus, he prepared his son Orodes for the part of avenger, gave him the Parthian forces, and sent men to hire auxiliary troops. Pharasmanes[5] replied by forming a league with the Albanians[5] and calling up the Sarmatians,[6] whose "wand-bearers,"[7] true to the national custom, accepted the gifts of both parties and enlisted in opposite camps. The Iberians, however, who con-

[7] Originally a name applied to the great eunuchs of the Persian Court. Its application to Scythian princelets is now attested by inscriptions.

Hiberi locorum potentes Caspia via Sarmatam in
Armenios raptim effundunt. At qui Parthis adventabant, facile arcebantur, cum alios incessus hostis
clausisset, unum reliquum mare inter et extremos
Albanorum montis aestas impediret, quia flatibus
etesiarum implentur vada: hibernus auster revolvit
fluctus pulsoque introrsus freto brevia litorum
nudantur.

XXXIV. Interim Oroden sociorum inopem auctus
auxilio Pharasmanes vocare ad pugnam et detrectan-
tem incessere, adequitare castris, infensare pabula;
ac saepe *in* modum obsidii stationibus cingebat,
donec Parthi contumeliarum insolentes circum-
sisterent regem, poscerent proelium. Atque illis
sola in equite vis: Pharasmanes et pedite valebat.
Nam Hiberi Albanique saltuosos locos incolentes
duritiae patientiaeque magis insuevere; feruntque
se Thessalis ortos, qua tempestate Iaso post avectam
Medeam genitosque ex ea liberos inanem mox
regiam Aeetae vacuosque Colchos repetivit. Multaque de nomine eius et oraclum Phrixi celebrant;
nec quisquam ariete sacrificaverit, credito vexisse
Phrixum, sive id animal seu navis insigne fuit.

---

[1] The misnamed ' Caspian Gate '—the famous Pass of
Dariel in the Terek valley, traversed to-day by the military
road between Tiflis and Vladikavkaz (Ordzhonikidze). It
was of sinister importance (*metuendaque portae Limina Cas-
piacae*, Stat. *Silv.* IV. 4) as the highroad for Sarmatian and,
later, Hunnish inroads into the plains of Parthia and the
eastern provinces of the empire: *cf.* Procop. *B.P.* I. 10;
B.G. IV. 3.—The *Caspiae Portae* proper lay far eastward, north
of Teheran.

[2] Between Derbend and Baku, on the west shore of the
Caspian.

[3] Σ Ap. Rh. I. 256, ἔνιοι δέ φασιν αὐτὸν ἐπὶ κριοπρῴρου
σκάφους πλεῦσαι. This convenient hypothesis was freely
applied by the rationalists to resolve such cases of conscience

trolled the important positions, hastily poured their own Sarmatians into Armenia by the Caspian Way:[1] those advancing to the support of the Parthians were held back without difficulty; for other passes had been closed by the enemy, and the one remaining,[2] between the sea and the extremity of the Albanian mountains, was impracticable in summer, as the shallows are flooded by the Etesian gales. In winter the waves are rolled back by southerly winds, and the recoil of the water inward leaves the beach uncovered.

XXXIV. Meanwhile Orodes was devoid of allies; and Pharasmanes, strong in his reinforcements, began to challenge him to engage and to harass him as he drew off, to ride up to his encampments and to ravage the foraging grounds. Frequently he encircled him with outposts almost in the manner of a formal siege; till the Parthians, unaccustomed to these insolences, surrounded the king and demanded battle. Their one strength lay in the cavalry: Pharasmanes was formidable also in infantry, for life in a highland district has trained the Iberians and Albanians to superior hardiness and endurance. They claim to have originated from Thessaly, at the time when Jason, after the departure of Medea with the children she had borne him, retraced his steps, a little later, to the empty palace of Aeëtes and the kingless realm of Colchis. His name survives in many of their institutions, which include an oracle of Phrixus; and, as the belief is held that Phrixus was carried by a ram (whether the word denotes the animal or the figurehead of a ship),[3] it is inadmissible to offer one in sacrifice.

as Europa's bull, Ganymede's eagle—though here the standard of a legion was an alternative—and the like.

Ceterum derecta utrimque acie Parthus imperium Orientis, claritudinem Arsacidarum contraque ignobilem Hiberum, mercennario milite disserebat; Pharasmanes integros semet a Parthico dominatu, quanto maiora peterent, plus decoris victores aut, si terga darent, flagitii atque periculi laturos; simul horridam suorum aciem, picta auro Medorum agmina, hinc viros, inde praedam ostendere.

XXXV. Enimvero apud Sarmatas non una vox ducis: se quisque stimulant, ne pugnam per sagittas sinerent: impetu et comminus praeveniendum. Variae hinc bellantium species, cum Parthus sequi vel fugere pari arte suetus distraheret turmas, spatium ictibus quaereret, Sarmatae omisso arcu, quo brevius valent, contis gladiisque ruerent; modo equestris proelii more frontis et tergi vices, aliquando ut conserta acie [1] corporibus et pulsu armorum pellerent pellerentur. Iamque et Albani Hiberique prensare, detrudere, ancipitem pugnam hostibus facere, quos super eques et propioribus vulneribus pedites adflictabant. Inter quae Pharasmanes Orodesque, dum strenuis adsunt aut dubitantibus subveniunt, conspicui eoque gnari, clamore telis equis concurrunt,

---

[1] acie *Heinsius*: acies.

---

[1] The Sarmatians. The tactics of these ancient Cossacks are shortly described at *Hist.* I. 79. The long sword and heavy cavalry pike—often used as a missile—were national weapons.

However, when the line of battle had been drawn up on either side, the Parthian dilated on the empire of the East and the lustre of the Arsacian house, as contrasted with the obscure Iberian and his hired soldiery: Pharasmanes called on his troops to remember that they had never felt the Parthian yoke; that the higher their emprize, the greater the honour they would reap from victory, the greater their disgrace and danger if they turned their backs. At the same time, he pointed to his own grim host and to the Median columns in their embroidery of gold—"men on the one hand, booty on the other."

XXXV. In the Sarmatian ranks, however, speech was not limited to a leader: man encouraged man not to permit a battle of archers; better to anticipate matters by a charge and a hand-to-hand struggle! The encounter, in consequence, wore a variety of aspects. For the Parthians, habituated to pursue or flee with equal art, spread out their squadrons and manoeuvred for room for their flights of missiles: the Sarmatians, ignoring their shorter-ranged bows, rushed on with pike and sword. At times, advance and retreat alternated in the traditional style of a cavalry engagement: then, as though in a locked line of battle, the combatants struggled breast to breast, with a clash of steel, repulsing and repulsed. Then came the Albanians and Iberians, gripping the enemy, unsaddling him, and placing him in double jeopardy between the horsemen [1] striking from above and the infantry dealing closer wounds below. In the meantime, Pharasmanes and Orodes were carrying support to the resolute or succour to the wavering. Conspicuous figures, they recognized each other: a shout, an exchange of javelins, and

215

instantius Pharasmanes; nam vulnus per galeam adegit. Nec iterare valuit, praelatus equo et fortissimis satellitum protegentibus saucium: fama tamen occisi falso credita exterruit Parthos victoriam-que concessere.

XXXVI. Mox Artabanus tota mole regni ultum iit. Peritia locorum ab Hiberis melius pugnatum; nec ideo abscedebat, ni contractis legionibus Vitellius et subdito rumore, tamquam Mesopotamiam inva-surus, metum Romani belli fecisset. Tum omissa Armenia versaeque Artabani res, inliciente Vitellio de-sererent regem saevum in pace et adversis proeliorum exitiosum. Igitur Sinnaces, quem antea infensum memoravi, patrem Abdagaesen aliosque occultos consilii et tunc continuis cladibus promptiores ad defectionem trahit, adfluentibus paulatim, qui metu magis quam benevolentia subiecti repertis auctoribus sustulerant animum. Nec iam aliud Artabano reliquum, quam si qui externorum corpori custodes aderant, suis quisque sedibus extorres, quis neque boni intellectus neque mali cura, sed mercede aluntur ministri sceleribus. His adsumptis in longinqua et contermina Scythiae fugam maturavit, spe auxilii,

---

[1] They had been in Armenia for the better part of a year.

[2] East of the Caspian. At the southern extremity lay the Hyrcanians, and immediately to their north the Dahae, among whom Artabanus' youth was passed (II. 3). Carmania—the name survives in that of the desert of Kirmân—touched the Persian gulf.

they spurred to the charge—Pharasmanes with the
greater fury, as he wounded his opponent through
the helmet. He failed to repeat the blow, his horse
carrying him too far past while the bravest of his
guards interposed to protect the wounded prince.
Still, a falsely credited report of his death demoralized
the Parthians, and they conceded the victory.

XXXVI. It was not long before Artabanus sought
his revenge with the full powers of his empire.
The Iberians, with their knowledge of the country,[1]
had the better of the campaign; but, in spite of that
fact, he showed no signs of withdrawal, had not
Vitellius, by assembling the legions and circulating
a report that he was on the point of invading Armenia, inspired him with fears of a Roman war.
There followed the evacuation of Armenia and the
collapse of Artabanus' fortunes, Vitellius tempting
his subjects to abandon a king merciless in peace
and fatally unfortunate in the field. Sinnaces, therefore, whose hostility, as I have mentioned, was of
earlier date, induced his father Abdagaeses, to revolt,
along with others, accessory to the project, and now
the readier for action owing to the series of reverses;
and these were joined by a gradual stream of recruits,
whose submission had been due more to fear than to
goodwill, and whose spirit had risen with the discovery of responsible leaders. Nothing now remained to Artabanus but the few foreigners acting
as his body-guard—homeless and landless men,
members of a class neither comprehending good
nor regarding evil but feed and fed as the agents of
crime. Taking these with him, he hurriedly fled to
the remote districts adjoining Scythia;[2] where
he hoped that his marriage connections with the

quia Hyrcanis Carmaniisque per adfinitatem innexus
erat: atque interim posse Parthos absentium aequos
praesentibus mobilis, ad paenitentiam mutari.

XXXVII. At Vitellius profugo Artabano et flexis
ad novum regem popularium animis, hortatus
Tiridaten parata capessere, robur legionum sociorumque ripam ad Euphratis ducit. Sacrificantibus,
cum hic more Romano suovetaurilia daret, ille
equum placando amni adornasset, nuntiavere accolae
Euphraten nulla imbrium vi sponte et inmensum
attolli, simul albentibus spumis in modum diadematis
sinuare orbes, auspicium prosperi transgressus.
Quidam callidius interpretabantur, initia conatus
secunda neque diuturna, quia eorum, quae terra
caelove portenderentur, certior fides, fluminum
instabilis natura simul ostenderet omina raperetque.

Sed ponte navibus effecto tramissoque exercitu
primus Ornospades multis equitum milibus in castra
venit, exul quondam et Tiberio, cum Delmaticum
bellum conficeret, haud inglorius auxiliator eoque
civitate Romana donatus, mox repetita amicitia
regis multo apud eum honore, praefectus campis,
qui Euphrate et Tigre [1] inclutis amnibus circumflui

---

[1] Tigre] Tigri *Halm* (as at XII. 13).

---

[1] A purificatory offering of a boar, ram, and bull on behalf
of the army.

[2] The principal Persian victim, usually offered to the Sun
(Xen. *An.* IV. 5; Just. I. 10); to the Strymon, however, in
Hdt. VII. 113.

[3] The white band—hence *albentibus spumis*—round the
tiara of an oriental monarch.

[4] The great rebellion, crushed by Tiberius, after extraordinary efforts, in 6–9 A.D.

Hyrcanians and Carmanians would find him allies: in the interval, the Parthians, tolerant of princes when absent and fickle to them when present, might turn to the ways of penitence.

XXXVII. But Vitellius, now that Artabanus was in flight and the sentiments of his countrymen were inclining to a change of sovereigns, advised Tiridates to embrace the opportunity presented, and marched the flower of his legions and auxiliaries to the bank of the Euphrates. During the sacrifice, while the Roman was paying the national offering [1] to Mars and the Parthian had prepared a horse [2] to placate the river, word was brought by the people of the neighbourhood that, without any downpour of rain, the Euphrates was rising spontaneously and to a remarkable height: at the same time, the whitening foam was wreathing itself into circles after the fashion of a diadem [3]—an omen of a happy crossing. Others gave a more skilled interpretation: the first results of the venture would be favourable, but fleeting; for the presages given by the earth or the sky had a surer warranty, but rivers, unstable by nature, exhibited an omen, and in the same instant swept it away.

However, when a bridge of boats had been constructed and the army taken over, the first man to appear in the camp was Ornospades at the head of several thousand cavalry. Once an exile and a not inglorious coadjutor of Tiberius when he was stamping out the Dalmatic war,[4] he had been rewarded by a grant of Roman citizenship: later, he had regained the friendship of his king, stood high in his favour, and held the governorship of the plains, which, encircled by the famous streams of Tigris

Mesopotamiae nomen acceperunt. Neque multo post Sinnaces auget copias, et columen partium Abdagaeses gazam et paratus regios adicit. Vitellius ostentasse Romana arma satis ratus monet Tiridaten primoresque, hunc, Phraatis avi,[1] altoris Caesaris quae [2] utrobique pulchra meminerit, illos, obsequium in regem, reverentiam in nos, decus quisque suum et fidem retinerent. Exim cum legionibus in Suriam remeavit.

XXXVIII. Quae duabus aestatibus gesta coniunxi, quo requiesceret animus a domesticis malis; non enim Tiberium, quamquam triennio post caedem Seiani, quae ceteros mollire solent, tempus preces satias mitigabant, quin incerta vel abolita pro gravissimis et recentibus puniret. Eo metu Fulcinius Trio, ingruentis accusatores haud perpessus, supremis tabulis multa et atrocia in Macronem ac praecipuos libertorum Caesaris conposuit, ipsi fluxam senio mentem et continuo abscessu velut exilium obiectando. Quae ab heredibus occultata recitari Tiberius iussit, patientiam libertatis alienae ostentans et contemptor suae infamiae, an scelerum Seiani diu nescius mox quoquo modo dicta vulgari malebat veritatisque, cui adulatio officit, per probra

---

[1] avi *Becher* : aviut *Med.*, avi et *Rhenanus, vulg.*
[2] quae] quaeque *Neue, vulg.*

---

[1] The narrative of the second is not complete, and is taken up in chap. 41.
[2] Oct. 18, 31 A.D.   [3] V. 11; VI. 4.

and Euphrates, have received the name of Mesopotamia. Before long, Tiridates' forces were augmented by Sinnaces; and Abdagaeses, the pillar of his cause, added the treasure and appurtenances of the crown. Vitellius, persuaded that to have displayed the Roman arms was enough, bestowed his advice on Tiridates and the nobles: the former was to remember his grandfather Phraates, his foster-father the Caesar, and the great qualities of both; the latter, to retain their obedience to the king, their respect to ourselves, their personal honour and good faith. He then returned with the legions to Syria.

XXXVIII. I have conjoined the events of two summers,[1] in order to allow the mind some respite from domestic horrors. For, notwithstanding the three years elapsed since the execution of Sejanus,[2] not time nor prayers nor satiety, influences that soften other breasts, could mollify Tiberius or arrest his policy of avenging half-proved or forgotten delinquencies as heinous and freshly committed crimes. This alarmed Fulcinius Trio;[3] and, instead of awaiting passively the imminent onslaught of the accusers, he drew up in his last will a long and appalling indictment of Macro and the chief imperial freedmen, and taunted their master with the mental decrepitude of age and the virtual exile of his continuous absence. The heirs would have suppressed the passage: Tiberius commanded it to be read, in token of his tolerance of freedom in others and in contempt of his own ill fame; unless, possibly, he had so long been unaware of the crimes of Sejanus that he now preferred to have publicity given to attacks, however worded, and by insult, if not otherwise, to become acquainted with that truth

saltem gnarus fieri. Isdem diebus Granius Marcianus senator, a C. Graccho maiestatis postulatus, vim vitae suae attulit, Tariusque Gratianus praetura functus lege eadem extremum ad supplicium damnatus.

XXXIX. Nec dispares Trebelleni [1] Rufi et Sextii Paconiani exitus : nam Trebellenus [1] sua manu cecidit, Paconianus in carcere ob carmina illic in principem factitata strangulatus est. Haec Tiberius non mari, ut olim, divisus neque per longinquos nuntios accipiebat, sed urbem iuxta, eodem ut die vel noctis interiectu litteris consulum rescriberet, quasi aspiciens undantem per domos sanguinem aut manus carnificum.

Fine anni Poppaeus Sabinus concessit vita, modicus originis, principum amicitia consulatum ac triumphale decus adeptus maximisque provinciis per quattuor et viginti annos inpositus, nullam ob eximiam artem, sed quod par negotiis neque supra erat.

XL. Q. Plautius Sex. Papinius consules sequuntur. Eo anno neque quod L. Aruseius . . .[2] morte adfecti forent, adsuetudine malorum ut atrox advertebatur, sed exterruit quod Vibulenus Agrippa eques Romanus cum perorassent accusatores, in ipsa curia depromptum sinu venenum hausit, prolapsusque ac mori-

---

[1] Trebelleni . . . Trebellenus *Andresen* : trebellieni . . . trebellienus.

[2] . . . *Doederlein*.

---

[1] II. 67. [2] VI. 3. [3] IV. 46 n.

[4] Probably the accuser of L. Arruntius (see chap. 7). In that case, the lacuna must have contained the mention of a favour shown to him (presumably a remission of his penalty), then a second *neque quod*, followed by the names of at least two reputable persons put to death.

which adulation stifles.—In these same days, the senator Granius Marcianus, accused of treason by Gaius Gracchus, took his own life; and Tarius Gratianus, who had held the praetorship, was sentenced under the same law to the final penalty.

XXXIX. Trebellenus Rufus[1] and Sextius Paconianus[2] made not dissimilar endings: for Trebellenus fell by his own hand; Paconianus was strangled in prison for verses which he had there indited against the sovereign.—These tidings Tiberius now received, not as formerly across the dividing sea nor by messengers from afar, but hard under the walls of Rome, where, on the same day or with the interval of a night, he could pen his answer to the consular reports and all but rest his eyes upon the blood that streamed in the houses of his victims, or upon the handiwork of his executioners.

At the close of the year, Poppaeus Sabinus[3] breathed his last. Of modest origin, he had by the friendship of emperors attained a consulate and triumphal honours, and for twenty-four years had governed the great provinces, thanks to no shining ability but to the fact that he was adequate to his business, and no more.

XL. There followed the consulate of Quintus Plautius and Sextus Papinius. In this year, the horrors had become too familiar for either the ⟨pardon⟩ of Lucius Aruseius[4] or the infliction of the death penalty on . . . and . . . to be noticed as an atrocity; but there was a moment of terror when, in the senate-house itself, the Roman knight Vibulenus Agrippa, after his accusers had closed their case, drew poison from the folds of his robe, swallowed it, and, as he fell dying, was rushed to the dungeon

A.v.c. 789 = A.D. 36

bundus festinatis lictorum manibus in carcerem raptus est, faucesque iam exanimis laqueo vexatae. Ne Tigranes quidem, Armenia quondam potitus ac tunc reus, nomine regio supplicia civium effugit. At C. Galba consularis et duo Blaesi voluntario exitu cecidere, Galba tristibus Caesaris litteris provinciam sortiri prohibitus : Blaesis sacerdotia, integra eorum domo destinata, convulsa distulerat, tunc ut vacua contulit in alios, quod signum mortis intellexere et exsecuti sunt. Et Aemilia Lepida, quam iuveni Druso nuptam rettuli, crebris criminibus maritum insectata, quamquam intestabilis, tamen impunita agebat, dum superfuit pater Lepidus : post a delatoribus corripitur ob servum adulterum, nec dubitabatur de flagitio : ergo omissa defensione finem vitae sibi posuit.

XLI. Per idem tempus Cietarum natio Cappadoci Archelao subiecta, quia nostrum in modum deferre census, pati tributa adigebatur, in iuga Tauri montis abscessit locorumque ingenio sese contra imbelles regis copias tutabatur, donec M. Trebellius legatus, a Vitellio praeside Suriae cum quattuor milibus legionariorum et delectis auxiliis missus, duos collis, quos barbari insederant (minori Cadra, alteri Davara

---

[1] Tigranes IV (a grandson of Herod the Great), whose brief reign is omitted by Tacitus at II. 4, but mentioned in the *Monumentum Ancyranum* and by Josephus (*A.J.* XVIII. 5, 4).

[2] Elder brother of the future emperor; consul in 22 A.D. (III. 52), and ruined by extravagance (Suet. *Galb.* 3).

[3] Sons of Sejanus' uncle.

[4] In a lost passage. She was the daughter of Marcus Lepidus (III. 32), not of Manius (chap. 5 n.).

[5] On the coast of Cilicia Trachea.

by quick-handed lictors, and his throat—though he had now ceased to breathe—tormented by a halter. Not even Tigranes,[1] once monarch of Armenia and now a defendant, was preserved by his royal title from the doom of Roman citizens. On the other hand, the consular Gaius Galba,[2] with the two Blaesi,[3] perished by self-slaughter. Galba had been excluded from the allotment of a province by an ominous epistle from the Caesar: in the case of the Blaesi, the priesthoods destined for them before the family lost its head had been deferred by Tiberius after the blow fell; he now treated them as vacant and assigned them to others—an intimation of death which was understood and acted upon. So also with Aemilia Lepida, whose marriage to the young Drusus I have already recorded.[4] After persecuting her husband with a succession of calumnies, she lived, detested but unpunished, while her father Lepidus survived; then the informers attacked her on the ground of adultery with a slave. Of her guilt no doubt was entertained; she therefore waived her defence and put an end to her life.

XLI. About this date, the Cietae,[5] a tribe subject to Archelaus of Cappadocia, pressed to conform with Roman usage by making a return of their property and submitting to a tribute, migrated to the heights of the Tauric range, and, favoured by the nature of the country, held their own against the unwarlike forces of the king; until the legate Marcus Trebellius, despatched by Vitellius from his province of Syria with four thousand legionaries and a picked force of auxiliaries, drew his lines round the two hills which the barbarians had occupied (the smaller is known as Cadra, the other as Davara) and reduced

nomen est), operibus circumdedit et erumpere ausos
ferro, ceteros siti ad deditionem coegit.

At Tiridates volentibus Parthis Nicephorium et
Anthemusiada ceterasque urbes, quae Macedonibus [1]
sitae Graeca vocabula usurpant, Halumque et
Artemitam Parthica oppida recepit, certantibus
gaudio qui Artabanum Scythas inter eductum ob
saevitiam exsecrati come Tiridatis ingenium Romanas
per artis sperabant.

XLII. Plurimum adulationis Seleucenses induere,
civitas potens, saepta muris neque in barbarum
corrupta, sed conditoris Seleuci retinens. Trecenti
opibus aut sapientia delecti ut senatus, sua populo
vis. Et quotiens concordes agunt, spernitur Parthus :
ubi dissensere, dum sibi quisque contra aemulos
subsidium vocant, accitus in partem adversum
omnes valescit. Id nuper acciderat Artabano
regnante, qui plebem primoribus tradidit ex suo usu :
nam populi imperium iuxta libertatem, paucorum
dominatio regiae libidini propior est. Tum adven-
tantem Tiridaten extollunt veterum regum honoribus
et quos recens aetas largius invenit ; simul probra
in Artabanum fundebant, materna origine Arsaciden,
cetera degenerem. Tiridates rem Seleucensem po-

---

[1] Macedonibus] ⟨a⟩ Macedonibus *Faërnus* (*cf.* III. 38).

---

[1] The narrative reverts to the end of chap. 37.

[2] Both towns were in Mesopotamia; Artemita—and, doubtless, Halus—lay across the Tigris.

[3] One of the great cities of the ancient world, built on the
western bank of the Tigris, some twenty miles south of Bagdad,
and facing its Parthian rival, Ctesiphon, across the stream.
Its decline dates from its sack and burning by the troops of
Avidius Cassius (165 A.D.).

them to surrender—those who ventured to make a sally, by the sword, the others by thirst.

Meanwhile,[1] with the acquiescence of the Parthians, Tiridates took over Nicephorium, Anthemusias,[2] and the other cities of Macedonian foundation, carrying Greek names, together with the Parthic towns of Halus and Artemita; enthusiasm running high, as Artabanus, with his Scythian training, had been execrated for his cruelty and it was hoped that Roman culture had mellowed the character of Tiridates.

XLII. The extreme of adulation was shown by the powerful community of Seleucia,[3] a walled town which, faithful to the memory of its founder Seleucus,[4] has not degenerated into barbarism. Three hundred members, chosen for wealth or wisdom, form a senate: the people has its own prerogatives. So long as the two orders are in unison, the Parthian is ignored: if they clash, each calls in aid against its rival; and the alien, summoned to rescue a part, overpowers the whole. This had happened lately in the reign of Artabanus, who consulted his own ends by sacrificing the populace to the aristocrats: for supremacy of the people is akin to freedom; between the domination of a minority and the whim of a monarch the distance is small. They now celebrated the arrival of Tiridates with the honours paid to the ancient kings, along with the innovations of which a later age has been more lavish: at the same time, they poured abuse on Artabanus as an Arsacid on the mother's side, but otherwise of ignoble blood.—Tiridates handed over the government of Seleucia to

[4] The marshal of Alexander, founder of the dynasty bearing his name.

pulo permittit. Mox consultans, quonam die sollemnia regni capesseret, litteras Phraatis et Hieronis, qui validissimas praefecturas optinebant, accipit, brevem moram precantium. Placitumque opperiri viros praepollentis, atque interim Ctesiphon sedes imperii petita: sed ubi diem ex die prolatabant, multis coram et adprobantibus Surena patrio more Tiridaten insigni regio evinxit.

XLIII. Ac si statim interiora ceterasque nationes petivisset, oppressa cunctantium dubitatio et omnes in unum cedebant: adsidendo castellum, in quod pecuniam et paelices Artabanus contulerat, dedit spatium exuendi pacta. Nam Phraates et Hiero et si qui alii delectum capiendo diademati diem haut concelebraverant, pars metu, quidam invidia in Abdagaesen, qui tum aula et novo rege potiebatur, ad Artabanum vertere; isque in Hyrcanis repertus est, inluvie obsitus et alimenta arcu expediens. Ac primo tamquam dolus pararetur territus, ubi data fides reddendae dominationi venisse, adlevatur animum et quae repentina mutatio exquirit. Tum Hiero pueritiam Tiridatis increpat, neque penes Arsaciden imperium, sed inane nomen apud inbellem externa mollitia, vim in Abdagaesis domo.

---

[1] Opposite Seleucia; originally a village used as a royal winter-residence διὰ τὸ εὐαέριον (Strab. 743), then the capital both of the Arsacids and of the Sassanids. It sank into obscurity after its capture and sack by Omar (March, 637 A.D.).

[2] The hereditary commander-in-chief, the name being at once personal and official, like the Roman *Caesar* or the Parthian *Arsaces*.

the democracy; then, as he was debating what day to fix for his formal assumption of sovereignty, he received letters from Phraates and Hiero, holders of the two most powerful satrapies, asking for a short postponement. It was decided to wait for men of their high importance, and in the interval a move was made to the seat of government at Ctesiphon.[1] However, as day after day found them still procrastinating, the Surena,[2] before an applauding multitude, fastened, in the traditional style, the royal diadem upon the brows of Tiridates.

XLIII. And, had he marched at once upon the interior and the remaining tribes, he must have overborne the doubts of the hesitant, and the nation would have been his own; but, by investing the fortress in which Artabanus had bestowed his money and his harem, he allowed a breathing-space in which agreements could be repudiated. For Phraates and Hiero, with others who had taken no share in the solemnities of the day fixed for the assumption of the diadem, some in fear, a few in jealousy of Abdagaeses (now master of the court and the newly crowned king), passed over to Artabanus; who was discovered in Hyrcania, a filth-covered figure, procuring his daily bread by his bow. His first terrified expectation of treachery gave way to relief on a solemn assurance that they had come to restore him to his throne, and he inquired the reason for the sudden change. Hiero then inveighed against the boyish years of Tiridates:—" It was no Arsacid that held sway: the unsubstantial title was born by a weakling whose foreign effeminacy unfitted him for the sword; the power was vested in the house of Abdagaeses."

XLIV. Sensit vetus regnandi falsos in amore odia
non fingere. Nec ultra moratus, quam dum Scytha-
rum auxilia conciret, pergit properus et praeveniens
inimicorum astus, amicorum paenitentiam; neque
exuerat paedorem, ut vulgum miseratione adverteret.
Non fraus, non preces, nihil omissum, quo ambiguos
inliceret, prompti firmarentur. Iamque multa manu
propinqua[1] Seleuciae adventabat, cum Tiridates
simul fama atque ipso Artabano perculsus distrahi
consiliis, iret contra an bellum cunctatione tractaret.
Quibus proelium et festinati casus placebant, disiectos et longinquitate itineris fessos ne animo quidem
satis ad obsequium coaluisse disserunt, proditores
nuper hostisque eius, quem rursum foveant. Verum
Abdagaeses regrediendum in Mesopotamiam cense-
bat, ut amne obiecto, Armeniis interim Elymaeisque
et ceteris a tergo excitis, aucti copiis socialibus et
quas dux Romanus misisset fortunam temptarent.
Ea sententia valuit, quia plurima auctoritas penes
Abdagaesen et Tiridates ignavus ad pericula erat.
Sed fugae specie discessum; ac principio a gente
Arabum facto ceteri domos abeunt vel in castra Artabani, donec Tiridates cum paucis in Suriam revectus
pudore proditionis omnis exsolvit.

---

¹ propinqua] propinquans *Madvig.*

---

¹ The Tigris.
² Presumably the people at the head of the Persian Gulf;
but, in that case, *a tergo* must be due to a misapprehension.
³ From Osroëne in N. Mesopotamia: cf. XII. 12 n.

XLIV. The veteran monarch realized that, if they were false in love, they were not hypocritical in their hatreds. Waiting only to collect auxiliaries in Scythia, he took the field with a speed that baffled the machinations of his foes and the vacillation of his friends: his squalor he retained as likely to attract the multitude through their sympathies. Neither fraud nor entreaty—nothing that could entice the doubtful or confirm the resolute—was neglected. He was already nearing the outskirts of Seleucia at the head of a numerous force, when Tiridates, unnerved at once by news of Artabanus and by Artabanus in person, began to waver between the two plans of a counter-advance or a strategy of delay. The partisans of battle and a quick decision of their fate argued that not even in thought had those scattered and wayworn bands coalesced into a loyal whole, betrayers and enemies as they had been but yesterday of the very prince whose cause they were again espousing. Abdagaeses, however, advised a return to Mesopotamia; where, behind the barrier of the river,[1] they might in the interval raise the Armenians, Elymaeans[2] and other nations in their rear; then, reinforced by the contingents of their allies and by any which the Roman commander might have despatched, submit their fortunes to the test. This view prevailed, as the dominant influence was that of Abdagaeses and Tiridates had little appetite for danger. But the withdrawal was effected in the style of a flight, and, with the Arabian tribesmen[3] setting the example, the rest left for their homes or the camp of Artabanus; till at last Tiridates with a few attendants retraced his way to Syria and freed all from the disgrace of desertion.

XLV. Idem annus gravi igne urbem adfecit,[1]
deusta parte circi, quae Aventino contigua, ipsoque
Aventino; quod damnum Caesar ad gloriam vertit
exsolutis domuum et insularum pretiis. Miliens
sestertium in munificentia ea[2] conlocatum, tanto
acceptius in vulgum, quanto modicus privatis aedi-
ficationibus ne publice quidem nisi duo opera struxit,
templum Augusto et scaenam Pompeiani theatri;
eaque perfecta, contemptu ambitionis an per senectutem, haud dedicavit. Sed aestimando cuiusque
detrimento quattuor progeneri Caesaris, Cn. Domitius, Cassius Longinus, M. Vinicius, Rubellius
Blandus delecti additusque nominatione consulum
P. Petronius. Et pro ingenio cuiusque quaesiti
decretique in principem honores; quos omiserit
receperitve, in incerto fuit ob propinquum vitae
finem. Neque enim multo post supremi Tiberio
consules, Cn. Acerronius C. Pontius, magistratum
occepere, nimia iam potentia Macronis, qui gratiam
Gai Caesaris numquam sibi neglectam acrius in dies
fovebat impuleratque post mortem Claudiae, quam
nuptam ei rettuli, uxorem suam Enniam imitando
amorem iuvenem inlicere pactoque matrimonii

---

[1] adfecit *Wurm* : adficit.　　　　　⟨ea⟩ *Otto*.

---

[1] The Circus Maximus, in the hollow (*vallis Murcia*) between
the Palatine and Aventine.
[2] IV. 7 n.—The *scaena* had been destroyed by fire in 22 A.D.
(III. 72).
[3] IV. 75; VI. 15, 27.
[4] At chap. 20 above.
[5] Dio agrees (LVIII. 28); Philo, after enlarging on Macro's
intrigues, asserts his innocence in this particular (t. II. 551 M.);
Suetonius attributes the advances to Gaius (*Cal.* 12).

XLV. The same year saw the capital visited by a
serious fire, the part of the Circus[1] adjoining the
Aventine being burnt down along with the Aventine
itself: a disaster which the Caesar converted to his
own glory by paying the full value of the mansions
and tenement-blocks destroyed. One hundred
million sesterces were invested in this act of munificence, which came the more acceptably to the
multitude that he was far from extravagant in build-
ing on his own behalf; whilst, even on the public
account, the only two works he erected were the
temple of Augustus and the stage of Pompey's
theatre,[2] and in each case he was either too scornful
of popularity or too old to dedicate them after
completion. To estimate the losses of the various
claimants, four husbands of the Caesar's grand-
daughters[3] were appointed: Gnaeus Domitius,
Cassius Longinus, Marcus Vinicius, and Rubellius
Blandus. Publius Petronius was added by nomina-
tion of the consuls. Honours varying with the
ingenuity of their authors were invented and voted
to the sovereign. Which of these he rejected or
accepted remained unknown, since the end of his
days was at hand.

For shortly afterwards the last consuls of Tiberius, A.V.C. 790 =
Gnaeus Acerronius and Gaius Petronius, inaugurated A.D. 37
their term of office. By this time the influence of
Macro exceeded all bounds. Never careless of the
good graces of Gaius Caesar, he was now courting
them with daily increasing energy; and after the
death of Claudia, whose espousal to the prince has
been mentioned earlier,[4] he had induced his wife
Ennia to captivate the youth by a mockery of love
and to bind him by a promise of marriage.[5] Caligula

vincire, nihil abnuentem, dum dominationis apisceretur; nam etsi commotus ingenio simulationum tamen falsa in sinu avi perdidicerat.

XLVI. Gnarum hoc principi, eoque dubitavit de tradenda re publica, primum inter nepotes, quorum Druso genitus sanguine et caritate propior, sed nondum pubertatem ingressus, Germanici filio robur iuventae, vulgi studia, eaque apud avum odii causa. Etiam de Claudio agitanti, quod is conposita aetate bonarum artium cupiens erat, inminuta mens eius obstitit. Sin extra domum successor quaereretur, ne memoria Augusti, ne nomen Caesarum in ludibria et contumelias verterent, metuebat: quippe illi non perinde curae gratia praesentium quam in posteros ambitio. Mox incertus animi, fesso corpore, consilium, cui impar erat, fato permisit, iactis tamen vocibus, per quas intellegeretur providus futurorum; namque Macroni non abdita ambage occidentem ab eo deseri, orientem spectari exprobravit. Et Gaio Caesari, forte orto sermone L. Sullam inridenti, omnia Sullae vitia et nullam eiusdem virtutem habiturum praedixit. Simul crebris cum lacrimis minorem ex nepotibus conplexus, truci alterius vultu, "Occides hunc tu" inquit "et te alius." Sed gravescente valetudine nihil e libidinibus omittebat,

---

[1] Tiberius Gemellus, the survivor of the twins (II. 84); born in 19 A.D.

[2] Gaius, born in 12 A.D.

[3] He was in his forty-sixth year.

[4] Tiberius Gemellus.

[5] The first part of the prediction was fulfilled by Caligula within a year, the second by Cassius Chaerea in 41 A.D.

objected to no conditions, provided that he could reach the throne: for, wild though his temper was, he had none the less, at his grandfather's knee, mastered in full the arts of hypocrisy.

XLVI. This the emperor knew; and he hesitated therefore with regard to the succession—first between his grandchildren. Of these, the issue of Drusus [1] was the nearer to him in blood and by affection, but had not yet entered the years of puberty: the son of Germanicus [2] possessed the vigour of early manhood, but also the affections of the multitude—and that, with his grandsire, was a ground of hatred. Even Claudius with his settled years [3] and aspirations to culture came under consideration: the obstacle was his mental imbecility. Yet, if a successor were sought outside the imperial family, he dreaded that the memory of Augustus—the name of the Caesars— might be turned to derision and to contempt. For the care of Tiberius was not so much to enjoy popularity in the present as to court the approval of posterity. Soon, mentally irresolute, physically outworn, he left to fate a decision beyond his competence; though remarks escaped him which implied a foreknowledge of the future. For, with an allusion not difficult to read, he upbraided Macro with forsaking the setting and looking to the rising sun; and to Caligula, who in some casual conversation was deriding Lucius Sulla, he made the prophecy that he would have all the vices of Sulla with none of the Sullan virtues. At the same time, with a burst of tears, he embraced the younger of his grandsons; [4] then, at the lowering looks of the other:—" Thou wilt slay him," he said, " and another thee." [5] Yet, in defiance of his failing health,

in patientia firmitudinem simulans solitusque eludere medicorum artes atque eos, qui post tricesimum aetatis annum ad internoscenda corpori suo utilia vel noxia alieni consilii indigerent.

XLVII. Interim Romae futuris etiam post Tiberium caedibus semina iaciebantur. Laelius Balbus Acutiam, P. Vitellii quondam uxorem, maiestatis postulaverat; qua damnata cum praemium accusatori decerneretur, Iunius Otho tribunus plebei intercessit, unde illis odia, mox Othoni exitium.[1] Dein multorum amoribus famosa Albucilla, cui matrimonium cum Satrio Secundo coniurationis indice fuerat, defertur inpietatis in principem; conectebantur ut conscii et adulteri eius Cn. Domitius, Vibius Marsus, L. Arruntius. De claritudine Domitii supra memoravi; Marsus quoque vetustis honoribus et inlustris studiis erat. Sed testium interrogationi, tormentis servorum Macronem praesedisse commentarii ad senatum missi ferebant, nullaeque in eos imperatoris litterae suspicionem dabant, invalido ac fortasse ignaro ficta pleraque ob inimicitias Macronis notas in Arruntium.

XLVIII. Igitur Domitius defensionem meditans,

---

[1] exitium *Nipperdey* : exilium.

---

[1] Plutarch twice makes the figure sixty (*Praec. san. tuend.* 136 D, *An seni gerenda resp.* 794 B).

[2] I. 70 n.; V. 8.

[3] No doubt the son of the schoolmaster-praetor of III. 66.

[4] The *novissimum consilium* (chap. 8) of Sejanus—to assassinate Tiberius and Caligula and seize the empire. Details are scanty and uncertain; but, as the plot was apparently disclosed to Tiberius by Claudius' mother Antonia (Jos. *A.J.* XVIII. 6, 6), it is conjectured that Satrius (IV. 34) supplied her with the information which she forwarded to Capreae.

he relinquished no detail of his libertinism: he was striving to make endurance pass for strength; and he had always had a sneer for the arts of the physicians, and for men who, after thirty [1] years of life, needed the counsel of a stranger in order to distinguish things salutary to their system from things deleterious.

XLVII. Meanwhile, at Rome the seeds were being sown of bloodshed destined to outlast Tiberius. Laelius Balbus had brought a charge of treason against Acutia, formerly the wife of Publius Vitellius.[2] After her condemnation, a reward was on the point of being decreed to the accuser, when Junius Otho,[3] the plebeian tribune, opposed his veto: whence a feud between the pair, terminated later by the destruction of Otho. Next, Albucilla, made notorious by a multitude of lovers, and at one time married to Satrius Secundus, the divulger of the plot,[4] was arraigned for a breach of piety towards the sovereign: associated in the indictment as her accomplices and adulterers were Gnaeus Domitius, Vibius Marsus, Lucius Arruntius. On the nobility of Domitius I have touched above;[5] Marsus also could claim ancestral honours as well as some distinction in letters.[6] But the documents forwarded to the senate stated that Macro had presided at the examination of witnesses and the torture of the slaves; and the absence of the emperor's usual letter against the accused gave rise to a suspicion that much of the evidence had been fabricated during his illness, and possibly without his knowledge, on account of the prefect's well-known hostility to Arruntius.

XLVIII. Domitius and Marsus, therefore, con-

[5] IV. 75.   [6] II. 74 n.

Marsus tamquam inediam destinavisset, produxere
vitam: Arruntius, cunctationem et moras suadenti-
bus amicis, non eadem omnibus decora respondit:
sibi satis aetatis, neque aliud paenitendum, quam
quod inter ludibria et pericula anxiam senectam
toleravisset, diu Seiano, nunc Macroni, semper alicui
potentium invisus, non culpa, sed ut flagitiorum
inpatiens. Sane paucos ad[1] suprema principis dies
posse vitari: quem ad modum evasurum imminentis
iuventam? An, cum Tiberius post tantam rerum
experientiam vi dominationis convulsus et mutatus
sit, Gaium Caesarem vix finita pueritia, ignarum
omnium aut pessimis innutritum, meliora capessi-
turum Macrone duce, qui ut deterior ad oppri-
mendum Seianum delectus plura per scelera rem
publicam conflictavisset? Prospectare iam se acrius
servitium, eoque fugere simul acta et instantia.
Haec vatis in modum dictitans venas resolvit. Docu-
mento sequentia erunt bene Arruntium morte usum.
Albucilla inrito ictu ab semet vulnerata iussu senatus
in carcerem fertur. Stuprorum eius ministri, Carsidius Sacerdos praetorius ut in insulam deportaretur,
Pontius Fregellanus amitteret ordinem senatorium,
et eaedem poenae in Laelium Balbum decernuntur,

[1] ad *Madvig*: et.

tinued to live—the former studying his defence, the latter ostensibly bent on self-starvation. Arruntius, whose friends advised procrastination and delays, replied that " not the same things were becoming to all men. For himself he had lived long enough; and it was his one regret that he had borne with an old age of anxieties amid flouts and perils, long detested by Sejanus, now by Macro, always by one or other of the mighty, not through his fault, but because he was impatient of villanies. True, he might steer through the few days before the passing of the sovereign: but how to escape the youth of the sovereign who loomed ahead? Or, if absolute sway had power to convulse and transform the character of Tiberius after his vast experience of affairs, would Gaius Caesar, barely out of his boyhood, ignorant of all things or nurtured amid the worst, apply himself to better ways under the tutelage of Macro; who had been chosen, as the worse villain of the pair, to crush Sejanus, and had tormented the state by crimes more numerous than his? Even now he foresaw a yet harder servitude, and for that reason he was fleeing at once from the past and from the future." So speaking, with something of a prophetic accent, he opened his veins.—That Arruntius did well to die the sequel will demonstrate. Albucilla, after dealing herself an ineffective wound, was borne to the dungeon by order of the senate. Of those who had subserved her amours, Carsidius Sacerdos, an ex-praetor, was condemned to deportation to an island, Pontius Fregellanus to forfeiture of his senatorial rank; and the same penalties were decreed against Laelius Balbus: one verdict, at least, which was pronounced with

id quidem a laetantibus, quia Balbus truci eloquentia habebatur, promptus adversum insontis.

XLIX. Isdem diebus Sex. Papinius consulari familia repentinum et informem exitum delegit, iacto in praeceps corpore. Causa ad matrem referebatur, quae pridem repudiata adsentationibus atque luxu perpulisset iuvenem ad ea, quorum effugium non nisi morte inveniret. Igitur accusata in senatu, quamquam genua patrum advolveretur luctumque communem et magis inbecillum tali super casu feminarum animum aliaque in eundem dolorem maesta et miseranda diu ferret, urbe tamen in decem annos prohibita est, donec minor filius lubricum iuventae exiret.

L. Iam Tiberium corpus, iam vires, nondum dissimulatio deserebat: idem animi rigor; sermone ac vultu intentus quaesita interdum comitate quamvis manifestam defectionem tegebat. Mutatisque saepius locis tandem apud promunturium Miseni consedit in villa, cui L. Lucullus quondam dominus. Illic eum adpropinquare supremis tali modo compertum. Erat medicus arte insignis, nomine Charicles, non quidem regere valetudines principis solitus, consilii tamen copiam praebere. Is velut propria ad negotia digrediens et per speciem officii manum complexus pulsum venarum attigit. Neque fefellit:

---

[1] The vicissitudes of this famous palace, which in its earliest days housed Marius and Lucullus and in its latest Romulus Augustulus and the bones of St. Severinus, are summarized by Gibbon (t. IV. 52 sq. Bury). Phaedrus lays the scene of one of his fables (II. 5) at the villa during a visit of Tiberius.

joy, since he was regarded as the master of a truculent eloquence—the ever-ready foe of innocence.

XLIX. During these days, Sextus Papinius, member of a consular family, chose an abrupt and indecent end by throwing himself from a window. The motive was referred to his mother, long ago divorced, who, by flattering his taste for dissipation, was supposed to have driven the youth to extremities from which he could find no issue except by death. Arraigned accordingly in the senate, though she threw herself at the knees of the Fathers and pleaded at length the common heritage of grief and the greater weakness of the female heart under such a blow, with much else in the same harrowing strain, she was nevertheless forbidden the capital for ten years, till her younger son should leave behind him the slippery period of youth.

L. By now his constitution and his strength were failing Tiberius, but not yet his powers of dissimulation. The unbending mind remained; still energetic in word and look, he strove every now and then to cover the manifest breaking-up by a forced sociability. After repeated changes of residence, he came to rest at last on the promontory of Misenum, in a villa which once had Lucius Lucullus for its master.[1] There it was discovered, by the following means, that he was nearing the end. There was a doctor, of repute in his calling, by the name of Charicles, who had been accustomed not to treat the illnesses of the emperor but to offer him opportunities for consulting him. While taking his departure on the plea of private business, he clasped the Caesar's hand, apparently as an act of respect, and felt the pulse. The device was detected.

nam Tiberius, incertum an offensus tantoque magis
iram premens, instaurari epulas iubet discumbitque
ultra solitum, quasi honori abeuntis amici tribueret.
Charicles tamen labi spiritum nec ultra biduum
duraturum Macroni firmavit. Inde cuncta conloquiis
inter praesentes, nuntiis apud legatos et exercitus
festinabantur. Septimum decimum kal. Aprilis
interclusa anima credıtus est mortalitatem exple-
visse; et multo gratantum concursu ad capienda
imperii primordia Gaius Caesar egrediebatur, cum
repente adfertur redire Tiberio vocem ac visus
vocarique qui recreandae defectioni cibum adferrent.
Pavor hinc in omnes, et ceteri passim dispergi, se
quisque maestum aut nescium fingere; Caesar in
silentium fixus a summa spe novissima expectabat.
Macro intrepidus opprimi senem iniectu multae
vestis iubet discedique ab limine. Sic Tiberius
finivit [1] octavo et septuagesimo aetatis anno.

LI. Pater ei Nero et utrimque origo gentis Claudiae, quamquam mater in Liviam et mox Iuliam
familiam adoptionibus transierit. Casus prima ab
infantia ancipites; nam proscriptum patrem exul
secutus, ubi domum Augusti privignus introiit,
multis aemulis conflictatus est, dum Marcellus et

---

[1] finivit] finivit ⟨vitam⟩ *Heinsius*, ⟨vitam⟩ finivit *Ritter*.

---

[1] The inevitable variations will be found in Suetonius
(*Tib.* 73) and Dio (LVIII. 28). The circumstantial and un-
sensational account quoted by the former from ' Seneca '—
presumably the elder—is noteworthy.

[2] Ti. Claudius Nero : see V. 1 with the notes.

Tiberius—possibly offended, and therefore making a special effort to conceal his anger—ordered the dinner to proceed, and, ostensibly out of compliment to a departing friend, remained at table until after his usual hour. Still, Charicles assured Macro that the respiration was failing and that he would not last above a couple of days. Immediately all arrangements were hurried through; at interviews, if the parties were present; by courier, in the case of the generals and the armies. On the sixteenth of March, owing to a stoppage in his breathing, it was believed that he had paid the debt of nature; and Gaius Caesar, in the midst of a gratulatory crowd, was leaving the villa to enter on the preliminaries of empire, when suddenly word came that Tiberius was recovering his speech and sight and calling for someone to bring him food as a restorative after his swoon. A general panic followed: the others began to scatter in all directions, each face counterfeiting grief or ignorance; only the Caesar, frozen into silence, stood dashed from the height of hope and expecting the worst. Macro, undaunted, ordered the old man to be suffocated under a pile of bed-clothes, while all left the threshold.[1]—Thus Tiberius made an end in the seventy-eighth year of his age.

LI. The son of Nero,[2] on both sides he traced his origin to the Claudian house, though his mother, by successive acts of adoption, had passed into the Livian and, later, the Julian families. From earliest infancy he experienced the hazards of fortune. At first the exiled attendant of a proscribed father, he entered the house of Augustus in the quality of step-son; only to struggle against numerous rivals during the heyday of Marcellus and Agrippa and,

Agrippa, mox Gaius Luciusque Caesares viguere;
etiam frater eius Drusus prosperiore civium amore
erat. Sed maxime in lubrico egit accepta in matrimonium Iulia, inpudicitiam uxoris tolerans aut
declinans. Dein Rhodo regressus vacuos principis
penatis duodecim annis, mox rei Romanae arbitrium
tribus ferme et viginti obtinuit. Morum quoque
tempora illi diversa: egregium vita famaque, quoad
privatus vel in imperiis sub Augusto fuit; occultum
ac subdolum fingendis virtutibus, donec Germanicus
ac Drusus superfuere; idem inter bona malaque
mixtus incolumi matre; intestabilis saevitia, sed
obtectis libidinibus, dum Seianum dilexit timuitve:
postremo in scelera simul ac dedecora prorupit,
postquam remoto pudore et metu suo tantum
ingenio utebatur.

---

[1] By his retirement to Rhodes (I. 53).

[2] From 2 A.D. to 14 A.D., Gaius Caesar being still alive in the
first two years, but absent in the East.

[3] So the *advocatus diaboli* sums up his case, which has not
always been regarded as conclusive against canonization, or at
least beatification ! The evidence on both sides of the endlessly
debated question may be found carefully collected and coolly
judged in the eighth chapter of Furneaux' *Introduction*.

later, of Gaius and Lucius Caesar; while even
his brother Drusus was happier in the love of his
countrymen. But his position was the most precarious after his preferment to the hand of Julia,
when he had to tolerate, or to elude,[1] the infidelities
of his wife. Then came the return from Rhodes;
and he was master of the heirless imperial house for
twelve years,[2] and later arbiter of the Roman world
for virtually twenty-three. His character, again, has
its separate epochs. There was a noble season in
his life and fame while he lived a private citizen
or a great official under Augustus; an inscrutable
and disingenuous period of hypocritical virtues
while Germanicus and Drusus remained: with his
mother alive, he was still an amalgam of good and
evil; so long as he loved, or feared, Sejanus, he was
loathed for his cruelty, but his lust was veiled;
finally, when the restraints of shame and fear were
gone, and nothing remained but to follow his own
bent, he plunged impartially into crime and into
ignominy.[3]

BOOK XI

LIBER XI

I. . . . . nam Valerium Asiaticum, bis consulem,
fuisse quondam adulterum eius credidit; pariterque
hortis inhians, quos ille a Lucullo coeptos insigni
magnificentia extollebat, Suillium accusandis utrisque immittit. Adiungitur Sosibius Britannici edu-
cator, qui per speciem benevolentiae moneret
Claudium cavere vim atque opes principibus infensas:
praecipuum auctorem Asiaticum interficiendi *Gai*[1]
Caesaris non extimuisse contione in[2] populi Romani
fateri gloriamque facinoris ultro petere; clarum ex

---

[1] <Gai> *Al. Ruperti.*
[2] contione in *Halm :* contionem.

---

[1] For the rest of the Annals, as for the whole of the Histories,
the only independent authority is the eleventh-century Lango-
bardic manuscript, *Med<iceus II>* (Laurentianus, plut. 68, 2),
which offers a tradition distinctly inferior to that of the first
Medicean in Books I-VI. The events dealt with in the lost
books (VII-X, together with the first half of XI) are
summarized in the Chronological Table (pp. 419-22). The
narrative reopens midway in the seventh year of Claudius
(47 A.D.).

[2] The *dramatis personae* are :—1. Valeria Messalina, the
too famous cousin and third wife of Claudius : 2. Poppaea
Sabina, daughter of Tiberius' " competent but not over-com-
petent " friend and lieutenant (VI. 39); the ruling beauty of
the period, and mother, by Titus Ollius, of Nero's Poppaea
(XIII. 45); now married to Publius Scipio (III. 74?):
3. Mnester, the leading pantomimist of the day; freedman
of Tiberius, minion of Caligula (Suet. *Cal.* 36, 55, 57), and
lover of Messalina, by whom he is suspected of an intrigue
with Poppaea : 4. Valerius Asiaticus, a wealthy consular from

BOOK XI[1]

I. . . . For she believed that Valerius Asiaticus,[2] twice a consul, had formerly been her paramour; A.V.C. 800 — A.D. 47 and, as she coveted equally the gardens which Lucullus had laid down and Asiaticus was embellishing with conspicuous splendour, she unleashed Suillius to indict the pair. With him was associated Britannicus'[3] tutor Sosibius; who, ostensibly out of good-will, was to warn Claudius to be on his guard against a power and a purse which boded no good to emperors:—" The prime mover in the killing of Gaius Caesar, Asiaticus had not trembled to avow his complicity in a gathering of the Roman people and even to arrogate the glory of the assassination.[4] Famous, in consequence, at Rome, with a

Vienne; selected by Messalina in place of Mnester, as the putative adulterer to be struck down along with Poppaea: 5. P. Suillius Rufus, now returned from his exile (IV. 31 n.), and chosen to conduct the accusation: 6. L. Vitellius (VI. 32 n.), at the zenith of his influence with Claudius; colleague with him in the consulate and censorship this year, and present as assessor at Asiaticus' trial before the private court of the emperor.

[3] Ti. Claudius Britannicus, son of Claudius and Messalina; now five years old. Sosibius—executed later by Agrippina on a charge of conspiracy (D. Cass. LX. 32)—was doubtless a Greek freedman.

[4] The tale goes that at a stormy meeting of the people (Jos. *A.J.* XIX. 1), or the praetorians (D. Cass. LIX. 30), he answered the shouted question, " Who was the slayer? " with the words, *Utinam ego* (εἴθε γὰρ ἔγωγε). Of his actual complicity there is no evidence.

eo in urbe, didita per provincias fama parare iter ad Germanicos exercitus, quando genitus Viennae multisque et validis propinquitatibus subnixus turbare gentiles nationes promptum haberet. At Claudius nihil ultra scrutatus citis cum militibus tamquam opprimendo bello Crispinum praetorii praefectum misit, a quo repertus est apud Baias vinclisque inditis in urbem raptus.

II. Neque data senatus copia: intra cubiculum auditur, Messalina coram, et Suillio corruptionem militum, quos pecunia et stupro in omne flagitium obstrictos arguebat, exim adulterium Poppaeae, postremum mollitiam corporis obiectante. Ad quod victo silentio prorupit reus et "Interroga" inquit, "Suilli, filios tuos: virum esse me fatebuntur." ingressusque defensionem, commoto maiorem in modum Claudio, Messalinae quoque lacrimas excivit. Quibus abluendis cubiculo egrediens monet Vitellium, ne elabi reum sineret: ipsa ad perniciem Poppaeae festinat, subditis qui terrore carceris ad voluntariam mortem propellerent, adeo ignaro Caesare, ut paucos post dies epulantem apud se maritum eius Scipionem, percontaretur, cur sine uxore discubuisset, atque ille functam fato responderet.

III. Sed consultanti super absolutione Asiatici flens Vitellius, commemorata vetustate amicitiae

reputation that pervaded the provinces, he was preparing an excursion to the armies of Germany; for the reason that, born as he was at Vienne and backed by a multitude of powerful connections, he had every facility for creating trouble among the peoples of his native land." Claudius made no further scrutiny; but, as though to quell an incipient war, despatched at full speed a body of soldiers under the praetorian prefect Crispinus, who found Asiaticus at Baiae, threw him into irons, and haled him to the capital.

II. Nor was access to the senate allowed: he was heard inside a bedroom, with Messalina looking on and Suillius formulating the charges: corruption of the military, who, he alleged, were bound in return for money—and worse—to every form of infamy; adultery with Poppaea; and, finally, sexual effeminacy. The last imputation was too much for the defendant's taciturnity:—"Question thy sons, Suillius, he broke out; "they will confess me man!" And entering on his defence, he moved Claudius deeply, and even elicited tears from Messalina; who, on quitting the room to wash them away, cautioned Vitellius not to let the prisoner slip through their fingers. She herself set hurriedly about the destruction of Poppaea, and suborned agents to drive her to a voluntary death by the menace of the dungeon; the ignorance of the Caesar being so complete that, when her husband Scipio dined with him a few days later, he inquired why he had taken his place without his wife, and received the answer that she had gone the way of all flesh.

III. When, however, Claudius requested his advice as to the acquittal of Asiaticus, Vitellius

utque Antoniam principis matrem pariter observavissent, dein percursis Asiatici in rem publicam officiis recentique adversus Britanniam militia, quaeque alia conciliandae misericordiae videbantur, liberum mortis arbitrium ei permisit; et secuta sunt Claudii verba in eandem clementiam. Hortantibus dehinc quibusdam inediam et lenem exitum, remittere beneficium Asiaticus ait: et usurpatis quibus insueverat exercitationibus, lauto corpore, hilare epulatus, cum se honestius calliditate Tiberii vel impetu Gai Caesaris periturum dixisset, quam quod fraude muliebri et inpudico Vitellii ore caderet, venas exsolvit, viso tamen ante rogo iussoque transferri partem in aliam, ne opacitas arborum vapore ignis minueretur: tantum illi securitatis novissimae fuit.

IV. Vocantur post haec patres, pergitque Suillius addere reos equites Romanos inlustres, quibus Petra cognomentum. At causa necis ex eo, quod domum suam Mnesteris et Poppaeae congressibus praebuissent. Verum nocturnae quietis species alteri obiecta, tamquam vidisset Claudium spicea corona evinctum, spicis retro conversis, eaque imagine gravitatem annonae *prae*dixisset. Quidam pampineam coronam albentibus foliis visam atque ita

---

[1] Presumably in the expedition of 43 A.D.

[2] Claudius describes him as a ' palaestric prodigy ' (*Or. Claud.* II. 14).

[3] In his Lucullan Gardens on the Pincian Hill (*Collis Hortulorum*).

[4] A point upon which Claudius—whose accession had coincided with a threatened famine—remained peculiarly sensitive.

tearfully recalled their long-standing friendship and
the equal devotion they had shown to the sovereign's
mother Antonia: then, running over the services of
Asiaticus to the state, his recent work in the field
against the Britons,[1] and all else that seemed calculated to inspire compassion, he proposed that he
should be allowed a free choice as to the form of his
death; and a pronouncement from Claudius followed
in the same spirit of clemency. When some of his
friends then recommended the gradual exit by
starvation, Asiaticus remarked that he was declining
that boon; went through the gymnastic exercises
which had become habitual with him;[2] bathed;
dined in good spirits; and, after observing that it
would have been more respectable to perish by the
subtlety of Tiberius or the onslaught of Gaius Caesar
than to fall by female fraud and the lecherous
tongue of Vitellius, opened his arteries; but not
before he had visited his pyre[3] and given orders for
it to be moved to another site, so that his trees with
their shady leafage might not be affected by the
heat. So complete was his composure to the end!

IV. The Fathers were then convened; and
Suillius proceeded to add to the list of accused two
Roman knights of the highest rank, surnamed
Petra. The cause of death lay in the allegation
that they had lent their house as a trysting-place
for Mnester and Poppaea. It was, however, for
a vision during his night's sleep that one of them was
indicted, the charge being that he had seen Claudius
crowned with a wheaten diadem, the ears inverted,
and on the strength of his vision had predicted a
shortage in the corn-supply.[4] It has been stated by
some that the thing seen was a vine-wreath with

interpretatum tradidere, vergente autumno mortem
principis ostendi. Illud haud ambigitur, qualicum-
que insomnio ipsi fratrique perniciem adlatam.
Sestertium quindeciens et insignia praeturae Crispino
decreta. Adiecit Vitellius sestertium deciens Sosi-
bio, quod Britannicum praeceptis, Claudium consiliis
iuvaret. Rogatus sententiam et Scipio, "Cum idem "
inquit " de admissis Poppaeae sentiam quod omnes,
putate me idem dicere quod omnes," eleganti
temperamento inter coniugalem amorem et sena-
toriam necessitatem.

V. Continuus inde et saevus accusandis reis
Suillius multique audaciae eius aemuli; nam cuncta
legum et magistratuum munia in se trahens princeps
materiam praedandi patefecerat. Nec quicquam
publicae mercis tam venale fuit quam advocatorum
perfidia, adeo ut Samius,[1] insignis eques Romanus,
quadringentis nummorum milibus Suillio datis et
cognita praevaricatione ferro in domo eius incu-
buerit. Igitur incipiente C. Silio consule designato,
cuius de potentia *et* exitio in tempore memorabo,
consurgunt patres legemque Cinciam flagitant, qua
cavetur antiquitus, ne quis ob causam orandam
pecuniam donumve accipiat.

VI. Deinde obstrepentibus iis, quibus ea contumelia parabatur, discors Suillio Silius acriter incubuit,

[1] <T.> Samius *Ritter.*

---

[1] The external distinctions of the office without the office
itself; which, in this case, was not even accessible to Crispinus,
since, as praetorian prefect, he was necessarily a knight.
[2] See chaps. 12 and 35.

whitening leaves; which he read as an indication of the emperor's decease at the wane of autumn. The point not disputed is that it was a dream, whatever its character, which brought ruin to himself and to his brother. A million and a half sesterces, with the decorations of the praetorship,[1] were voted to Crispinus. Vitellius proposed a million more for Sosibius, for assisting Britannicus by his instructions and Claudius by his counsels. Scipio, who was also asked for his view, replied: " As I think what all think of Poppaea's offences, take me as saying what all say ! "—an elegant compromise between conjugal love and senatorial obligation.

V. And now Suillius, steady and pitiless, continued his prosecutions, his boldness finding a multitude of imitators: for the concentration of all legal and magisterial functions in the person of the sovereign had opened a wide field to the plunderer. Nor was any public ware so frankly on sale as the treachery of advocates: so much so that Samius, a Roman knight of distinction, after paying Suillius four hundred thousand sesterces and finding him in collusion with the opponents, fell on his sword in the house of his counsel. Hence, following the lead of the consul designate, Gaius Silius, whose power and whose ruin I shall describe in their place,[2] the Fathers rose in a body, demanding the Cincian law,[3] with its ancient stipulation that no person shall accept either money or gift for pleading a cause.

VI. Then, as the members for whom the stigma was designed began to protest, Silius, who was at

[3] The *lex Cincia de donis atque muneribus* (204 B.C.), revived by Augustus in 17 B.C. Suillius' second collision with it had graver results (XIII. 42 sq.).

veterum oratorum exempla referens, qui famam et
posteros praemia eloquentiae cogitavissent. Pulcherrimam [1] alioquin et bonarum artium principem
sordidis ministeriis foedari; ne fidem quidem integram manere, ubi magnitudo quaestuum spectetur.
Quodsi in nullius mercedem negotia agantur,[2]
pauciora fore: nunc inimicitias, accusationes, odia
et iniurias foveri, ut quo modo vis morborum pretia
medentibus, sic fori tabes pecuniam advocatis ferat.
Meminissent Asinii, Messalae ac recentiorum
Arruntii et Aesernini: ad summa provectos incorrupta vita et facundia. Talia dicente consule
designato, consentientibus aliis, parabatur sententia,
qua lege repetundarum tenerentur, cum Suillius et
ceteri, qui non iudicium, quippe in manifestos, sed
poenam statui videbant, circumsistunt Caesarem,
ante acta deprecantes.

VII. Et postquam adnuit, agere incipiunt: quem
illum tanta superbia esse, ut aeternitatem famae spe
praesumat? usui et reis [3] subsidium praeparari, ne
quis inopia advocatorum potentibus obnoxius sit.
Neque tamen eloquentiam gratuito contingere:

[1] pulcherrimam *Nipperdey*: pulcherrima.
[2] negotia agantur *Heinsius* (negotia fiant *Bezzenberger*):
negotiant *Med.*, *with an erasure following.*
[3] reis *Jacob*: rebus.

---

[1] For Asinius Pollio (*insigne maestis praesidium reis,* Hor.
Carm. II. 1) and Messala Corvinus, see IV. 34 n., III. 34 n.; for
L. Arruntius, VI. 5 n.; and for M. Claudius Marcellus Aeserninus, grandson of Pollio, III. 11.
[2] Cossutianus Capito, one of the most active accusers of the
period. Banished for extortion in Cilicia (XIII. 33), he was
restored to the senate by the intervention of his father-in-law
Tigellinus (XIV. 48), was a prime mover in the prosecution of
Thrasea (XVI. 21 sqq.), and then disappears from the stage.

variance with Suillius, delivered a bitter attack and
appealed to the example of the old orators, who had
regarded fame and the future as the only wages of
eloquence :—" What would otherwise be the fairest
and foremost of the liberal arts was degraded by
mercenary service : even good faith could not
remain unaffected, when the size of the fees was
the point regarded. If lawsuits were so conducted
that no one profited by them, lawsuits would be
fewer : as matters stood, enmities and accusations,
ill blood and injustice, were being fostered, in order
that, as the prevalence of disease brought rewards
to the physician, so the corruption of the courts
should bring money to the advocate. Let them
remember Asinius, Messala, and, of the moderns,
Arruntius and Aeserninus : [1] they had reached the
summits of their profession without a stain upon
their life or their eloquence ! " With the consul
designate speaking in this strain and others indicating
assent, steps were being taken to draft a resolution
making offenders liable under the law of extortion,
when Suillius, Cossutianus, [2] and the rest, who saw
that to them the vote implied not trial—their guilt
was too manifest for that—but punishment, surrounded the emperor, imploring an amnesty for the
past.

VII. At his signal of consent, they began to state
their case :—" Where was the man whose pre-
sumption was such that he could anticipate in hope
an eternity of fame ? It was a boon to defendants
themselves that help should be made available, so
that no one need be left at the mercy of the strong
through the lack of an advocate. But eloquence was
not a happy accident costing nothing : private

omitti curas familiaris, ut quis se alienis negotiis intendat. Multos militia, quosdam exercendo agros tolerare vitam : nihil a quoquam expeti, nisi cuius fructus ante providerit. Facile Asinium et Messalam inter Antonium et Augustum bellorum praemiis refertos, aut ditium familiarum heredes Aeserninos et Arruntios magnum animum induisse. Prompta sibi exempla, quantis mercedibus P. Clodius aut C. Curio contionari soliti sint. Se modicos senatores, *qui* quieta[1] re publica nulla nisi pacis emolumenta peterent. Cogitaret plebem, quae toga enitesceret : sublatis studiorum pretiis etiam studia peritura. Ut minus decora haec, ita haud frustra dicta princeps ratus, capiendis pecuniis *statuit*[2] modum usque ad dena sestertia, quem egressi repetundarum tenerentur.

VIII. Sub idem tempus Mithridates, quem imperitasse Armeniis *iussuque Gai*[3] Caesaris vinctum memoravi, monente Claudio in regnum remeavit, fisus

---

[1] <qui> quieta *Halm* : qui et a *Med.* quieta . . . petere *Pichena.*

[2] <statuit> *Orelli,* <posuit> *dett.*

[3] <iussuque Gai> *Urlichs : lac.*

---

[1] Two questionable sponsors, the former being the notorious enemy of Cicero, killed in the affray with Milo; the latter, the equally notorious tribune purchased by Caesar.

[2] The last extant notices of eastern affairs (VI. 31–37, 41–45) closed with the Roman nominee, Mithridates on the throne of Armenia, and the veteran Artabanus III. of Parthia repossessed of his kingdom. On the accession of Caligula, even the half-success achieved by Tiberius was cancelled : Mithridates was summoned to Rome and placed under arrest, and Armenia allowed to relapse under Parthian influence or suzerainty.

business was neglected in proportion as a man applied
himself to the affairs of others. Many supported
themselves by military service; not a few by the
cultivation of their estates: no man embraced any
avocation, unless he had made sure that it would
yield him a return. It was easy for Asinius and
Messala, glutted with the prizes of the duel between
Antony and Augustus, or for the heirs of wealthy
houses—Aeserninus, Arruntius, and their like—to
assume a pose of magnanimity: they had themselves
obvious precedents in the rewards for which Publius
Clodius or Gaius Curio [1] were in the habit of delivering
their harangues. Personally, they were senators of
modest means, who, in a tranquil state, sought
none but the emoluments of peace: Let him consider also the common people who won distinction by
the gown! If the rewards of the art they studied
were annulled, the art too would perish."—The
emperor, who considered that these arguments, if
less high-minded, were still not pointless, fixed ten
thousand sesterces as the maximum fee to be
accepted; those exceeding it to be liable on the count
of extortion.

VIII.[2] Nearly at the same time,[3] Mithridates, whose
tenure of the Armenian crown and arrest by order of
Caligula I have already mentioned, followed the
advice of Claudius and returned to his kingdom, in

The situation, however, was altered again by the death of
Artabanus III. (40 A.D.) and the outbreak of civil war between
his sons Gotarzes and Vardanes, a third brother (Artabanus
IV.) having been summarily despatched.—It should be borne
in mind that these chapters (8–10) contain, not the events of
47 A.D., but an epitome of the events from 42 or 43 A.D. to
48 A.D. The narrative is then resumed in XII. 10.

[3] In reality, about five years earlier.

Pharasmanis opibus. Is rex Hiberis idemque Mithridatis frater nuntiabat discordare Parthos summaque imperii ambigua, minora sine cura haberi. Nam Gotarzes inter[1] pleraque saeva[2] necem fratri Artabano coniugique ac filio eius paraverat,[3] unde metus in ceteros, et accivere Vardanen. Ille, ut erat magnis ausis promptus, biduo tria milia stadiorum invadit ignarumque et exterritum Gotarzen proturbat; neque cunctatur quin proximas praefecturas corripiat, solis Seleucensibus dominationem eius abnuentibus. In quos, ut patris sui quoque[4] defectores, ira magis quam ex usu praesenti accensus, inplicatur obsidione urbis validae et munimentis obiecti amnis muroque et commeatibus firmatae. Interim Gotarzes Daharum Hyrcanorumque opibus auctus bellum renovat, coactusque Vardanes omittere Seleuciam Bactrianos apud campos castra contulit.

IX. Tunc distractis Orientis viribus et quonam inclinarent incertis, casus Mithridati datus est occupandi Armeniam, vi militis Romani ad excin-

---

[1] Gotarzes inter *Doederlein :* inter Gotharzes.

[2] saeva *Halm :* saeva qui *Med. The original is hardly recoverable.*

[3] paraverat *Halm :* praeparaberat.

[4] sui quoque] quoque sui *Urlichs,* suique *Wurm.*

---

[1] VI. 32 etc.

[2] About 350 miles—an impossible distance for any considerable body of men, even Parthians. If Vardanes travelled with a few attendants—the question of fresh horses would present no difficulty—the speed still approximates to, or surpasses, that of the most famous journies of Roman couriers over good roads, with the resources of the *cursus publicus* behind them.

reliance on the powers of Pharasmanes.[1] That prince, king of Iberia and also brother of Mithridates, kept announcing that the Parthians were divided among themselves—the crown was in question, minor matters unregarded. For Gotarzes, among his numerous cruelties, had procured the murder of his brother Artabanus and his wife and son, with the result that the rest took alarm and called in Vardanes. He, with his usual alacrity for great adventures, covered three thousand stadia [2] in two days; drove the unsuspecting and terrified Gotarzes into flight, and without hesitation seized the nearest satrapies—Seleucia [3] alone refusing to acknowledge his supremacy. Less from considerations of his immediate interest than from anger at a community which had also deserted his father, he hampered himself with the siege of a powerful city, secured by the barrier of an intervening river, fortified, and provisioned. Meanwhile, Gotarzes, strengthened by the forces of the Dahae and Hyrcanians,[4] renewed hostilities; and Vardanes, compelled to abandon Seleucia, pitched his camp opposite to him on the plains of Bactria.[5]

IX. This juncture, when the powers of the East were divided and it was still uncertain which way the scales would fall, gave Mithridates his opportunity of seizing Armenia. thanks to the energy of the Roman troops in demolishing the hill fortresses,

[3] VI. 42 n.

[4] VI. 36 n.

[5] E. of Parthia proper (Khorasân), on the upper reaches of the Amu-darya and Syr-darya, with the Hindu Kush to the south, the capital being Bactra (Balkh). It had formerly been the seat of a Graeco-Indian kingdom.

denda[1] castellorum ardua, simul Hibero exercitu
campos persultante. Nec enim restitere Armenii,
fuso qui proelium ausus erat Demonacte praefecto.
Paululum cunctationis attulit rex minoris Armeniae
Cotys, versis illuc quibusdam procerum; dein litteris
Caesaris coercitus, et cuncta in Mithridaten fluxere,
quam*quam* atrociorem quam novo regno conduceret.
At Parthi imperatores cum pugnam pararent, foedus
repente iciunt[2] cognitis popularium insidiis, quas
Gotarzes fratri patefecit; congressique primo cunctanter, dein complexi dextras apud altaria deum
pepigere fraudem inimicorum ulcisci atque ipsi inter
se concedere. Potiorque Vardanes visus retinendo
regno: at Gotarzes, ne quid aemulationis exsisteret,
penitus in Hyrcaniam abiit. Regressoque Vardani
deditur Seleucia septimo post defectionem anno,
non sine dedecore Parthorum, quos una civitas tam
diu eluserat.

X. Exim validissimas praefecturas invisit; et
reciperare Armeniam avebat, ni a Vibio Marso,
Suriae legato, bellum minitante cohibitus foret.
Atque interim Gotarzes paenitentia concessi regni
et vocante nobilitate, cui in pace durius servitium est,
contrahit copias. Et hinc contra itum ad amnem
Erinden;[3] in cuius transgressu multum certato pervicit Vardanes, prosperisque proeliis medias nationes

---

[1] excindenda *Halm* : excidenda.
[2] iciunt *Agricola* : iaciunt.
[3] Erinden] Charindam *Ryck* (*from Ptol.* VI. 2, 2 Χαρίνδα
ποταμοῦ ἐκβολαί, *and Amm. Marc. XXIII.* 6, 40 amnes . . .
Choaspes et Gyndes et Amardus et Charinda).

---

[1] Head of one of the 120 *praefecturae* (στρατηγίαι) into
which Armenia was divided (Plin. *H.N.* VI. 9, 27).
[2] W. of Armenia proper.   [3] 43 A.D.

while the Iberian army overran the plains; for the natives offered no resistance after the rout of the prefect Demonax,[1] who had risked a battle. Some little delay was occasioned by Cotys, the king of Lesser Armenia,[2] to whom a section of the nobles had turned: then he was repressed by a despatch from the Caesar, and the current set full towards Mithridates, who showed more severity than was conducive to the stability of his new throne.—Meanwhile, as the Parthian commanders were preparing for battle, they suddenly concluded an agreement on their discovery of a national conspiracy, disclosed by Gotarzes to his brother. They met, hesitantly at first; then, with right hands clasped, they pledged themselves before the altars of the gods to avenge the treachery of their enemies and each to make concessions to the other. Vardanes was considered the better fitted to retain the crown: Gotarzes, to avoid all chance of rivalry, withdrew into the depths of Hyrcania. On the return of Vardanes, Seleucia capitulated[3] in the seventh year after its revolt; not without some dishonour to the Parthians, whom a single town had so long defied.

X. Vardanes then visited the principal satrapies, and was burning to recover Armenia, when he was checked by a threat of war from Vibius Marsus, the legate of Syria. In the meantime, Gotarzes, repenting of his cession of the throne, and invited by the grandees, whose vassalage is always more irksome in peace, gathered an army. On the other side, a counter-advance brought Vardanes to the river Erindes. A severe struggle at the crossing ended in his complete victory, and in successful actions he reduced the intervening tribes up to the

subegit ad flumen Sinden, quod Dahas Ariosque
disterminat. Ibi modus rebus secundis positus:
nam Parthi quamquam victores longinquam militiam
aspernabantur. Igitur exstructis monimentis, quibus opes suas testabatur nec cuiquam ante Arsacidarum tributa illis de gentibus parta, regreditur
ingens gloria atque eo ferocior et subiectis intoleran-
tior; qui dolo ante conposito incautum venationique
intentum interfecere, primam intra iuventam, sed
claritudine paucos inter senum regum, si perinde
amorem inter populares quam metum apud hostes
quaesivisset.

Nece Vardanis turbatae Parthorum res inter
ambiguos, quis in regnum acciperetur. Multi ad
Gotarzen inclinabant, quidam ad Meherdaten prolem
Phraatis, obsidio nobis datum: dein praevaluit
Gotarzes. Potitusque regiam, per saevitiam ac
luxum adegit Parthos mittere ad principem Romanum occultas preces, quis permitti Meherdaten
patrium ad fastigium orabant.

XI. Isdem consulibus ludi saeculares octingente-
simo post Romam conditam, quarto et sexagensimo,
quam Augustus ediderat, spectati sunt. Utriusque
principis rationes praetermitto, satis narratas libris,

---

[1] The scene of the campaign is indeterminable, as the
Erindes and Sindes are equally unknown, while the Arii
(S.W. of Bactria) were far removed from the Dahae.

[2] He was son of Vonones and grandson of Phraates IV
(VI. 31 n.).

[3] That of Claudius and Vitellius (47 A.D.).

[4] Details may be found in the commentaries. Roughly
speaking the games were instituted in 249 B.C. as centennial,
were celebrated again—three years late—in 146 B.C., and
omitted in 46 B.C. Augustus, by availing himself of a Sibylline
saeculum of 110 years and the traditions of the quindecimviral

Sindes, which forms the boundary-line between the Dahae and Arians.[1] There his triumphs came to a close, as the Parthians, though victorious, were in no mood for a distant campaign. Consequently, after raising a number of monuments recording his power and the fact that no Arsacid before him had levied tribute from those nations, he returned full of glory and therefore more arrogant and more arbitrary towards his subjects; who, by a prearranged act of treachery, assassinated him while off his guard and absorbed in his hunting,—a prince still in his earliest manhood, but in renown, had he sought the love of his people as he sought the fear of his enemies, unequalled but by a few of veteran kings.

By the murder of Vardanes Parthian affairs were thrown into confusion, as there was no unanimity with regard to his successor. Many leaned to Gotarzes; some to Phraates' descendant Meherdates,[2] who had been given in hostage to ourselves. Then Gotarzes carried the day, made himself master of the palace, and by dint of cruelty and debauchery drove the Parthians to send a secret petition to the Roman emperor, pleading that Meherdates might be set free to ascend the throne of his fathers.

XI. Under the same consulate,[3] eight hundred years from the foundation of Rome, sixty-four from their presentation by Augustus, came a performance of the Secular Games. The calculations [4] employed by the two princes I omit, as they have been suffi-

college, contrived to celebrate them in 17 B.C., one year too soon according to his own data. Claudius reverted to the *saeculum* of 100 years, but treated the festival as the eighth centenary of Rome (753 + 47 = 800). Domitian followed Augustus, but held his *ludi* six years before the date (88 A.D.).

quibus res imperatoris Domitiani composui. Nam is quoque edidit ludos saecularis iisque intentius adfui sacerdotio quindecimvirali praeditus ac tunc praetor, quod non iactantia refero, sed quia collegio quindecimvirum antiquitus ea cura et magistratus potissimum exsequebantur officia caerimoniarum. Sedente Claudio circensibus ludis, cum pueri nobiles equis ludicrum Troiae inirent interque eos Britannicus imperatore genitus et L. Domitius adoptione mox in imperium et cognomentum Neronis adscitus, favor plebis acrior in Domitium loco praesagii acceptus est. Vulgabaturque adfuisse infantiae eius dracones in modum custodum, fabulosa et externis miraculis adsimilata: nam ipse, haudquaquam sui detractator[1] unam omnino anguem in cubiculo visam narrare solitus est.

XII. Verum inclinatio populi supererat ex memoria Germanici, cuius illa reliqua suboles virilis; et matri Agrippinae miseratio augebatur ob saevitiam Messalinae, quae semper infesta et tunc commotior, quo minus strueret crimina et accusatores, novo et furori proximo amore distinebatur. Nam in C. Silium, iuventutis Romanae pulcherrimum, ita exarserat, ut Iuniam Silanam, nobilem feminam, matri-

---

[1] detractator Burmann: detractor Med. (cf. Liv. XXXIV. 15 fin., where the same variant exists).

---

[1] The closing books, now lost, of the Histories.
[2] III. 64 n.
[3] The sham fight of patrician youths on horseback, best known from the description in the Aeneid (V. 545 sqq.).
[4] The future emperor Nero, son of Cn. Domitius Ahenobarbus and Germanicus' daughter Agrippina (IV. 75 n.)
[5] The consul designate of chap. 5; son of the conqueror of Sacrovir (I. 31; III. 42; IV. 18).

cently explained in the books which I have devoted
to the reign of Domitian.[1] For he too exhibited
Secular Games, and, as the holder of a quindecimviral
priesthood [2] and as praetor at the time, I followed
them with more than usual care: a fact which I
recall not in vanity, but because from of old this
responsibility has rested with the Fifteen, and
because it was to magistrates in especial that the
task fell of discharging the duties connected with
the religious ceremonies. During the presence
of Claudius at the Circensian Games, when a caval-
cade of boys from the great families opened the
mimic battle of Troy,[3] among them being the emperor's son, Britannicus, and Lucius Domitius,[4]—soon
to be adopted as heir to the throne and to the
designation of Nero,—the livelier applause given by
the populace to Domitius was accepted as prophetic.
Also there was a common tale that serpents had
watched over his infancy like warders: a fable
retouched to resemble foreign miracles, since
Nero—certainly not given to self-depreciation—used
to say that only a single snake had been noticed in
his bedroom.

XII. However, the memory of Germanicus left
him with a residue of popularity as the one male off-
shoot left of the family; and growing pity was felt for
his mother Agrippina in view of her persecution by
Messalina; who, always her enemy and now more
than usually excited, was only withheld from mar-
shalling accusations and accusers by a fresh amour
verging upon insanity. For her passion for Gaius
Silius,[5] most handsome of Roman youths, had burned
so high that she drove his distinguished wife, Junia
Silana, from under her husband's roof, and entered

monio eius exturbaret vacuoque adultero poteretur.
Neque Silius flagitii aut periculi nescius erat: sed
certo, si abnueret, exitio et nonnulla fallendi spe,
simul magnis praemiis, opperiri futura et praesentibus
frui pro solacio habebat. Illa non furtim, sed
multo comitatu ventitare domum, egressibus ad-
haerescere, largiri opes, honores, postremo, velut
translata iam fortuna, servi liberti paratus principis
apud adulterum visebantur.

XIII. At Claudius matrimonii sui ignarus et munia
censoria usurpans, theatralem populi lasciviam severis
edictis increpuit, quod in P. Pomponium consularem
(is carmina scaenae dabat) inque feminas inlustres
probra iecerat. Et lege lata saevitiam creditorum
coercuit, ne in mortem parentum pecunias filiis
familiarum faenori darent. Fontisque aquarum
Simbruinis collibus deductos urbi intulit. Ac novas
litterarum formas addidit vulgavitque, comperto
Graecam quoque[1] litteraturam non simul coeptam
absolutamque.

XIV. Primi per figuras animalium Aegyptii sensus
mentis effingebant—ea antiquissima monimenta
memoriae humanae inpressa saxis cernuntur—, et
litterarum semet inventores perhibent; inde Phoeni-

---

[1] Graecam quoque *Frobeniana :* quoque Graecam.

---

[1] The office, in abeyance since 23 B.C., was resuscitated by
Claudius and held by himself and Vitellius after resignation
of their joint consulate in this year.

[2] V. 8 n.

[3] Two supplies, the *aqua Claudia* (from the little lakes
formed by the Anio on the hills above Subiaco) and the
Anio novus (taken off from the river itself); though they
entered the city on the same arches.

upon the possession of a now unfettered adulterer. Silius was blind neither to the scandal nor to the danger, but, since refusal was certain death, since there was some little hope of avoiding exposure, and since the rewards were high, he consoled himself by closing his eyes to the future and enjoying the present. Messalina, with no attempt at concealment, went incessantly to the house with a crowd of retainers; abroad, she clung to his side; wealth and honours were showered upon him; finally, as though the transference of sovereignty was complete, slaves, freedmen, and furnishings of the palace were to be seen in the house of an adulterer.

XIII. Claudius, meanwhile, ignorant of his own matrimonial fortune and engrossed by his censorial functions,[1] reprimanded in austere edicts the licence shown in theatres by the populace, which had directed its ribaldry upon the consular Publius Pomponius [2] (he composed pieces for the stage), and upon several of rank. He checked by legislation extortion on the part of creditors, prohibiting loans to a minor, repayable at the father's death: he brought the spring-water down from the Simbruine hills,[3] and introduced it into the capital; and, after making the discovery that not even the Greek alphabet was begun and completed in the same instant, he invented and gave to the world some additional Latin characters.

XIV. The Egyptians, in their animal-pictures, were the first people to represent thought by symbols: these, the earliest documents of human history, are visible to-day, impressed upon stone. They describe themselves also as the inventors of the alphabet: from Egypt, they consider, the

269

cas, quia mari praepollebant, intulisse Graeciae gloriamque adeptos, tamquam reppererint quae acceperant. Quippe fama est Cadmum classe Phoenicum vectum rudibus adhuc Graecorum populis artis eius auctorem fuisse. Quidam Cecropem Atheniensem vel Linum Thebanum et temporibus Troianis Palamedem Argivum memorant sedecim litterarum formas, mox alios ac praecipuum Simoniden ceteras repperisse. At in Italia Etrusci ab Corinthio Demarato, Aborigines Arcade ab Evandro didicerunt; et forma litteris Latinis quae veterrimis Graecorum. Sed nobis quoque paucae primum fuere, deinde additae sunt. Quo exemplo Claudius tres litteras adiecit, quae usui imperitante eo, post oblitteratae, aspiciuntur etiam nunc in aere publico [1] per fora ac templa fixo.

XV. Rettulit deinde ad senatum super collegio haruspicum, ne vetustissima Italiae disciplina per desidiam exolesceret: saepe adversis rei publicae temporibus accitos, quorum monitu redintegratas caerimonias et in posterum rectius habitas; primoresque Etruriae sponte aut patrum Romanorum inpulsu retinuisse scientiam et in familias propagasse: quod

---

[1] publico *Nipperdey:* publico dis plebiscitis *Med. No emendation has any likelihood.*

---

[1] 1. An inverted digamma, ⅃, for the consonantal *u* (⅃VLGVS = VVLGVS); 2. an "antisigma," Ɔ, equivalent to the Greek Ψ; 3. the Greek sign for the *spiritus asper*, Ⱶ, to express the *y*-sound, between *u* and *i*, heard in such words

Phoenicians, who were predominant at sea, imported the knowledge into Greece, and gained the credit of discovering what they had borrowed. For the tradition runs that it was Cadmus, arriving with a Phoenician fleet, who taught the art to the still uncivilized Greek peoples. Others relate that Cecrops of Athens (or Linus of Thebes) and, in the Trojan era, Palamedes of Argos, invented sixteen letters, the rest being added later by different authors, particularly Simonides. In Italy the Etruscans learned the lesson from the Corinthian Demaratus, the Aborigines from Evander the Arcadian; and in form the Latin characters are identical with those of the earliest Greeks. But, in our case too, the original number was small, and additions were made subsequently: a precedent for Claudius, who appended three more letters,[1] which had their vogue during his reign, then fell into desuetude, but still meet the eye on the official bronzes fixed in the forums and temples.

XV. He next consulted the senate on the question of founding a college of diviners,[2] so that "the oldest art of Italy should not become extinct through their indolence. Often, in periods of public adversity, they had called in diviners, on whose advice religious ceremonies had been renewed and, for the future, observed with greater correctness; while the Etruscan nobles, voluntarily or at the instance of the Roman senate, had kept up the art and propagated it in certain families. Now that work was

as *maximus* (*maxumus*) (= MAXIⱵMVS). Many instances of (1), survive, some of (3), none—or possibly one—of (2).

[2] Soothsayers—of far lower standing than the augurs—practising, *inter alia*, the Etruscan art of divination by inspection of entrails (*extispicium*).

271

nunc segnius fieri publica circa bonas artes socordia,
et quia externae superstitiones valescant. Et laeta
quidem in praesens omnia, sed benignitati deum
gratiam referendam, ne ritus sacrorum inter ambigua
culti per prospera oblitterarentur. Factum ex eo
senatus consultum, viderent pontifices quae retinenda
firmandaque haruspicum.

XVI. Eodem anno Cheruscorum gens regem Roma
petivit, amissis per interna bella nobilibus et uno
reliquo stirpis regiae, qui apud urbem habebatur
nomine Italicus. Paternum huic genus e Flavo
fratre Arminii, mater ex Actumero principe Chattorum erat; ipse forma decorus et armis equisque
in patrium nostrumque morem exercitus. Igitur
Caesar auctum pecunia, additis stipatoribus, horta-
tur gentile decus magno animo capessere: illum
primum Romae ortum nec obsidem, sed civem ire
externum ad imperium. Ac primo laetus Germanis
adventus atque eo, quod nullus discordiis imbutus
pari in omnes studio ageret, celebrari, coli, modo
comitatem et temperantiam, nulli invisa, saepius
vinolentiam ac libidines, grata barbaris, usurpans.
Iamque apud proximos, iam longius clarescere, cum

---

[1] Principally Judaism and the Egyptian cults of Isis and
Serapis, though Christianity and Mithraism were on the way.

[2] North-east of the Chatti, between the Weser and the Elbe,
the tribe of Arminius.

[3] II. 9–10. He had served in the Roman army as a
mounted scout; whence the taunt below (*exploratoris* (*Flavi*).

done more negligently through the public indifference to all liberal accomplishments, combined with the progress of alien superstitions.[1] For the moment, indeed, all was flourishing; but they must show their gratitude to the favour of Heaven by making sure that the sacred rituals observed in the time of hazard were not forgotten in the day of prosperity." A senatorial decree was accordingly passed, instructing the pontiffs to consider what points in the discipline of the haruspices needed to be maintained or strengthened.

XVI. In the same year the tribe of the Cherusci[2] applied to Rome for a king, as intestine strife had exterminated their nobility, and of the royal house there survived one member, who was kept at Rome and bore the name of Italicus. On the father's side he sprang from Arminius' brother Flavus,[3] his mother being the daughter of the Chattan chieftain Actumerus: he himself was a handsome figure, trained to arms and horsemanship on both the German and the Roman systems. The Caesar, therefore, made him a grant of money, added an escort, and encouraged him to enter on his family honours with a high heart:— " He was the first man born at Rome, and not a hostage but a citizen, to leave for a foreign throne." At the outset, indeed, his arrival was greeted by the Germans with enthusiasm; and, as he was imbued with no party animosities and showed himself equally anxious to oblige all men, admirers flocked round a prince who practised occasionally the inoffensive foibles of courtesy and restraint, but more frequently the drunkenness and incontinence dear to barbarians. His fame was already beginning to reach, and to transcend, the neighbouring states,

potentiam eius suspectantes, qui factionibus floruerant
discedunt ad conterminos populos ac testificantur
adimi veterem Germaniae libertatem et Romanas
opes insurgere. Adeo neminem isdem in terris
ortum, qui principem locum impleat, nisi exploratoris
Flavi progenies super cunctos attollatur? Frustra
Arminium praescribi: cuius si filius hostili in solo
adultus in regnum venisset, posse extimesci, infectum
alimonio, sevitio, cultu, omnibus externis: at si
paterna Italico mens esset, non alium infensius arma
contra patriam ac deos penatis quam parentem eius
exercuisse.

XVII. His atque talibus magnas copias coegere,
nec pauciores Italicum sequebantur. Non enim in-
rupisse ad invitos, sed accitum memorabat, quando
nobilitate ceteros anteiret: virtutem experirentur,
an dignum se patruo Arminio, avo Actumero[1]
praeberet. Nec patrem rubori, quod fidem adversus
Romanos volentibus Germanis sumptam numquam
omisisset. Falso libertatis vocabulum obtendi ab iis,
qui privatim degeneres, in publicum exitiosi, nihil
spei nisi per discordias habeant. Adstrepebat huic
alacre vulgus; et magno ut[2] inter barbaros proelio
victor rex, dein secunda fortuna ad superbiam

---

[1] Actumero *Muellenhoff:* catumero.   [2] ⟨ut⟩ *Lipsius.*

when, in jealousy of his power, the men who had flourished upon faction made their way to the adjacent tribes and there took up their testimony :—
" The ancient freedom of Germany was being filched away, and Roman power was mounting. Was it so indisputable that there was not a man born upon the same soil as themselves who was competent to fill the princely station, without this offspring of the scout Flavus being exalted above them all ? It was idle to invoke the name of Arminius. Had a son of Arminius returned to govern them after being reared in the enemy's country, they might well have dreaded a youth infected by foreign nurture, servitude, and dress,—in a word, by all things foreign ! As for Italicus, if he had the family disposition, no man had waged a more implacable war against country and home than had his father ! "

XVII. With these and similar appeals they collected a large force; nor was Italicus' following inferior :—" He had not," he reminded them, " taken an unwilling people by storm, but had been summoned because in nobility he stood higher than his rivals : as to his courage, let them test it and see if he proved himself worthy of his uncle Arminius, his grandsire Actumerus ! Nor did he blush for his father—that he had never renounced the obligations to Rome which he contracted with German assent. The name of liberty was being used as a dishonest pretext by men who, base-born themselves and a curse to the realm, had no hope but in civil dissensions." The crowd shouted applause, and in a battle, great as barbarian battles go, victory rested with the king. Then, flushed by success, he lapsed into arrogance, was expelled, was restored a second

prolapsus pulsusque, ac rursus Langobardorum opibus refectus, per laeta per adversa res Cheruscas adflictabat.

XVIII. Per idem tempus Chauci, nulla dissensione domi, et morte Sanquinii alacres, dum Corbulo adventat, inferiorem Germaniam incursavere duce Gannasco, qui natione Canninefas, auxiliare stipendium meritus,[1] post transfuga, levibus navigiis praedabundus Gallorum maxime oram vastabat, non ignarus ditis et inbellis esse. At Corbulo provinciam ingressus magna cum cura et mox gloria, cui principium illa militia fuit, triremis alveo Rheni, ceteras navium, ut quaeque habiles, per aestuaria et fossas adegit; luntribusque hostium depressis et exturbato Gannasco, ubi praesentia satis composita sunt, legiones operum et laboris ignavas, populationibus laetantis, veterem ad morem reduxit, ne quis agmine decederet nec pugnam nisi iussus iniret. Stationes, vigiliae, diurna nocturnaque munia in armis agitabantur. Feruntque militem, quia vallum non accinctus, atque alium, quia pugione tantum accinctus foderet, morte punitos. Quae nimia et incertum an falso iacta originem tamen e severitate

---

[1] auxiliare stipendium meritus *Bipontina* : auxiliare ex diu meritis *Med.—Possibly* :—auxiliare diu<stipendiū>meritus.

---

[1] East of the Elbe, north of Bohemia.
[2] The "Lesser Chauci," between the Ems and the Weser.
[3] Sanquinius Maximus (VI. 4). His death as *legatus pro praetore* of Lower Germany and his replacement by Corbulo (XIII. 8 n.) must have been noticed in the lost part of this book.
[4] IV. 73 n.

time by the Langobard[1] arms, and in his prosperity and in his adversity remained the scourge of the Cheruscan nation.

XVIII. During the same period, the Chauci,[2] untroubled by domestic strife and elated by the death of Sanquinius,[3] forestalled the arrival of Corbulo by raiding Lower Germany under the leadership of Gannascus,—a Canninefate[4] by extraction, once an auxiliary in the Roman service, then a deserter, and now with a piratical fleet of light vessels engaged in ravaging principally the coast of Gaul, with the wealth of whose peaceful communities he was well acquainted. On his entry into the province, however, Corbulo, showing extreme care and soon acquiring that great reputation which dates from this campaign, brought up his triremes[5] by the Rhine channel and the rest of his vessels, according to their draughts, by the estuaries and canals. Sinking the hostile boats, he ejected Gannascus, and, after adequately settling affairs on the spot, recalled the legions, as lethargic in their toils and duties as they were ardent in pillage, to the old code with its prohibitions against falling out on march or beginning an action without orders. Outpost and sentry work, duties of the day and the night, were carried out under arms; and it is on record that two soldiers were punished by death, one for digging soil for the rampart without sidearms, the other for doing so with none but his dagger. Exaggerated and possibly false as the tales may be, their starting-point is still the severity of the com-

---

[5] Belonging to the Rhine flotilla (*classis Germanica*), instituted by Drusus who cut for it the military canal (*fossa, Drusiana*) from the Rhine to the Zuyder Zee.

ducis traxere; intentumque et magnis delictis inexorabilem scias, cui tantum asperitatis etiam adversus levia credebatur.

XIX. Ceterum is terror milites hostisque in diversum adfecit: nos virtutem auximus, barbari ferociam infregere. Et natio Frisiorum, post rebellionem clade L. Apronii coeptam infensa aut male fida, datis obsidibus consedit apud agros a Corbulone descriptos: idem senatum, magistratus, leges inposuit. Ac ne iussa exuerent, praesidium immunivit, missis qui maiores Chaucos ad deditionem pellicerent, simul Gannascum dolo adgrederentur. Nec inritae aut degeneres insidiae fuere adversus transfugam et violatorem fidei. Sed caede eius motae Chaucorum mentes, et Corbulo semina rebellionis praebebat, ut laeta apud plerosque, ita apud quosdam sinistra fama. Cur hostem conciret? Adversa in rem publicam casura: sin prospere egisset, formidolosum paci virum insignem et ignavo principi praegravem. Igitur Claudius adeo novam in Germanias vim prohibuit, ut referri praesidia cis Rhenum iuberet.

XX. Iam castra in hostili solo molienti Corbuloni eae litterae redduntur. Ille re subita, quamquam multa simul offunderentur, metus ex imperatore,

---

[1] IV. 72 n.

[2] Between the Weser (which divided them from the *minores*) and the Elbe.

mander; and the man may safely be taken as strict and, to grave offences, inexorable, who was credited with such rigour in regard to trifles.

XIX. However, the terror he inspired had opposite effects on the soldiers and on the enemy: to us it meant a revival of courage, to the barbarians a weakening of confidence. So, the Frisian clan,[1] hostile or disaffected since the rebellion inaugurated by the defeat of Lucius Apronius, gave hostages and settled in the reservation marked out by Corbulo: who also imposed on them a senate, a magistracy, and laws. To guard against neglect of his orders, he built a fortified post in the district, while despatching agents to persuade the Greater Chauci[2] to surrender, and to attempt the life of Gannascus by ruse. The trap was neither ineffective nor, against a deserter and a violator of his faith, dishonourable; yet the killing of Gannascus unsettled the temper of the Chauci, and Corbulo was sowing the seeds of rebellion. Hence the news, though acceptable to many, was by some regarded as sinister:— "Why was he raising up an enemy? Any losses would fall upon the state: if success attended him, then a distinguished soldier, intolerable as such to a nervous emperor, constituted a threat to peace."— Claudius, therefore, so firmly prohibited fresh aggression against Germany that he ordered our garrisons to be withdrawn to the west bank of the Rhine.

XX. Corbulo was already arranging for his encampment on hostile ground, when the despatch was delivered. He was taken by surprise; but although a multitude of consequences poured upon his mind—danger from the emperor, contempt from the

contemptio ex barbaris, ludibrium apud socios, nihil
aliud prolocutus quam " Beatos quondam duces
Romanos," signum receptui dedit. Ut tamen
miles otium exueret, inter Mosam Rhenumque trium
et viginti milium spatio fossam perduxit, qua incerta
Oceani vitarentur. Insignia tamen triumphi indulsit
Caesar, quamvis bellum negavisset.

Nec multo post Curtius Rufus eundem honorem
adipiscitur, qui in agro Mattiaco recluserat specus
quaerendis venis argenti; unde tenuis fructus nec
in longum fuit: at legionibus cum damno labor,
effodere rivos, quaeque in aperto gravia, humum
infra moliri. Quis subactus miles, et quia plures per
provincias similia tolerabantur, componit occultas
litteras nomine exercituum, precantium imperatorem,
ut, quibus permissurus esset exercitus, triumphalia
ante tribueret.

XXI. De origine Curtii Rufi, quem gladiatore genitum quidam prodidere, neque falsa prompserim et
vera exsequi pudet. Postquam adolevit, sectator
quaestoris, cui Africa obtigerat, dum in oppido
Adrumeto vacuis per medium diei porticibus secretus
agitat, oblata ei species muliebris ultra modum
humanum et audita est vox :—" Tu es, Rufe, qui in
hanc provinciam pro consule venies." Tali omine in
spem sublatus degressusque in urbem[1] largitione

----

[1] urbem *Nipperdey :* urbe et.

----

[1] The difficult voyage between the mouths of the two rivers.
[2] *Legatus pro praetore* of Upper Germany; identified by
Lipsius and Ryck with Q. Curtius Rufus, the historian of
Alexander, but more probably his father.
[3] The Wiesbaden and Homburg district.
[4] So as to relieve him from the need of earning them by
the exertions of his troops.

barbarians, ridicule on the side of the provincials—he made no remark except: "Happy the Roman generals before my time!" and gave the signal for retreat. To give the troops occupation, however, he ran a canal, twenty-three miles in length, between the Meuse and Rhine, thus making it possible to evade the hazards of the North Sea.[1] The Caesar, though refusing him a war, conceded him none the less the insignia of a triumph.

Nor was it long before the same distinction was gained by Curtius Rufus,[2] who had opened a mine, in search of silver-lodes, in the district of Mattium.[3] The profits were slender and short-lived, but the legions lost heavily in the work of digging out water-courses and constructing underground workings which would have been difficult enough in the open. Worn out by the strain—and also because similar hardships were being endured in a number of provinces—the men drew up a private letter in the name of the armies, begging the emperor, when he thought of entrusting an army to a general, to assign him triumphal honours in advance.[4]

XXI. As to the origin of Curtius Rufus, whom some have described as the son of a gladiator, I would not promulgate a falsehood and I am ashamed to investigate the truth. On reaching maturity, he joined the train of a quaestor to whom Africa had been allotted, and, in the town of Adrumetum, was loitering by himself in an arcade deserted during the mid-day heat, when a female form of superhuman size rose before him, and a voice was heard to say: "Thou, Rufus, art he that shall come into this province as proconsul." With such an omen to raise his hopes, he left for the capital, and, thanks

amicorum, simul acri ingenio quaesturam et mox
nobilis inter candidatos praeturam principis suffragio
adsequitur, cum hisce verbis Tiberius dedecus natali-
um eius velavisset: " Curtius Rufus videtur mihi ex
se natus." Longa post haec senecta, et adversus
superiores tristi adulatione, adrogans minoribus,
inter pares difficulis, consulare imperium, triumphi
insignia ac postremo Africam obtinuit; atque ibi
defunctus fatale praesagium implevit.

XXII. Interea Romae, nullis palam neque cognitis
mox causis, Cn. Nonius eques Romanus ferro accinctus
reperitur in coetu salutantum principem. Nam
postquam tormentis dilaniabatur, de se non *infitiatus*
conscios non edidit, incertum an occultans.

Isdem consulibus P. Dolabella censuit spectaculum
gladiatorum per omnes annos celebrandum pecunia
eorum, qui quaesturam adipiscerentur. Apud maiores
virtutis id praemium fuerat, cunctisque civium, si
bonis artibus fiderent, licitum petere magistratus;
ac ne aetas quidem distinguebatur, quin prima
iuventa consulatum et dictaturas inirent. Sed quaestores regibus etiam tum imperantibus instituti
sunt, quod lex curiata ostendit ab L. Bruto repetita.
Mansitque consulibus potestas deligendi, donec

---

[1] The quaestors designate (XIII. 5 n.).

[2] The age of eligibility for the higher magistracies was
fixed by the *lex Villia annalis* (180 B.C.).

[3] The *lex curiata de imperio*—in the later republic, the merest
formality, but none the less indispensable—conferred *im-*

to the bounty of his friends backed by his own energy of character, attained the quaestorship, followed—in spite of patrician competitors—by a praetorship due to the imperial recommendation; for Tiberius had covered the disgrace of his birth by the remark: "Curtius Rufus I regard as the creation of himself." Afterwards, long of life and sullenly cringing to his betters, arrogant to his inferiors, unaccommodating among his equals, he held consular office, the insignia of triumph, and finally Africa; and by dying there fulfilled the destiny foreshadowed.

XXII. At Rome, in the meantime, for no reason then evident or afterwards ascertained, the Roman knight Gnaeus Nonius was discovered with a sword at his side amid the throng at the emperor's levée. Lacerated by the torturer, he admitted his own guilt, but divulged no accomplices: whether he concealed any is uncertain.

Under the same consuls, Publius Dolabella proposed that an exhibition of gladiators should be given yearly at the expense of the men who obtained a quaestorship.[1] With our ancestors, office had been the prize of merit, and all citizens who had confidence in their qualities could legitimately seek a magistracy; nor was there even a distinction of age, to preclude entrance upon a consulate or dictatorship in early youth.[2] The quaestorship itself was instituted while the kings still reigned, as shown by the renewal of the curiate law [3] by Lucius Brutus; and the power of selection remained with the consuls,

perium, during the regal period, upon the kings after election, and therefore, after the fall of the monarchy, on the two consuls as the king's successors.

eum quoque honorem populus mandaret. Creatique primum Valerius Poti*t*us et Aemilius Mamercus sexagensimo tertio anno post Tarquinios exactos, ut rem militarem comitarentur. Dein gliscentibus negotiis duo additi, qui Romae curarent: mox duplicatus numerus, stipendiaria iam Italia et accedentibus provinciarum vectigalibus: post lege Sullae viginti creati supplendo senatui, cui iudicia tradiderat. Et quamquam equites iudicia reciperavissent, quaestura tamen ex dignitate candidatorum aut facilitate tribuentium gratuito concedebatur, donec sententia Dolabellae velut venundaretur.

XXIII. A. Vitellio L. Vipstano consulibus cum de supplendo senatu agitaretur primoresque Galliae, quae Comata appellatur, foedera et civitatem Romanam pridem adsecuti ius adipiscendorum in urbe honorum expeterent, multus ea super re variusque rumor. Et studiis diversis apud principem certabatur, adseverantium non adeo aegram Italiam, ut senatum suppeditare urbi suae nequiret. Suffe-

---

[1] In 447 B.C., two years after the fall of the decemvirate, during which the quaestorship had been in abeyance.

[2] Actually, there can be little doubt, the urban quaestorship was older than the military (Liv. IV. 43).

[3] By the addition of four *quaestores classici* in 267 B.C., when Rome, after the Pyrrhic Wars, had become supreme in Italy.

[4] In 81 B.C.—As to the contests of the knights and senate for the *iudicia*, see XII. 60 n.

[5] The future emperor.

[6] " Long-haired Gaul " (the three imperial provinces of Aquitania, Lugdunensis, and Belgica), as opposed to "trousered Gaul" (the senatorial and completely romanized Gallia Narbonensis).

until this office, with the rest, passed into the bestowal of the people. The first election, sixty-three
years after the expulsion of the Tarquins,[1] was that
of Valerius Potitus and Aemilius Mamercus, as
finance officials attached to the army in the field.
Then, as their responsibilities grew, two were
added to take duty at Rome ;[2] and before long, with
Italy now contributory and revenues accruing from
the provinces, the number was again doubled.[3]
Later still, by a law of Sulla,[4] twenty were appointed
with a view to supplementing the senate, to the
members of which he had transferred the jurisdiction
in the criminal courts ; and, even when that jurisdiction had been reassumed by the knights, the
quaestorship was still granted without fee, in
accordance with the dignity of the candidates or by
the indulgence of the electors, until by the pro-
position of Dolabella it was virtually put up to
auction.

XXIII. In the consulate of Aulus Vitellius[5] and A.V.C. 801 =
Lucius Vipstanus, the question of completing the A.D. 48
numbers of the senate was under consideration, and
the leading citizens of Gallia Comata,[6] as it is termed,
who had long before obtained federate rights and
Roman citizenship,[7] were claiming the privilege of
holding magistracies in the capital. Comments on
the subject were numerous and diverse ; and in the
imperial council the debate was conducted with
animation on both sides :—" Italy," it was asserted,
" was not yet so moribund that she was unable to
supply a deliberative body to her own capital. The

---

[7] Their clans were *foederati* ; they themselves, full Roman
citizens, but without senatorial rank, and therefore ineligible
for the official career.

cisse olim indigenas consanguineis populis, nec
paenitere veteris rei publicae. Quin adhuc memorari
exempla, quae priscis moribus ad virtutem et gloriam
Romana indoles prodiderit. An parum quod Veneti
et Insubres curiam inruperint, nisi coetu[1] alienigena-
rum velut capitivitas inferatur? Quem ultra honorem
residuis nobilium, aut si quis pauper e Latio senator
foret? Oppleturos omnia divites illos, quorum avi
proavique hostilium nationum duces exercitus nostros
ferro vique cediderint, divum Iulium apud Alesiam
obsederint. Recentia haec: quid si memoria
eorum oreretur,[2] qui Capitolio et arce Romana
manibias deorum deripere conati sint[3]? Fruerentur
sane vocabulo civitatis: insignia patrum, decora
magistratuum ne vulgarent.

XXIV. His atque talibus haud permotus princeps
et statim contra disseruit et vocato senatu ita exorsus
est: " Maiores mei, quorum antiquissimus Clausus
origine Sabina simul in civitatem Romanam et in
familias patriciorum adscitus est, hortantur uti

---

[1] coetu *Ritter :* coetus.   [2] oreretur *Bach :* moreretur.
[3] manibias deorum deripere conati sint *Nipperdey (after
Heinsius)* : manibus eorundem per se satis *Med. The passage
is hopeless.*

---

[1] The Latin and Italian communities.
[2] Types of the Gallic population north of the Po, enfran-
chised by Caesar at the outbreak of the Civil War (49 B.C.).
[3] The scene of the siege, in 52 B.C., of Vercingetorix by Caesar
and of Caesar by the relieving Gaulish army (Caes. *B.G.* VII.
68 etc.); now Alise-Sainte-Reine, a village of some 600
inhabitants, between Semur and Dijon.
[4] The text is desperate, but refers to the capture of Rome
and siege of the Capitol by the Senonian Gauls after Allia
(390 B.C.).
[5] Large fragments of the actual speech, here re-written, re-
arranged, and condensed by Tacitus, were discovered at Lyons,

time had been when a Roman-born senate was enough for nations[1] whose blood was akin to their own; and they were not ashamed of the old republic. Why, even to-day men quoted the patterns of virtue and of glory which, under the old system, the Roman character had given to the world! Was it too little that Venetians and Insubrians[2] had taken the curia by storm, unless they brought in an army of aliens to give it the look of a taken town? What honours would be left to the relics of their nobility or the poor senator who came from Latium? All would be submerged by those opulent persons whose grandfathers and great-grandfathers, in command of hostile tribes, had smitten our armies by steel and the strong hand, and had besieged the deified Julius at Alesia.[3] But those were recent events! What if there should arise the memory of the men who essayed to pluck down the spoils, sanctified to Heaven, from the Capitol and citadel of Rome?[4] Leave them by all means to enjoy the title of citizens: but the insignia of the Fathers, the glories of the magistracies,—these they must not vulgarize!"

XXIV. Unconvinced by these and similar arguments, the emperor not only stated his objections there and then, but, after convening the senate, addressed it as follows:[5]—" In my own ancestors, the eldest of whom, Clausus,[6] a Sabine by extraction, was made simultaneously a citizen and the head of a patrician house, I find encouragement to employ

---

in 1524, and printed by Lipsius in an excursus to his famous edition fifty years later. They may be conveniently consulted in Orelli, Nipperdey, or Furneaux.

[6] IV. 9 n.

paribus consiliis in re publica [1] capessenda, trans-
ferendo huc quod usquam egregium fuerit. Neque
enim ignoro Iulios Alba, Coruncanios Camerio,
Porcios Tusculo, et ne vetera scrutemur, Etruria
Lucaniaque et omni Italia in senatum accitos,
postremo ipsam ad Alpes promotam, ut non modo
singuli viritim, sed terrae, gentes in nomen nostrum
coalescerent. Tunc solida domi quies et adversus
externa floruimus, cum Transpadani in civitatem
recepti, cum specie deductarum per orbem terrae
legionum additis provincialium validissimis fesso
imperio subventum est. Num paenitet Balbos ex
Hispania nec minus insignis viros e Gallia Narbonensi
transivisse? Manent posteri eorum nec amore in
hanc patriam nobis concedunt. Quid aliud exitio
Lacedaemoniis et Atheniensibus fuit, quamquam
armis pollerent, nisi quod victos pro alienigenis
arcebant? At conditor nostri Romulus tantum
sapientia valuit, ut plerosque populos eodem die
hostis, dein civis habuerit. Advenae in nos regna-
verunt: libertinorum filiis magistratus mandare [2]
non, ut plerique falluntur, repens, sed priori populo
factitatum est. At cum Senonibus pugnavimus:

---

[1] in re publica *Halm, Weissenborn:* rem publica (*with an erasure before* rem).

[2] mandare *Ritter:* mandaret.

---

[1] In Latium, like Alba and Tusculum; but the site is uncertain.

[2] In virtue of the extension of the franchise to all Italy south of the Po, at the end of the Social War.

the same policy in my administration, by trans-
ferring hither all true excellence, let it be found
where it will. For I am not unaware that the Julii
came to us from Alba, the Coruncanii from Camerium,[1]
the Porcii from Tusculum; that—not to scrutinize
antiquity—members were drafted into the senate
from Etruria, from Lucania, from the whole of Italy;[2]
and that finally Italy itself was extended to the
Alps,[3] in order that not individuals merely but
countries and nationalities should form one body
under the name of Romans. The day of stable
peace at home and victory abroad came when
the districts beyond the Po were admitted to citizenship, and, availing ourselves of the fact that our
legions were settled throughout the globe, we added
to them the stoutest of the provincials, and succoured
a weary empire. Is it regretted that the Balbi
crossed over from Spain and families equally distinguished from Narbonese Gaul? Their descendants remain; nor do they yield to ourselves in
love for this native land of theirs. What else proved
fatal to Lacedaemon and Athens, in spite of their
power in arms, but their policy of holding the conquered aloof as alien-born? But the sagacity of
our own founder Romulus was such that several
times he fought and naturalized a people in the
course of the same day! Strangers have been
kings over us: the conferment of magistracies on
the sons of freedmen is not the novelty which it is
commonly and mistakenly thought, but a frequent
practice of the old commonwealth.—' But we fought

[3] The reference is to Caesar's grant of the *civitas* to the
Gallic communities north of the Po, in 49 B.C., a date which
makes the following *tunc solida domi quies* curious.

scilicet Vulsci et Aequi numquam adversam nobis aciem instruxere. Capti a Gallis sumus: sed et Tuscis obsides dedimus et Samnitium iugum subii- mus.[1] Ac tamen,[2] si cuncta bella recenseas, nullum breviore spatio quam adversus Gallos confectum: continua inde ac fida pax. Iam moribus artibus adfinitatibus nostris mixti aurum et opes suas inferant potius quam separati habeant. Omnia, patres conscripti, quae nunc vetustissima creduntur, nova fuere: plebeii magistratus post patricios, Latini post plebeios, ceterarum Italiae gentium post Latinos. Inveterascet hoc quoque, et quod hodie exemplis tuemur, inter exempla erit."

XXV. Orationem principis secuto patrum consulto primi Aedui senatorum in urbe ius adepti sunt. Datum id foederi antiquo, et quia soli Gallorum fraternitatis nomen cum populo Romano usurpant.

Isdem diebus in numerum patriciorum adscivit Caesar vetustissimum quemque e senatu aut quibus

---

[1] subiimus *Orelli :* subimus.
[2] ac tamen *Halm :* attamen.

---

[1] Southern and eastern neighbours respectively of ancient Rome; associated with the legends of Coriolanus and Cincin- natus.

[2] After the surrender of Rome to Porsenna (*Hist.* III. 72; Plin. *H.N.* XXXIV. 14, 39).

with the Senones.'—Then, presumably, the Volscians and Aequians [1] never drew up a line of battle against us.—'We were taken by the Gauls.'—But we also gave hostages to the Tuscans [2] and underwent the yoke of the Samnites.[3]—And yet, if you survey the whole of our wars, not one was finished within a shorter period [4] than that against the Gauls: thenceforward there has been a continuous and loyal peace. Now that customs, culture, and the ties of marriage have blended them with ourselves, let them bring among us their gold and their riches instead of retaining them beyond the pale! All, Conscript Fathers, that is now believed supremely old has been new: plebeian magistrates followed the patrician; Latin, the plebeian; magistrates from the other races of Italy, the Latin. Our innovation, too, will be parcel of the past, and what to-day we defend by precedents will rank among precedents."

XXV. The emperor's speech was followed by a resolution of the Fathers, and the Aedui [5] became the first to acquire senatorial rights in the capital: a concession to a long-standing treaty and to their position as the only Gallic community enjoying the title of brothers to the Roman people.

Much at the same time, the Caesar adopted into the body of patricians all senators of exceptionally

[3] At the Caudine Forks in 321 B.C. (Liv. IX. init.).

[4] In ten years (59–50 B.C.). There were many shorter conquests; and, in his actual speech, Claudius emphasizes the obstinacy of their resistance (*Or. Claud.* ii. 31).

[5] Between the Loire and Saône, the capital being Augustodunum (Autun). The date of the treaty mentioned is unknown, but they were *socii populi Romani* in the Gracchan period (Liv. *Epit.* 61): the lapse under Sacrovir (III. 40 sqq.) is ignored.

clari parentes fuerant, paucis iam reliquis familiarum,
quas Romulus maiorum et L. Brutus minorum gentium appellaverant, exhaustis etiam quas dictator
Caesar lege Cassia et princeps Augustus lege Saenia
sublegere; laetaque haec in rem publicam munia
multo gaudio censoris inibantur. Famosos probris
quonam modo senatu depelleret anxius, mitem et
recens repertam quam ex severitate prisca rationem
adhibuit, monendo, secum quisque de se consultaret
peteretque ius exuendi ordinis: facilem eius rei
veniam. Et motos senatu excusatosque simul
propositurum, ut iudicium censorum[1] ac pudor
sponte cedentium permixta[2] ignominiam mollirent.
Ob ea Vipstanus consul rettulit patrem senatus
appellandum esse Claudium: quippe promiscum
patris patriae cognomentum; nova in rem publicam
merita non usitatis vocabulis honoranda: sed ipse
cohibuit consulem ut nimium adsentantem. Con-
diditque lustrum, quo censa sunt civium quinquagiens
noviens centena octoginta quattuor milia septuaginta
duo. Isque illi finis inscitiae erga domum suam fuit:
haud multo post flagitia uxoris noscere ac punire
adactus, ut deinde ardesceret in nuptias incestas.

---

[1] censorum] censorium *Faërnus*.
[2] permixta *Ritter :* permixti.

---

[1] A variant from the conventional account which describes
the hundred *patres maiorum gentium*, forming the senate of
Romulus, as supplemented by Tarquinius Priscus with a
hundred *minorum gentium*, and by L. Brutus with a hundred
conscripti from the equestrian order (Liv. I. 8, 35; II. 1).

[2] *Censu perfecto . . . instructum exercitum omnem suove-
taurilibus lustravit; idque conditum lustrum appellatum, quia
is censendo finis factus est*, Liv. I. 44.

[3] Jerome and Syncellus give 6,844,009 and 6,941,000

long standing or of distinguished parentage: for
by now few families remained of the Greater and
Lesser Houses, as they were styled by Romulus
and Lucius Brutus;[1] and even those selected to fill
the void, under the Cassian and Saenian laws, by the
dictator Caesar and the emperor Augustus were
exhausted. Here the censor had a popular task,
and he embarked upon it with delight.   How to
remove members of flagrantly scandalous character,
he hesitated; but adopted a lenient method,
recently introduced, in preference to one in the
spirit of old-world severity, advising each offender
to consider his case himself and to apply for the
privilege of renouncing his rank: that leave would
be readily granted; and he would publish the names
of the expelled and the excused together, so that
the disgrace should be softened by the absence of
anything to distinguish between censorial condemnation and the modesty of voluntary resignation.
In return, the consul Vipstanus proposed that
Claudius should be called Father of the Senate:—
" The title Father of his Country he would have to
share with others: new services to the state ought to
be honoured by unusual phrases." But he personally checked the consul as carrying flattery to
excess.   He also closed the lustrum,[2] the census
showing 5,984,072 citizens.[3]   And now came the end
of his domestic blindness: before long, he was
driven to note and to avenge the excesses of his
wife—only to burn afterwards for an incestuous
union.

respectively; but the figures of the *Mediceus* seem to represent
a more natural rate of increase upon the totals for 28 B.C.,
8 B.C., and 14 A.D. (4,063,000; 4,233,000; 4,937,000).

XXVI. Iam Messalina facilitate adulteriorum in
fastidium versa ad incognitas libidines profluebat,
cum abrumpi dissimulationem etiam Silius, sive [1]
fatali vaecordia an imminentium periculorum remedium ipsa pericula ratus, urguebat: quippe non eo
ventum, ut senectam principis opperirentur. In-
sontibus innoxia consilia, flagitiis manifestis subsidium ab audacia petendum. Adesse conscios paria
metuentes. Se caelibem, orbum, nuptiis et adoptan-
do Britannico paratum. Mansuram eandem Messalinae potentiam, addita securitate, si praevenirent
Claudium, ut insidiis incautum, ita irae properum.
Segniter eae voces acceptae, non amore in maritum,
sed ne Silius summa adeptus sperneret adulteram
scelusque inter ancipitia probatum veris mox pretiis
aestimaret. Nomen tamen matrimonii concupivit ob
magnitudinem infamiae, cuius apud prodigos novissima voluptas est. Nec ultra exspectato, quam dum
sacrificii gratia Claudius Ostiam proficisceretur,
cuncta nuptiarum sollemnia celebrat.

XXVII. Haud sum ignarus fabulosum visum iri tantum ullis mortalium securitatis fuisse in civitate omnium gnara et nihil reticente, nedum consulem designatum cum uxore principis, praedicta die, adhibitis
qui obsignarent, velut suscipiendorum liberorum
causa convenisse, atque illam audisse auspicum verba,

[1] <sive . . .> sive *Nipperdey.*

---

[1] Probably for the safety of the corn-fleet, as was inferred
by Lipsius from Dio's πρὸς ἐπίσκεψιν σίτου (LX. 31),
compared with Amm. Marc. XIX. 10, 4.

[2] *Id etiam tabulae* (the marriage contract) *indicant, ubi
scribitur:* '*liberorum procreandorum causa*' (S. Aug. *Serm.* 96).

[3] Now such in name alone (*nuptiarum auspices . . . qui re
omissa nomen tantum tenent,* Cic. *De div.* I. 16, 28).

XXVI. By now the ease of adultery had cloyed on Messalina and she was drifting towards untried debaucheries, when Silius himself, blinded by his fate, or convinced perhaps that the antidote to impending danger was actual danger, began to press for the mask to be dropped:—" They were not reduced to waiting upon the emperor's old age: deliberation was innocuous only to the innocent; detected guilt must borrow help from hardihood. They had associates with the same motives for fear. He himself was celibate, childless, prepared for wedlock and to adopt Britannicus. Messalina would retain her power unaltered, with the addition of a mind at ease, could they but forestall Claudius, who, if slow to guard against treachery, was prompt to anger." She took his phrases with a coolness due, not to any tenderness for her husband, but to a misgiving that Silius, with no heights left to scale, might spurn his paramour and come to appreciate at its just value a crime sanctioned in the hour of danger. Yet, for the sake of that transcendent infamy which constitutes the last delight of the profligate, she coveted the name of wife; and, waiting only till Claudius left for Ostia to hold a sacrifice,[1] she celebrated the full solemnities of marriage.

XXVII. It will seem, I am aware, fabulous that, in a city cognizant of all things and reticent of none, any human beings could have felt so much security; far more so, that on a specified day, with witnesses to seal the contract, a consul designate and the emperor's wife should have met for the avowed purposes of legitimate marriage;[2] that the woman should have listened to the words of the auspices,[3]

subisse *flammeum*,[1] sacrificasse apud deos; discubi-
tum inter convivas, oscula complexus, noctem
denique actam licentia coniugali. Sed nihil compositum miraculi causa, verum audita scriptaque
senioribus tradam.

XXVIII. Igitur domus principis inhorruerat, maximeque quos penes potentia et, si res verterentur,
formido, non iam secretis conloquiis, sed aperte fre-
mere, dum histrio cubiculum principis insultaverit,[2]
dedecus quidem inlatum, sed excidium procul afuisse:
nunc iuvenem nobilem dignitate formae, vi mentis ac
propinquo consulatu maiorem ad spem adcingi;
nec enim occultum, quid post tale matrimonium
superesset. Subibat sine dubio metus reputantes
hebetem Claudium et uxori devinctum multasque
mortes iussu Messalinae patratas: rursus ipsa
facilitas imperatoris fiduciam dabat, si atrocitate
criminis praevaluissent, posse opprimi damnatam
ante quam ream; sed in eo discrimen verti, si
defensio audiretur, utque clausae aures etiam
confitenti forent.

XXIX. Ac primo Callistus, iam mihi circa necem

---

[1] <flammeum> *Urlichs* (*from* XV 37).
[2] insultaverit *Bipontina :* exultabero.

---

[1] The great freedmen—nominally chief secretaries in the
emperor's household; in reality, heads of the executive, and
masters of Claudius and the empire. They are particularized
in the next chapter.
[2] Mnester (chap. 1 n.).

have assumed the veil, have sacrificed in the face of
Heaven; that both should have dined with the
guests, have kissed and embraced, and finally have
spent the night in the licence of wedlock. But I
have added no touch of the marvellous: all that I
record shall be the oral or written evidence of
my seniors.

XXVIII. A shudder, then, had passed through the
imperial household. In particular, the holders of
power[1] with all to fear from a reversal of the established
order, gave voice to their indignation, no longer in
private colloquies, but without disguise :—" Whilst
an actor [2] profaned the imperial bedchamber, humiliation might have been inflicted, but destruction
had still been in the far distance. Now, with his
stately presence, his vigour of mind, and his impending consulate, a youthful noble was girding
himself to a greater ambition—for the sequel of
such a marriage was no mystery ! " Fear beyond
doubt came over them when they considered the
hebetude of Claudius, his bondage to his wife, and
the many murders perpetrated at the fiat of Messalina. Yet, again, the very pliancy of the emperor
gave ground for confidence that, if they carried the
day thanks to the atrocity of the charge, they might
crush her by making her condemnation precede her
trial. But the critical question, they realized, was
whether Claudius would give a hearing to her defence,
and whether they would be able to close his ears
even to her confession.

XXIX. At the outset, Callistus [3] (whom I have

[3] Sold originally by a private owner (Sen. *Ep.* 47) to Caligula, over whom his influence was unbounded; now Secretary
of Petitions—*libertus a libellis*—to Claudius.

THE ANNALS OF TACITUS

Gai Caesaris narratus, et Appianae caedis molitor
Narcissus flagrantissimaque eo in tempore gratia
Pallas agitavere, num Messalinam secretis minis
depellerent amore Silii, cuncta alia dissimulantes.
Dein metu, ne ad perniciem ultro traherentur,
desistunt, Pallas per ignaviam, Callistus prioris
quoque regiae peritus et potentiam cautis quam
acribus consiliis tutius haberi : perstitit Narcissus,
solum [1] id immutans, ne quo sermone praesciam
criminis et accusatoris faceret. Ipse ad occasiones
intentus, longa apud Ostiam Caesaris mora, duas
paelices, quarum is corpori maxime insueverat, largitione ac promissis et uxore deiecta plus potentiae
ostentando perpulit delationem subire.

XXX. Exim Calpurnia (id enim [2] paelici nomen),
ubi datum secretum, genibus Caesaris provoluta
nupsisse Messalinam Silio exclamat; simul Cleo-
patram, quae id opperiens adstabat, an comperisset
interrogat, atque illa adnuente cieri Narcissum
postulat. Is veniam in praeteritum petens, quod
ei Vettios, Plautios [3] dissimulavisset, nec nunc

---

[1] solum *Agricola :* ut solum.
[2] id enī *Jackson :* idem *Med.*, id *vulg.* For enim *compare*
X V !. 30, Serviliae (id enim nomen puellae fuit) : *for the con-*
fusion, Liv. I. 17, 9 (idem *F³ϛ* : id enim Ω).
[3] Vettios, Plautios *Nipperdey :* cis uetticis plautio.

---

[1] The Secretary of State (*libertus ab epistulis*); μέγιστον
τῶν τότε ἀνθρώπων δυνηθείς (D. Cass. LX. 34), and the most
striking figure of the triumvirate. His partnership with
Messalina in the destruction of Ap. Junius Silanus (IV. 68 n.)
is described by Suetonius (*Claud.* 37). For his later career,
see the remainder of this book, with XII. 1, 57, 65; XIII. 1.
[2] Freedman of the emperor's mother Antonia; Financial

already noticed in connection with the killing of
Gaius Caesar), together with Narcissus,[1] the contriver
of the Appian murder, and Pallas,[2] then in the high
noon of his favour, discussed the chances of diverting
Messalina from her amour with Silius by private
threats, while suppressing their knowledge of all
other circumstances. Then, lest failure should
involve their own destruction, Pallas and Callistus
desisted; Pallas, through cowardice; the other,
because he had expert knowledge of the last court
as well and believed power to be held more securely
by cautious than by vigorous counsels. Narcissus
stood firm, making only one modification of the
plan: there was to be no interview to forewarn her
of the accusation or of the accuser. Himself on the
alert for opportunities, as the Caesar lingered long at
Ostia, he induced the pair of concubines, to whose
embraces Claudius was the most habituated, by
gifts, promises, and demonstrations of the power
which would accrue to them from the fall of the wife,
to undertake the task of delation.

XXX. As the next step, Calpurnia—for so the
woman was called—secured a private audience, and,
falling at the Caesar's knee, exclaimed that Messalina had wedded Silius. In the same breath, she
asked Cleopatra, who was standing by ready for
the question, if she had heard the news; and, on her
sign of assent, requested that Narcissus should be
summoned. He, entreating forgiveness for the past,
in which he had kept silence to his master on the
subject of Vettius, Plautius,[3] and their like, said that

Secretary (*libertus a rationibus*), and brother of the Felix of
Acts xxiii. sq.
[3] Chaps. 31, 35 sq.

adulteria obiecturum ait, ne*dum* domum[1] servitia et
ceteros fortunae paratus reposceret. Frueretur
immo his, set redderet uxorem rumperetque tabulas
nuptiales. " An discidium " inquit " tuum nosti?
Nam matrimonium Silii vidit populus et senatus et
miles; ac ni propere agis, tenet urbem maritus."

XXXI. Tum potissimum *quemque* amicorum vocat,
primumque rei frumentariae praefectum Turranium,
post Lusium Getam praetorianis inpositum percon-
tatur. Quis fatentibus certatim ceteri circumstre-
punt, iret in castra, firmaret praetorias cohortes,
securitati ante quam vindictae consuleret. Satis
constat eo pavore offusum Claudium, ut identidem
interrogaret, an ipse imperii potens, an Silius privatus
esset. At Messalina non alias solutior luxu, adulto
autumno simulacrum vindemiae per domum cele-
brabat. Urgueri prela, fluere lacus; et feminae
pellibus accinctae adsultabant ut sacrificantes vel
insanientes Bacchae; ipsa crine fluxo thyrsum
quatiens, iuxtaque Silius hedera vinctus, gerere
cothurnos, iacere caput, strepente circum procaci
choro. Ferunt Vettium Valentem lascivia in praeal-

---

[1] nedum domum *Halm :* ne domum.

[1] Οἰκίαν αὐτῷ (Silius) βασιλικὴν ἐχαρίσατο (Messalina),
πάντα τὰ τιμιώτατα τῶν τοῦ Κλαυδίου κειμηλίων συμφορήσασα
ἐς αὐτήν (D. Cass. LX. 31).

[2] This *exactae diligentiae senex*, now a nonagenarian (Sen.
Brev. vit. 20), had held his office for at least thirty-four years
(I. 7).

[3] Colleague of Rufrius Crispinus (chap. 1).

not even now would he reproach the lady with her adulteries, far less reclaim the palace, the slaves, and other appurtenances of the imperial rank.[1] No, these Silius might enjoy—but let him restore the bride and cancel the nuptial contract! " Are you aware," he demanded, " of your divorce? For the nation, the senate, and the army, have seen the marriage of Silius; and, unless you act with speed, the new husband holds Rome! "

XXXI. The Caesar now summoned his principal friends; and, in the first place, examined Turranius,[2] head of the corn-department; then the praetorian commander Lusius Geta.[3] They admitted the truth; and from the rest of the circle came a din of voices :—" He must visit the camp, assure the fidelity of the guards, consult his security before his vengeance." Claudius, the fact is certain, was so bewildered by his terror that he inquired intermittently if he was himself emperor—if Silius was a private citizen.

But Messalina had never given voluptuousness a freer rein. Autumn was at the full, and she was celebrating a mimic vintage through the grounds of the house. Presses were being trodden, vats flowed; while, beside them, skin-girt women were bounding like Bacchanals excited by sacrifice or delirium. She herself was there with dishevelled tresses and waving thyrsus; at her side, Silius with an ivy crown,[4] wearing the buskins and tossing his head, while around him rose the din of a wanton chorus. The tale runs that Vettius Valens,[5] in some freak of

---

[4] He was impersonating Bacchus.

[5] A lover of Messalina, and a doctor of celebrity (Plin. *H.N.* XXIX. 1, 8).

tam arborem conisum, interrogantibus quid aspiceret, respondisse tempestatem ab Ostia atrocem, sive coeperat ea species, seu forte lapsa vox in praesagium vertit.

XXXII. Non rumor interea, sed undique nuntii incedunt, qui gnara Claudio cuncta et venire promptum ultioni adferrent. Igitur Messalina Lucullianos in hortos, Silius dissimulando metu ad munia fori digrediuntur. Ceteris passim dilabentibus adfuere centuriones, inditaque sunt vincla, ut quis reperiebatur in publico aut per latebras. Messalina tamen, quamquam res adversae consilium eximerent, ire obviam et aspici a marito, quod saepe subsidium habuerat, haud segniter intendit misitque[1] ut Britannicus et Octavia in complexum patris pergerent Et Vibidiam, virginum Vestalium vetustissimam, oravit pontificis maximi auris adire, clementiam expetere. Atque interim, tribus omnino comitantibus—id repente solitudinis erat—spatium urbis pedibus emensa, vehiculo, quo purgamenta hortorum excipiuntur,[2] Ostiensem viam intrat, nulla cuiusquam misericordia, quia flagitiorum deformitas praevalebat.

XXXIII. Trepidabatur nihilo minus a Caesare: quippe Getae praetorii praefecto haud satis fidebant, ad honesta seu prava iuxta levi. Ergo Narcissus, adsumptis quibus idem metus, non aliam spem in-

---

[1] misitque *Halm* : misique *Med.*, missique *Med²*.
[2] excipiuntur *Heinsius*: eripiuntur *Med.*, *Fisher.*

---

[1] The emperor himself (III. 58 n.). For the weight attached to the intercession of any Vestal, see the close of Cicero's *Pro Fonteio* (46 sqq.).

humour, clambered into a tall tree, and to the
question, " What did he spy ? " answered : " A
frightful storm over Ostia "—whether something of
the kind was actually taking shape, or a chance-
dropped word developed into a prophecy.

XXXII. In the meanwhile, not rumour only but
messengers were hurrying in from all quarters,
charged with the news that Claudius knew all and
was on the way, hot for revenge. They parted therefore ; Messalina to the Gardens of Lucullus ; Silius—
to dissemble his fear—to the duties of the forum.
The rest were melting away by one road or other,
when the centurions appeared and threw them into
irons as discovered, some in the open, some in hiding.
Messalina, though the catastrophe excluded thought,
promptly decided for the course which had so often
proved her salvation, to meet her husband and be
seen by him : also, she sent word that Britannicus
and Octavia were to go straight to their father's
arms. Further, she implored Vibidia, the senior
Vestal Virgin, to gain the ear of the Supreme Pontiff [1]
and there plead for mercy. In the interval, with
three companions in all (so complete, suddenly, was
her solitude), she covered the full breadth of the city
on foot, then mounted a vehicle used as a receptacle
for garden refuse, and took the Ostian road, without
a being to pity her, since all was outweighed by the
horror of her crimes.

XXXIII. Quite equal agitation prevailed on the
imperial side ; as implicit confidence was not felt
in the praetorian commandant Geta, who veered
with equal levity to the good and to the evil.
Narcissus, therefore, with the support of others who
shared his alarms, stated formally that there was no

columitatis Caesaris adfirmat, quam si ius militum
uno illo die in aliquem libertorum transferret, seque
offert suscepturum. Ac ne, dum in urbem revehitur,[1]
ad paenitentiam a L. Vitellio et [2] Largo Caecina
mutaretur, in eodem gestamine sedem poscit
adsumiturque.[3]

XXXIV. Crebra post haec fama fuit, inter diversas
principis voces, cum modo incusaret flagitia uxoris,
aliquando ad memoriam coniugii et infantiam liberorum revolveretur, non aliud prolocutum Vitellium
quam " O facinus! o scelus! " Instabat quidem
Narcissus aperiret [4] ambages et veri copiam faceret:
sed non ideo pervicit, quin suspensa et quo
ducerentur inclinatura responderet exemploque eius
Largus Caecina uterétur.

Et iam erat in aspectu Messalina clamitabatque
audiret Octaviae et Britannici matrem, cum obstre-
pere accusator, Silium et nuptias referens; simul
codicillos libidinum indices tradidit, quis visus
Caesaris averteret. Nec multo post urbem ingredienti
offerebantur communes liberi, nisi Narcissus amoveri
eos iussisset. Vibidiam depellere nequivit, quin
multa cum invidia flagitaret, ne indefensa coniunx
exitio daretur. Igitur auditurum principem et fore

---

[1] revehitur *Orelli :* refertur uehitur.
[2] et *Nipperdey :* P.
[3] assumiturque *Walther :* assumitque.
[4] aperiret . . . faceret *Madvig :* aperire . . . facere.

---

[1] Colleague of Claudius in the consulship six years earlier.
[2] A *cri du cœur* which might, of course, have been wrung
from him either by the conduct of Messalina or by that of
Narcissus.

hope of saving the emperor, unless, for that day only, the command of the troops was transferred to one of the freedmen; the responsibility he offered to take himself. Furthermore, that Claudius, while being conveyed to the city, should not be swayed to repentance by Lucius Vitellius and Caecina Largus,[1] he demanded a seat in the same litter, and took his place along with them.

XXXIV. It was a persistent tradition later that, amid the self-contradictory remarks of the emperor, who at one moment inveighed against the profligacies of his wife, and, in the next, recurred to memories of his wedded life and to the infancy of his children, Vitellius merely ejaculated: " Ah, the crime—the villainy ! "[2] Narcissus, it is true, urged him to explain his enigma and favour them with the truth; but urgency was unavailing; Vitellius responded with incoherent phrases, capable of being turned to any sense required, and his example was copied by Caecina Largus.

And now Messalina was within view. She was crying to the emperor to hear the mother of Octavia and Britannicus, when the accuser's voice rose in opposition with the history of Silius and the bridal: at the same time, to avert the Caesar's gaze, he handed him the memoranda exposing her debaucheries. Shortly afterwards, at the entry into Rome, the children of the union were on the point of presenting themselves, when Narcissus ordered their removal. Vibidia he could not repulse, nor prevent her from demanding in indignant terms that a wife should not be given undefended to destruction. He therefore replied that the emperor would hear her and there would be opportunities for

diluendi criminis facultatem respondit : iret interim
virgo et sacra capesseret.

XXXV. Mirum inter haec silentium Claudi, Vitellius ignaro propior : omnia liberto oboediebant. Pate-
fieri domum adulteri atque illuc deduci imperatorem
iubet. Ac primum in vestibulo effigiem patris Silii
consulto senatus abolitam demonstrat, tum quidquid
avitum Neronibus et Drusis in pretium probri cessisse.
Incensumque et ad minas erumpentem castris infert,
parata contione militum; apud quos praemonente
Narcisso pauca verba fecit : nam iustum dolorem
pudor impediebat. Continuus dehinc cohortium
clamor nomina reorum et poenas flagitantium;
admotusque Silius tribunali non defensionem, non
moras temptavit, precatus ut mors adceleraretur.
Eadem constantia et inlustres equites Romani
[cupido maturae necis fuit].[1] Et Titium Proculum,
custodem a Silio Messalinae datum et indicium
offerentem, Vettium Valentem confessum et Pompeium Urbicum ac Saufeium Trogum ex consciis tradi
ad supplicium iubet. Decrius quoque Calpurnianus
vigilum praefectus, Sulpicius Rufus ludi procurator,
Iuncus Vergilianus senator eadem poena adfecti.

---

[1] [cupido . . . fuit] *Nipperdey. But the words have no
resemblance to a gloss ; the* equites illustres *ought to be named ;
and it would be preferable to mark a lacuna after* Romani.

---

[1] Its destruction had evidently been ordered at the condemnation of Silius (IV. 18–20).

[2] The appointment of such guardians of conjugal fidelity
was not uncommon under the empire. Here the detail is at
least in keeping with the general insanity of the proceedings.

[3] The semi-military night police and fire-brigade of Rome.
The force, instituted by Augustus, comprised seven cohorts
(each responsible for two of the fourteen wards), recruited in
the main from freedmen.

[4] For the maintenance and training of the bands, required

rebutting the charge: meanwhile, the Virgin would do well to go and attend to her religious duties.

XXXV. Throughout the proceedings Claudius maintained a strange silence, Vitellius wore an air of unconsciousness: all things moved at the will of the freedman. He ordered the adulterer's mansion to be thrown open and the emperor to be conducted to it. First he pointed out in the vestibule an effigy—banned by senatorial decree [1]—of the elder Silius; then he demonstrated how the heirlooms of the Neros and the Drusi had been requisitioned as the price of infamy. As the emperor grew hot and broke into threats, he led him to the camp, where a mass-meeting of the troops had been prearranged. After a preliminary address by Narcissus, he spoke a few words: for, just as his resentment was, shame denied it utterance. There followed one long cry from the cohorts demanding the names and punishment of the criminals. Set before the tribunal, Silius attempted neither defence nor delay, and asked for an acceleration of death. His firmness was imitated by a number of Roman knights of the higher rank. Titius Proculus, appointed by Silius as "custodian" [2] of Messalina, and now proffering evidence, was ordered for execution, together with Vettius Valens, who confessed, and their accomplices Pompeius Urbicus and Saufeius Trogus. The same penalty was inflicted also on Decrius Calpurnianus, prefect of the city-watch; [3] on Sulpicius Rufus, procurator of the school of gladiators; [4] and on the senator Juncus Vergilianus.

at games exhibited by the emperor. The procurator was of equestrian rank, and the post a stepping-stone to financial offices of some importance.

THE ANNALS OF TACITUS

XXXVI. Solus Mnester cunctationem attulit, dilaniata veste clamitans, aspiceret verberum notas, reminisceretur vocis, qua se obnoxium iussis Messalinae dedisset: aliis largitione aut spei magnitudine, sibi ex necessitate culpam; nec cuiquam ante pereundum fuisse, si Silius rerum poteretur. Commotum his et pronum ad misericordiam Caesarem perpulere liberti, ne tot inlustribus viris interfectis histrioni consuleretur: sponte an coactus tam magna peccavisset, nihil referre. Ne Trauli quidem Montani equitis Romani defensio recepta est. Is modesta iuventa, sed corpore insigni, accitus ultro noctemque intra unam a Messalina proturbatus erat, paribus lasciviis ad cupidinem et fastidia. Suillio Caesonino et Plautio Laterano mors remittitur, huic ob patrui egregium meritum: Caesoninus vitiis protectus est, tamquam in illo foedissimo coetu passus muliebria.

XXXVII. Interim Messalina Lucullianis in hortis prolatare vitam, componere preces, nonnulla spe et aliquando ira; tantum inter extrema superbiae gerebat.[1] Ac ni caedem eius Narcissus properavisset, verterat pernicies in accusatorem. Nam Claudius domum regressus et tempestivis epulis delenitus, ubi vino incaluit, iri iubet nuntiarique miserae (hoc

---

[1] superbiae gerebat *Bezzenberger :* superbia egebat.

---

[1] His orders were brief but comprehensive—ὅσα ἂν προστάττηται ὑπὸ τῆς Μεσσαλίνης ποιεῖν (D. Cass. LX. 22).
[2] See chap. 2.
[3] Nephew of A. Plautius Silvanus, the conqueror of Britain. See XIII. 11; XV. 49, 60.

XXXVI. Only Mnester caused some hesitation, as, tearing his garments, he called to Claudius to look at the imprints of the lash and remember the phrase by which he had placed him at the disposal of Messalina.[1] "Others had sinned through a bounty or a high hope; he, from need; and no man would have had to perish sooner, if Silius gained the empire." The Caesar was affected, and leaned to mercy; but the freedmen decided him, after so many executions of the great, not to spare an actor: when the transgression was so heinous, it mattered nothing whether it was voluntary or enforced. Even the defence of the Roman knight Traulus Montanus was not admitted. A modest but remarkably handsome youth, he had within a single night received his unsought invitation and his dismissal from Messalina, who was equally capricious in her desires and her disdains. In the cases of Suillius Caesoninus[2] and Plautius Lateranus,[3] the death penalty was remitted. The latter was indebted to the distinguished service of his uncle: Suillius was protected by his vices, since in the proceedings of that shameful rout his part had been the reverse of masculine.

XXXVII. Meanwhile, in the Gardens of Lucullus, Messalina was fighting for life, and composing a petition; not without hope, and occasionally—so much of her insolence she had retained in her extremity—not without indignation. In fact, if Narcissus had not hastened her despatch, the ruin had all but fallen upon the head of the accuser. For Claudius, home again and soothed by an early dinner, grew a little heated with the wine, and gave instructions for someone to go and inform "the poor woman"—the exact phrase which he is stated to have

enim verbo usum ferunt) dicendam ad causam postero
die adesset. Quod ubi auditum et languescere ira,
redire amor ac, si cunctarentur, propinqua nox et
uxorii cubiculi memoria timebantur, prorumpit
Narcissus denuntiatque centurionibus et tribuno,
qui aderat, exsequi caedem : ita imperatorem iubere.
Custos et exactor e libertis Euodus datur. Isque
raptim in hortos praegressus repperit fusam humi,
adsidente matre Lepida, quae florenti filiae haud
concors supremis eius necessitatibus ad miserationem
evicta erat suadebatque, ne percussorem opperiretur :
transisse vitam neque aliud quam morti decus
quarendum. Sed animo per libidines corrupto
nihil honestum inerat : lacrimaeque et quaestus
inriti ducebantur, cum impetu venientium pulsae
fores adstititque tribunus per silentium, at libertus
increpans multis et servilibus probris.

XXXVIII. Tunc primum fortunam suam intro-
spexit ferrumque accepit, quod frustra iugulo aut
pectori per trepidationem admovens ictu tribuni tran-
sigitur. Corpus matri concessum. Nuntiatiumque
Claudio epulanti perisse Messalinam, non distincto
sua an aliena manu. Nec ille quaesivit, poposcitque
poculum et solita convivio celebravit. Ne secutis

---

[1] Nero's aunt, Domitia Lepida (XII. 64 n.).

[2] By Suetonius the unfortunate lapse of memory in the
case of Poppaea Sabina (chap. 2) is transferred to this occasion:
*Occisa Messalina, paulo post quam in triclinio decubuit, 'cur
domina non venisset' requisiit (Claud.* 39). Seneca, too, makes
play with the emperor's lack of interest in the affair :—*Dic
mihi, dive Claudi,* says Augustus (*Apocol.* 10), . . . *tu Messalinam, cuius aeque avunculus maior eram quam tuus, occidisti?
' Nescio,' inquis.*

used—that she must be in presence next day to plead her cause. The words were noted: his anger was beginning to cool, his love to return; and, if they waited longer, there was ground for anxiety in the approaching night with its memories of the marriage-chamber. Narcissus, accordingly, burst out of the room, and ordered the centurions and tribune in attendance to carry out the execution: the instructions came from the emperor. Evodus, one of the freedmen, was commissioned to guard against escape and to see that the deed was done. Hurrying to the Gardens in advance of the rest, he discovered Messalina prone on the ground, and, seated by her side, her mother Lepida;[1] who, estranged from her daughter during her prime, had been conquered to pity in her last necessity, and was now advising her not to await the slayer:—" Life was over and done; and all that could be attempted was decency in death." But honour had no place in that lust-corrupted soul, and tears and lamentations were being prolonged in vain, when the door was driven in by the onrush of the new-comers, and over her stood the tribune in silence, and the freedman upbraiding her with a stream of slavish insults.

XXXVIII. Now for the first time she saw her situation as it was, and took hold of the steel. In her agitation, she was applying it without result to her throat and again to her breast, when the tribune ran her through. The corpse was granted to her mother; and word was carried to Claudius at the table that Messalina had perished: whether by her own or a strange hand was not specified. Nor was the question asked:[2] he called for a cup and went through the routine of the banquet. Even in the

quidem diebus odii gaudii, irae tristitiae, ullius denique humani adfectus signa dedit, non cum laetantis accusatores aspiceret, non cum filios maerentis. Iuvitque oblivionem eius senatus censendo nomen et effigies privatis ac publicis locis demovendas. Decreta Narcisso quaestoria insignia, levissimum fastidio[1] eius, cum super Pallantem et Callistum ageret . . . honesta quidem, sed ex quis deterrima orerentur tristitiis multis.[2]

[1] fastidio *Ernesti*: fastidii *Med.*, fastigii *dett.*
[2] *The sentence is both defective and corrupt.*

days that followed, he betrayed no symptoms of
hatred or of joy, of anger or of sadness, or, in fine, of
any human emotion; not when he saw the accusers
rejoicing, not when he saw his children mourning.
His forgetfulness was assisted by the senate, which
decreed that the name and statues of the empress
should be removed from private and public places.
The decorations of the quaestorship were voted to
Narcissus: baubles to the pride of one who bore
himself as the superior of Pallas and Callistus!
. . . . . . Meritorious actions, it is true, but
fated to produce the worst of results. . . . . .

BOOK XII

LIBER XII

I. Caede Messalinae convulsa principis domus, orto apud libertos certamine, quis deligeret uxorem Claudio, caelibis vitae intoleranti et coniugum imperiis obnoxio. Nec minore ambitu feminae exarserant: suam quaeque nobilitatem formam opes contendere ac digna tanto matrimonio ostentare. Sed maxime ambigebatur inter Lolliam Paulinam M. Lollii[1] consularis et Iuliam Agrippinam Germanico genitam: huic Pallas, illi Callistus fautores aderant; at Aelia Paetina e familia Tuberonum Narcisso fovebatur. ipse huc modo, modo illuc, ut quemque suadentium audierat, promptus,[2] discordantis in consilium vocat ac promere sententiam et adicere rationes iubet.

II. Narcissus vetus matrimonium, filiam[3] communem (nam Antonia ex Paetina erat), nihil in penatibus eius novum disserebat, si sueta coniunx rediret, haudquaquam novercalibus odiis visura Britannicum,

---

[1] ⟨M. Lollio, filio⟩ M. Lollii *Madvig.*
[2] promptus] pronus *Muretus.*
[3] filiam *Muretus*: familiam.

---

[1] Granddaughter of M. Lollius (III. 48 n.); taken from her husband, Memmius Regulus, by Caligula, but quickly divorced. succumbed to the jealousy of Agrippina (chap. 22, XIV. 12). The elder Pliny had seen her at an ordinary dinner in jewels valued at 40,000,000 sesterces (*H.N.* IX. 35, 58).

BOOK XII

I. THE execution of Messalina shook the imperial household: for there followed a conflict among the freedmen, who should select a consort for Claudius, with his impatience of celibacy and his docility under wifely government. Nor was competition less fierce among the women: each paraded for comparison her nobility, her charms, and her wealth, and advertised them as worthy of that exalted alliance. The question, however, lay mainly between Lollia Paulina,[1] daughter of the consular Marcus Lollius, and Julia Agrippina, the issue of Germanicus. The latter had the patronage of Pallas; the former, of Callistus; while Aelia Paetina,[2] a Tubero by family, was favoured by Narcissus. The emperor, who leaned alternately to one or the other, according to the advocate whom he had heard the last, called the disputants into council, and ordered each to express his opinion and to add his reasons.

II. Narcissus discoursed on his early marriage, on the daughter who had blessed that union (for Antonia was Paetina's child), on the fact that no innovation in his domestic life would be entailed by the return of a spouse, who would regard Britannicus and Octavia —pledges of affection, next in dearness to her own

---

[2] Already married to Claudius, but divorced *ex levibus offensis* (Suet. *Claud.* 26). For their daughter, Claudia Antonia, cf. XV. 53.

Octaviam, proxima suis pignora. Callistus inprobatam longo discidio, ac si rursum adsumeretur, eo ipso superbam; longeque rectius Lolliam induci, quando nullos liberos genuisset, vacuam aemulatione et privignis parentis loco futuram. At Pallas id maxime in Agrippina laudare, quod Germanici nepotem secum traheret, dignum prorsus imperatoria fortuna: stirpem nobilem et familiae *Iuliae* Claudiaeque [1] posteros coniungeret, ne femina expertae fecunditatis, integra iuventa, claritudinem Caesarum aliam in domum ferret.

III. Praevaluere haec adiuta Agrippinae inlecebris: ad eum per speciem necessitudinis crebro ventitando pellicit patruum, ut praelata ceteris et nondum uxor potentia uxoria iam uteretur. Nam ubi sui matrimonii certa fuit, struere maiora nuptiasque Domitii, quem ex Cn. Ahenobarbo genuerat, et Octaviae Caesaris filiae moliri; quod sine scelere perpetrari non poterat, quia L. Silano desponderat Octaviam Caesar iuvenemque et alia clarum insigni triumphalium et gladiatorii muneris magnificentia protulerat ad studia vulgi. Sed nihil arduum videbatur in animo principis, cui non iudicium, non odium erat nisi indita et iussa.

---

[1] ⟨Iuliae⟩ Claudiaeque *Freinsheim, Heinsius*: Claudiae quae.

---

[1] The present L. Domitius Ahenobarbus—the future Nero (XI. 11).

[2] As daughter of the elder Agrippina and Germanicus, Agrippina was a member, on the mother's side, of the Julian house; on the father's, of the Claudian. See the stemmata, vol. ii. p. 240 sq.

[3] Son of M. Silanus (II. 59; *Hist.* IV. 48) and Aemilia Lepida, granddaughter of Augustus.

—with anything rather than stepmotherly aversion. Callistus held that she was disqualified by her long-standing divorce, and, if recalled, would by the very fact be inclined to arrogance. A far wiser course was to bring in Lollia, who, as she had never known motherhood, would be immune from jealousy, and could take the place of a parent to her step-children. Pallas, in his eulogy of Agrippina, insisted on the point that she brought with her the grandson of Germanicus,[1] who fully deserved an imperial position: let the sovereign unite to himself a famous stock, the posterity of the Julian and Claudian races,[2] and ensure that a princess of tried fecundity, still in the vigour of youth, should not transfer the glory of the Caesars into another family!

III. His arguments prevailed, with help from the allurements of Agrippina. In a succession of visits, cloaked under the near relationship, she so effectually captivated her uncle that she displaced her rivals and anticipated the position by exercising the powers of a wife. For, once certain of her marriage, she began to amplify her schemes, and to intrigue for a match between Domitius, her son by Gnaeus Ahenobarbus, and the emperor's daughter Octavia. That result was not to be achieved without a crime, as the Caesar had plighted Octavia to Lucius Silanus,[3] and had introduced the youth (who had yet other titles to fame) to the favourable notice of the multitude by decorating him with the triumphal insignia and by a magnificent exhibition of gladiators. Still, there seemed to be no insuperable difficulty in the temper of a prince who manifested neither approval nor dislike except as they were imposed upon him by orders.

IV. Igitur Vitellius, nomine censoris servilis
fallacias obtegens ingruentiumque dominationum
provisor, quo gratiam Agrippinae pararet, consiliis
eius implicari, ferre crimina in Silanum, cui*us* sane
decora et procax soror, Iunia Calvina, haud multum [1]
ante Vitellii nurus fuerat.   Hinc initium accusationis;
fratrumque non incestum, sed incustoditum amorem
ad infamiam traxit.   Et praebebat Caesar auris,
accipiendis adversus generum suspicionibus caritate
filiae promptior.   At Silanus insidiarum nescius ac
forte eo anno praetor, repente per edictum Vitellii
ordine senatorio movetur, quamquam lecto pridem
senatu lustroque condito.   Simul adfinitatem Claudius
diremit, adactusque Silanus eiurare magistratum, et
reliquus praeturae dies in Eprium Marcellum
conlatus est.

V. C. Pompeio Q. Veranio consulibus pactum inter
Claudium et Agrippinam matrimonium iam fama,
iam amore inlicito firmabatur; necdum celebrare
sollemnia nuptiarum audebant, nullo exemplo de-
ductae in domum patrui fratris filiae: quin et
incestum ac, si sperneretur, ne in malum publicum
erumperet, metuebatur.   Nec ante omissa cunctatio,
quam Vitellius suis artibus id perpetrandum sumpsit.
Percontatusque   Caesarem   an   iussis   populi,   an

---

[1] multum] multo *Halm*.

---

[1] See XI. 23 sqq.
[2] The earliest mention of the famous *delator*, for whom see
XIII. 33 n.

IV. Vitellius, therefore, able to screen his servile knaveries behind the title of Censor, and with a prophetic eye for impending tyrannies, wooed the good graces of Agrippina by identifying himself with her scheme and by producing charges against Silanus, whose sister—fair and wayward, it is true—had until recently been his own daughter-in-law. This gave him the handle for his accusation, and he put an infamous construction on a fraternal love which was not incestuous but unguarded. The Caesar lent ear, affection for his daughter increasing his readiness to harbour doubts of her prospective husband. Silanus, ignorant of the plot, and, as it happened, praetor for the year, was suddenly by an edict of Vitellius removed from the senatorial order, though the list had long been complete and the lustrum closed.[1] At the same time, Claudius cancelled the proposed alliance: Silanus was compelled to resign his magistracy, and the remaining day of his praetorship was conferred on Eprius Marcellus.[2]

V. In the consulate of Gaius Pompeius and Quintus Veranius, the union plighted between Claudius and Agrippina was already being rendered doubly sure by rumour and by illicit love. As yet, however, they lacked courage to celebrate the bridal solemnities, no precedent existing for the introduction of a brother's child into the house of her uncle. Moreover, the relationship was incest; and, if that fact were disregarded, it was feared that the upshot would be a national calamity. Hesitation was dropped only when Vitellius undertook to bring about the desired result by his own methods. He began by asking the Caesar if he would yield to the mandate of the people?—to the authority of the

A.V.C. 802 = A.D. 49

auctoritati senatus cederet, ubi ille unum se civium et consensui imparem respondit, opperiri intra palatium iubet. Ipse curiam ingreditur, summamque rem publicam agi obtestans veniam dicendi ante alios exposcit orditurque:—Gravissimos principis labores, quis orbem terrae capessat, egere adminiculis, ut domestica cura vacuus in commune consulat. Quod porro honestius censoriae mentis levamentum quam adsumere coniugem, prosperis dubiisque sociam, cui cogitationes intimas, cui parvos liberos tradat, non luxui aut voluptatibus adsuefactus, sed qui prima ab iuventa legibus obtemperavisset.

VI. Postquam haec favorabili oratione praemisit multaque patrum adsentatio sequebatur, capto rursus initio, quando maritandum principem cuncti suaderent, deligi oportere feminam nobilitate puer- periis sanctimonia insignem. Nec diu anquirendum quin Agrippina claritudine generis anteiret: datum ab ea fecunditatis experimentum et congruere artis honestas. Id vero egregium, quod provisu deum vidua iungeretur principi sua tantum matrimonia experto. Audivisse a parentibus, vidisse ipsos abripi[1] coniuges ad libita Caesarum: procul id a praesenti

---

[1] abripi *Ritter*: arripi.

---

[1] Britannicus, eight years of age, and Octavia, about a year older.

[2] Her second husband, Passienus Crispus (VI. 20), was now dead—*per fraudem Agrippinae, quam heredem reliquerat*, according to a scholium on Juv. IV. 81.

[3] The reference is to Augustus (V. 1) and Caligula (Suet. *Cal.* 24 sq.).

senate? On receiving the answer that he was a citizen among citizens, and incompetent to resist their united will, he ordered him to wait inside the palace. He himself entered the curia. Asseverating that a vital interest of the country was in question, he demanded leave to speak first, and began by stating that " the extremely onerous labours of the sovereign, which embraced the management of a world, stood in need of support, so that he might pursue his deliberations for the public good, undisturbed by domestic anxiety. And what more decent solace to that truly censorian spirit than to take a wife, his partner in weal and woe, to whose charge might be committed his inmost thoughts and the little children [1] of a prince unused to dissipation or to pleasure, but to submission to the law from his early youth? "

VI. As this engagingly worded preface was followed by flattering expressions of assent from the members, he took a fresh starting-point :—" Since it was the universal advice that the emperor should marry, the choice ought to fall on a woman distinguished by nobility of birth, by experience of motherhood, and by purity of character. No long inquiry was needed to convince them that in the lustre of her family Agrippina came foremost : she had given proof of her fruitfulness, and her moral excellences harmonized with the rest. But the most gratifying point was that, by the dispensation of providence, the union would be between a widow [2] and a prince with experience of no marriage-bed but his own. They had heard from their fathers, and they had seen for themselves, how wives were snatched away at the whim of the Caesars : [3] such

modestia. Statueretur immo documentum, quo uxorem imperator *a patribus*[1] acciperet. At enim nova nobis in fratrum filias coniugia : sed aliis gentibus sollemnia, neque lege ulla prohibita ; et sobrinarum[2] diu ignorata tempore addito percrebruisse. Morem accommodari, prout conducat, et fore hoc quoque in iis quae mox usurpentur.

VII. Haud defuere qui certatim, si cunctaretur Caesar, vi acturos testificantes erumperent curia. Conglobatur promisca multitudo populumque Romanum eadem orare clamitat. Nec Claudius ultra exspectato obvius apud forum praebet se gratantibus, senatumque ingressus decretum postulat, quo iustae inter patruos fratrumque filias nuptiae etiam in posterum statuerentur. Nec tamen repertus est nisi unus talis matrimonii cupitor, Alledius[3] Severus eques Romanus, quem plerique Agrippinae gratia inpulsum ferebant. Versa ex eo civitas et cuncta feminae oboediebant, non per lasciviam, ut Messalina, rebus Romanis inludenti. Adductum et quasi virile servitium : palam severitas ac saepius superbia ;

[1] ⟨a patribus⟩ *Ritter* : *lac.* (*of six or seven letters*).
[2] sobrinarum ⟨et consobrinarum⟩ *Nipperdey. See note.*
[3] Al'edius *Ritter* : talledius *Med.*, T. Alledius *Lipsius.*

[1] As it would be absurd for Vitellius to mention only second cousins (*sobrini*), when the marriage of cousins (*consobrini*) had long been permissible, and equally absurd to assume that because " cousin " can be used loosely for " second cousin," therefore " second cousin " can be used loosely for " cousin," Nipperdey's emendation is plausible.—In any case, the Roman prejudice against such alliances remained invincible : Julian, for instance, finds no better name for the marriages between his own cousins than γάμοι οὐ γάμοι (228 C).

violence was far removed from the orderliness of the present arrangement. They were, in fact, to establish a precedent by which the emperor would accept his consort from the Roman people !—Still, marriage with a brother's child, it might be said, was a novelty in Rome.—But it was normal in other countries, and prohibited by no law ; while marriage with ⟨cousins and⟩ second cousins,[1] so long unknown, had with the progress of time become frequent. Usage accommodated itself to the claims of utility, and this innovation too would be among the conventions of to-morrow."

VII. Members were not lacking to rush from the curia, with emulous protestations that, if the emperor hesitated, they would proceed by force. A motley crowd flocked together, and clamoured that such also was the prayer of the Roman people. Waiting no longer, Claudius met them in the Forum, and offered himself to their felicitations, then entered the senate, and requested a decree legitimizing for the future also the union of uncles with their brothers' daughters. None the less, only a single enthusiast for that form of matrimony was discovered—the Roman knight Alledius Severus,[2] whose motive was generally said to have been desire for the favour of Agrippina.—From this moment it was a changed state, and all things moved at the fiat of a woman —but not a woman who, as Messalina, treated in wantonness the Roman empire as a toy. It was a tight-drawn, almost masculine tyranny : in public, there was austerity and not infrequently arrogance ;

---

[2] He had attained his rank by rising to leading-centurion, and enjoyed at least the satisfaction of numbering the emperor and empress among his wedding-guests (Suet. *Claud.* 26).

nihil domi inpudicum, nisi dominationi expediret. Cupido auri immensa obtentum habebat, quasi subsidium regno pararetur.

VIII. Die nuptiarum Silanus mortem sibi conscivit, sive eo usque spem vitae produxerat, seu delecto die augendam ad invidiam. Calvina soror eius Italia pulsa est. Addidit Claudius sacra ex legibus Tulli regis piaculaque apud lucum Dianae per pontifices danda, inridentibus cunctis, quod poenae procurationesque incesti id temporis exquirerentur. At Agrippina, ne malis tantum facinoribus notesceret, veniam exilii pro Annaeo Seneca, simul praeturam impetrat, laetum in publicum rata ob claritudinem studiorum eius, utque Domitii pueritia tali magistro adolesceret et consiliis eiusdem ad spem dominationis uterentur, quia Seneca fidus in Agrippinam memoria beneficii et infensus Claudio dolore iniuriae credebatur.

IX. Placitum dehinc non ultra cunctari, sed designatum consulem Mammium [1] Pollionem ingentibus promissis inducunt sententiam expromere, qua oraretur Claudius despondere Octaviam Domitio, quod aetati utriusque non absurdum et maiora patefacturum erat. Pollio haud disparibus verbis ac

---

[1] Mammium *Andresen*: Memmium.

---

[1] No doubt, the famous grove of the *rex Nemorensis*—the "priest who slew the slayer And shall himself be slain"—on lake Nemi, near Aricia.

[2] He had been relegated to Corsica eight years earlier, on the charge of adultery with Germanicus' daughter Julia Livilla, wife of M. Vinicius. Of his works, the *Consolatio ad Helviam* and the *Consolatio ad Polybium* date from this period.

at home, no trace of unchastity, unless it might contribute to power. A limitless passion for gold had the excuse of being designed to create a bulwark of despotism.

VIII. On the wedding-day Silanus committed suicide; whether he had preserved his hope of life till then, or whether the date was deliberately chosen to increase the odium of his death. His sister Calvina was expelled from Italy. Claudius, in addition, prescribed sacrifices in accordance with the legislation of King Tullus, and expiatory ceremonies to be carried out by the pontiffs in the grove of Diana;[1] universal derision being excited by this choice of a period in which to unearth the penalties and purifications of incest. Agrippina, on the other hand, not to owe her reputation entirely to crime, procured a remission of banishment for Annaeus Seneca,[2] along with a praetorship: his literary fame, she conceived, would make the act popular with the nation; while she was anxious to gain so distinguished a tutor for Domitius in his transit from boyhood to adolescence, and to profit by his advice in their designs upon the throne. For the belief was that Seneca was attached to Agrippina by the memory of her kindness and embittered against Claudius by resentment of his injury.

IX. The decision was now taken to delay no further; and the consul designate, Mammius Pollio, was induced by extraordinary promises to put forward a motion entreating Claudius to affiance Octavia to Domitius: an arrangement plausible enough on the score of their ages and likely to clear the way to higher things. Pollio proposed his resolution in nearly the same phrases which had

nuper Vitellius censet; despondeturque Octavia, ac
super priorem necessitudinem sponsus iam et gener
Domitius aequari Britannico studiis matris, arte
eorum, quis ob accusatam Messalinam ultio ex filio
timebatur.

X. Per idem tempus legati Parthorum ad ex-
petendum, ut rettuli, Meherdaten missi senatum in-
grediuntur mandataque in hunc modum incipiunt:—
Non se foederis ignaros nec defectione a familia
Arsacidarum venire, set filium Vononis, nepotem
Phraatis accersere adversus dominationem Gotarzis
nobilitati plebique iuxta intolerandam.   Iam fratres,
iam propinquos, iam longius sitos caedibus exhaustos;
adici coniuges gravidas, liberos parvos, dum socors
domi, bellis infaustus ignaviam saevitia tegat.
Veterem sibi ac publice coeptam nobiscum amicitiam,
et subveniendum sociis virium aemulis cedentibusque
per reverentiam.   Ideo regum liberos obsides[1] dari,
ut, si domestici imperii taedeat, sit regressus ad
principem patresque, quorum moribus adsuefactus
rex melior adscisceretur.

XI. Ubi haec atque talia dissertavere, incipit
orationem Caesar de fastigio Romano Parthorumque

---

[1] liberos obsides *Draeger*: obsides liberos.

---

[1] Claudius was his great-uncle, his stepfather, and now his
prospective father-in-law.
[2] For Meherdates and the situation generally, see XI. 8–10,
with the notes.

lately been employed by Vitellius; Octavia's engagement followed; and Domitius—who, over and above his former relationship [1] to the Emperor, was now his plighted son-in-law—began to assume equality with Britannicus, thanks to the zeal of his mother, and to the art of those who, in return for their arraignment of Messalina, apprehended the vengeance of her son.

X. About this date, the Parthian envoys, despatched, as I have mentioned, to sue for the return of Meherdates,[2] entered the senate, and opened with the following statement of their commission:—" They were not ignorant of the existing treaty, nor did they come in rebellion against the family of the Arsacids: they were summoning the son of Vonones, the grandson of Phraates, to redress the tyranny of Gotarzes, which was insufferable equally to the nobles and to the commons. Already brothers, near relatives, distant connections had been annihilated by his butcheries; pregnant wives and infant children were being added to the list; whilst, inert at home and disastrous in the field, he sought to disguise his cowardice by his cruelty. With us they had an old friendship, begun by national agreement, and it was our part to assist an allied country, which rivalled our power, but allowed our primacy out of respect. The object of giving the sons of kings in hostage for their fathers was that, if the government at home became obnoxious, recourse could be had to the emperor and senate, and a more enlightened prince, imbued with their manners, be called to the throne."

XI. In reply to these and similar representations, the emperor began a speech upon Roman pre-

obsequiis, seque divo Augusto adaequabat, petitum ab eo regem referens, omissa Tiberii memoria, quamquam is quoque miserat. Addidit praecepta (etenim aderat Meherdates), ut non dominationem et servos, sed rectorem et cives cogitaret, clementiamque ac iustitiam, quanto ignota[1] barbaris, tanto laetiora capesseret. Hinc versus ad legatos extollit laudibus alumnum urbis, spectatae ad id modestiae: ac tamen ferenda regum ingenia, neque usui crebras mutationes. Rem Romanam huc satietate gloriae provectam, ut externis quoque gentibus quietem velit. Datum posthac C. Cassio, qui Suriae praeerat, deducere iuvenem ripam ad Euphratis.

XII. Ea tempestate Cassius ceteros praeminebat peritia legum: nam militares artes per otium ignotae, industriosque aut ignavos pax in aequo tenet. Ac tamen quantum sine bello dabatur, revocare priscum morem, exercitare legiones, cura provisu perinde agere, ac si hostis ingrueret: ita dignum maioribus suis et familia Cassia *ratus*[2] per illas quoque gentes celebrata. Igitur excitis quorum de sententia

---

[1] ignota *or* ignara *dett.* : ignata.
[2] ⟨ratus⟩ *Med.*[2] : *lac.* (*of six or seven letters*).

---

[1] Meherdates' father, Vonones (II. 1). For the princes sent out by Tiberius—Phraates and Tiridates—see VI. 31 sq.

[2] C. Cassius Longinus, one of the most famous names in Roman jurisprudence (*Cassianae scholae princeps et parens*, Plin. *Ep.* VII. 24); consul (*suffectus*) in 30 A.D.; proconsul of Asia some ten years later; succeeded Vibius Marsus (XI. 10) as *legatus pro praetore* of Syria; banished by Nero to Sardinia in 65 A.D.; recalled by Vespasian (Pompon. *Dig.* I. 2, 2, § 51).

[3] He belonged to the school (*Sabiniani, Cassiani*) of Masurius Sabinus and Ateius Capito (III. 75 n.).

eminence and the signs of deference evinced by
Parthia. He claimed parity with the deified Augustus, to whom, as he pointed out, they had applied
for a king;[1] but he omitted to mention Tiberius,
though he too had sent out sovereigns. As Meherdates was present, he subjoined a few maxims:—
" Let him form the idea not of a despotism and
slaves but of a governor and citizens, and practise
mercy and justice—qualities unknown to barbarians,
and as such doubly welcome." Then, turning to
the deputies, he eulogized the foster-child of the
city, " who so far had given every proof of moderation. Still, the character of kings had to be borne
with, and frequent changes served no purpose.
Rome, in her satiety of glory, had reached the stage
when she desired tranquillity for foreign countries
as well as herself." Gaius Cassius,[2] the governor of
Syria, was then commissioned to escort the youth
to the bank of the Euphrates.

XII. In that period, Cassius stood unrivalled as a
jurist:[3] for the arts of war are lost in a quiet world,
and peace maintains on a single level the man of
action and the sluggard. Still, so far as was possible,
he reintroduced the old code of discipline, constantly
exercised his legions, and acted with the same care
and forethought as if an enemy had been at hand:
in his view, the only conduct worthy of his ancestry
and of the Cassian family, which had gained celebrity
even in those regions.[4] Accordingly, he called up
the persons who had suggested the application for a

[4] His ancestor, the "tyrannicide," an officer of Crassus, had
foiled the Parthian invasion of Syria after Carrhae (Mommsen,
R.H. V. 160 sqq., E.T.).

petitus rex, positisque castris apud Zeugma, unde
maxime pervius amnis, postquam inlustres Parthi
rexque Arabum Acbarus [1] advenerat, monet Meherdaten, barbarorum impetus acres cunctatione languescere aut in perfidiam mutari : ita urgueret coepta.
Quod spretum fraude Acbari, qui iuvenem ignarum [2]
et summam fortunam in luxu ratum multos per dies
attinuit apud oppidum Edessam.   Et vocante Carene
promptasque res ostentante, si citi advenissent, non
comminus Mesopotamiam, sed flexu Armeniam
petivit,[3] id temporis inportunam, quia hiems occi-
piebat.

XIII. Exim nivibus et montibus fessi, postquam
campos [4] propinquabant, copiis Carenis adiunguntur,
tramissoque amne Tigri permeant Adiabenos, quorum
rex Izates societatem Meherdatis palam induerat, in
Gotarzen per occulta et magis fida inclinabat.   Sed
capta in transitu urbs Ninos, vetustissima sedes
Assyriae, *et* castellum insigne fama, quod postremo
inter Darium atque Alexandrum proelio Persarum
illic opes conciderant.   Interea   Gotarzes   apud
montem, cui nomen Sanbulos, vota dis loci suscipie-

---

[1] Acbarus] Abgarus *Ryck* (*from the coins and inscriptions*).
[2] ignarum] ignavum *Madvig.*
[3] petivit] petunt *Lipsius, al.*
[4] campos] campis *dett.* (*cf.* I. 63 etc.).

---

[1] Built by Seleucus Nicator, together with Apamea on the
eastern bank, to command the main crossing of the Euphrates
into N. Mesopotamia.
[2] King of Osroëne—the fertile northern part of Mesopotamia
between the Euphrates and Tigris (VI. 44 n.).
[3] The capital of Osroëne—more famous in the day of Justin-
ian and Chosroës than in that of Claudius and Gotarzes.
[4] Evidently satrap (*praefectus*) of Mesopotamia.
[5] N. Assyria.

king; pitched his camp at Zeugma,[1] the most convenient point for crossing the river; and, after the arrival of the Parthian magnates and the Arab prince Acbarus,[2] cautioned Meherdates that the enthusiasm of barbarians, though lively, grows chill with delay or changes into treachery: let him therefore press on with his adventure. The advice was ignored through the dishonesty of Acbarus, by whom the inexperienced youth—who identified kingship with dissipation—was detained day after day in the town of Edessa.[3] Even when invited by Carenes,[4] who pointed out that all was easy if they arrived quickly, he took, not the short road into Mesopotamia, but a circuitous route to Armenia, at that time an impracticable district, as winter was setting in.

XIII. At last, when, outworn by snows and mountains, they were nearing the plains, they effected a junction with the forces of Carenes, and, crossing the Tigris, struck through the country of the Adiabeni,[5] whose king, Izates, had in public leagued himself with Meherdates, whilst in private, and with more sincerity, he inclined to Gotarzes. In passing, however, they captured Nineveh, the time-honoured capital of Assyria, together with a fortress, known to fame as the site on which the Persian empire fell in the last battle between Darius and Alexander.[6]—Meanwhile, Gotarzes, at a mountain by the name of Sanbulos,[7] was offering

[6] *In hac Adiabena Ninus est civitas . . . et Arbela et Gaugamela ubi Dareum Alexander . . . incitato Marte prostravit* (331 B.C.), Amm. Marc. XXIII. 6, 22. But neither Arbela nor Gaugamela was a *castellum*, and the text is not too certain.

[7] The mountain and the deity are unknown.

bat, praecipua religione Herculis, qui tempore stato
per quietem monet sacerdotes, ut templum iuxta
equos venatui adornatos sistant. Equi ubi pharetras
telis onustas accepere, per saltus vagi nocte demum
vacuis pharetris multo cum anhelitu redeunt.
Rursum deus, qua silvas pererraverit, nocturno visu
demonstrat, reperiunturque fusae passim ferae.

XIV. Ceterum Gotarzes, nondum satis aucto
exercitu, flumine Corma pro munimento uti, et
quamquam per insectationes et nuntios ad proelium
vocaretur, nectere moras, locos mutare et missis
corruptoribus exuendam ad fidem hostes emercari.
Ex quis Izates Adiabeno,[1] mox Acbarus [2] Arabum
cum exercitu abscedunt, levitate gentili, et quia
experimentis cognitum est barbaros malle Roma
petere reges quam habere. At Meherdates validis
auxiliis nudatus, ceterorum proditione suspecta, quod
unum reliquum, rem in casum dare proelioque
experiri statuit. Nec detrectavit pugnam Gotarzes
deminutis hostibus ferox; concursumque magna
caede et ambiguo eventu, donec Carenem profligatis
obviis [3] longius evectum integer a tergo globus
circumveniret. Tum omni spe perdita Meherdates,
promissa Parracis paterni clientis secutus, dolo eius
vincitur traditurque victori. Atque ille non pro-

---

[1] Adiabeno *J. F. Gronovius*: adiabenus.
[2] Acbarus] abbarus *Med.*
[3] obviis *Andresen* (*Med.*[1] ?): obusis *Med.*, obversis *det.*,
vulg.

---

[1] An unidentified eastern tributary of the Tigris.

vows to the local deities; the chief cult being that
of Hercules, who at fixed intervals warns his priests
by dream to place beside his temple a number of
horses equipped for hunting. These, after being
furnished with quivers full of arrows, run loose in
the forest glades, and only at night return, panting
hard, and with quivers emptied. In a second
nightly vision, the god points out the course he
held through the forest, and all along it wild beasts
are discovered strewing the ground.

XIV. Gotarzes, whose army had not as yet reached
adequate strength, made use of the river Corma [1] as
a natural barrier, and, in spite of derisive messages
challenging him to battle, continued to interpose
delays, to change his quarters, and, by despatching
bribery-agents, to bid for the defection of his enemies.
First Izates and the contingents of Adiabene, then
Acbarus with those of the Arabs, took their departure,
in accordance with the levity of their race and with
the fact, proved by experience, that barbarians are
more inclined to seek their kings from Rome than to
keep them. Stripped of these powerful auxiliaries,
and apprehending treason from the rest, Meherdates
took the one course remaining and decided to stake
his fortune upon a trial of arms. Gotarzes, emboldened by the depletion of the enemy, did not
decline an engagement, and the armies met, with
great slaughter and dubious success; until Carenes,
who had broken the forces opposed to him, carried
his advance too far and was cut off by fresh troops
in his rear. With all hope lost, Meherdates now
listened to the promises of his father's vassal Parraces,
and, by an act of perfidy on his part, was thrown into
chains and surrendered to the victor; who, up-

pinquum neque Arsacis de gente, sed alienigenam et Romanum increpans, auribus decisis vivere iubet, ostentui clementiae suae et in nos dehonestamento. Dein Gotarzes morbo obiit, accitusque in regnum Vonones Medos tum praesidens. Nulla huic prospera aut adversa, quis memoraretur: brevi et inglorio imperio perfunctus est, resque Parthorum in filium eius Vologesen translatae.

XV. At Mithridates Bosporanus amissis opibus vagus, postquam Didium ducem Romanum roburque exercitus abisse cognoverat, relictos in novo regno Cotyn iuventa rudem et paucas cohortium cum Iulio Aquila equite Romano, spretis utrisque concire nationes, inlicere perfugas; postremo exercitu coacto regem Dandaridarum exturbat imperioque eius potitur. Quae ubi cognita et iam iamque Bosporum invasurus habebatur, diffisi propriis viribus Aquila et Cotys, quia Zorsines Siracorum rex hostilia resumpserat, externas et ipsi gratias quaesivere missis legatis ad Eunonen, qui Aorsorum[1] genti *rex potentia*[2] praecellebat. Nec fuit in arduo societas potentiam Romanam adversus rebellem Mithridaten ostentantibus. Igitur pepigere, equestribus proeliis Eunones certaret, obsidia urbium Romani capesserent.

[1] Aorsorum *Lipsius*: adorsorum *Med. (as throughout).*
[2] ⟨rex potentia⟩ *Nipperdey.*

---

[1] A small dependent kingdom of considerable antiquity, including roughly the Crimea and a number of tribes to the east of the Cimmerian Bosporus (*Straits of Kertch*). The throne, vacant by the transfer of Polemo to Cilicia, had in 41 A.D. been conferred by Claudius on Mithridates (D. Cass. LX. 8). Some five years later, for reasons doubtless given in the lost part of Book XI, he was ejected by A. Didius Gallus, and replaced by his brother Cotys.

braiding him as no relative of his, nor a member of
the Arsacian house, but an alien and a Roman,
struck off his ears and commanded him to live—an
advertisement of his own mercy and of our dishonour. Next came the death of Gotarzes by disease,
and Vonones, then viceroy of Media, was called to
the throne. No successes and no reverses entitled
him to mention: he completed a short, inglorious
and perfunctory reign, and the Parthian empire
devolved upon his son Vologeses.

XV. Meanwhile, Mithridates of Bosporus,[1] a wan-
derer since the loss of his throne, learned that the
Roman commander Didius[2] had departed with the
main body of his army, leaving the young and simple
Cotys in his novel kingdom, with a few cohorts under
the Roman knight, Julius Aquila. Scornful of both,
he proceeded to raise the tribes and attract deserters:
finally, mustering an army, he ejected the king of
the Dandaridae,[3] and seized his dominions. When
this had become known and his invasion of Bosporus
was expected from day to day, Aquila and Cotys
—diffident of their own strength, as the Siracene
prince Zorsines had resumed hostilities—followed
his example, and sought outside support by sending
envoys to the powerful Aorsian prince, Eunones.
An alliance presented little difficulty, when they
could exhibit the power of Rome ranged against the
rebel Mithridates. It was arranged, therefore, that
Eunones should be responsible for the cavalry fighting, the Romans undertaking the siege of all towns.

[2] At this time, probably *legatus* of Moesia; later, of Britain
(chap. 40).
[3] The Dandaridae, Siraci, and Aorsi, were Sarmatian tribes
between the Caspian and Sea of Azov, with the Don and
Caucasus as northern and southern limits.

XVI. Tunc composito agmine incedunt, cuius frontem et terga Aorsi, media cohortes et Bosporani tutabantur nostris in armis. Sic pulsus hostis, ventumque Sozam, oppidum Dandaricae, quod desertum a Mithridate ob ambiguos popularium animos optineri relicto ibi praesidio visum. Exim in Siracos pergunt, et transgressi amnem Pandam circumveniunt urbem Uspen, editam loco et moenibus ac fossis munitam, nisi quod moenia non saxo, sed cratibus et vimentis ac media humo adversum inrumpentis invalida erant; eductaeque altius turres facibus atque hastis turbabant obsessos. Ac ni proelium nox diremisset, coepta patrataque expugnatio eundem intra diem foret.

XVII. Postero misere legatos, veniam liberis corporibus orantes: servitii decem milia offerebant. Quod aspernati sunt victores, quia trucidare deditos saevum, tantam multitudinem custodia cingere arduum: belli potius iure caderent, datumque militibus, qui scalis evaserant, signum caedis. Excidio Uspensium metus ceteris iniectus, nihil tutum ratis, cum arma, munimenta, impediti vel eminentes loci amnesque et urbes iuxta perrumperentur. Igitur Zorsines, diu pensitato, Mithridatisne rebus extremis

---

[1] Soza, the Panda, and Uspe are alike unknown.

XVI. They then advanced with combined forces, the front and rear held by the Aorsi, the centre by the cohorts and by Bosporan troops armed on our model. In this order they inflicted a reverse on the enemy and reached Soza,[1] a town of Dandarica evacuated by Mithridates, which, in view of the doubtful sympathies of the population, it was thought advisable to secure by leaving a garrison. They next advanced on the Siraci, and, crossing the stream of the Panda, invested Uspe, a city built on a height and fortified with walls and moats—the drawback being that, as the walls were not of stone but of wickerwork hurdles with soil between, they were too weak to sustain an attack, while our siege towers, with their greater elevation, threw the garrison into disorder by discharges of firebrands and spears. In fact, if the struggle had not been interrupted by night, the beginning and end of the attack would have fallen within the limits of one day.

XVII. On the morrow, deputies were sent out asking terms for the free population, but making an offer of ten thousand slaves. The composition was rejected by the victors, on the ground that it was cruelty to massacre surrendered men, and extremely difficult to maintain a ring of guards round such a multitude: better they should perish by the law of war! And the troops, who had mounted by their ladders, received the signal for no quarter. The destruction of the inhabitants of Uspe struck dismay into the rest of the country; safety being considered impossible when armies and fortifications, high or difficult ground, rivers and cities, failed equally to stay the enemy. Zorsines, therefore, after long debating whether his first consideration was due

an patrio regno consuleret, postquam praevaluit gentilis utilitas, datis obsidibus apud effigiem Caesaris procubuit, magna gloria exercitus Romani, quem incruentum et victorem tridui itinere afuisse ab amne Tanai constitit. Sed in regressu dispar fortuna fuit, quia navium quasdam (quippe [1] mari remeabant) in litora Taurorum delatas circumvenere barbari, praefecto cohortis et plerisque auxiliarium [2] interfectis.

XVIII. Interea Mithridates nullo in armis subsidio consultat, cuius misericordiam experiretur. Frater Cotys, proditor olim, deinde hostis, metuebatur: Romanorum nemo id auctoritatis aderat, ut promissa eius magni penderentur. Ad Eunonen convertit, propriis odiis *non* infensum et recens coniuncta nobiscum amicitia validum. Igitur cultu vultuque quam maxime ad praesentem fortunam comparato regiam ingreditur genibusque eius provolutus, ' Mithridates ' inquit ' terra marique Romanis per tot annos quaesitus sponte adsum : utere, ut voles, prole magni Achaemenis, quod mihi solum hostes non abstulerunt.'

XIX. At Eunones claritudine viri, mutatione rerum et prece haud degeneri permotus, adlevat supplicem laudatque, quod gentem Aorsorum, quod

[1] quippe *Nipperdey* : quae.
[2] auxiliarium *Lipsius* : consiliarium.

---

[1] The Don.
[2] Of the Crimea (*Chersonesus Taurica*).
[3] The progenitor of the Persian royal family, from which Mithridates the Great, of Pontus, ancestor of his namesake of Bosporus, claimed descent (Just. XXXVIII. 7).

to the desperate case of Mithridates or to his own
ancestral kingdom, when once the interests of his
nation carried the day, gave hostages and prostrated
himself before the effigy of the Caesar—much to the
glory of the Roman army, which had indisputably
reached, bloodless and victorious, a point within
three days' march of the Tanais.[1] During their
withdrawal, however, fortune changed, as a few
of the ships—they were returning by sea—were
carried on to the Taurian coast[2] and there surrounded by the barbarians, who killed the prefect
of one cohort and many of the auxiliaries.

XVIII. In the interval, as there was no help in
arms, Mithridates debated the question whose mercy
he should put to the proof. His brother Cotys, once his
betrayer, then his declared enemy, inspired mistrust;
and, of the Romans, no one of sufficient authority
was on the scene for much weight to be attached to
his promises. He turned to Eunones, who was not
embittered against him by private animosities, and
whose power had been increased by his recently
formed friendship with ourselves. His dress and
features, then, adjusted so far as possible to his
present situation, he entered the palace and fell at
the king's knees with the words:—" Mithridates,
whom the Romans have sought for so many years
over land and sea, is here of his own accord. Use
as thou wilt the issue of the great Achaemenes[3]—
the one title of which my enemies have not bereft
me."

XIX. Eunones, moved by the fame of the man,
by the revolution in his fortunes, and by his not
ignoble prayer, raised the suppliant and commended
him for selecting the Aorsian people and his own

suam dextram petendae veniae delegerit. Simul legatos litterasque ad Caesarem in hunc modum mittit: populi Romani imperatoribus, magnarum nationum regibus primam ex similitudine fortunae amicitiam, sibi et Claudio etiam communionem victoriae esse. Bellorum egregios fines, quotiens ignoscendo transigatur: sic Zorsini victo nihil ereptum. Pro Mithridate, quando gravius mereretur, non potentiam neque regnum precari, sed ne triumpharetur neve poenas capite expenderet.

XX. At Claudius, quamquam nobilitatibus externis mitis dubitavit tamen, accipere captivum pacto salutis an repetere armis rectius foret. Hinc dolor iniuriarum et libido vindictae adigebat: sed disserebatur contra suscipi bellum avio itinere, inportuoso mari; ad hoc reges feroces, vagos populos, solum frugum egenum, taedium ex mora, pericula ex properantia, modicam victoribus laudem ac multum infamiae, si pellerentur. Quin arriperet oblata et servaret exulem, cui inopi quanto longiorem vitam, tanto plus supplicii fore. His permotus scripsit Eunoni, meritum quidem novissima exempla Mithridatem, nec sibi vim ad exsequendum deesse: verum ita maioribus placitum, quanta pervicacia in hostem,

342

right hand to which to address his appeal for
clemency. At the same time, he sent a legation
to the Caesar, with a letter to the following effect:—
" Between the emperors of the Roman nation and
the kings of great realms, friendship had its origin
in the similarity of rank: between himself and
Claudius there subsisted also a partnership in victory.
The noblest end of war was a settlement reached by
pardon; and it was thus that Zorsines had been
conquered, but not despoiled. On behalf of Mithridates, who deserved sterner treatment, he asked for
neither power nor royalty, but simply that he should
not be led in triumph nor expiate his faults with his
life."

XX. Claudius, however, lenient though he was to
foreign potentates, still doubted whether it was preferable to accept the captive, under a guarantee of
safety, or to reclaim him by arms. He was impelled
to the second course by resentment of his injuries and
by the desire of revenge; yet it was urged on the
other side that " he would be undertaking a war in a
roadless country and upon a harbourless sea. Consider, too, the martial kings, their nomadic peoples,
the unfruitful soil; the tedium consequent on delay,
the dangers consequent on haste; the modest
laurels of victory, the pronounced ignominy of
repulse! Better to embrace the proffered opportunity, and spare an exile to whom every extension
of his poverty-stricken life would be an extension
of punishment." Impressed by these arguments, he
wrote to Eunones that " Mithridates, it was true,
had earned the last penalties; nor was it out of his
power to exact them; but it had been a maxim of
his ancestors to display as much charity to suppliants

tanta beneficentia adversus supplices utendum; nam triumphos de populis regnisque integris acquiri.

XXI. Traditus posthac Mithridates vectusque Romam per Iunium Cilonem, procuratorem Ponti, ferocius quam pro fortuna disseruisse apud Caesarem ferebatur, elataque vox eius in vulgum hisce verbis:—
"Non sum remissus ad te, sed reversus: vel si non credis, dimitte et quaere." Vultu quoque interrito permansit, cum rostra iuxta custodibus circumdatus visui populo praeberetur. Consularia insignia Ciloni, Aquilae praetoria decernuntur.

XXII. Isdem consulibus atrox odii Agrippina ac Lolliae infensa, quod secum de matrimonio principis certavisset, molitur crimina et accusatorem, qui obiceret Chaldaeos, magos interrogatumque Apollinis Clarii simulacrum super nuptiis imperatoris. Exim Claudius inaudita rea multa de claritudine eius apud senatum praefatus, sorore L. Volusii genitam, maiorem ei patruum Cottam Messalinum esse, Memmio quondam Regulo nuptam (nam de Gai Caesaris nuptiis consulto reticebat), addidit perniciosa in rem publicam consilia et materiem sceleri detrahendam: proin publicatis bonis cederet Italia. Ita quinquagiens sestertium ex opibus immensis exuli relictum. Et Calpurnia inlustris femina pervertitur,

---

[1] Mithridates himself remained at Rome till the reign of Galba, when he was executed without trial as an accomplice of Nymphidius Sabinus (Plut. *Galb.* 15 init.).

[2] See chap. 1.

[3] For L. Volusius, see XIII. 30 fin.; for Cotta, IV. 20 n.; for Regulus, V. 11 n.; for Lollia's brief marriage to Caligula, chap. 1 n.

as pertinacity against the enemy: for it was at the expense of peoples and monarchies still undefeated that triumphs were earned."

XXI. Mithridates was handed over in due course and conveyed to Rome by Junius Cilo, the procurator of Pontus. The tale went that he spoke before the emperor's tribunal with a spirit not warranted by his situation, and one sentence came to the knowledge of the public, the words being: "I have not been returned to you; I return. If you doubt, let me go, and fetch me!" His features did not even lose their intrepidity, when he was being displayed beside the Rostra, in the midst of his warders, to the gaze of the populace.—Consular decorations were voted to Cilo, praetorian to Aquila.[1]

XXII. In the same consulate, Agrippina, fierce in her hatreds, and infuriated against Lollia as her rival for the emperor's hand,[2] arranged for her prosecution and her prosecutor, the charges to be traffic with Chaldaeans and magicians, and application to the image of the Clarian Apollo for information as to the sovereign's marriage. On this, Claudius—without hearing the defendant—delivered a long exordium in the senate on the subject of her family distinctions, pointing out that her mother had been the sister of Lucius Volusius, her great-uncle Cotta Messalinus, herself the bride formerly of Memmius Regulus (her marriage with Caligula was deliberately suppressed);[3] then added that her projects were pernicious to the state and she must be stripped of her resources for mischief: it would be best, therefore, to confiscate her property and expel her from Italy. Accordingly, out of her immense estate five million sesterces were spared to support her exile. Calpurnia also, a woman

345

quia formam eius laudaverat princeps, nulla libidine, sed fortuito sermone, unde ira Agrippinae citra ultima stetit. In Lolliam mittitur tribunus, a quo ad mortem adigeretur. Damnatus et lege repetundarum Cadius Rufus accusantibus Bithynis.

XXIII. Galliae Narbonensi ob egregiam in patres reverentiam datum, ut senatoribus eius provinciae non exquisita principis sententia, iure quo Sicilia haberetur, res suas invisere liceret. Ituraeique et Iudaei defunctis regibus, Sohaemo atque Agrippa, provinciae Suriae additi. Salutis augurium quinque et septuaginta[1] annis omissum repeti ac deinde continuari placitum. Et pomerium urbis auxit Caesar, more prisco, quo iis, qui protulere imperium, etiam terminos urbis propagare datur. Nec tamen duces Romani, quamquam magnis nationibus subactis, usurpaverant nisi L. Sulla et divus Augustus.

[1] septuaginta *Ritter*: viginti.

---

[1] Wild hill-country, adjoining Trachonitis, far east of the Jordan, and inhabited by Judaized Arab bowmen.

[2] Herod Agrippa I, grandson of Herod the Great and Mariamne, and an intimate friend, first of Caligula, then of Claudius. His death (see *Acts* xii. 23) must be dated some five years previously.

[3] They were henceforward under imperial procurators subordinate to the *legatus* of Syria.

[4] An obscure rite to ascertain whether it was permissible to offer prayers for the national safety—the day of intercession having to be one of absolute peace throughout the empire.

[5] If the text is right, a round number for seventy-eight, as the obsolescent ceremony was revived by Augustus in the year of his triple triumph, when he closed the temple of Janus for the first time (29 B.C.).

[6] A strip of consecrated ground outside (and, originally, inside) the wall, constituting the ideal boundary of the city.

of high rank, came to ruin because Claudius had
praised her appearance, not amorously, but in
a casual conversation, so that Agrippina's anger
stopped short of the last consequences: in Lollia's
case, a tribune was despatched to enforce her suicide.
Another condemnation was that of Cadius Rufus
under the law of extortion, the indictment being
brought by the Bithynians.

XXIII. For its exemplary deference to the senate,
Narbonese Gaul was so far privileged that members
from the province were allowed the right, obtaining
in the case of Sicily, of visiting their estates without
first ascertaining the pleasure of the emperor.
Ituraea[1] and Judaea, on the death of their sovereigns,
Sohaemus and Agrippa,[2] were attached to the
province of Syria.[3] A decision was taken that the
Augury of Safety,[4] disused for the last seventy-five[5]
years, should be reintroduced and continued for the
future. The Caesar also enlarged the pomerium,[6] in
consonance with the old custom, by which an expan-
sion of the empire[7] confers the right to extend
similarly the boundaries of the city: a right, however, which, even after the conquest of powerful
nations, had been exercised by no Roman commander
except Lucius Sulla and the deified Augustus.[8]

[7] In this case, the conquest of Britain. For it is fantastic
to question this interpretation on the strength of a statement
by the nameless pedant, whom Seneca derides in *De brev. vit.*
13–14, that the pomerium was extended *nunquam provinciali,
sed Italico agro acquisito.*

[8] This assertion, repeated in Dio, cannot stand in face of the
silence of the *Monumentum Ancyranum* and the words of the
lex de imperio Vespasiani (conferring on Vespasian the powers
of Augustus, Tiberius and Claudius) :—*utique ei fines pomeri
proferre promovere . . . liceat, ita uti licuit Ti. Claudio
Caesari Aug. Germanico* (14).

XXIV. Regum in eo ambitio vel gloria varie vulgata : sed initium condendi, et quod pomerium Romulus posuerit, noscere haud absurdum reor. Igitur a foro boario, ubi aereum tauri simulacrum aspicimus, quia id genus animalium aratro subditur, sulcus designandi oppidi coeptus, ut magnam Herculis aram amplecteretur ; inde certis spatiis interiecti lapides per ima montis Palatini ad aram Consi, mox curias veteres, tum ad sacellum Larum, *in*de forum Romanum ; forumque[1] et Capitolium non a Romulo, sed a Tito Tatio additum urbi credidere. Mox pro fortuna pomerium auctum. Et quos tum Claudius terminos posuerit, facile cognitu et publicis actis perscriptum.

XXV. C. Antistio M. Suillio consulibus adoptio in Domitium auctoritate Pallantis festinatur, qui obstrictus Agrippinae ut conciliator nuptiarum et mox stupro eius inligatus, stimulabat Claudium, consuleret rei publicae, Britannici pueritiam robore circumdaret : sic apud divum Augustum, quamquam

---

[1] Larum, inde forum Romanum ; forumque *Weissenborn* : larum de forumque Romanum *Med.*, Larundae, forumque Romanum *Orelli*.

---

[1] Between the Circus Maximus and the river. The brazen bull was an Aeginetan bronze, one of the spoils of Greece.

[2] *Oppida condebant in Latio Etrusco ritu ; id est, iunctis bobus, tauro et vacca interiore, circumagebant sulcum . . . Terram unde exsculpserant, fossam vocabant, et introrsum iactam,* 'murum' (Varro, *L.L.* V. § 143).

[3] The primitive town, *Roma quadrata*, occupied the Palatine ; and along the irregular trapezoid formed by its base the pomerium of Romulus was drawn, outside and below the city-walls. Of the four angular points, the south-western was marked by the Ara Maxima of Hercules, the south-eastern by the subterranean altar of Consus (each at an extremity of the Circus Maximus), the north-eastern and north-western by the

XXIV. As to the vanity or glory of the various
kings in that respect, differing accounts are given;
but the original foundation, and the character of the
pomerium as fixed by Romulus, seem to me a reasonable subject of investigation. From the Forum
Boarium,[1] then, where the brazen bull which meets
the view is explained by the animal's use in the
plough, the furrow to mark out the town[2] was cut so
as to take in the great altar of Hercules. From that
point, boundary-stones were interspersed at fixed
intervals along the base of the Palatine Hill[3] up to
the altar of Consus, then to the old curiae, then again
to the shrine of the Lares, and after that to the
Forum Romanum. The Forum and the Capitol, it
was believed, were added to the city, not by Romulus
but by Titus Tatius.[4] Later, the pomerium grew
with the national fortunes: the limits as now determined by Claudius are both easily identified and
recorded in public documents.

XXV. In the consulate of Gaius Antistius and
Marcus Suillius, the adoption of Domitius was
hurried forward by the influence of Pallas, who,
pledged to Agrippina as the agent in her marriage,
then bound to her by lawless love, kept goading
Claudius to consult the welfare of the country and
to supply the boyish years of Britannicus with a
stable protection:—" So, in the family of the divine
Augustus, though he had grandsons to rely upon, yet

A.v.c. 803 =
A.D. 50

old meeting-place of the *curiae* and the *sacellum Larum*
though the exact site of both is uncertain. The Forum
Romanum, as shown by the next sentence, was skirted but not
included.

[4] The Capitol is presumed to have been an outpost of the
Sabine settlement on the Quirinal; the Forum, the market-
place for that settlement and the Latin town on the Palatine.

nepotibus subnixum, viguisse privignos; a Tiberio super propriam stirpem Germanicum adsumptum: se quoque accingeret iuvene partem curarum capessituro. His evictus triennio [1] maiorem natu Domitium filio anteponit, habita apud senatum oratione eundem in quem a liberto acceperat modum. Adnotabant periti nullam antehac adoptionem inter patricios Claudios reperiri, eosque ab Atto Clauso continuos duravisse.

XXVI. Ceterum actae principi grates, quaesitiore in Domitium adulatione; rogataque lex, qua in familiam Claudiam et nomen Neronis transiret. Augetur et Agrippina cognomento Augustae. Quibus patratis nemo adeo expers misericordiae fuit, quem non Britannici fortuna maerore adficeret. Desolatus paulatim etiam servilibus ministeriis perintempestiva [2] novercae officia in ludibrium [3] vertebat, intellegens falsi. Neque enim segnem ei fuisse indolem ferunt, sive verum, seu periculis commendatus retinuit famam sine experimento.

XXVII. Sed Agrippina, quo vim suam sociis quoque nationibus ostentaret, in oppidum Ubiorum, in quo genita erat, veteranos coloniamque deduci impetrat, cui nomen inditum e vocabulo ipsius. Ac forte acciderat, ut eam gentem Rhenum [4] transgressam avus Agrippa in fidem acciperet.

---

[1] triennio *Freinsheim*: biennio.
[2] perintempestiva] puer intempestiva *Sirker*.
[3] ludibrium *Nipperdey*: ludibria.
[4] Rhenum *Sirker*: rheno.

---

[1] The "Sabine" branch, as opposed to the plebeian Claudii Marcelli.
[2] The formality of a *lex curiata* was necessary, since Nero, by the death of his father, was *sui iuris*.
[3] Cologne (*Colonia Agrippinensis*).

his step-children rose to power; Tiberius had issue of his own, but he adopted Germanicus: let Claudius also gird to himself a young partner, who would undertake a share of his responsibilities!" The emperor yielded to the pressure, and gave Domitius, with his three years' seniority, precedence over his son, reproducing in his speech to the senate the arguments furnished by his freedman. It was noted by the expert that, prior to this, there was no trace of an adoption in the patrician branch [1] of the Claudian house, which had lasted without interruption from Attus Clausus downward.

XXVI. Thanks, however, were returned to the sovereign; a more refined flattery was bestowed on Domitius; and the law [2] was carried providing for his adoption into the Claudian family and the designation of Nero. Agrippina herself was dignified by the title of Augusta. When the transaction was over, no one was so devoid of pity as not to feel compunction for the lot of Britannicus. Stripped little by little of the services of the very slaves, the boy turned into derision the officious importunities of his stepmother, whose hypocrisy he understood. For report credits him with no lack of intelligence, possibly with truth, or possibly through the sympathy inspired by his dangers he has retained a reputation which was never put to the proof.

XXVII. Agrippina, on the other hand, in order to advertise her strength to the provinces also, arranged for the plantation of a colony [3] of veterans in the Ubian town where she was born. The settlement received its title from her name; and, as chance would have it, it had been her grandfather Agrippa who extended Roman protection to the tribe on its migration across the Rhine.

Isdem temporibus in superiore Germania trepidatum adventu Chattorum latrocinia agitantium. Dein P.[1] Pomponius legatus auxiliaris Vangionas ac Nemetas, addito equite alario, *inmittit*,[2] monitos ut anteirent populatores vel dilapsis inprovisi circumfunderentur. Et secuta consilium ducis industria militum, divisique in duo agmina, qui laevum iter petiverant, recens reversos praedaque per luxum usos et somno gravis circumvenere. Aucta laetitia, quod quosdam e clade Variana quadragensimum post annum servitio exemerant.

XXVIII. At qui dextris et propioribus compendiis ierant, obvio hosti et aciem auso plus cladis faciunt, et praeda famaque onusti ad montem Taunum revertuntur, ubi Pomponius cum legionibus opperiebatur, si Chatti cupidine ulciscendi casum pugnae praeberent. Illi metu, ne hinc Romanus, inde Cherusci, cum quis aeternum discordant, circumgrederentur, legatos in urbem et obsides misere; decretusque Pomponio triumphalis honos, modica pars famae eius apud posteros, in quis carminum gloria praecellit.

XXIX. Per idem tempus Vannius Suebis a Druso Caesare inpositus pellitur regno, prima imperii aetate

---

[1] P. *Ritter*: L.
[2] ⟨inmittit⟩ *Doederlein, al. More probably a larger lacuna should be marked after* agitantium *above.*

---

[1] From the Hesse-Nassau district: the Vangiones and Nemetes lay on the west bank of the Rhine, their principal towns being the modern Worms and Spires.
[2] The *Höhe*, now again Taunus, between the Rhine and Nidda. For the Roman fort there, see I. 56.
[3] See V. 8 nn.

At the same period, a panic was caused in Upper Germany by an incursion of Chattan marauders.[1] Thereupon, the legate Publius Pomponius sent the auxiliary Vangiones and Nemetes, supported by allied cavalry, with instructions to head off the raiders, or, if they scattered, to envelop and surprise them. The general's plan was seconded by the activity of the troops. They separated into two columns; one of which, marching to the left, entrapped a newly-returned detachment of pillagers, who, after employing their booty in a debauch, were sleeping off the effects. The exultation of the men was heightened by the fact that, after forty years, they had redeemed from slavery a few survivors of the Varian disaster.

XXVIII. Their companions, who had taken the shorter route by the right, inflicted graver loss on the enemy, who met them and risked a set engagement. Laden with their spoils and honours, they returned to the heights of Taunus,[2] where Pomponius was waiting with the legions, in hopes that the Chatti, anxious for revenge, would afford him an opportunity for battle. They, however, afraid of being caught between the Romans on one side and their eternal adversaries, the Cherusci, on the other, sent a deputation to Rome with hostages, and triumphal honours were voted to Pomponius: a slender portion of his fame in the eyes of posterity, with whom the glory of his verse ranks higher.[3]

XXIX. Much at the same time, Vannius,[4] imposed on the Suebi by Drusus Caesar, was expelled from his kingdom. Esteemed and loved by his country-

---

[4] See II. 63, with the notes, and, for a clear account of the whole situation, Mommsen, *Prov.* i. 214 sqq.

carus [1] acceptusque popularibus, mox diuturnitate in superbiam mutans et odio accolarum, simul domesticis discordiis circumventus. Auctores fuere Vibilius Hemundurorum rex et Vangio ac Sido sorore Vannii geniti. Nec Claudius, quamquam saepe oratus, arma certantibus barbaris interposuit, tutum Vannio perfugium promittens, si pelleretur; scripsitque Palpellio Histro, qui Pannoniam praesidebat, legionem ipsaque e provincia lecta auxilia pro ripa componere, subsidio victis et terrorem adversus victores, ne fortuna elati nostram quoque pacem turbarent. Nam vis innumera, Lugii aliaeque gentes, adventabant, fama ditis regni, quod Vannius triginta per annos praedationibus et vectigalibus auxerat. Ipsi manus propria pedites, eques e Sarmatis Iazygibus erat, impar multitudini hostium, eoque castellis sese defensare bellumque ducere statuerat.

XXX. Sed Iazyges obsidionis impatientes et proximos per campos vagi necessitudinem pugnae attulere, quia Lugius Hermundurusque illic ingruerant. Igitur degressus castellis Vannius funditur proelio, quamquam rebus adversis laudatus, quod et pugnam manu capessivit et corpore adverso vulnera excepit. Ceterum ad classem in Danuvio opperientem perfugit; secuti mox clientes et acceptis agris

---

[1] carus *Wölfflin* : clarus.

---

[1] *Latissime patet Lugiorum nomen in pluris civitates diffusum* (*Germ.* 43). They are, at any rate, to be placed N.E. of Vannius' kingdom, which may be roughly taken as at least the Czecho-Slovakian provinces of Bohemia and Moravia.

[2] An emigrant branch (᾽Ιάζυγες μετανάσται) of the Iazyges on the Black Sea and Sea of Azov; now established in the plain between the Danube and Theiss, on the eastern frontier of Pannonia.

men in the first years of his sovereignty, then, by
continuous power, perverted to tyranny, he now
succumbed to his neighbours' hatred combined with
domestic discords. The authors of his fall were
Vibilius, king of the Hermunduri, and Vangio and
Sido, the children of his own sister. Nor did Claudius,
though often appealed to, interpose his arms between
the warring barbarians, but promised a secure retreat
to Vannius in the case of his expulsion, and wrote
to the governor of Pannonia, Palpellius Hister, to
station one legion, with a chosen body of auxiliaries
from the province itself, upon the Danube bank—
there to act as a support to the conquered and a
deterrent to the conquerors, lest in the elation of
success they should disturb the Roman peace as
well. For a countless horde was on the march—
Lugians[1] and other tribes, allured by the fame of
that wealthy monarchy, which Vannius, for thirty
years, had aggrandized by depredations and by
exactions. The king's own force of infantry and his
cavalry, recruited from the Sarmatian Iazyges,[2] were
unequal to the numbers of the enemy; and he had
consequently decided to hold out in his fortresses
and so to protract the campaign.

XXX. The Iazyges, however, impatient of confinement, spread over the adjacent plains and made
a battle imperative, as the Lugians and Hermunduri
had there rushed to the attack. Vannius accordingly
descended from his strongholds and was worsted in
the engagement, earning, despite his ill-success, a
meed of praise for fighting sword in hand and taking
his wounds in front. Still, he sought refuge with
the flotilla waiting in the Danube: his vassals, who
quickly followed, received a grant of lands and were

in Pannonia locati sunt. Regnum Vangio ac Sido
inter se partivere, egregia adversus nos fide, subiectis,
suone an servitii ingenio, dum adipiscerentur dominationis, multa caritate, et maiore odio, postquam
adepti sunt.

XXXI. At in Britannia P. Ostorius pro praetore
turbidae res excepere, effusis in agrum sociorum
hostibus eo violentius, quod novum ducem exercitu
ignoto et coepta hieme iturum obviam non rebantur.
Ille gnarus primis eventibus metum aut fiduciam
gigni, citas cohortis rapit, et caesis qui restiterant,
disiectos consectatus, ne rursus conglobarentur
infensaque et infida pax non duci, non militi requiem
permitteret, detrahere arma suspectis cunctaque cis
Trisantonam[1] et Sabrinam fluvios cohibere parat.
Quod primi Iceni abnuere, valida gens nec proeliis
contusi, quia societatem nostram volentes accesserant.
Hisque auctoribus circumiectae nationes locum
pugnae delegere, saeptum agresti aggere et aditu
angusto, ne pervius equiti foret. Ea munimenta
dux Romanus, quamquam sine robore legionum socialis copias ducebat, perrumpere adgreditur et

---

[1] cis Trisantonam *Heraeus, Bradley*: castris antonam *Med.*,
castris Avonam ⟨inter⟩ *Mannert, Heinsius. See note.*

---

[1] This confused account of British affairs from 47 A.D. to
58 A.D. gives rise to a number of problems, which cannot be
discussed in short footnotes. Only a few points, useful for a
comprehension of the narrative as it stands, are noticed.

[2] Successor of A. Plautius (leader of the invasion of 43 A.D.),
who is known to have returned to Rome for his ovation in
47 A.D.

[3] With the emendation in the text—the only plausible
attempt to cure the passage—the Trisantona must be taken
as the Trent; for which, it must be owned, no evidence exists.
The Τρισαντῶνος ποταμοῦ ἐκβολαί are, in fact, placed by
Ptolemy (II. 3, 4) on the S. coast, W. of the Καινὸς λιμήν and

settled in Pannonia. Vannius and Sido partitioned the kingdom between them, and to ourselves showed admirable loyalty: by their subjects—whether the fault lay in their own nature or in that of despotism—they were well loved whilst winning their power, better hated when their power was won.

XXXI. Meanwhile, in Britain[1] the propraetor Publius Ostorius[2] had a troubled reception, as the enemy had poured into the territory of our allies with a violence all the greater from their belief that a new commander would not take the field with an untried army and with winter begun. Ostorius, aware that first results are those which engender fear or confidence, swept his cohorts forward at speed, cut down the resisters, chased the broken bands and —to obviate a second rally, to be followed by a sullen and disloyal peace which would allow no rest either to the general or his troops—prepared to disarm the suspect and to overawe the whole district on this side of the Trent and Severn.[3] The first to become restive were the Iceni,[4] a powerful community not yet broken in battle, as they had voluntarily acceded to our alliance. At their suggestion, the surrounding tribes chose for their field of battle a position protected by a rustic embankment with a narrow approach, designed to be impervious to cavalry. This defence the Roman commander prepared to carry, though he was leading an auxiliary force without the strength of the legions, and

the Κάντιον ἄκρον (N. Foreland). It is argued on the other side that river-names tend to repeat themselves, that "Trisantona" may perhaps be found in the Tarannon of Montgomeryshire, and that the "Trannonus" of Nennius, in the ninth century, is demonstrably the Trent.

[4] In Norfolk, Suffolk, and Cambridgeshire.

distributis cohortibus turmas quoque peditum ad
munia accingit. Tunc dato signo perfringunt aggerem suisque claustris impeditos turbant. Atque
illi conscientia rebellionis et obsaeptis effugiis multa
et clara facinora fecere, qua pugna filius legati M.
Ostorius servati civis decus meruit.

XXXII. Ceterum clade Icenorum compositi qui
bellum inter et pacem dubitabant, et ductus in
Decangos [1] exercitus. Vastati agri, praedae passim
actae, non ausis aciem hostibus, vel si ex occulto
carpere agmen temptarent, punito dolo. Iamque
ventum haud procul mari, quod Hiberniam
insulam aspectat, cum ortae apud Brigantas discordiae retraxere ducem, destinationis certum, ne
nova moliretur nisi prioribus firmatis. Et Brigantes
quidem, paucis qui arma coeptabant interfectis, in
reliquos data venia, resedere: Silurum gens non
atrocitate, non clementia mutabatur, quin bellum
exerceret castrisque legionum premenda foret. Id
quo promptius veniret, colonia Camulodunum valida

---

[1] in Decangos *Bezzenberger*: inde Cangos *Med.*, in Ceangos
Andresen.

---

[1] The *corona civica* (III. 21 n.).

[2] As pigs of lead have been unearthed in Cheshire and
Staffordshire, inscribed DECEANG or the like, it is presumed
that the tribe occupied the lead district of Flintshire. Whether
the name was *Deceangi* or *Ceangi* depends on the unanswerable
question whether, in the inscriptions, DE is a preposition or
not. Ptolemy's Καιαγγανῶν ἄκρον (II. 3, 3) tells in favour of
the second form.

[3] A powerful tribe spread over the northern counties.

[4] In S. Wales, Monmouth, and Hereford.

distributing the cohorts in appropriate positions, turned even his mounted squadrons to infantry work. Then, on the signal, they broke through the embankment, and threw the enemy, hampered by his own barrier, into confusion. The Britons, with their rebellion on their conscience, and every egress closed, performed many remarkable feats; and during the engagement the legate's son, Marcus Ostorius, earned the reward for saving a Roman life.[1]

XXXII. By the Icenian defeat all who were wavering between war and peace were reduced to quietude, and the army was led against the Ceangi.[2] The country was devastated, booty collected everywhere, while the enemy declined to risk a battle, or, if he made a stealthy attempt to harass the marching columns, found his treachery punished. And now Ostorius was within measurable distance of the sea which looks towards Ireland, when an outbreak of sedition among the Brigantes[3] recalled a leader who was firm in his resolution to attempt new conquests only when he had secured the old. The Brigantian rising, it is true, subsided on the execution of a handful of men, who were beginning hostilities, and the pardon of the rest; but neither severity nor clemency converted the Silurian tribe,[4] which continued the struggle and had to be repressed by the establishment of a legionary camp.[5] To facilitate that result, a colony was settled on conquered lands at Camulodunum[6] by a strong detachment of

[5] Perhaps at Gloucester. The permanent establishment of the second legion at Isca Silurum—Caerleon (= castra legionis) on Usk—appears to have taken place under Vespasian.

[6] Colchester; formerly the capital of the Trinobantine king Cunobelinus ("Cymbeline"). The creation of the colony of veterans allowed the legions in Essex to be moved west.

veteranorum manu deducitur in agros captivos,
subsidium adversus rebelles et inbuendis sociis ad
officia legum.

XXXIII. Itum inde in Siluras, super propriam
ferociam Carataci viribus confisos, quem multa
ambigua, multa prospera extulerant, ut ceteros
Britannorum imperatores praemineret. Sed tum
astu, locorum fraude prior, vi militum inferior,
transfert bellum in Ordovicas, additisque qui pacem
nostram metuebant, novissimum casum experitur,
sumpto ad proelium loco, ut aditus, abscessus, cuncta
nobis inportuna et suis in melius essent, hinc[1] montibus arduis, et si qua clementer accedi poterant, in
modum valli saxa praestruit. Et praefluebat amnis
vado incerto, catervaeque armatorum pro munimentis constiterant.

XXXIV. Ad hoc gentium ductores circumire,
hortari, firmare animos minuendo metu, accendenda
spe aliisque belli incitamentis: enimvero Caratacus
huc illuc volitans illum diem, illam aciem testabatur
aut reciperandae libertatis aut servitutis aeternae
initium fore; vocabatque nomina maiorum, qui
dictatorem Caesarem pepulissent, quorum virtute
vacui a securibus et tributis intemerata coniugum et
liberorum corpora retinerent. Haec atque talia

----

[1] hinc *Halm*: tunc.

----

[1] Son of Cunobelinus. He had commanded against A.
Plautius in 43 A.D., and had apparently taken refuge among the
Silures.

[2] In central and northern Wales.

veterans, who were to serve as a bulwark against revolt and to habituate the friendly natives to their legal obligations.

XXXIII. The march then proceeded against the Silurians, whose native boldness was heightened by their confidence in the prowess of Caratacus;[1] whose many successes, partial or complete, had raised him to a pinnacle above the other British leaders. But on this occasion, favoured by the treacherous character of the country, though inferior in military strength, he astutely shifted the seat of war to the territory of the Ordovices;[2] where, after being joined by all who feared a Roman peace, he put the final chance to trial. The place fixed upon for the struggle was one where approaches, exits, every local feature would be unfavourable to ourselves and advantageous to his own forces. On one side the hills rose sheer; and wherever a point could be reached by a gentle ascent, the way was blocked with stones composing a sort of rampart. Along the front ran a river with a precarious ford, and bands of warriors were in position before the defences.

XXXIV. In addition, the tribal chieftains were going round, haranguing the men and confirming their spirits by minimizing fear, by kindling hope, and by applying the various stimulants of war. As for Caratacus, he flew hither and thither, protesting that this day—this field—would be the prelude to their recovery of freedom or their eternal servitude. He invoked the names of their ancestors, who had repelled the dictator Caesar, and by whose valour they were immune from the Axes and the tributes and still preserved inviolate the persons of their wives and children.—To these appeals and the like

361

dicenti adstrepere vulgus, gentili quisque religione obstringi, non telis, non vulneribus cessuros.

XXXV. Obstupefecit ea alacritas ducem Romanum; simul obiectus amnis, additum vallum, inminentia iuga, nihil nisi atrox et propugnatoribus frequens terrebat. Sed miles proelium poscere, cuncta virtute expugnabilia clamitare; praefectique *et* [1] tribuni paria disserentes ardorem exercitus intendebant. Tum Ostorius, circumspectis quae inpenetrabilia quaeque pervia, ducit infensos amnemque haud difficulter evadit. Ubi ventum ad aggerem, dum missilibus certabatur, plus vulnerum in nos et pleraeque caedes oriebantur: postquam facta testudine rudes et informes saxorum conpages distractae parque comminus acies, decedere barbari in iuga montium. Sed eo quoque inrupere ferentarius gravisque miles, illi telis adsultantes, hi conferto gradu, turbatis contra Britannorum ordinibus, apud quos nulla loricarum galearumve tegmina; et si auxiliaribus resisterent, gladiis ac pilis legionariorum, si huc verterent, spathis et hastis auxiliarium sternebantur. Clara ea victoria fuit, captaque uxor [2] et filia Carataci fratresque in deditionem accepti.

XXXVI. Ipse, ut ferme intuta sunt adversa, cum

---

[1] ⟨et⟩ *Bezzenberger.*
[2] uxor *Bezzenberger* : uxore.

the crowd shouted assent, and every man took his tribal oath to give way neither for weapons nor for wounds.

XXXV. This ardour disconcerted the Roman general; and he was daunted also by the intervening river, by the added rampart, the beetling hills, the absence of any point that was not defiant and thronged with defenders. But the soldiers insisted on battle; against courage, they clamoured, no place was impregnable; and prefects and tribunes, employing the same language, intensified the zeal of the army. After surveying the ground to discover its impenetrable and its vulnerable points, Ostorius now put himself at the head of the eager troops and crossed the river without difficulty. When the embankment was reached, so long as the struggle was carried on by missiles, most of the wounds, and numerous casualties, fell to our own lot. But a mantlet was formed; and, once the rude and shapeless aggregate of stones had been demolished and matters came to an equal encounter at close quarters, the barbarians withdrew to the hill-tops. Yet even there the light and heavy troops broke in, the former skirmishing with their darts, the latter advancing in close order, while the British ranks opposite were in complete confusion: for they lacked the protection of breastplates and helmets; if they offered a resistance to the auxiliaries, they were struck down by the swords and javelins of the legionaries; if they faced against the legionaries, they fell under the falchions and lances of the auxiliaries. It was a notable victory; and the wife and daughter of Caratacus were taken, his brothers being admitted to surrender.

XXXVI. Caratacus himself—for adversity seldom

fidem Cartimanduae reginae Brigantum petivisset,
vinctus ac victoribus traditus est, nono post anno,
quam bellum in Britannia coeptum. Unde fama
eius evecta insulas[1] et proximas provincias pervagata
per Italiam quoque celebrabatur, avebantque visere,
quis ille tot per annos opes nostras sprevisset. Ne
Romae quidem ignobile Carataci nomen erat; et
Caesar dum suum decus extollit, addidit gloriam
victo. Vocatus quippe ut ad insigne spectaculum
populus: stetere in armis praetoriae cohortes
campo, qui castra praeiacet. Tunc[2] incedentibus
regiis clientulis phalerae, torques[3] quaeque bellis
externis quaesiverat traducta, mox fratres et coniunx
et filia, postremo ipse ostentatus. Ceterorum preces
degeneres fuere ex metu: at non Caratacus aut vultu
demisso aut verbis misericordiam requirens, ubi
tribunali adstitit, in hunc modum locutus est :—

XXXVII. " Si quanta nobilitas et fortuna mihi
fuit, tanta rerum prosperarum moderatio fuisset,
amicus potius in hanc urbem quam captus venissem,
neque dedignatus esses claris maioribus ortum,
pluribus gentibus imperitantem foedere in pacem[4]
accipere. Praesens sors mea ut mihi informis, sic
tibi magnifica est. Habui equos viros, arma opes:
quid mirum, si haec invitus amisi? Nam[5] si vos
omnibus imperitare vultis, sequitur ut omnes servi-
tutem accipiant? Si statim deditus traherer,[6] neque

---

[1] insulas] insulam *Heinsius.*   [2] tunc] tum *Ernesti.*
[3] torques *Doederlein* : torquibus.
[4] in pacem *Doederlein* : * pacem.
[5] nam] num *Lipsius.*
[6] traherer *Bekker* : traderer.

---

[1] An exceptional circumstance at Rome : see III. 4 n.

finds a refuge—after seeking the protection of the Brigantian queen Cartimandua, was arrested and handed to the victors, in the ninth year from the opening of the war in Britain. Through that resistance, his reputation had gone beyond the islands, had overspread the nearest provinces, and was familiar in Italy itself; where there was curiosity to see what manner of man it was that had for so many years scorned our power. Even in Rome, the name of Caratacus was not without honour; and the Caesar, by attempting to heighten his own credit, added distinction to the vanquished. For the populace were invited as if to some spectacle of note; the praetorian cohorts stood under arms [1] upon the level ground in front of their camp. Then, while the king's humble vassals filed past, ornaments and neck-rings and prizes won in his foreign wars were borne in parade; next his brothers, wife, and daughter were placed on view; finally, he himself. The rest stooped to unworthy entreaties dictated by fear; but on the part of Caratacus not a downcast look nor a word requested pity. Arrived at the tribunal, he spoke as follows :—

XXXVII. "Had my lineage and my rank been matched by my moderation in success, I should have entered this city rather as a friend than as a captive; nor would you have scorned to admit to a peaceful league a king sprung from famous ancestors and holding sway over many peoples. My present lot, if to me a degradation, is to you a glory. I had horses and men, arms and riches: what wonder if I lost them with a pang? For if you would rule the world, does it follow that the world must welcome servitude? If I were dragged before you after

mea fortuna neque tua gloria inclaruisset; et supplicium mei oblivio sequeretur: at si incolumem
servaveris, aeternum exemplar clementiae ero."
Ad ea Caesar veniam ipsique et coniugi et fratribus
tribuit. Atque illi vinclis absoluti [1] Agrippinam
quoque, haud procul alio suggestu conspicuam, isdem
quibus principem laudibus gratibusque venerati sunt.
Novum sane et moribus veterum insolitum, feminam
signis Romanis praesidere: ipsa semet parti a
maioribus suis imperii sociam ferebat.

XXXVIII. Vocati posthac patres multa et magnifica super captivitate Carataci disseruere, neque
minus id clarum, quam quod Syphacem P. Scipio,
Persen L. Paulus, et si qui alii vinctos reges populo
Romano ostendere. Censentur Ostorio triumphi
insignia, prosperis ad id rebus eius, mox ambiguis,
sive amoto Carataco, quasi debellatum foret, minus
intenta apud nos militia fuit, sive hostes miseratione
tanti regis acrius ad ultionem exarsere. Praefectum
castrorum et legionarias cohortes exstruendis apud
Siluras praesidiis relictas circumfundunt. Ac ni cito
nuntiis [2] ex [3] castellis proximis subventum foret
copiarum obsidio, occidione [4] obcubuissent: praefectus tamen et octo centuriones ac promptissimus

---

[1] absoluti] exsoluti *Lipsius,* soluti *Ritter.*
[2] nuntiis ⟨dimissis⟩ *Wurm.*
[3] ex *Ruperti* (e *Lipsius*) : et.
[4] obsidio ⟨occidio⟩ne *Halm* : obsidione.

---

[1] The Numidian prince whose chequered career in the
Second Punic War was closed by his defeat at Cirta. Scipio's
triumph was in 201 B.C.: that Syphax appeared in it was
asserted by Polybius, doubted by Livy (XXX. 45).

[2] The last Macedonian king; defeated at Pydna by L.
Aemilius Paulus in 168 B.C., and exhibited in his triumph the
following year.

surrendering without a blow, there would have been little heard either of my fall or of your triumph: punishment of me will be followed by oblivion; but save me alive, and I shall be an everlasting memorial of your clemency." The answer was the Caesar's pardon for the prince, his wife, and his brothers; and the prisoners, freed from their chains, paid their homage to Agrippina also—a conspicuous figure on another tribunal not far away—in the same terms of praise and gratitude which they had employed to the emperor. It was an innovation, certainly, and one without precedent in ancient custom, that a woman should sit in state before Roman standards: it was the advertisement of her claim to a partnership in the empire which her ancestors had created.

XXXVIII. The Fathers, who were convened later, delivered long and florid orations on the capture of Caratacus—" an incident as glorious as the exhibition to the Roman people of Syphax[1] by Publius Scipio, of Perseus[2] by Lucius Paulus, of other manacled kings by other generals." Triumphal insignia were awarded to Ostorius; whose fortunes, so far unclouded, now became dubious—possibly because, with the removal of Caratacus, our energy in the field had been slackened in the belief that the war was won, or possibly sympathy with their great king had fired the enemy's zeal to avenge him. A camp-prefect and some legionary cohorts, left behind to construct garrison-posts in Silurian territory, were attacked from all quarters; and, if relief had not quickly reached the invested troops from the neighbouring forts—they had been informed by messenger —they must have perished to the last man. As it was, the prefect fell, with eight centurions and the

quisque e manipulis cecidere. Nec multo post
pabulantis nostros [1] missasque ad subsidium turmas
profligant.

XXXIX. Tum Ostorius cohortis expeditas opposuit; nec ideo fugam sistebat, ni legiones proelium
excepissent: earum robore aequata pugna, dein
nobis pro meliore fuit. Effugere hostes tenui
damno, quia inclinabat dies. Crebra hinc proelia, et
saepius in modum latrocinii per saltus per paludes, ut
cuique sors aut virtus, temere proviso,[2] ob iram
ob praedam, iussu et aliquando ignaris ducibus,
ac praecipua Silurum pervicacia. Quos accendebat
vulgata imperatoris Romani vox, ut quondam
Sugambri excisi aut in Gallias traiecti forent, ita
Silurum nomen penitus extinguendum. Igitur duas
auxiliaris cohortis avaritia praefectorum incautius
populantis intercepere; spoliaque et captivos largi-
endo ceteras quoque nationes ad defectionem trahebant, cum taedio curarum fessus Ostorius concessit
vita, laetis hostibus, tamquam ducem haud spernen-
dum etsi non proelium, at certe bellum absumpsisset.

XL. At Caesar cognita morte legati, ne provincia
sine rectore foret, A. Didium suffecit. Is propere
vectus non tamen integras res invenit, adversa interim
legionis pugna, cui Manlius Valens praeerat, auc-

---

[1] nostros *Puteolanus*: nos ipsos *Med. The alternative
is:* pabulantis nos⟨tros speculati⟩ ipsos missasque e.q.s., *or
the like.*

[2] proviso] provisu *Lipsius.*

---

[1] By Tiberius in 8 B.C.: cf. II. 26.
[2] See chap. 15.

boldest members of the rank and file.—Nor was it long before both a Roman foraging party and the squadrons despatched to its aid were totally routed.

XXXIX. Ostorius then interposed his light cohorts; but even so he failed to check the flight, until the legions took up the contest. Their strength equalized the struggle, which eventually turned in our favour; the enemy escaped with trivial losses, as the day was drawing to a close. Frequent engagements followed, generally of the irregular type, in woods and fens; decided by individual luck or bravery; accidental or prearranged; with passion or plunder for the motives; by orders, or sometimes without the knowledge of the leaders. Particularly marked was the obstinacy of the Silures, who were infuriated by a widely repeated remark of the Roman commander, that, as once the Sugambri had been exterminated or transferred to the Gallic provinces,[1] so the Silurian name ought once for all to be extinguished. They accordingly cut off two auxiliary cohorts which, through the cupidity of their officers, were ravaging the country too incautiously; and by presents of spoils and captives they were drawing into revolt the remaining tribes also, when Ostorius—broken by the weary load of anxiety— paid the debt of nature; to the delight of the enemy, who considered that, perhaps not a battle, but certainly a campaign had disposed of a general whom it was impossible to despise.

XL. On receiving the news of the legate's death, the Caesar, not to leave the province without a governor, appointed Aulus Didius[2] to the vacancy. In spite of a rapid crossing, he found matters deteriorated, as the legion under Manlius Valens had been

taque est [1] apud hostis eius rei fama, quo venientem
ducem exterrerent, atque illo augente audita, ut
maior laus compositis et,[2] si duravissent, venia iustior
tribueretur. Silures id quoque damnum intulerant
lateque persultabant, donec adcursu Didii pellerentur. Sed post captum Caratacum praecipuus
scientia rei militaris Venutius, e Brigantum civitate,
ut supra memoravi, fidusque diu et Romanis armis
defensus, cum Cartimanduam reginam matrimonio
teneret; mox orto discidio et statim bello etiam
adversus nos hostilia induerat. Sed primo tantum
inter ipsos certabatur, callidisque Cartimandua
artibus fratem ac propinquos Venutii ˙ intercepit.
Inde accensi hostes, stimulante ignominia, ne feminae
imperio subderentur, valida et lecta armis iuventus
regnum eius invadunt. Quod nobis praevisum, et
missae auxilio cohortes acre proelium fecere, cuius
initio ambiguo finis laetior fuit. Neque dispari
eventu pugnatum a legione, cui Caesius Nasica
praeerat; nam Didius, senectute gravis et multa
copia honorum, per ministros agere et arcere hostem
satis habebat. Haec, quamquam a duobus pro
praetoribus pluris per annos gesta, coniunxi, ne

---

[1] est *Nipperdey*: et.
[2] compositis et *Andresen*: compositi vel *Med.* (set *for* vel,
*mg. m.*1).

---

[1] The reference in the Annals is lost, but see *Hist.* III. 45.

defeated in the interval. Reports of the affair were exaggerated: among the enemy, with the hope of alarming the commander on his arrival; by the commander—who magnified the version he heard —with the hope of securing additional credit, if he settled the disturbances, and a more legitimate excuse, if the disturbances persisted. In this case, again, the loss had been inflicted by the Silurians, and they carried their forays far and wide, until repelled by the advent of Didius. Since the capture of Caratacus, however, the Briton with the best knowledge of the art of war was Venutius, whose Brigantian extraction has been mentioned earlier.[1] He had long been loyal, and had received the protection of the Roman arms during his married life with Queen Cartimandua: then had come a divorce, followed by immediate war, and he had extended his hostility to ourselves. At first, however, the struggle was confined to the pair; and Cartimandua adroitly entrapped the brother and family connections of Venutius. Incensed at her act, and smarting at the ignominious prospect of submitting to the sway of a woman, the enemy—a powerful body of young and picked warriors—invaded her kingdom. That event had been foreseen by us, and the cohorts sent to the rescue fought a sharp engagement, with dubious results at the outset but a more cheerful conclusion. The conflict had a similar issue in the case of the legion, which was commanded by Caesius Nasica; since Didius, retarded by his years and full of honours, was content to act through his subordinates and to hold the enemy at distance.—These operations, though conducted by two propraetors over a period of years, I have related consecutively, lest, if treated

divisa haud perinde ad memoriam sui valerent: ad temporum ordinem redeo.

XLI. Ti. Claudio quintum Servio Cornelio Orfito[1] consulibus virilis toga Neroni maturata, quo capessendae rei publicae habilis videretur. Et Caesar adulationibus senatus libens cessit, ut vicensimo aetatis anno consulatum Nero iniret atque interim designatus proconsulare imperium extra urbem haberet ac princeps iuventutis appellaretur. Additum nomine eius donativum militi, congiarium plebei. Et ludicro circensium, quod adquirendis vulgi studiis edebatur, Britannicus in praetexta, Nero triumphali veste travecti sunt: spectaret populus hunc decore imperatorio, illum puerili habitu, ac perinde fortunam utriusque praesumeret. Simul qui centurionum tribunorumque sortem Britannici miserabantur, remoti fictis causis et alii per speciem honoris; etiam libertorum si quis incorrupta fide, depellitur tali occasione. Obvii inter se Nero Britannicum nomine, ille Domitium salutavere. Quod ut discordiae initium Agrippina multo questu ad maritum defert: sperni quippe adoptionem,

----

[1] [Orfito] *Ritter, probably.*

----

[1] Nero was thirteen on Dec. 15 of the preceding year, and the minimum age for the assumption of the *toga virilis* was fourteen.

[2] Thirty-three appears to have been the age fixed by Augustus.

[3] The title conferred by Augustus on his grandsons, Gaius and Lucius Caesar (I. 3). Like the proconsular imperium and the rest of the honours, it was a method of indicating the emperor's choice of a successor—he had, in theory at least, no precise power to nominate him.

separately, they should leave an inadequate impression on the memory. I return to the chronological order.

XLI. In the consulate of Tiberius Claudius, his fifth term, and of Servius Cornelius, the manly toga was prematurely [1] conferred on Nero, so that he should appear qualified for a political career. The Caesar yielded with pleasure to the sycophancies of the senate, which desired Nero to assume the consulship in the twentieth year of his age,[2] and in the interval, as consul designate, to hold proconsular authority outside the capital and bear the title Prince of the Youth.[3] There was added a donative to the troops, with a largess to the populace, both under his name; while at the games in the Circus, exhibited to gain him the partialities of the crowd, Britannicus rode past in the juvenile white and purple, Nero in the robes of triumph. "Let the people survey the one in the insignia of supreme command, the other in his puerile garb, and anticipate conformably the destinies of the pair!" At the same time all centurions and tribunes who evinced sympathy with the lot of Britannicus were removed, some on fictitious grounds, others under cloak of promotion. Even the few freedmen of untainted loyalty were dismissed on the following pretext. At a meeting between the two boys, Nero greeted Britannicus by his name, and was himself saluted as "Domitius."[4] Representing the incident as a first sign of discord, Agrippina reported it with loud complaints to her husband:—"The act of adoption

_A.V.C. 804 =_
_A.D. 51_

---

[4] The offence lay in ignoring the fact that, since the adoption, there was no longer a "L. Domitius Ahenobarbus," but merely a "Ti. Claudius Nero Caesar."

quaeque censuerint patres, iusserit populus, intra
penates abrogari; ac nisi pravitas tam infensa
docentium arceatur, eruptura in publicam perniciem.
Commotus his quasi criminibus optimum quemque
educatorem filii exilio aut [1] morte adficit datosque a
noverca custodiae eius inponit.

XLII. Nondum tamen summa moliri Agrippina
audebat, ni praetoriarum cohortium cura exsolve-
rentur Lusius Geta et Rufrius [2] Crispinus, quos Messalinae memores et liberis eius devinctos credebat.
Igitur distrahi cohortes ambitu duorum et, si ab uno
regerentur, intentiorem fore disciplinam adseverante
uxore, transfertur regimen cohortium ad Burrum
Afranium, egregiae militaris famae, gnarum tamen
cuius sponte praeficeretur. Suum quoque fastigium
Agrippina extollere altius: carpento Capitolium
ingredi, qui honos sacerdotibus et sacris antiquitus
concessus venerationem augebat feminae, quam
imperatore genitam, sororem eius, qui rerum potitus
sit, et coniugem et matrem fuisse, unicum ad hunc
diem exemplum est. Inter quae praecipuus pro-
pugnator eius Vitellius, validissima gratia, aetate
extrema (adeo incertae sunt potentium res) accusatione corripitur, deferente Iunio Lupo senatore. Is

---

[1] aut *Petersen* : ac.
[2] Rufrius *Halm* : Rufius.

---

[1] A two-wheeled vehicle with an ornate cover. Its use had
already been permitted by the senate to Messalina (D. Cass.
LX. 21), as it was later to the wife and daughter of Vespasian,
and to others.

[2] Germanicus had received the title from Tiberius (I. 58 fin.).

[3] She was, of course, sister of Caligula, as well as wife of
Claudius and mother of Nero.

was flouted, the decision of the Fathers and the mandate of the people abrogated on the domestic hearth! And unless they removed the mischievous influence of those who inculcated this spirit of hostility, it would break out in a public catastrophe." Perturbed by these hinted accusations, the emperor inflicted exile or death on the best of his son's preceptors, and placed him under the custody of the substitutes provided by his stepmother.

XLII. As yet, however, Agrippina lacked courage to make her supreme attempt, unless she could discharge from the command of the praetorian cohorts both Lusius Geta and Rufrius Crispinus, whom she believed faithful to the memory of Messalina and pledged to the cause of her children. Accordingly, through her assertions to her husband that the cohorts were being divided by the intriguing rivalry of the pair, and that discipline would be stricter if they were placed under a single head, the command was transferred to Afranius Burrus; who bore the highest character as a soldier but was well aware to whose pleasure he owed his appointment. The exaltation of her own dignity also occupied Agrippina: she began to enter the Capitol in a carriage;[1] and that honour, reserved by antiquity for priests and holy objects, enhanced the veneration felt for a woman who to this day stands unparalleled as the daughter of an Imperator[2] and the sister, the wife, and the mother of an emperor.[3] Meanwhile, her principal champion, Vitellius, at the height of his influence and in the extremity of his age—so precarious are the fortunes of the mighty—was brought to trial upon an indictment laid by the senator Junius Lupus. The charges he preferred

crimina maiestatis et cupidinem imperii obiectabat; praebuissetque auris Caesar, nisi Agrippinae minis magis quam precibus mutatus esset, ut accusatori aqua atque igni interdiceret. Hactenus Vitellius voluerat.

XLIII. Multa eo anno prodigia evenere. Insessum diris avibus Capitolium, crebris terrae motibus prorutae domus, ac dum latius metuitur, trepidatione vulgi invalidus[1] quisque obtriti; frugum quoque egestas et orta ex eo fames in prodigium accipiebatur. Nec occulti tantum questus, sed iura reddentem Claudium circumvasere clamoribus turbidis, pulsumque in extremam fori partem vi urguebant, donec militum globo infensos perrupit. Quindecim dierum alimenta urbi, non amplius superfuisse constitit, magnaque deum benignitate et modestia hiemis rebus extremis subventum. At hercule olim Italia legionibus longinquas in provincias commeatus portabat, nec nunc infecunditate laboratur, sed Africam potius et Aegyptum exercemus, navibusque et casibus vita populi Romani permissa est.

XLIV. Eodem anno bellum inter Armenios Hiberosque exortum Parthis quoque ac Romanis gravissimorum inter se motuum causa fuit. Genti Par-

---

[1] invalidus] invalidissimus *Wölfflin.*

---

[1] Cf. Suet. *Dom.* 23:—*Ante paucos quam occideretur mensis, cornix in Capitolio elocuta est,* Ἔσται πάντα καλῶς. Only in the last five books of the Annals are such prodigies mentioned; a fact from which the natural inference is drawn that Tacitus has begun to utilize another source—possibly the history of his own times by the elder Pliny, who opened *a fine Aufidi Bassi* (probably in the reign of Claudius) and would

were treason and designs upon the empire; and to
these the Caesar would certainly have inclined his
ear, had not the prayers, or rather the threats of
Agrippina converted him to the course of formally
outlawing the prosecutor: Vitellius had desired no
more.

XLIII. Many prodigies occurred during the year.
Ominous birds took their seat on the Capitol;[1] houses
were overturned by repeated shocks of earthquake,
and, as the panic spread, the weak were trampled
underfoot in the trepidation of the crowd. A
shortage of corn, again, and the famine which
resulted, were construed as a supernatural warning.
Nor were the complaints always whispered. Claudius,
sitting in judgement, was surrounded by a wildly
clamorous mob, and, driven into the farthest corner
of the Forum, was there subjected to violent pressure,
until, with the help of a body of troops, he forced a
way through the hostile throng. It was established
that the capital had provisions for fifteen days, no
more; and the crisis was relieved only by the
especial grace of the gods and the mildness of the
winter. And yet, Heaven knows, in the past, Italy
exported supplies for the legions into remote
provinces; nor is sterility the trouble now, but we
cultivate Africa and Egypt by preference, and the
life of the Roman nation has been staked upon
cargo-boats and accidents.

XLIV. In the same year, an outbreak of war
between the Armenians and Iberians gave rise as
well to a very serious disturbance of the relations
between Parthia and Rome. The Parthian nation

indisputably have found space for the phenomena: see his
own references in *H.N.* II. §§ 199 and 232.

thorum Vologeses imperitabat, materna origine ex
paelice Graeca, concessu fratrum regnum adeptus;
Hiberos Pharasmanes vetusta possessione, Armenios
frater eius Mithridates optinebat opibus nostris.
Erat Pharasmani filius nomine Radamistus, decora
proceritate, vi corporis insignis et patrias artes
edoctus, claraque inter accolas fama. Is modicum
Hiberiae regnum senecta patris detineri ferocius
crebriusque iactabat, quam ut cupidinem occultaret.
Igitur Pharasmanes iuvenem potentiae promptum[1] et
studio popularium accinctum, vergentibus iam annis
suis metuens, aliam ad spem trahere et Armeniam
ostentare, pulsis Parthis datam Mithridati a semet
memorando; sed vim differendam et potiorem dolum,
quo incautum opprimerent. Ita Radamistus simu-
lata adversus patrem discordia tamquam novercae
odiis impar pergit ad patruum, multaque ab eo comitate in speciem liberum cultus primores Armeniorum ad res novas inlicit, ignaro et ornante insuper
Mithridate.

XLV. Reconciliationis specie adsumpta regres-
susque ad patrem, quae fraude confici potuerint,
prompta nuntiat, cetera armis exsequenda. Interim
Pharasmanes belli causas confingit: proelianti sibi

---

[1] promptum *Lipsius* : prompte.

---

[1] For Pharasmanes and Mithridates, see VI. 32 sqq., XI. 8 sq.

was now subject to Vologeses, who, on the mother's side, was the offspring of a Greek concubine and had obtained the crown with the acquiescence of his brothers : Iberia was held by its old master Pharasmanes ; Armenia—with our support—by his brother Mithridates.[1] There was a son of Pharasmanes by the name of Radamistus, tall and handsome, remarkable for his bodily strength, versed in the national accomplishments, and in high repute with the neighbouring peoples. That the modest kingdom of Iberia was being kept from him by his father's tenacity of life, was a statement which he threw out too boldly and too frequently for his desires to remain unguessed. Pharasmanes, therefore, who had his misgivings about a youth alert for power and armed with the sympathies of the country, while his own years were already on the wane, sought to attract him to other ambitions by pointing to Armenia ; which, he observed, he had, by his expulsion of the Parthians, himself bestowed on Mithridates. Force, however, must wait : some ruse, by which they could take him off his guard, was preferable. Radamistus, then, after a feigned rupture with his father, gave out that he was unable to face the hatred of his stepmother, and made his way to his uncle ; was treated by him with exceptional kindness as though he had been a child of his own ; and proceeded to entice the Armenian nobles to revolution, undetected, and in fact honoured, by Mithridates.

XLV. Assuming the character of a reconciled son, he returned to his father, and announced that all which it had been possible to effect by fraud was ready : what remained must be achieved by arms. Meanwhile, Pharasmanes fabricated pretexts for

adversus regem Albanorum et Romanos auxilio
vocanti fratrem adversatum, eamque iniuriam excidio
ipsius ultum iturum; simul magnas copias filio
tradidit. Ille inruptione subita territum exutumque
campis Mithridaten compulit in castellum Gorneas,
tutum loco ac praesidio militum, quis Caelius Pollio
praefectus, centurio Casperius praeerat. Nihil tam
ignarum barbaris quam machinamenta et astus op-
pugnationum: at nobis ea pars militiae maxime
gnara est.[1] Ita Radamistus frustra vel cum damno
temptatis munitionibus obsidium incipit; et cum vis
neglegeretur, avaritiam praefecti emercatur, obtes-
tante Casperio, ne socius rex, ne Armenia donum
populi Romani scelere et pecunia verterentur.
Postremo quia multitudinem hostium Pollio, iussa
patris Radamistus obtendebant, pactus indutias
abscedit, ut, nisi Pharasmanem bello absterruisset,
Ummidium[2] Quadratum praesidem Suriae doceret,
quo in statu Armenia foret.

XLVI. Digressu centurionis velut custode exsolutus praefectus hortari Mithridaten ad sanciendum
foedus, coniunctionem fratrum ac priorem aetate
Pharasmanen et cetera necessitudinum nomina referens, quod filiam eius in matrimonio haberet, quod
ipse Radamisto socer esset: non abnuere pacem
Hiberos, quamquam in tempore validiores; et satis

---

[1] [at . . . gnara est] *Ritter*.
[2] Ummidium *Ritter*: tummidium.

---

[1] VI. 33 n.
[2] Of an auxiliary cohort.—Casperius reappears at XV. 5
and possibly at *Hist.* III. 73.

war :—" During his conflict with the king of Albania,[1] his appeal for Roman help had been opposed by his brother, and he would now avenge that injury by his destruction." At the same time, he entrusted a large force to his son ; who, by a sudden incursion, unnerved Mithridates, beat him out of the plains, and forced him into Gorneae, a fort protected by the nature of the ground and a garrison under the command of the prefect[2] Caelius Pollio and the centurion Casperius. Nothing is so completely unknown to barbarians as the appliances and refinements of siege operations—a branch of warfare perfectly familiar to ourselves. Hence, after several attacks, fruitless or worse, upon the fortifications, Radamistus began a blockade : then, as force was ignored, he bribed the avarice of the prefect, though Casperius protested against the subversion, by guilt and gold, of an allied monarch and of Armenia, his gift from the Roman people. At last, as Pollio continued to plead the numbers of the enemy and Radamistus the orders of his father, he stipulated for a truce, and left with the intention of either deterring Pharasmanes from his campaign or acquainting the governor of Syria, Ummidius Quadratus, with the state of matters in Armenia.

XLVI. With the centurion's departure, the prefect found himself rid of his warder, and he now pressed Mithridates to conclude a treaty. He enlarged upon the link of brotherhood, upon Pharasmanes' priority in age, upon the other titles of kinship,— the fact that he was married to his brother's daughter and was himself the father-in-law of Radamistus. "The Iberians," he said, "though for the time being the stronger party, were not disinclined to peace.

381

cognitam Armeniorum perfidiam, nec aliud subsidii quam castellum commeatu egenum: ne dubia *ten*tare armis quam incruentas condiciones mallet.[1] Cunctante ad ea Mithridate et suspectis praefecti consiliis, quod paelicem regiam polluerat inque omnem libidinem venalis habebatur, Casperius interim ad Pharasmanen pervadit, utque Hiberi obsidio decedant expostulat. Ille propalam incerta et saepius molliora respondens, secretis nuntiis monet Radamistum obpugnationem quoquo modo celerare. Augetur flagitii merces, et Pollio occulta corruptione inpellit milites, ut pacem flagitarent seque praesidium omis*suros* minitarentur. Qua necessitate Mithridates diem locumque foederi accepit castelloque egreditur.

XLVII. Ac primo Radamistus in amplexus eius effusus simulare obsequium, socerum ac parentem appellare; adicit ius iurandum, non ferro, non veneno vim adlaturum. Simul in lucum propinquum trahit, provisum illic sacrificii paratum [2] dictitans. ut dis testibus pax firmaretur. Mos est regibus, quotiens in societatem coëant, implicare dextras pollicesque inter se vincire nodoque praestringere: mox ubi sanguis in artus *se* extremos suffuderit, levi ictu cruorem eliciunt atque invicem lambunt. Id foedus arcanum habetur quasi mutuo

[1] dubia tentare . . . mallet *Sirker*: dubitare . . . malle.
[2] sacrificii paratum *Pflugk*: sacrificium imperatum *Med.*, sacrificum paratum *Bezzenberger*.

He was familiar enough already with Armenian treachery, and his only defence was a badly provisioned fort. Let him not decide for the doubtful experiment of arms in preference to a bloodless compact!" While Mithridates hesitated in spite of these arguments—the prefect's advice being suspect, as he had seduced one of the royal concubines and was considered capable of any villainy for a price—Casperius in the interval made his way to Pharasmanes and demanded that the Iberians should raise the siege. In public, the king's replies were vague and usually bland; in private, he warned Radamistus by courier to hurry on the siege by any and all means. The wage of dishonour was accordingly increased; and by secret bribery Pollio induced the troops to demand a peace under threat of abandoning the post. Mithridates had now no option; he accepted the place and day suggested for the treaty, and left the fort.

XLVII. The first act of Radamistus was to throw himself into his arms with affected devotion and to address him as father-in-law and parent. He followed with an oath that neither by steel nor by poison would he practise against his life. At the same moment, he hurried him into a neighbouring grove, where, he informed him, the apparatus of sacrifice had been provided in order that their peace might be ratified before the attesting gods. The procedure in the case of two kings meeting to conclude an alliance is to unite their right hands, tie the thumbs together, and tighten the pressure by a knot: then, when the blood has run to the extremities, a slight incision gives it outlet, and each prince licks it in turn. A mystical character is attached to the agree-

cruore sacratum. Sed tunc qui ea vincla admovebat, decidisse simulans genua Mithridatis invadit ipsumque prosternit; simulque concursu plurium iniciuntur catenae. Ac compede, quod dedecorum barbaris, trahebatur; mox quia vulgus duro imperio habitum, probra ac verbera intentabat. Et erant contra, qui tantam fortunae commutationem miserarentur; secutaque cum parvis liberis coniunx cuncta lamentatione complebat. Diversis et contectis vehiculis abduntur, dum Pharasmanis iussa exquirerentur. Illi cupido regni fratre et filia potior animusque sceleribus paratus; visui tamen consuluit, ne coram interficeret. Et Radamistus, quasi iuris iurandi memor, non ferrum, non venenum in sororem et patruum expromit, sed proiectos in humum et veste multa gravique opertos necat. Filii quoque Mithridatis, quod caedibus parentum inlacrimaverant, trucidati sunt.

XLVIII. At Quadratus cognoscens proditum Mithridaten et regnum ab interfectoribus optineri, vocat consilium, docet acta et an ulcisceretur consultat. Paucis decus publicum curae, plures tuta disserunt: omne scelus externum cum laetitia habendum; semina etiam odiorum iacienda, ut saepe

ment thus sealed and counter-sealed in blood. But, on this occasion, the person who was fastening the bonds feigned to slip, and, grasping Mithridates by the knees, threw him prostrate : at the same instant, a number of men rushed up and put him in irons. He was dragged off by his shackles, to barbarians a supreme indignity ; and before long the populace, which had experienced the rigour of his sway, was levelling against him its insults and its blows. There were also, on the other hand, some found to pity so complete a reversal of fortune ; and his wife, who followed with their infant children, filled the place with her laments. The prisoners were stowed out of sight in separate and covered vehicles, until the orders of Pharasmanes should be ascertained. To him the desire of a crown outweighed a brother and a daughter, and his temper was prompt to crime : still he shewed consideration for his eyes by not having them killed in his presence. Radamistus, too, mindful apparently of his oath, produced neither steel nor poison for the destruction of his sister and uncle, but had them tossed on the ground and smothered under a heavy pile of clothes. Mithridates' sons were also slaughtered, since they had shed tears at the murder of their parents.

XLVIII. Quadratus, gathering that Mithridates was betrayed and his kingdom held by the murderers, convened his council, laid the incidents before it, and asked for an opinion whether he should take punitive measures. A few showed some concern for the national honour ; the majority inculcated safety :—" Alien crime in general was to be hailed with pleasure ; it was well, even, to sow the seeds of hatred, precisely as on many occasions a Roman

principes Romani eandem Armeniam specie largitionis turbandis barbarorum animis praebuerint:
poteretur Radamistus male partis, dum invisus,
infamis, quando id magis ex usu, quam si cum gloria
adeptus foret. In hanc sententiam itum. Ne
tamen adnuisse facinori viderentur et diversa Caesar
iuberet, missi ad Pharasmanen nuntii, ut abscederet a
finibus Armeniis filiumque abstraheret.

XLIX. Erat Cappadociae procurator Iulius Paelignus, ignavia animi et derisiculo corporis iuxta
despiciendus, sed Claudio perquam familiaris, cum
privatus olim conversatione scurrarum iners otium
oblectaret. Is Paelignus[1] auxiliis provincialium contractis tamquam reciperaturus Armeniam, dum
socios magis quam hostis praedatur, abscessu
suorum et incursantibus barbaris praesidii egens ad
Radamistum venit; donisque eius evictus ultro
regium insigne sumere cohortatur sumentique adest
auctor et satelles. Quod ubi turpi fama divulgatum,
ne ceteri quoque ex Paeligno coniectarentur, Helvidius Priscus legatus cum legione mittitur, rebus
turbidis pro tempore ut consuleret. Igitur propere
montem Taurum transgressus moderatione plura
quam vi composuerat, cum rediret in Suriam iubetur,
ne initium belli adversus Parthos existeret.

---

[1] [Paelignus] *Freinsheim.*

---

[1] Not the son-in-law of Thrasea (XVI. 28 n.), leader of the
Stoic opposition under Vespasian, but conceivably, as Nipperdey suggested, an elder brother.

emperor, ostensibly as an act of munificence, had given away this same Armenia, merely to unsettle the temper of the barbarians. Let Radamistus hold his ill-gotten gains, so long as he held them at the price of detestation and of infamy : it was better for us than if he had won them with glory! " This opinion was adopted. But, to avoid the appearance of having acquiesced in the crime, when the imperial orders might be to the contrary effect, messengers were sent to Pharasmanes, requesting him to evacuate Armenian territory and withdraw his son.

XLIX. The procurator of Cappadocia was Julius Paelignus, a person made doubly contemptible by hebetude of mind and grotesqueness of body, yet on terms of the greatest intimacy with Claudius during the years of retirement when he amused his sluggish leisure with the society of buffoons. This Paelignus had mustered the provincial militia, with the avowed intention of recovering Armenia ; but, while he was plundering our subjects in preference to the enemy, the secession of his troops left him defenceless against the barbarian incursions, and he made his way to Radamistus, by whose liberality he was so overpowered that he voluntarily advised him to assume the kingly emblem, and assisted at its assumption in the quality of sponsor and satellite. Ugly reports of the incident spread; and, to make it clear that not all Romans were to be judged by the standard of Paelignus, the legate Helvidius Priscus [1] was sent with a legion to deal with the disturbed situation as circumstances might require. Accordingly, after crossing Mount Taurus in haste, he had settled more points by moderation than by force, when he was ordered back to Syria, lest he should give occasion for a Parthian war.

L. Nam Vologeses casum invadendae Armeniae obvenisse ratus, quam a maioribus suis possessam externus rex flagitio optineret, contrahit copias fratremque Tiridaten deducere in regnum parat, ne qua pars domus sine imperio ageret. Incessu Parthorum sine acie pulsi Hiberi, urbesque Armeniorum Artaxata et Tigranocerta iugum accepere. Deinde atrox hiems seu parum provisi commeatus et orta ex utroque tabes perpellunt Vologesen omittere praesentia. Vacuamque rursus Armeniam Radamistus invasit, truculentior quam antea, tamquam adversus defectores et in tempore rebellaturos. Atque illi, quamvis servitio sueti, patientiam abrumpunt armisque regiam circumveniunt.

LI. Nec aliud Radamisto subsidium fuit quam pernicitas equorum, quis seque et coniugem abstulit. Sed coniunx gravida primam utcumque fugam ob metum hostilem et mariti caritatem toleravit; post festinatione continua, ubi quati uterus et viscera vibrantur, orare ut morte honesta contumeliis captivitatis eximeretur. Ille primo amplecti adlevare adhortari, modo virtutem admirans, modo timore aeger, ne quis relicta poteretur. Postremo violentia amoris et facinorum non rudis destringit acinacen vulneratamque ripam ad Araxis trahit, flumini tradit,

---

[1] The reference is probably to the Arsacian dynasty of Armenia in the second and first centuries B.C.

[2] The other brother, Pacorus, had been established in Media Atropatene (Azerbeidjân), which was in practice, as Armenia was in theory, an appanage of the Arsacidae.

[3] II. 56 n.

[4] The second city of Armenia, lying in the extreme south, though the site is disputed (XV. 5 n.).

[5] The Arâs, on which Artaxata stood.

L. For Vologeses, convinced that the chance was come for an attack on Armenia, once the property of his ancestors,[1] now usurped by a foreign monarch in virtue of a crime, collected a force, and prepared to settle his brother Tiridates on the throne; so that no branch of his family should lack its kingdom.[2] The Parthian invasion forced back the Iberians without a formal battle, and the Armenian towns of Artaxata[3] and Tigranocerta[4] accepted the yoke. Then a severe winter, the inadequate provision of supplies, and an epidemic due to both of these causes, forced Vologeses to abandon the scene of action; and Armenia, masterless once again, was occupied by Radamistus, more truculent than ever towards a nation of traitors whom he regarded as certain to rebel when opportunity offered. They were a people inured to bondage; but patience broke, and they surrounded the palace in arms.

LI. The one salvation for Radamistus lay in the speed of the horses which swept himself and his wife away. His wife, however, was pregnant; and though fear of the enemy and love of her husband sustained her more or less in the first stages of the flight, yet before long, with the continuous gallop jarring her womb and vibrating through her system, she began to beg for an honourable death to save her from the degradations of captivity. At first, he embraced her, supported her, animated her, one moment wondering at her courage, the next sick with fear at the thought of abandoning her to the possession of another. At last, overmastered by his love, and no stranger to deeds of violence, he drew his sabre, dragged her bleeding to the bank of the Araxes,[5] and, bent on removing even

ut corpus etiam auferretur: ipse praeceps Hiberos [1]
ad patrium regnum pervadit. Interim Zenobiam
(id mulieri nomen) placida in eluvie [2] spirantem ac
vitae manifestam advertere pastores, et dignitate
formae haud degenerem reputantes obligant vulnus,
agrestia medicamina adhibent cognitoque nomine
et casu in urbem Artaxata ferunt; unde publica
cura deducta ad Tiridaten comiterque excepta cultu
regio habita est.

LII. Fausto Sulla Salvio Othone consulibus Furius
Scribonianus in exilium agitur, quasi finem principis
per Chaldaeos scrutaretur. Adnectebatur crimini
Vibia mater eius, ut casus prioris (nam relegata
erat) inpatiens. Pater Scriboniani Camillus arma
per Delmatiam moverat; idque ad clementiam
trahebat Caesar, quod stirpem hostilem iterum con-
servaret. Neque tamen exuli longa posthac vita
fuit: morte fortuita an per venenum extinctus esset,
ut quisque credidit, vulgavere. De mathematicis
Italia pellendis factum senatus consultum atrox et
inritum. Laudati dehinc oratione principis, qui ob
angustias familiares ordine senatorio sponte cede-
rent, motique, qui remanendo inpudentiam pauper-
tati adicerent.

LIII. Inter quae refert ad patres de poena feminarum, quae servis coniungerentur; statuiturque, ut

---

[1] [Hiberos] *Heraeus.*
[2] in eluvie *Madvig* : inluvie.

---

[1] Son-in-law of Claudius; killed at Marseilles by order of
Nero (XIV. 57).
[2] Brother of the future emperor.
[3] Consul in 32 A.D. His rising, ten years later, broke down
within five days (Suet. *Claud.* 13 fin.).

her corpse, consigned her to the current: he himself rode headlong through to his native kingdom of Iberia. Meanwhile, Zenobia (to give his wife her name) was noticed by a few shepherds in a quiet backwater, still breathing and showing signs of life. Arguing her high birth from the distinction of her appearance, they bound up her wound, applied their country remedies, and, on discovering her name and misfortune, carried her to the town of Artaxata; from which, by the good offices of the community, she was escorted to Tiridates, and, after a kind reception, was treated with royal honours.

LII. In the consulate of Faustus Sulla [1] and Salvius Otho, [2] Furius Scribonianus was driven into exile, on a charge of inquiring into the end of the sovereign by the agency of astrologers: his mother Vibidia was included in the arraignment, on the ground that she had not acquiesced in her former misadventure —she had been sentenced to relegation. Camillus, [3] the father of Scribonianus, had taken arms in Dalmatia: a point placed by the emperor to the credit of his clemency, since he was sparing this hostile stock for a second time. The exile, however, did not long survive: the question whether he died by a natural death or from poison was answered by the gossips according to their various beliefs. The expulsion of the astrologers from Italy was ordered by a drastic and impotent decree of the senate. Then followed a speech by the emperor, commending all who voluntarily renounced senatorial rank owing to straitened circumstances: those who, by remaining, added impudence to poverty were removed.

LIII. At the same time, he submitted a motion to the Fathers, penalizing women who married

391

ignaro domino ad id prolapsae in servitute, sin consensisset, pro libertis haberentur. Pallanti, quem repertorem eius relationis ediderat Caesar, praetoria insignia et centiens quinquagiens sestertium censuit consul designatus Barea Soranus. Additum a Scipione Cornelio gratis publice agendas, quod regibus Arcadiae ortus veterrimam nobilitatem usui publico postponeret seque inter ministros principis haberi sineret. Adseveravit Claudius contentum honore Pallantem intra priorem paupertatem subsistere. Et fixum est aere publico senatus consultum, quo libertinus sestertii ter miliens possessor antiquae parsimoniae laudibus cumulabatur.

LIV. At non frater eius, cognomento Felix, pari moderatione agebat, iam pridem Iudaeae inpositus et cuncta malefacta sibi inpune ratus tanta potentia subnixo. Sane praebuerant Iudaei speciem motus orta seditione, postquam . . .[1] cognita caede eius haud obtemperatum esset, manebat metus, ne quis

[1] postquam ⟨a C. Caesare iussi erant effigiem eius in templo locare : et quamquam⟩ cognita e.q.s. *Haase (from Hist.* V. 9).

---

[1] The Stoic martyr (XVI. 21 n., 23, 30 sqq.).

[2] He made the freedman descend from Evander's ancestor Pallas (Virg. *Aen.* VIII. 51 sqq.). Whatever may be thought of the genealogy, his brother Felix was husband of three queens.

[3] The phrase, stereotyped in this connection, was read half a century later by the younger Pliny on Pallas' tomb (*Ep.* VII. 29) :—*Huic senatus ob fidem pietatemque erga patronos ornamenta praetoria decrevit et sestertium centies quinquagies, cuius honore contentus fuit.*

[4] Fixed side by side with a statue of the Dictator Julius in armour. Pliny consulted the decree itself, and found it *tam*

slaves; and it was resolved that anyone falling so far without the knowledge of the slave's owner should rank as in a state of servitude; while, if he had given sanction, she was to be classed as a freed-woman. That Pallas, whom the Caesar had specified as the inventor of his proposal, should receive the praetorian insignia and fifteen million sesterces, was the motion of the consul designate, Barea Soranus.[1] It was added by Cornelius Scipio that he should be accorded the national thanks, because, descendant though he was of the kings of Arcadia,[2] he postponed his old nobility to the public good, and permitted himself to be regarded as one among the servants of the emperor. Claudius passed his word that Pallas, contented with the honour,[3] declined to outstep his former honest poverty. And there was engraved on official brass [4] a senatorial decree lavishing the praises of old-world frugality upon a freedman, the proprietor of three hundred million sesterces.

LIV. The like moderation, however, was not shewn by his brother, surnamed Felix;[5] who for a while past had held the governorship of Judaea, and considered that with such influences behind him all malefactions would be venial. The Jews, it is true, had given signs of disaffection in the rioting prompted ⟨by the demand of Gaius Caesar for an effigy of himself in the Temple; and though⟩ the news of his murder had made compliance needless, the fear remained

---

copiosum et effusum ut ille superbissimus titulus (on the tomb) *modicus atque etiam demissus videretur* (*Ep.* VIII. 6).

[5] The procurator of *Acts* xxiv; like his brother, a freed-man of Claudius' mother Antonia, and therefore bearing the name Antonius Felix. The account which follows of the Judaeo-Samaritan disturbances cannot be reconciled with that of Josephus (*A.J.* XX. 5–6, 7 init.).

principum eadem imperitaret. Atque interim Felix
intempestivis remediis delicta accendebat, aemulo
ad deterrima Ventidio *Cumano*, cui pars provinciae
habebatur, ita divisis, ut huic Galilaeorum natio,
Felici Samaritae parerent, discordes olim et tum
contemptu regentium minus coërcitis odiis. Igitur
raptare inter se, immittere latronum globos, componere insidias et aliquando proeliis congredi, spoliaque et praedas ad procuratores referre. Hique
primo laetari, mox gliscente pernicie cum arma
militum interiecissent, caesi milites; arsissetque
bello provincia, ni Quadratus Suriae rector sub-
venisset. Nec diu adversus Iudaeos, qui in necem
militum proruperant, dubitatum quin capite poenas
luerent: Cumanus et Felix cunctationem adferebant, quia Claudius causis rebellionis auditis ius
statuendi etiam de procuratoribus dederat. Sed
Quadratus Felicem inter iudices ostentavit, recep-
tum in tribunal, quo studia accusantium deterreren-
tur; damnatusque flagitiorum, quae duo deliquerant,
Cumanus, et quies provinciae reddita.

LV. Nec multo post agrestium Cilicum nationes,
quibus Cietarum[1] cognomentum, saepe et alias com-
motae, tunc Troxobore[2] duce montis asperos castris
cepere atque inde decursu in litora aut urbes vim

---

[1] Cietarum *VI*. 41 : Clitarum.
[2] Troxobore] Troxoboro *Haase*.

---

[1] VI. 41 n.

that some emperor might issue an identical mandate. In the interval, Felix was fostering crime by misconceived remedies, his worst efforts being emulated by Ventidius Cumanus, his colleague in the other half of the province—which was so divided that the natives of Galilee were subject to Ventidius, Samaria to Felix. The districts had long been at variance, and their animosities were now under the less restraint, as they could despise their regents. Accordingly, they harried each other, unleashed their troops of bandits, fought an occasional field, and carried their trophies and their thefts to the procurators. At first, the pair rejoiced; then, when the growth of the mischief forced them to interpose the arms of their troops, the troops were beaten, and the province would have been ablaze with war but for the intervention of Quadratus, the governor of Syria. With regard to the Jews, who had gone so far as to shed the blood of regular soldiers, there were no protracted doubts as to the infliction of the death penalty : Cumanus and Felix were answerable for more embarrassment, as Claudius, on learning the motives of the revolt, had authorized Quadratus to deal with the case of the procurators themselves. Quadratus, however, displayed Felix among the judges, his admission to the tribunal being intended to cool the zeal of his accusers : Cumanus was sentenced for the delinquencies of two, and quietude returned to the province.

LV. Shortly afterwards, the tribes of wild Cilicians, known under the name of Cietae,[1] who had already broken the peace on many occasions, now formed a camp, under the leadership of Troxobor, on their precipitous hills ; and, descending to the coast or the

cultoribus et oppidanis ac plerumque in mercatores et navicularios audebant. Obsessaque civitas Anemuriensis, et missi e Suria in subsidium equites cum praefecto Curtio Severo turbantur, quod duri circum loci peditibusque ad pugnam idonei equestre proelium haud patiebantur. Dein rex eius orae Antiochus blandimentis adversum plebem, fraude in ducem cum barbarorum copias dissociasset, Troxobore[1] paucisque primoribus interfectis ceteros clementia composuit.

LVI. Sub idem tempus inter lacum Fucinum amnemque Lirim perrupto monte, quo magnificentia operis a pluribus viseretur, lacu in ipso navale proelium adornatur, ut quondam Augustus structo trans[2] Tiberim stagno, sed levibus navigiis et minore copia ediderat. Claudius triremis[3] quadriremisque et undeviginti hominum milia armavit, cincto ratibus ambitu, ne vaga[4] effugia forent, ac tamen spatium amplexus ad vim remigii, gubernantium artes, impetus navium et proelio solita. In ratibus praetoriarum cohortium manipuli turmaeque adstiterant,

[1] Troxobore] Troxoboro *Med.*, *Haase*.
[2] trans *Urlichs* : cis *Med.*, circa *Zumpt*.
[3] ⟨C⟩ triremis *Lipsius*.   [4] vaga] vacua *Heinsius*.

---

[1] Of Commagene : see XIII. 7 n.

[2] The Lago di Celano (Fucino); lying among the Apennines, E. of Rome, in the Marsian country. As it had no visible outlet and its level varied enormously with the stoppage or opening of the subterranean channel, it was decided to carry out a project of Julius Caesar, and to drain it into the Liris (Garigliano) by driving a tunnel through the intervening height (Monte Salviano).

[3] A brick-lined tunnel, 3 metres high and 1·80 wide, was driven in eleven years, by 30,000 workmen, a distance of 5,595 metres, hammer and chisel having to be employed for half the way on solid limestone.

cities, ventured to attack the peasants and towns-people, and, very frequently, the merchants and shipmasters. The city of Anemurium was invested; and a troop of horse sent to its relief from Syria under the prefect Curtius Severus was put to flight, as the rough ground in the vicinity, though suited to an infantry engagement, did not admit of cavalry fighting. Eventually, Antiochus [1]—in whose kingdom that part of the coast was included—by cajolery of the crowd and duplicity towards their leader dissolved the union of the barbarian forces, and, after executing Troxobor and a few chiefs, quieted the remainder by clemency.

LVI. Nearly at this date, the tunnelling of the mountain between Lake Fucinus [2] and the river Liris had been achieved; and, in order that the impressive character of the work [3] might be viewed by a larger number of visitants, a naval battle was arranged upon the lake itself, on the model of an earlier spectacle given by Augustus—though with light vessels and a smaller force [4]—in his artificial lagoon adjoining the Tiber. Claudius equipped triremes, quadriremes, and nineteen thousand combatants: the lists he surrounded with rafts, so as to leave no unauthorized points of escape, but reserved space enough in the centre to display the vigour of the rowing, the arts of the helmsmen, the impetus of the galleys, and the usual incidents of an engage-ment. On the rafts were stationed companies and squadrons of the praetorian cohorts, covered by a

[4] Thirty triremes or biremes, according to the *Monumentum Ancyranum*, with smaller vessels and a total of about 3,000 combatants, as distinct from rowers. Suetonius gives an impossibly low number for Claudius' fleet: Dio puts it at fifty vessels a side (LX. 33).

antepositis propugnaculis, ex quis catapultae ballistaeque tenderentur. Reliqua lacus classiarii tectis
navibus obtinebant. Ripas et colles montium*que* [1]
edita in modum theatri multitudo innumera complevit, proximis e municipiis et alii urbe ex ipsa, visendi
cupidine aut officio in principem. Ipse insigni
paludamento neque procul Agrippina chlamyde
aurata praesedere. Pugnatum quamquam inter
sontis fortium virorum animo, ac post multum
vulnerum occidioni exempti sunt.

LVII. Sed perfecto spectaculo apertum aquarum
iter. Incuria operis manifesta fuit, haud satis depressi ad lacus ima vel media. Eoque, tempore
interiecto, altius effossi specus, et contrahendae
rursus multitudini gladiatorum spectaculum editur,
inditis pontibus pedestrem ad pugnam. Quin et
convivium effluvio lacus adpositum magna formidine
cunctos adfecit, quia vis aquarum prorumpens
proxima trahebat, convulsis ulterioribus aut fragore
et sonitu exterritis. Simul Agrippina trepidatione
principis usa ministrum operis Narcissum incusat
cupidinis ac praedarum. Nec ille reticet, inpotentiam
muliebrem nimiasque spes eius arguens.

---

[1] montiumque *Heraeus*: montium *Med.*, ac montium
Puteolanus.

---

[1] The passage, according to Pliny, was deliberately neglected by Nero (*destitutum successoris odio*), and, though reopened by Hadrian (Spart. *Vit. Hadr.* 22), was useless in the
time of Dio (LX. 11). The lake was finally drained in 1874.

[2] Modern investigations point, in fact, to fraud on the part
of the contractors.

breastwork from which to operate their catapults
and ballistae: the rest of the lake was occupied by
marines with decked vessels. The shores, the hills,
the mountain-crests, formed a kind of theatre, soon
filled by an untold multitude, attracted from the
neighbouring towns, and in part from the capital
itself, by curiosity or by respect for the sovereign.
He and Agrippina presided, the one in a gorgeous
military cloak, the other—not far distant—in a
Greek mantle of cloth of gold. The battle, though
one of criminals, was contested with the spirit and
courage of freemen; and, after much blood had flowed,
the combatants were exempted from destruction.

LVII. On the conclusion of the spectacle, however,
the passage was opened for the waters. Carelessness
was at once evident in the construction of the tunnel,
which had not been sunk to the maximum or even
the mean depth of the lake. An interval of time
was therefore allowed for the channel to be cleared
to a lower level;[1] and, with a view to collecting a
second multitude, a gladiatorial exhibition was given
on pontoons laid for an infantry battle. A banquet,
even, had been served near the efflux of the lake;
only to result, however, in a general panic, as the
outrushing volume of water carried away the adjoining portions of the work, while those at a greater
distance experienced either the actual shock or the
terror produced by the crash and reverberation. At
the same moment, Agrippina profited by the
emperor's agitation to charge Narcissus, as director
of the scheme, with cupidity and embezzlement.[2]
He was not to be silenced, and retorted with an
attack on her feminine imperiousness and the
extravagance of her ambitions.

LVIII. D. Iunio Q. Haterio consulibus sedecim annos natus Nero Octaviam Caesaris filiam in matrimonium accepit. Utque studiis honestis *et* eloquentiae gloria enitesceret, causa Iliensium suscepta Romanum Troia demissum et Iuliae stirpis auctorem Aeneam aliaque haud procul fabulis vetera facunde exsecutus perpetrat, ut Ilienses omni publico munere solverentur. Eodem oratore Bononiensi coloniae igni haustae subventum centiens sestertii largitione. Reddita[1] Rhodiis libertas, adempta saepe aut firmata, prout bellis externis meruerant aut domi seditione deliquerant; tributumque Apamensibus terrae motu convolsis in quinquennium remissum.

LIX. At Claudius saevissima quaeque promere adigebatur eiusdem Agrippinae artibus, quae Statilium Taurum opibus inlustrem hortis eius inhians pervertit accusante Tarquitio Prisco. Legatus is Tauri Africam imperio proconsulari regentis, postquam revenerant, pauca repetundarum crimina, ceterum magicas superstitiones obiectabat. Nec ille diutius falsum accusatorem, indignas sordes[2] perpessus vim vitae suae attulit ante sententiam senatus. Tarquitius tamen curia exactus est, quod patres odio delatoris contra ambitum Agrippinae pervicere.

---

[1] reddita *Nipperdey* : redditur.
[2] indigna*sque* sordes *Heinsius* : indigna sortes.

---

[1] D. Junius Silanus Torquatus, brother of M. and L. Silanus (XII. 3; XIII. 1), and a great-grandson of Augustus. For his death, see XV. 35.
[2] Bologna.
[3] 'Απάμεια Κιβωτός on the Maeander.

LVIII. In the consulate of Decimus Junius [1] and Quintus Haterius, Nero, at the age of sixteen, received in marriage the emperor's daughter Octavia. Desirous to shine by his liberal accomplishments and by a character for eloquence, he took up the cause of Ilium, enlarged with grace on the Trojan descent of the Roman nation; on Aeneas, the progenitor of the Julian line; on other traditions not too far removed from fable; and secured the release of the community from all public obligations. By his advocacy, again, the colony of Bononia,[2] which had been destroyed by fire, was assisted with a grant of ten million sesterces; the Rhodians recovered their liberties, so often forfeited or confirmed as the balance varied between their military services abroad or their seditious offences at home; and Apamea,[3] which had suffered from an earthquake shock, was relieved from its tribute for the next five years.

LIX. Claudius, in contrast, was being forced to a display of sheer cruelty, still by the machinations of Agrippina. Statilius Taurus, whose wealth was famous, and whose gardens aroused her cupidity, she ruined with an accusation brought by Tarquitius Priscus. He had been the legate of Taurus when he was governing Asia with proconsular powers, and now on their return charged him with a few acts of malversation, but more seriously with addiction to magical superstitions. Without tolerating longer a lying accuser and an unworthy humiliation, Taurus took his own life before the verdict of the senate. Tarquitius, none the less, was expelled from the curia —a point which the Fathers, in their detestation of the informer, carried in the teeth of Agrippina's intrigues.

LX. Eodem anno saepius audita vox principis, parem vim rerum habendam a procuratoribus suis iudicatarum, ac si ipse statuisset. Ac ne fortuito prolapsus videretur, senatus quoque consulto cautum plenius quam antea et uberius. Nam divus Augustus apud equestres,[1] qui Aegypto praesiderent, lege agi decretaque eorum perinde haberi iusserat, ac si magistratus Romani constituissent; mox alias per provincias et in urbe pleraque concessa sunt, quae olim a praetoribus noscebantur. Claudius omne ius tradidit, de quo totiens seditione aut armis certatum, cum Semproniis rogationibus equester ordo in possessione iudiciorum locaretur, aut rursum Serviliae leges senatui iudicia redderent,[2] Mariusque et Sulla olim de eo vel praecipue bellarent. Sed tunc ordinum diversa studia, et quae vicerant[3] publice

[1] equestres] equites illustres *A. Schmidt.*
[2] redderent ⟨vel adimerent⟩ *Nipperdey.*
[3] vicerant] evicerant *Heinsius.*

---

[1] Those principally affected were the *procuratores rei privatae*—financial agents of equestrian rank, responsible throughout the empire for the management and supervision of imperial property. Till now they had possessed no judicial powers (cf. IV. 6, 15), and their claims had been prosecuted in ordinary courts ἐξ ἴσου τοῖς ἰδιώταις (D. Cass. LVII. 23).

[2] See II. 59, with the note.

[3] The term includes not only praetors in the ordinary sense of the word, but provincial governors.—What follows is scarcely relevant. For "the privilege at issue in the contests of knights and senators under the republic was that of furnishing the jurors in the criminal *quaestiones perpetuae*; the question now dealt with is that of the jurisdiction of an individual

LX. Several times in this year, the emperor was heard to remark that judgments given by his procurators [1] ought to have as much validity as if the ruling had come from himself. In order that the opinion should not be taken as a chance indiscretion, provision—more extensive and fuller than previously—was made to that effect by a senatorial decree as well. For an order of the deified Augustus had conferred judicial powers on members of the equestrian order, holding the government of Egypt; [2] their decisions to rank as though they had been formulated by the national magistrates. Later, both in other provinces and in Rome, a large number of cases till then falling under the cognizance of the praetors [3] were similarly transferred; and now Claudius handed over in full the judicial power so often disputed by sedition or by arms—when, for instance, the Sempronian rogations [4] placed the equestrian order in possession of the courts; or the Servilian laws retroceded those courts to the senate; or when, in the days of Marius and Sulla, the question actually became a main ground of hostilities. But the competition was then between class and class, and the results of victory were universally valid. [5] Gaius

procurator, usually of equestrian rank, without jurors, in civil actions between the princeps and individuals " (Furneaux).

[4] The *lex Sempronia iudiciaria* of C. Gracchus, 122 B.C.— The first *lex Servilia* (of Q. Servilius Caepio, 106 B.C.) restored the *iudicia* in some measure to the senate; the second (of C. Servilius Glaucia, a few years later) returned them to the knights. Other stages of the controversy are left unnoticed by Tacitus, nor is the statement justified that it was a main issue between Marius and Sulla.

[5] Whereas, in the present case, not the powers of the equestrian order as a whole, but those of certain members of that order, holding certain positions, were being extended.

valebant. C. Oppius et Cornelius Balbus primi
Caesaris opibus potuere condiciones pacis et arbitria
belli tractare. Matios posthac et Vedios et cetera
equitum Romanorum praevalida nomina referre
nihil attinuerit, cum Claudius libertos, quos reɪ
familiari praefecerat, sibique et legibus adaequaverit.

LXI. Rettulit dein de inmunitate Cois tribuenda,
multaque super antiquitate eorum memoravit:
Argivos vel Coeum Latonae parentem vetustissimos
insulae cultores; mox adventu Aesculapii artem
medendi inlatam maximeque inter posteros eius
celebrem fuisse, nomina singulorum referens et
quibus quisque aetatibus viguissent. Quin etiam
dixit Xenophontem, cuius scientia ipse uteretur,
eadem familia ortum, precibusque eius dandum, ut
omni tributo vacui in posterum Coi sacram et tantum
dei ministram insulam colerent. Neque dubium
habetur multa eorundem in populum Romanum
merita sociasque victorias potuisse tradi: set Claudius, facilitate solita quod uni concesserat, nullis
extrinsecus adiumentis velavit.

---

[1] Both intimate friends of Caesar.

[2] C. Matius, a friend first of Caesar, then of Augustus. The
author of a frank and admirable letter to Cicero, preserved at
ad Fam. XI. 28, he appears to be most unfairly coupled with
Vedius Pollio, for whom see I. 10 n.

[3] The caste of Asclepiadae, its most famous member being
Hippocrates, who claimed descent from the god at eighteen
removes.

[4] C. Stertinius Xenophon, who was suspected later of ad-
ministering the *coup de grâce* to his patron. He is known from

Oppius and Cornelius Balbus [1] were the first individuals who, supported by the might of Caesar, were able to take for their province the conditions of a peace or the determination of a war. It would serve no purpose to mention their successors, a Matius [2] or a Vedius or the other all too powerful names of Roman knights, when the freedmen whom he had placed in charge of his personal fortune were now by Claudius raised to an equality with himself and with the law.

LXI. He next proposed to grant immunity to the inhabitants of Cos. Of their ancient history he had much to tell:—" The earliest occupants of the island had," he said, " been Argives—or, possibly, Coeus, the father of Latona. Then the arrival of Aesculapius had introduced the art of healing, which attained the highest celebrity among his descendants " [3]—here he gave the names of the descendants and the epochs at which they had all flourished. " Xenophon," [4] he observed again, " to whose knowledge he himself had recourse, derived his origin from the same family; and, as a concession to his prayers, the Coans ought to be exempted from all forms of tribute for the future and allowed to tenant their island as a sanctified place subservient only to its god." There can be no doubt that a large number of services rendered by the islanders to Rome, and of victories in which they had borne their part, could have been cited; but Claudius declined to disguise by external aids a favour which, with his wonted complaisance, he had accorded to an individual.

inscriptions to have served with credit in the army and to have been in high honour in his native island.

LXII. At Byzantii data dicendi copia, cum magnitudinem onerum apud senatum deprecarentur, cuncta repetivere. Orsi a foedere, quod nobiscum icerant, qua tempestate bellavimus adversus regem Macedonum, cui ut degeneri Pseudophilippi vocabulum inpositum, missas posthac copias in Antiochum, Persen, Aristonicum, et piratico bello adiutum Antonium memorabant, quaeque Sullae aut Lucullo aut Pompeio obtulissent, mox recentia in Caesares merita, quando ea loca insiderent, quae transmeantibus terra marique ducibus exercitibusque, simul vehendo commeatu opportuna forent.

LXIII. Namque artissimo inter Europam Asiamque divortio Byzantium in extremo [1] Europae posuere Graeci, quibus Pythium Apollinem consulentibus, ubi conderent urbem, redditum oraculum est, quaererent sedem caecorum terris adversam. Ea ambage Chalcedonii monstrabantur, quod priores illuc advecti, praevisa locorum utilitate, peiora legissent. Quippe Byzantium fertili solo, fecundo mari, quia vis piscium inmensa,[2] Pontum erumpens et obliquis subter undas saxis exterrita, omisso alterius litoris flexu hos ad portus defertur. Unde primo quaes-

---

[1] extremo *Agricola* : extrema.
[2] inmensa *Ruperti* : in meta.

---

[1] The pretender Andriscus (Liv. *Epit.* 49).   [2] IV. 55 n.
[3] The father of the triumvir.
[4] The Megarian colony opposite, near the modern Scutari. The story is first told by Herodotus (IV. 144), who makes the epigrammatist, not Apollo, but Megabazus.
[5] *Pelamydes*, a variety of tunny. The ancient theory was that they were native to the Atlantic, made their way along the French and Spanish coasts to the Mediterranean and thence to the Sea of Azov, returning in vast shoals after the breeding-season.

LXII. On the other hand, the Byzantians, who had been granted an audience and were protesting in the senate against the oppressiveness of their burdens, reviewed their entire history. Starting from the treaty concluded with ourselves at the date of our war against the king of Macedonia whose doubtful birth earned him the title of pseudo-Philip,[1] they mentioned the forces they had sent against Antiochus, Perseus and Aristonicus;[2] their assistance to Antonius[3] in the Pirate War; their offers of help at various times to Sulla, Lucullus, and Pompey; then their recent services to the Caesars—services possible because they occupied a district conveniently placed for the transit of generals and armies by land or sea, and equally so for the conveyance of supplies.

LXIII. For it was upon the extreme verge of Europe, at the narrowest part of the waters which divorce the continent from Asia, that Byzantium was planted by the Greeks; who, on consulting the Pythian Apollo where to found a city, were advised by the oracle to " seek a home opposite the country of the blind." That enigma pointed to the inhabitants of Chalcedon;[4] who had arrived at the place before them, had surveyed in advance the opportunities of the site, and had decided for a worse. For Byzantium is favoured with a fertile soil and with a prolific sea, since huge shoals of fish[5]—alarmed, as they emerge from the Euxine, by shelving rocks under the surface—make from the winding Asiatic coast, and find their way to the harbours opposite.[6] A thriving and wealthy community had thus arisen;

[6] In the sixteenth century, women and children still caught them in the Golden Horn by the simple expedient of lowering a basket into the water.

tuosi et opulenti; post magnitudine onerum urguente finem aut modum orabant, adnitente principe, qui Thraecio Bosporanoque bello recens fessos iuvandosque rettulit. Ita tributa in quinquennium remissa.

LXIV. M. Asinio M'. Acilio consulibus mutationem rerum in deterius portendi cognitum est crebris prodigiis. Signa ac tentoria militum igni caelesti arsere. Fastigio[1] Capitolii examen apium insedit. Biformis hominum partus et suis fetum editum, cui accipitrum ungues inessent. Numerabatur inter ostenta deminutus omnium magistratuum numerus, quaestore, aedili, tribuno ac praetore et consule paucos intra menses defunctis. Sed in praecipuo pavore Agrippina, vocem Claudii, quam temulentus iecerat, fatale sibi ut coniugum flagitia ferret, dein puniret, metuens, agere et celerare statuit, perdita prius Domitia Lepida muliebribus causis, quia Lepida minore Antonia genita, avunculo Augusto, Agrippinae sobrina prior[2] ac Gnaei mariti eius soror, parem sibi claritudinem credebat. Nec forma aetas opes multum distabant; et utraque inpudica, infamis, violenta, haud minus vitiis aemulabantur, quam si qua ex fortuna prospera acce-

---

[1] fastigio] fastigium *Nipperdey*.
[2] prior] propior *Vertranius Maurus* (*cf. Dig.* XXXVIII. 10, 10, § 16).

---

[1] The hostilities resulting, in 46 A.D., in the conversion of Thrace into a province. They must have been noticed in the lost part of Book XI.
[2] Messalina's mother.

but now, under stress of their financial burdens, they applied for exemption or an abatement, and were supported by the emperor; who pointed out to the senate that they had been recently exhausted by the Thracian [1] and Bosporan wars and were entitled to relief. Their tribute was therefore remitted for the next five years.

LXIV. In the consulate of Marcus Asinius and Manius Acilius, it was made apparent by a sequence of prodigies that a change of conditions for the worse was foreshadowed. Fire from heaven played round the standards and tents of the soldiers; a swarm of bees settled on the pediment of the Capitol; it was stated that hermaphrodites had been born, and that a pig had been produced with the talons of a hawk. It was counted among the portents that each of the magistracies found its numbers diminished, since a quaestor, an aedile, and a tribune, together with a praetor and a consul, had died within a few months. But especial terror was felt by Agrippina. Disquieted by a remark let fall by Claudius in his cups, that it was his destiny first to suffer and finally to punish the infamy of his wives, she determined to act—and speedily. First, however, she destroyed Domitia Lepida [2] on a feminine quarrel. For, as the daughter of the younger Antonia, the grand-niece of Augustus, the first cousin once removed of Agrippina, and also the sister of her former husband Gnaeus Domitius, Lepida regarded her family distinctions as equal to those of the princess. In looks, age, and fortune there was little between the pair; and since each was as unchaste, as disreputable, and as violent as the other, their competition in the vices was not less keen than in such advantages as they had received

perant. Enimvero certamen acerrimum, amita potius an mater apud Neronem praevaleret: nam Lepida blandimentis ac largitionibus iuvenilem animum devinciebat, truci contra ac minaci Agrippina, quae filio dare imperium, tolerare imperitantem nequibat.

LXV. Ceterum obiecta sunt, quod coniugem principis devotionibus petivisset quodque parum coërcitis per Calabriam servorum agminibus pacem Italiae turbaret. Ob haec mors indicta, multum adversante Narcisso, qui Agrippinam magis magisque suspectans prompsisse inter proximos ferebatur certam sibi perniciem, seu Britannicus rerum seu Nero poteretur; verum ita de se meritum Caesarem, ut vitam usui eius inpenderet. Convictam Messalinam et Silium; pares iterum accusandi causas esse [si Nero imperitaret]; [1] Britannico successore nullum principi metum: [2] at [3] novercae insidiis domum omnem convelli, maiore flagitio, quam si inpudicitiam prioris coniugis reticuisset. Quamquam ne inpudicitiam quidem nunc abesse Pallante adultero, ne quis ambigat decus pudorem corpus, cuncta regno viliora habere. Haec atque talia dictitans amplecti Britannicum, robur aetatis quam maturrimum pre-

---

[1] [si Nero imperitaret] *Furneaux tentatively.—Freinsheim retaining* meritum *proposed to cancel* si Nero . . . successore; *but the problems of the passage remained unsolved.*

[2] metum *Ferrarius*: meritum.

[3] at *Muretus*: ad *Med.* ('*obscurata* d *littera*'), ac *ed. princ.*

---

[1] See II. 69 n.   [2] IV. 27 n.

from the kindness of fortune. But the fiercest struggle was on the question whether the dominant influence with Nero was to be his aunt or his mother: for Lepida was endeavouring to captivate his youthful mind by a smooth tongue and an open hand, while on the other side Agrippina stood grim and menacing, capable of presenting her son with an empire but not of tolerating him as emperor.

LXV. However, the charges preferred were that Lepida had practised by magic [1] against the life of the emperor's consort, and, by her neglect to coerce her regiments of slaves in Calabria,[2] was threatening the peace of Italy. On these grounds the death-sentence was pronounced, in spite of the determined opposition of Narcissus; who, with his ever-deepening suspicions of Agrippina, was said to have observed among his intimates that " whether Britannicus or Nero came to the throne, his own doom was sure; but the Caesar's kindness to him had been such that he would sacrifice life to his interests. Messalina and Silius had received their condemnation—and there was again similar material for a similar charge. With the succession vested in Britannicus, the emperor's person was safe; but the stepmother's plot aimed at overthrowing the whole imperial house—a darker scandal than would have resulted, if he had held his peace about the infidelities of her predecessor. Though, even now, infidelity was not far to seek, when she had committed adultery with Pallas, in order to leave no doubt that she held her dignity, her modesty, her body, her all, cheaper than a throne! " This and the like he repeated frequently, while he embraced Britannicus, prayed for his speedy maturity, and, extending his hands now to heaven

cari, modo ad deos, modo ad ipsum tendere manus, adolesceret, patris inimicos depelleret, matris etiam interfectores ulcisceretur.

LXVI. In tanta mole curarum valetudine adversa corripitur, refovendisque viribus mollitia caeli et salubritate aquarum Sinuessam pergit. Tum Agrippina, sceleris olim certa et oblatae occasionis propera nec ministrorum egens, de genere veneni consultavit, ne repentino et praecipiti facinus proderetur; si lentum et tabidum delegisset, ne admotus supremis Claudius et dolo intellecto ad amorem filii rediret. Exquisitum aliquid placebat, quod turbaret mentem et mortem differret. Deligitur artifex talium vocabulo Locusta, nuper veneficii damnata et diu inter instrumenta regni habita. Eius mulieris ingenio paratum virus, cuius minister e spadonibus fuit Halotus, inferre epulas et explorare gustu solitus.

LXVII. Adeoque cuncta mox pernotuere, ut temporum illorum scriptores prodiderint infusum delectabili cibo *boleto*[1] venenum, nec vim medica-

---

[1] boleto *Jac. Gronovius*: leto *Med.*, [boleto] *Orelli*, [cibo] *Wurm.*

and now to the prince, implored that "he would hasten to man's estate, cast out the enemies of his father—and even take vengeance on the slayers of his mother!"

LXVI. Under the weight of anxiety, his health broke down, and he left for Sinuessa,[1] to renovate his strength by the gentle climate and the medicinal springs. At once, Agrippina—long resolved on murder, eager to seize the proffered occasion, and at no lack for assistants—sought advice upon the type of poison. With a rapid and drastic drug, the crime, she feared, would be obvious: if she decided for a slow and wasting preparation, Claudius, face to face with his end and aware of her treachery, might experience a return of affection for his son. What commended itself was something recondite, which would derange his faculties while postponing his dissolution. An artist in this domain was selected —a woman by the name of Locusta, lately sentenced on a poisoning charge, and long retained as part of the stock-in-trade of absolutism.[2] Her ingenuity supplied a potion, administered by the eunuch Halotus, whose regular duty was to bring in and taste the dishes.

LXVII. So notorious, later, were the whole proceedings that authors of the period have recorded that the poison was sprinkled on an exceptionally fine mushroom; though, as a result of his natural

---

[1] At the southern extremity of the Latian coast.
[2] She survived till the reign of Galba, who executed her along with others τῶν ἐπὶ Νέρωνος ἐπιπολασάντων (D. Cass. LXIV. 3). In the interval, she had removed Britannicus (XIII. 15): the drug she concocted for Nero in his last hours was stolen by his slaves (Suet. *Ner.* 47).

minis statim intellectam, socordiane an vinolentia;[1] simul soluta alvus subvenisse videbatur.
Igitur exterrita Agrippina, et quando ultima timebantur, spreta praesentium invidia provisam iam
sibi Xenophontis medici conscientiam adhibet. Ille
tamquam nisus evomentis adiuvaret, pinnam rapido
veneno inlitam faucibus eius demisisse creditur, haud
ignarus summa scelera incipi cum periculo, peragi
cum praemio.

LXVIII. Vocabatur interim senatus votaque pro
incolumitate principis consules et sacerdotes nuncu-
pabant, cum iam exanimis vestibus et fomentis
obtegeretur, dum quae res ferret[2] firmando Neronis
imperio componuntur. Iam primum Agrippina,
velut dolore evicta et solacia conquirens, tenere
amplexu Britannicum, veram paterni oris effigiem
appellare ac variis artibus demorari, ne cubiculo
egrederetur. Antoniam quoque et Octaviam sorores

---

[1] See note.

[2] res ferret *Jackson*: re forent *Med.*, e re forent *Heinsius*,
quae forent *Ernesti, alii alia*.

---

[1] His constitutional lethargy made him an unpromising
subject at best for a drug intended to produce delirium : its
effectiveness, moreover, would, by ancient ideas, be lessened
by his condition at the time (*impletae cibis vinoque venae minus
efficacem in maturanda morte vim veneni fecerunt*, Liv. XXVI.
14).—The tradition is :—*socordiane an Claudii vi. an vinolentia*, which implies for its origin a dittography of the first four
letters of *an vinolentia* and a superscribed *Claudii* (" socordiane aɲ ɣi an vinolentia "). The choice, therefore, lies between
Rhenanus' *socordiane Claudii an vinolentia* and the excision of
Claudii as in the text. *Intellectum* then bears the common
meaning suggested for it by Merivale (cf. Ov. *Met.* IX. 456,
nullos intellegit ignis, and the like). The usual course is to read

sluggishness or intoxication, the effects of the drug were not immediately felt by Claudius.[1] At the same time, a motion of his bowels appeared to have removed the danger. Agrippina was in consternation: as the last consequences were to be apprehended, immediate infamy would have to be braved; and she fell back on the complicity—which she had already assured—of the doctor Xenophon. He, it is believed, under cover of assisting the emperor's struggles to vomit, plunged a feather, dipped in a quick poison, down his throat: for he was well aware that crimes of the first magnitude are begun with peril and consummated with profit.[2]

LXVIII. Meanwhile, the senate was convened, and consuls and priests formulated their vows for the imperial safety, at a moment when the now lifeless body was being swathed in blankets and warming bandages, while the requisite measures were arranged for securing the accession of Nero. In the first place, Agrippina, heart-broken apparently and seeking to be comforted, held Britannicus to her breast, styled him the authentic portrait of his father, and, by this or the other device, precluded him from leaving his room. His sisters, Antonia and Octavia,

---

socordiane an Claudii vinolentia, and to refer the stupidity to the observers. But, apart from technical objections, *socordia* is the last quality to be attributed to Agrippina at the crisis of her fate, and the first to be attributed—at least by his countrymen and contemporaries—Claudius: cf. e.g. Sidon. Apoll. *Ep.* 7 fin. *Tiberius callidior, Claudius socordior, Nero impurior.*

[2] His belief would appear to have been justified, as he and his brother, Q. Stertinius, left between them 30,000,000 sesterces (Plin. XXIX. 1, 8). Halotus, too, went so far in the world as to be coupled in the public detestation with Tigellinus and to be rewarded with an *amplissima procuratio* by Galba (Suet. *Galb.* 15).

eius attinuit, et cunctos aditus custodiis clauserat, crebroque vulgabat ire in melius valetudinem principis, quo miles bona in spe ageret tempusque prosperum ex monitis Chaldaeorum adventaret.

LXIX. Tunc medio diei tertium ante Idus Octobris, foribus palatii repente diductis, comitante Burro Nero egreditur ad cohortem, quae more militiae excubiis adest. ibi monente praefecto faustis [1] vocibus exceptus inditur lecticae. Dubitavisse quosdam ferunt, respectantis rogitantisque ubi Britannicus esset: mox nullo in diversum auctore quae offere: bantur secuti sunt. Inlatusque castris Nero et congruentia tempori praefatus, promisso donativo ad exemplum paternae largitionis, imperator consalutatur. Sententiam militum secuta patrum consulta, nec dubitatum est apud provincias. Caelestesque honores Claudio decernuntur et funeris sollemne perinde ac divo Augusto celebratur, aemulante Agrippina proaviae Liviae magnificentiam. Testamentum tamen haud recitatum, ne antepositus filio privignus iniuria et invidia animos vulgi turbaret.

---

[1] faustis *Ernesti*: festis *Med. But cf. Amm. Marc. XVII.* 13, 33 vocibus festis in laudum imperatoris adsurgens: *Housman on Luc. III.* 101.

---

[1] Claudius on his accession set the disastrous precedent of presenting the praetorians with 15,000 sesterces a man.

she similarly detained. She had barred all avenues of approach with pickets, and ever and anon she issued notices that the emperor's indisposition was turning favourably: all to keep the troops in good hope, and to allow time for the advent of the auspicious moment insisted upon by the astrologers.

LXIX. At last, at midday, on the thirteenth of October, the palace gates swung suddenly open, and Nero, with Burrus in attendance, passed out to the cohort, always on guard in conformity with the rules of the service. There, at a hint from the prefect, he was greeted with cheers and placed in a litter. Some of the men are said to have hesitated, looking back and inquiring:—" Where was Britannicus ? " Then, as no lead to the contrary was forthcoming, they acquiesced in the choice presented to them: Nero was carried into the camp; and, after a few introductory words suited to the time, promised a donative on the same generous scale as that of his father,[1] and was saluted as *Imperator*. The verdict of the troops was followed by senatorial decrees; nor was any hesitation evinced in the provinces. Divine honours were voted to Claudius, and his funeral solemnities were celebrated precisely as those of the deified Augustus, Agrippina emulating the magnificence of her great-grandmother Livia. His will, however, was not read, lest the preference of the stepson to the son should leave a disquieting impression of injustice and invidiousness upon the mind of the common people.

TABLE OF DATES

The following list includes the more important events, which must have been related in the lost parts of the *Annals* :—

Annals V. 5—fin., VI. init.

29 A.D. Trial and condemnation of Agrippina and her son Nero ; the former banished to Pandateria, the latter to Pontia. Drusus spared for the moment, and married to Aemilia Lepida (cf. VI. 40).

30 A.D. Condemnation of Asinius Gallus, who is not permitted to die (cf. VI. 23). Drusus pronounced a public enemy and immured in an underground chamber of the Palatium (cf. VI. 23). Sejanus now apparently omnipotent.

31 A.D. Sejanus consul with Tiberius ; leaves Capreae for Rome. Deaths of Curtius Atticus (IV. 58), Fufius Geminus (V. 2 = Ῥοῦφος Γεμίνιος, D. Cass. LVIII. 4), and Drusus ; Sejanus' tool, Fulcinius Trio, *consul suffectus* in July. Signs that suspicions are entertained of Sejanus, who determines to remove both the emperor and Gaius (Caligula). Plot

divulged to Tiberius, who takes counter-measures. Sejanus struck down on Oct. 18, the principal agents being Memmius Regulus (*cos. suff.* Oct. 1), Cn. Sertorius Macro (privately appointed *praefectus praetorio*), and Graecinus Laco (*praefectus vigilum*). News signalled to Tiberius in Capreae. Many executions. Apicata reveals the circumstances of Drusus' death eight years previously. Livia put to death.

Annals VI.—X. (*with part of XI.*).

37 A.D. Accession of Gaius (March 18) amid universal enthusiasm. Exiles recalled ; prosecutions under the *lex maiestatis* nominally abjured ; Tiberius Gemellus favoured ; Claudius introduced to public life ; Nero born. Great financial extravagance. Illness of the emperor in October, followed by symptoms of mental derangement. Tiberius Gemellus and M. Junius Silanus (father-in-law of the emperor) forced to suicide.

38 A.D. The *comitia* restored in name. Death and deification of the emperor's sister and mistress, Drusilla. Executions and confiscations frequent. Macro compelled to commit suicide. Serious rioting between Jews and Gentiles at Alexandria, caused by attempt to introduce into the synagogues images of the emperor, whose belief in his own divinity becomes more and more pronounced.

39 A.D. Further executions and confiscations. Herod Antipas and Herodias banished to

Lyons; Mithridates of Armenia summoned to Rome and detained; bridge of boats—largely grain-ships—thrown across Gulf of Baiae. The emperor in Gaul: conspiracy and death of his brother-in-law Aemilius Lepidus and Lentulus Gaetulicus, legatus of Lower Germany. His sisters, Agrippina and Julia Livilla, banished for complicity in the plot. Auction of imperial heirlooms at Lyons.

40 A.D. The emperor at Lyons; sole consul for a time. Makes a fantastic demonstration against Britain; returns to Rome on Aug. 31. Orders to place his image in the Holy of Holies at Jerusalem temporarily cancelled at the intercession of the legate of Syria and Herod Agrippa, who has received the dominions of Philip the Tetrarch (37 A.D.) and Herod Antipas (39 A.D.). Deputation of Alexandrian Jews to Rome, including Philo, who describes it in the *Legatio ad Gaium.*

41 A.D. Assassination of Gaius (Jan. 24); Claudius proclaimed by the praetorians, who are accorded a donative of 15,000 sesterces a man. Herod Agrippa rewarded for his services at the crisis by the grant of Judaea, which ceases to be a procuratorial province. Agrippina and Julia Livilla recalled; but the latter again banished, at the instigation of Messalina, on a charge of adultery with Seneca, who is exiled to Corsica. Birth of Britannicus (Feb. 13).

TABLE OF DATES

42 A.D. Reduction of Mauretania, which is made into two procuratorial provinces (*M. Caesariensis*, *M. Tingitana*). Messalina, with the help of Narcissus, procures the death of her step-father Ap. Iunius Silanus. Conspiracy of Annius Vinicianus, supported by Furius Camillus Scribonianus, legatus of Dalmatia ; rising collapses immediately. Many executions.

43 A.D. Invasion of Britain under A. Plautius Silvanus, who defeats Caratacus and captures Camulodunum ; Claudius present for sixteen days. ? Mithridates recovers Armenia.

44 A.D. Triumph of Claudius. Achaia and Macedonia transferred to the senate. Judaea, after the death of Herod Agrippa, again placed under procurators.

45 A.D. ? Rebellion of Mithridates of Bosporus, crushed by A. Didius Gallus.

47 A.D. Censorship of Claudius and Vitellius. Ovation of A. Plautius Silvanus, who is succeeded as legatus of Britain by P. Ostorius Scapula. Extant portion of Book XI. opens with the death of Valerius Asiaticus.

Annals XVI. 35—XVIII. See Intro., vol. III, p. 234.

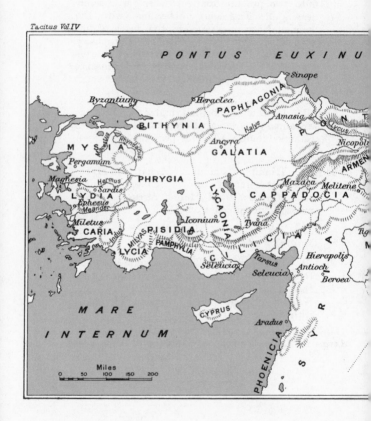